DICTIONARY OF FOREIGN TERMS

Mario Pei and Salvatore Ramondino

in collaboration with Laura Torbet

DELACORTE PRESS/NEW YORK

Copyright © 1974 by Mario Pei, Salvatore Ramondino
and Laura Robbins Torbet

Manufactured in the United States of America

First Delacorte printing

Library of Congress Cataloging in Publication Data

Pei, Mario Andrew, 1901–
Dictionary of foreign terms.

1. English language—Foreign words and phrases—
Dictionaries. I. Ramondino, Salvatore, joint author.
II. Title.
PE1670.P44   1975   422′.4   74-34091
ISBN 0-440-01779-3

Contents

Introduction

The average educated English speaker with little or no knowledge of foreign languages often is baffled by foreign terms and phrases that occur, without translation, in the books, magazines and newspapers that he reads, or that he may hear by way of television, radio, films and theater. Unless he has a large reference library at his immediate disposal, he will have no idea of their meaning or of how to pronounce them (in the spoken media, more often than not, he will hear them mispronounced!). This dictionary aims to assist him by telling him from what languages these terms and phrases come, often with some further interesting information about their history. It will also tell him how they are pronounced and what they mean. He will often find further reference to related terms and phrases that will round out the picture for him. For example, a reader who looks up *Nisei* in this dictionary and learns that it means a second-generation Japanese-American may naturally be curious to know how first-generation and third-generation Japanese-Americans are called. The cross-reference under *Nisei* will direct him to the related terms *Issei* and *Sansei*.

The pronunciations provided in this dictionary are designed to achieve the greatest simplicity and usability with the minimum loss of accuracy. The definitions are as concise and accurate as careful research could make them. The etymologies furnish at least the primary source and often, within the limitations of space, provide further pertinent and interesting information. The cross-references are copious for a work of this size, because the authors have felt, on the one hand, that the reader's curiosity should be satisfied when it is aroused, and on the other hand, that he will be grateful to have his attention directed to further pertinent and useful information.

In selecting the entries to be included in this dictionary the authors have had to consider and reject far more than could be included. The aim has been at all times to include only useful, interesting and timely material. Obscure classical quotations, highly technical terms, personal and geographical names, titles or opening lines of songs and arias, and terms that have become wholly naturalized in English have been omitted. In their quest for the most useful, most common and most timely material, the authors have combed through current books, magazines and newspapers published in English. All points of information have been rigorously checked with the most competent authorities in each of the many languages involved.

The authors have included terms and phrases not only from the more familiar languages such as French, Spanish, Italian, German and Latin, but also from Greek, Russian, Sanskrit, Hebrew, Arabic, and from little-known languages such as Malay, Tagalog, Afrikaans and scores of others.

Guide to the Use
of the Dictionary

1. ENTRY WORD OR PHRASE. Each article begins with the entry word or phrase, which is printed in boldface type.

   abajo . . .

2. ETYMOLOGY. The etymology is enclosed in square brackets. It includes the languages from which the entry is derived, and sometimes earlier source languages. Names of languages in the etymology are often abbreviated, without a following period. (See the list of abbreviations.) If the form or the meaning of the entry is different in the source language, the original form and/or meaning will be given. Source words cited in the etymology are printed in italics, unless they are themselves entries in the dictionary, when they are printed in boldface. Within the brackets are also included variant forms of the main entry, such as feminines, plurals and abbreviations. These are printed in boldface type.

   anomie [Fr, from Gk *a*, without + *nomos*, law] . . .

3. PRONUNCIATION. The pronunciation is printed in italics following the etymology. Syllables are separated by hyphens. Stressed syllables are shown in capital letters. Pronunciations of variant forms that appear within the etymology brackets are enclosed in parentheses following the pronunciation of the main entry. Normally pronunciation is given only for that portion of the variant form that differs from the main entry. The

simplified pronunciation used in this dictionary contains only letters of our own alphabet, with a minimum of diacritical marks. (See the pronunciation key.)

accademia [It] *ahk-kah-DEH-myah.* **. . .**

4. LITERAL MEANING. If the entry has a meaning in the source language that differs markedly from the meaning generally accepted in English, this is shown in parentheses preceding the accepted meaning and is introduced by the abbreviation *lit.* in italics.

a buena hambre no hay pan duro . . . (*lit.,* to a good hunger there is no hard bread) **. . .**

5. QUALIFYING LABELS. Where applicable, a qualifying label indicating the level of usage (e.g., *slang*), or the part of speech (e.g., *adj.*), or the special area of usage (e.g., *music*) precedes the definition. If the qualifying label applies to only one of two or more meanings of the entry, the label will precede that meaning. Qualifying labels are enclosed in parentheses and printed in italics, and may be abbreviated.

bis . . . (*interj.*) again! encore! **. . .**
blague . . . (*slang*) hogwash, humbug **. . .**
a capriccio . . . (*music*) at will; at whim **. . .**

6. DEFINITION. The meaning or meanings of the entry word or phrase are printed in lightface type. Related meanings are grouped together, separated only by commas. Distinct meanings or groups of meanings are separated by semicolons.

Abendessen . . . evening meal; supper.

7. SUBSIDIARY ENTRIES. Words or phrases that contain the main entry or are closely related to it are listed as subsidiary or run-on entries. These are printed in boldface type and are separated from the main entry and from one another by semicolons. A boldface dash in a subsidiary entry is to be read as a repetition of the main entry. Following each subsidiary entry is a pronunciation in parentheses of that part of it that has not

already been pronounced in the pronunciation of the main entry or of a preceding subsidiary entry.

chargé . . . **—d'affaires** (*-dah-FEHR*) . . .

8. CROSS-REFERENCES. These include variant forms or spellings of the main entry or related or contrasted entries. Cross-referenced terms are printed in boldface type. If they are not alphabetically adjacent, they will be found as separate entries in their proper alphabetical place.

A.D. See **anno Domini.**
adagio . . . a tempo between **andante** and **largo;** . . .
affresco. See **fresco.**
Nisei . . . Cf. **Issei, Sansei.**

List of Abbreviations

Only those abbreviations that are especially pertinent to the use of this dictionary are included. Standard abbreviations such as *U.S.*, *i.e.*, *e.g.*, and *etc.* are omitted.

abbr.	abbreviation	colloq.	colloquial
abl.	ablative	contr.	contraction
acc.	accusative	Dan	Danish
adj.	adjective	dat.	dative
adv.	adverb	dial.	dialect(al)
aero.	aeronautics	dim.	diminutive
Afr	African	Du	Dutch
AmerInd	American Indian	E	east(ern)
		Eng	English
AmerSp	American Spanish	equiv.	equivalent
		esp.	especially
Anglo-Fr	Anglo-French	fem.	feminine
Anglo-Ind	Anglo-Indian	Finn	Finnish
approx.	approximately	Flem	Flemish
Ar	Arabic	Fr	French
archit.	architecture	Gael	Gaelic
arith.	arithmetic	gen.	genitive
AS	Anglo-Saxon	geom.	geometry
bot.	botany	Ger	German
Bulg	Bulgarian	Gk	Greek
cap.	capitalized	Heb	Hebrew
Cat	Catalan	Hung	Hungarian
Celt	Celtic	Icel	Icelandic
cf.	compare	imper.	imperative
chem.	chemistry	interj.	interjection
Chin	Chinese	Ir	Irish

It	Italian	Pol	Polish
Jap	Japanese	Port	Portuguese
Lat	Latin	p.p.	past participle
l.c.	lower case	prep.	preposition
ling.	linguistics	prob.	probably
lit.	literal(ly)	Prov	Provençal
LL	Late Latin	pr.p.	present
masc.	masculine		participle
math.	mathematics	psych.	psychology
med.	medicine	p.t.	past tense
MedL	Medieval Latin	rel.	related
MexSp	Mexican	Rum	Rumanian
	Spanish	Russ	Russian
MF	Middle	S	south(ern)
	French	SAmer	South
MHG	Middle High		American
	German	Scand	Scandinavian
mil.	military	Scot	Scottish
Mod	Modern	sculp.	sculpture
N	north(ern)	sing.	singular
n.	noun	Skt	Sanskrit
naut.	nautical	Sp	Spanish
neut.	neuter	Swed	Swedish
NL	New Latin	Turk	Turkish
nom.	nominative	typog.	typography
Norw	Norwegian	usu.	usually
O	Old	var.	variant
obs.	obsolete	voc.	vocative
OF	Old French	W	west(ern)
orig.	original(ly)	WIndSp	West Indian
perh.	perhaps		Spanish
Pers	Persian	Yid	Yiddish
philos.	philosophy	zool.	zoology
pl.	plural		

Pronunciation Key

Pronunciations are printed in italics. Syllables are separated by hyphens. Capital letters indicate stressed syllables. Pronunciations for principal entries follow the etymology without parentheses. Pronunciations for variant forms, subsidiary entries, and cross-references are given in parentheses following the entries to which they apply. Generally, pronunciations in parentheses contain only the portion that has not been previously pronounced in the pronunciation of the principal entry or of a preceding subsidiary entry.

SYMBOL	DESCRIPTION (*if necessary*)	EXAMPLES
a		Eng b*a*t
ã	a nasalized vowel	Fr fl*an*
ah	"broad" *a*	Eng f*a*ther
ar		Eng b*ar*
aw		Eng l*aw*
ay		Eng d*a*y
b		Eng *b*it
ç	a voiceless palatal fricative	Ger i*ch*
ch		Eng *ch*in
d		Eng *d*o
e		Eng m*e*t
ẽ	a nasalized vowel	Fr bi*en*
ee		Eng n*ee*d
eh		Eng b*ea*r
ehr		Eng th*ere*
f		Eng *f*at
g		Eng *g*et

gh	a voiced guttural fricative (strong clearing of throat accompanied by vibration of vocal cords)	Turk a*gh*a
h		Eng *h*at
i		Eng p*i*n
j		Eng *j*ug
k		Eng *k*eep
kh	a voiceless guttural fricative	Ger a*ch*
ks	the sound of the letter *x*	Eng si*x*
l		Eng *l*ow
ly	a palatalized *l*	Sp ca*ll*e
m		Eng *m*an
n		Eng *n*et
ng		Eng si*ng*
ny	a palatalized *n*	Sp se*ñ*or
o		Eng n*o*t
õ	a nasalized vowel	Fr b*on*
ö	a middle vowel, produced by placing the lips in position for *oh* and the tongue in position for *e*	Fr p*eu*, p*eur*
oh		Eng r*o*de
oo		Eng f*oo*t, f*oo*d
or		Eng f*or*
ow		Eng h*ow*
p		Eng *p*at
r	a trilled *r* in most languages other than English; in French and usually in German, a uvular *r* (gentle clearing of throat)	Sp pe*r*o, Fr ché*ri*
s		Eng *s*it
sh		Eng *sh*oe
t		Eng *t*in
th		Eng *th*in, *th*en
u		Eng b*u*t
ũ	a nasalized vowel	Fr chac*un*
ü	a middle vowel, produced by placing the lips in position	Fr l*u*ne Ger K*ü*mmel

	for *oo* and the tongue in position for *ee*	
uh		Eng sof*a*
ur		Eng f*ur*
v		Eng *v*an
w		Eng *w*et, s*w*eet
y	represents any of three different sounds, depending on its surroundings:	
	1) when forming a syllable by itself or when there is no other vowel in the syllable, *y* represents a "long *i*" diphthong	Eng m*y*, m*i*ne Ger s*ei*n Sp ba*i*le
	2) when standing at the beginning of a syllable or following a consonant in the same syllable, *y* represents a consonant	Eng *y*et Sp b*i*en Fr ch*i*en
	3) when following a vowel in the same syllable, *y* represents a semivowel	Eng ba*y*, bo*y* Sp le*y*, ho*y*
z		Eng *z*ero, do*z*e
zh		Eng a*z*ure
'	1) an elided vowel	Eng heav'n Ger ab*e*nd
	2) in Russian words, indicates palatalization of the preceding consonant	Russ oblast'

A

a [Lat, var. of **ab**] *ah.* [It, Sp, Port] at; to; by; in, into; for; with; until.

à [Fr] *ah.* at; to, in, into; for; by; with; until; after the manner of; according to.

ab [Lat] *ahb.* from; away from; out of; since; after; by; by means of, with; [Ger] *ahp.* from; off; away; down; out.

abajo [Sp] *ah-BAH-hoh.* down, below, downstairs; down with . . . !

abanico [Sp] *ah-bah-NEE-koh.* fan.

à bas [Fr] *ah-BAH.* down!; down with . . . !

abat-jour [Fr] *ah-bah-ZHOOR.* lampshade; reflector; skylight; basement or ground-level window; aperture that deflects light downward.

abat-son(s) [Fr] *ah-bah-SŎ.* a louvered construction in a belfry or concert hall that directs sound downward.

a battuta [It] *ah-baht-TOO-tah.* (*music*) according to the beat; in strict time.

abat-vent [Fr] *ah-bah-VÃ.* wind deflector.

abat-voix [Fr] *ah-bah-VWAH.* voice deflector; a device placed over a rostrum or pulpit to direct the speaker's voice downward.

Abendessen [Ger] *AH-b'nt-es-s'n.* evening meal; supper.

Abendland [Ger] *AH-b'nt-lahnt.* the West; Occident.

Abendlied [Ger] *Ah-b'nt-leet.* evening song.

Abendstern [Ger] *AH-b'nt-shtehrn.* evening star.

a beneplacito [It] *ah-beh-nay-PLAH-chee-toh.* (*music*) at (one's) pleasure; at the performer's discretion.

Aberglaube [Ger] *AH-buh-GLOW-beh.* superstition; reverent belief in the unknown.

abest [Lat] *AHB-est.* he (she, it) is absent.

ab extra [Lat] *ahb-EKS-trah.* from outside.

abgekürzt [Ger] *AHP-guh-kürtst.* shortened; abridged.

Abhandlung [Ger: *pl.* **Abhandlungen**] *AHP-hahnt-loong* (*-'n*) treatise; (*pl.*) transactions, esp. of a learned society.

ab imo pectore [Lat] *ahb-EE-moh-PEK-toh-reh*. from the bottom of (one's) heart.

ab initio [Lat] *ahb-ee-NEE-tee-oh*. from the beginning.

Ablaut [Ger] *AHP-lowt*. vowel change or mutation.

abogado [Sp] *ah-boh-GAH-doh*. lawyer; advocate.

à bon chat, bon rat [Fr] *ah-bõ-SHAH-bõ-RAH*. (*lit.*, to a good cat, a good rat) tit for tat.

à bon cheval, point d'éperon [Fr] *ah-bõ-sh'VAHL-pwē-day-p'RÕ*. don't spur a willing horse.

à bon droit [Fr] *ah-bõ-DRWAH*. with good reason; justly.

à bon marché [Fr] *ah-bõ-mar-SHAY*. at a bargain, cheap.

abonnement [Fr] *ah-bun-MÃ*. subscription.

à bon vin point d'enseigne [Fr] *ah-bõ-VĒ-pwē-dã-SEH-nyuh*. (*lit.*, to a good wine, no signboard) a good product needs no advertising.

ab origine [Lat] *ahb-oh-REE-gee-neh*. from the beginning.

ab ovo [Lat] *ahb-OH-voh*. (*lit.*, from the egg) from the beginning.

ab ovo usque ad mala [Lat] *ahb-OH-voh-OOS-kweh-ahd-MAH-lah*. (*lit.*, from egg to apples) from soup to nuts; from beginning to end.

abrazo [Sp] *ah-BRAH-so*. embrace; cordial welcome.

abrégé [Fr] *ah-bray-ZHAY*. abridgment; summary.

Abreise [Ger] *AHP-ry-zeh*. departure.

abri [Fr] *ah-BREE*. shelter.

Abriss [Ger] *AHP-ris*. outline; sketch.

Abschied [Ger] *AHP-sheet*. departure; leave-taking.

Abschiedslied [Ger] *AHP-sheets-leet*. farewell song.

Abschnitt [Ger] *AHP-shnit*. section; paragraph; segment.

absence d'esprit [Fr] *ahp-SÃS-des-PREE*. absentmindedness.

absit invidia [Lat] *AHB-seet-een-VEE-dee-ah*. no offense.

absit omen [Lat] *AHB-seet-OH-men*. may the omen cause no evil.

absolvo [Lat] *ahb-SOHL-voh*. I absolve; I acquit.

absque [Lat] *AHBS-kweh*. without.

absque hoc [Lat] *HOHK*. without this; (*law*) a term used in a formal denial.

abuelo [Sp] *ah-BWEH-loh.* grandfather; **abuela** (*-lah*) grandmother.

a buena hambre no hay pan duro [Sp] *ah-BWEH-nah-AHM-breh-noh-y-PAHN-DOO-roh.* (*lit.*, to a good hunger there is no hard bread) hunger is the best sauce.

ab uno disce omnes [Lat] *ahb-OO-noh-DEES-keh-OHM-nes.* from one (example) learn (about) all.

a buon intenditor poche parole [It] *ah-BWOH-neen-ten-dee-TOR-POH-keh-pah-ROH-leh.* a word to the wise is sufficient.

ab urbe condita [Lat: abbr. **A.U.C.**] *ahb-OOR-beh-KOHN-dee-tah.* from the (date of the) founding of the city: referring to Rome, founded about 753 B.C.

Abwehr [Ger] *AHP-vehr* (*lit.*, defense) German counter-espionage agency in World War II.

A.C. See **ante Christum.**

acaba de publicarse [Sp] *ah-KAH-bah-deh-poo-blee-KAR-seh.* just published.

a caballo [Sp] *ah-kah-BAH-lyoh.* on horseback.

a capriccio [It] *ah-kah-PREE-choh.* (*music*) at will; at whim; at the performer's pleasure.

accablé [Fr] *ah-kah-BLAY.* crushed; overwhelmed.

accademia [It] *ahk-kah-DEH-myah.* academy.

accelerando [It] *ah-cheh-leh-RAHN-doh.* (*music*) gradually faster.

acciaccatura [It] *ah-chahk-kah-TOO-rah.* (*music*) a short grace note.

accompagnamento [It] *ahk-kohm-pah-nyah-MAYN-toh.* (*music*) accompaniment.

accompagnatore [It: *fem.* **-trice**] *ahk-kohm-pah-nyah-TOH-reh* (*-TREE-cheh*) accompanist.

accordo [It] *ahk-KOR-doh.* agreement, harmony; (*music*) chord.

accouchement [Fr] *ah-koosh-MÃ.* lying-in; confinement.

accoucheur [Fr: *fem.* **-euse**] *ah-koo-SHÖR* (*-ÖZ*) obstetrician; midwife.

accueil [Fr] *ah-KÖ-yuh.* reception; welcome.

aceituna [Sp] *ah-sey-TOO-nah.* olive.

acepipes [Port] *ah-suh-PEE-push.* appetizers, hors d'oeuvres.

acequia [Sp] *ah-SEH-kyah.* ditch; irrigation canal.

acera [Sp] *ah-SEH-rah.* sidewalk; footwalk.

ac etiam [Lat] *ahk-EH-tee-ahm.* and also; and even.

ach [Ger] *ahkh.* oh!; alas!

acharné [Fr] *ah-shar-NAY.* fierce; furious, bloodthirsty; tenacious.

acharnement [Fr] *ah-shar-nuh-MÃ.* ferocity; fury; tenacity.

achat [Fr] *ah-SHAH.* purchase.

à cheval [Fr] *ah-sh'VAHL.* on horseback.

Ach-laut [Ger] *ahkh-lowt.* the velar sound of *ch* in German after back vowels (*a, o, u*); the sound of *ch* in Scottish **loch.** Cf. **Ich-laut.**

Achtung [Ger] *AHKH-toong.* admiration; respect; (*mil.*) attention!; look out!, beware!, careful!

à compte [Fr] *ah-KÕT.* on account; in part payment.

à contre-coeur [Fr] *ah-KÕ-truh-KÖR.* reluctantly; against one's will.

à coup sûr [Fr] *ah-KOO-SÜR.* unerringly; without fail.

acqua [It] *AHK-kwah.* water.

a cruce salus [Lat] *ah-KROO-keh-SAH-loos.* salvation (comes) from the Cross.

Acta (Populi Romani) Diurna [Lat] *AHK-tah-(POH-poo-lee-roh-MAH-nee)-dee-OOR-nah.* daily doings or happenings (of the Roman people); daily news bulletin, posted in the Forum for the information of the people.

acta sanctorum [Lat] *AHK-tah-sahnk-TOH-room.* deeds of the saints.

acte authentique [Fr] *AHKT-oh-tã-TEEK.* notarized document.

Action Française [Fr] *ahk-SYÕ-frã-SEZ.* French monarchist party in early 20th century; name of its official newspaper.

actionnaire [Fr] *ahk-syuh-NEHR.* stockholder.

actualité [Fr] *ahk-tü-ah-lee-TAY.* present affair; matter of present interest; (*pl.*) **actualités** newsreel.

actuel [Fr] *ahk-tü-EL.* present; real; actual.

actus [Lat] *AHK-toos.* act; deed.

actus Dei [Lat] *AHK-toos-DEH-ee.* act of God.

a cuenta [Sp] *ah-KWEN-tah.* on account.

ad [Lat] *ahd.* to; by; at; for; up to, as far as; until; near; toward; according to.

A.D. See **anno Domini.**

ad absurdum [Lat] *ahd-ahb-SOOR-doom.* to the point of absurdity.

adagietto [It] *ah-dah-JAYT-toh.* (*music*) slower than **adagio**; a short piece in **adagio** time.

adagio [It] *ah-DAH-joh.* slowly, easily; (*music*) a tempo between **andante** and **largo**; dance movement in which the male swings the female slowly through the air.

Adam [Heb] *ah-DAHM.* man

ad arbitrium [Lat] *ahd-ar-BEE-tree-oom.* at pleasure; at will.

ad astra [Lat] *ahd-AHS-trah.* to the stars; to high position; **per ardua—** or **—per aspera** (*pehr-AHR-doo-ah-*) (*-pehr-AHS-peh-rah*) Through adversities to the stars (motto of Kansas).

ad calendas graecas [Lat] *ahd-kah-LEN-dahs-GRY-kahs.* (to put off) to the Greek calends; never.

ad captandum vulgus [Lat] *ahd-kahp-TAHN-doom-VOOL-goos.* to appeal to the crowd.

ad clerum [Lat] *ahd-KLEH-room.* to the clergy.

addio [It] *ahd-DEE-oh.* good-bye; farewell.

adelante [Sp] *ah-deh-LAHN-teh.* ahead; before; forward!; come in!

adelphos [Gk] *ah-del-FOHS.* brother.

à demi [Fr] *ah-duh-MEE.* half; halfway; by halves.

a Deo et rege [Lat] *ah-DEH-oh-et-REH-geh.* from God and the King.

à dessein [Fr] *ah-day-SẼ.* deliberately; on purpose; by design.

Adeste Fideles [Lat] *ah-DES-teh-fee-DEH-les.* O come, all ye faithful.

ad eundem(gradum) [Lat] *ahd-eh-OON-dem(GRAH-doom).* to the same degree.

adeus [Port] *ah-DEH-oosh.* good-bye; farewell.

à deux [Fr] *ah-DÖ.* for or between two; intimate, private; two at a time.

ad extremum [Lat] *ahd-eks-TREH-moom.* to the extreme; at last, finally.

ad finem [Lat: *abbr.* **ad fin.**] *ahd-FEE-nem.* to, at or toward the end; finally.

ad gustum [Lat] *ahd-GOOS-toom.* to taste.

ad hoc [Lat] *ahd-HOHK.* for this (situation or purpose).

ad hominem [Lat] *ahd-HOH-mee-nem.* (*lit.,* to the man) appealing to the emotions rather than the intellect; in a dispute, attacking the person of an opponent by slander and innuendo, obscuring the real issues.

ad idem [Lat] *ahd-EE-dem.* to the same point.

adieu [Fr] *ah-DYŎ.* farewell; good-bye.

ad infinitum [Lat] *ad-in-fi-NY-tum* (*ahd-een-fee-NEE-toom*) on and on; to infinity.

ad interim [Lat] *ad-IN-tuh-rim* (*ahd-EEN-teh-reem*) in the meantime; temporarily.

adiós [Sp] *ah-DYOHS.* good-bye; farewell.

à discrétion [Fr] *ah-dees-kray-SYŎ.* at will; without limit.

ad kalendas graecas. See **ad calendas graecas.**

ad libitum [Lat: *abbr.* **ad lib**] *ahd-LEE-bee-toom.* at pleasure; freely; extemporaneously.

ad majorem Dei gloriam [Lat: *abbr.* **A.M.D.G.**] *ahd-mah-YOH-rem-DEH-ee-GLOH-ree-ahm.* For the greater glory of God (motto of the Society of Jesus).

ad nauseam [Lat] *ad-NAW-see-uhm* (*ahd-NOW-seh-ahm*) to the point of nausea or disgust; on and on.

Adonai [Heb] *ah-doh-NY.* God; Lord.

ad patres [Lat] *ahd-PAH-tres.* (*lit.,* to the fathers) dead.

ad populum [Lat] *ahd-POH-poo-loom.* to the populace; appealing to the masses.

ad quem [Lat] *ahd-KWEM.* to or for whom or which.

ad rem [Lat] *ahd-REM.* (*lit.,* to the thing) to the point; to the question or matter.

à droite [Fr] *ah-DRWAHT.* to or on the right.

adsum [Lat] *AHD-soom.* (*lit.,* I am here) present!

aduana [Sp] *ah-DWAH-nah.* customhouse; customs.

a due voci [It] *ah-DOO-eh-VOH-chee.* with or for two voices.

ad utrumque paratus [Lat] *ahd-oo-TROOM-kweh-pah-RAH-toos.* ready for either (of two eventualities).

ad valorem [Lat] *ahd-vah-LOH-rem.* in proportion to the value.

advienne que pourra [Fr] *ahd-VYEN-kuh-poo-RAH.* come what may.

ad vitam [Lat] *ahd-VEE-tahm.* for life.

advocatus diaboli [Lat] *ahd-voh-KAH-toos-dee-AH-boh-lee.* devil's advocate.

aequam servare mentem [Lat] *Y-kwahm-sehr-VAH-reh-MEN-tem.* to keep a level head.

aequo animo [Lat] *Y-kwoh-AH-nee-moh.* with calm mind; with equanimity.

aere perennius [Lat] *Y-reh-peh-REN-nee-oos.* more enduring than bronze.

Aeroflot [Russ] *ah-eh-ruh-FLAWT.* the principal Soviet airline.

aes alienum [Lat] *YS-ah-lee-EH-noom.* another's money; borrowed money; debt.

aetas [Lat] *Y-tahs.* age.

aetatis suae [Lat] *y-TAH-tees-SOO-y.* of or at his or her age.

aetheling [AS] *ATH-uh-ling.* nobleman.

aevum [Lat] *Y-voom.* age; eon; eternity.

a favor de [Sp] *ah-fah-VOR-deh.* in favor of; for; for the benefit of.

afectísimo [Sp] *ah-fek-TEE-see-moh.* very affectionately: close of a letter.

afectuoso [Sp] *ah-fek-TWOH-soh.* affectionate.

affabile [It] *ahf-FAH-bee-leh.* (*music*) in a pleasing manner; affable.

affaire [Fr] *ah-FEHR.* affair; matter; transaction; dealing; —**d'amour** (*-dah-MOOR*) love affair; —**de coeur** (*-duh-KÖR*) affair of the heart; love affair; —**d'honneur** (*-duh-NÖR*) a matter of honor.

affaires [Fr] *ah-FEHR.* affairs; matters; business.

affetto [It] *ahf-FET-toh.* affection; warmth; passion.

affettuoso [It] *ahf-fet-TWOH-soh.* tender; tenderly; with feeling.

affiche [Fr] *ah-FEESH*. poster; billboard; placard; notice.

afflatus [Lat] *ahf-FLAH-toos*. breath; wind, breeze; inspiration.

affresco. See **fresco.**

affrettando [It] *ahf-fret-TAHN-doh*. (*music*) speeding up in tempo; quickening.

aficionado [Sp] *ah-fee-syoh-NAH-doh*. enthusiast; buff; fan.

à fond [Fr] *ah-FŎ*. at or to the bottom; thoroughly.

a fortiori [Lat] *ah-for-tee-OH-ree*. for a stronger reason; all the more.

aga [Turk] *AH-ghah*. ruler; leader; commander. Also, **agha.**

à gauche [Fr] *ah-GOHSH*. to or on the left.

agent provocateur [Fr] *ah-ZHĂ-proh-voh-kah-TŎR*. instigator; agitator; secret agent assigned to incite suspected persons to commit overt illegal acts in order to expose them.

ager [Lat] *AH-gehr*. field; district; territory; **—romanus** (*-roh-MAH-noos*) the original Roman territory.

agevole [It] *ah-JAY-voh-leh*. (*music*) lightly; with ease.

Aggadah [Heb] *ahg-gah-DAH*. tale; narrative; parts of the Talmud other than the laws. Also, **Haggadah.**

aggiornamento [It] *ah-jor-nah-MAYN-toh*. a bringing up to date; updating; modernization.

agha [Turk] *AH-ghah*. See **aga.**

agio [It *aggio*] *AH-joh*. fee for conversion of currency; difference in value between currencies.

agitato [It] *ah-jee-TAH-toh*. (*music*) with agitation; fast.

aglio [It] *AH-lyoh*. garlic.

agnellotti [It] *ah-nyel-LOHT-tee* (*lit.*, fat lambs) stuffed macaroni.

Agnus Dei [Lat] *AHG-noos-DEH-ee*. Lamb of God.

à gogo [Fr] *ah-goh-GOH*. (*slang*) aplenty; in abundance. See **gogo.**

agora [Gk] *AH-goh-rah*. marketplace; open market; assembly.

agrégation [Fr] *ah-gray-gah-SYŎ*. competitive examination for highest teaching posts in French lycées and universities.

agrégé [Fr] *ah-gray-ZHAY*. person certified to teach in a

French lycée or university after successfully competing in the **agrégation**.

agrément [Fr] *ah-gray-MÃ*. agreement; consent; agreeable quality; (*diplomacy*) the receiving country's agreement to another country's envoy.

agua [Sp] *AH-gwah*. water; —**caliente** (*-kah-LYEN-teh*) warm or hot water; —**fresca** (*-FRES-kah*) cool or fresh water; —**fría** (*-FREE-ah*) cold or ice water.

aguacate [Sp] *ah-gwah-KAH-teh*. avocado.

aguador [Sp] *ah-gwah-DOR*. water carrier.

aguardiente [Sp] *ah-gwar-DYEN-teh*. (*lit.*, fire water) coarse brandy or native whiskey.

à haute voix [Fr] *ah-OHT-VWAH*. aloud.

ahimsa [Skt] *uh-HIM-suh*. principle of nonviolence.

ahora [Sp] *ah-OH-rah*. now.

à huis clos [Fr] *ah-ÜEE-KLOH*. behind closed doors; in secret or private.

aide-de-camp [Fr] *EHD-duh-KÃ*. officer who serves as confidential assistant to a superior officer.

aide-mémoire [Fr] *EHD-may-MWAR*. memory aid; outline of discussion or agreement.

aide-toi, le ciel t'aidera [Fr] *ed-TWAH-luh-SYEL-ted'RAH*. God helps those who help themselves.

aigre-doux [Fr: *fem.* **aigre-douce**] *EH-gruh-DOO* (*-DOOS*) sour-sweet; semisour.

aigrette [Fr] *eh-GRET*. egret; plume of feathers or hair; feather boa; spray of precious stones.

aiguille [Fr] *ay-GÜEE-yuh*. needle; spire, needlelike mountain peak.

aiguillette [Fr] *eh-güee-YET*. shoulder braid loop; strip of meat or fish; (*naut.*) lanyard.

aîné [Fr] *eh-NAY*. elder; senior.

ainsi de suite [Fr] *ē-SEE-duh-SÜEET*. and so on; and so forth; etc.

ainsi soit-il [Fr] *ē-SEE-swah-TEEL*. so be it; amen.

air champêtre [Fr] *EHR-shã-PEH-truh*. (*music*) country tune.

air distingué [Fr] *EHR-dees-tē-GAY*. distinguished appearance or mien.

aire libre [Sp] *Y-reh-LEE-breh.* open air.

A.K. Abbr. of **alter kacker.**

Akademiya Nauk [Russ] *uh-kuh-DYEH-mee-yuh-nah-OOK.* Soviet Academy of Sciences.

Aktiengesellschaft [Ger] *AHK-tsyen-guh-zel-shahft.* joint stock company.

al [Ar] *ahl.* the.

al [It, Sp] *ahl.* to, at or in the.

ala [Lat] *AH-lah.* wing.

à la [Fr] *ah-lah.* in the manner of; after the style of. See **au.**

à l'abandon [Fr] *ah-lah-bā-DŎ.* carelessly; freely; uninhibitedly; at random.

à la belle étoile [Fr] *ah-lah-BEL-ay-TWAHL.* out in the open; under the stars.

à la bonne heure [Fr] *ah-lah-buh-NŎR.* (*lit.*, at the right time) very good! fine!

à la bourgeoise [Fr] *ah-lah-boor-ZHWAHZ.* middle-class fashion; family style.

à la broche [Fr] *ah-lah-BROHSH.* cooked on a skewer or spit.

à la campagne [Fr] *ah-lah-kā-PAH-nyuh.* in the country.

à la carte [Fr] *ah-lah-KART.* according to the menu; each item ordered individually. Cf. **table d'hôte.**

à la créole [Fr] *ah-lah-kray-AWL.* (*cookery*) Creole style, usu. with tomatoes, peppers and onions, and highly seasoned.

à la diable [Fr] *ah-lah-DYAH-bluh.* (*cookery*) deviled.

à la française [Fr] *ah-lah-frā-SEZ.* French style.

à la lanterne [Fr] *ah-lah-lā-TEHR-nuh.* to the lamppost!: a slogan of the French Revolution, when persons were hanged from the chains supporting the street lights.

à la lyonnaise [Fr] *ah-lah-lyuh-NEZ.* Lyon style; cooked with finely sliced onions.

à la maison [Fr] *ah-lah-meh-ZŎ.* at home; indoors.

à la maître d'hôtel [Fr] *ah-lah-MEH-truh-doh-TEL.* (*cookery*) very simply prepared with parsley, butter and lemon juice.

alameda [Sp] *ah-lah-MEH-dah.* avenue or mall lined with trees, esp. poplars.

álamo [Sp] *AH-lah-moh.* poplar tree.

à la mode [Fr] *ah-lah-MOHD.* in the (current) fashion; modish; (*U.S. colloq.*, of pie or other dessert) with ice cream; (of beef) larded and braised with vegetables and served with a thick brown gravy.

à la rigueur [Fr] *ah-lah-ree-GÖR.* in a strict sense; strictly speaking; if absolutely necessary.

à la russe [Fr] *ah-lah-RÜS.* Russian style.

alba [Prov] *AHL-bah.* dawn; song sung at dawn.

albergo [It] *ahl-BEHR-goh.* hotel; inn.

alborada [Sp] *ahl-boh-RAH-dah.* song or music performed at dawn.

albus [Lat] *AHL-boos.* white.

alcalde [Sp] *ahl-KAHL-deh.* mayor; magistrate; justice of the peace.

alcázar [Sp] *ahl-KAH-sar.* castle; fortified palace.

aldea [Sp] *ahl-DEH-ah.* village; hamlet.

al dente [It] *ahl-DEN-teh.* (*lit.*, to the tooth) not overcooked (pasta).

al doppio burro [It] *ahl-DOHP-pyoh-BOOR-roh.* with double butter (said of fettuccine served with butter and cheese).

alea jacta est [Lat] *AH-leh-ah-YAHK-tah-est.* the die is cast.

alegría [Sp] *ah-leh-GREE-ah.* happiness, joy; a flamenco dance.

alemán [Sp] *ah-leh-MAHN.* German.

alfândega [Port] *ahl-FUN-duh-guh.* customhouse.

al fine [It] *ahl-FEE-neh.* (*music*) to the end.

alforja [Sp] *ahl-FOR-hah.* saddlebag; pack.

al fresco [It] *ahl-FRAYS-koh.* outdoors; in the open air.

algodón [Sp] *ahl-goh-DOHN.* cotton.

alguacil [Sp] *ahl-gwah-SEEL.* constable; bailiff.

alianza [Sp] *ah-LYAHN-sah.* alliance.

aliquando bonus dormitat Homerus [Lat] *ah-lee-KWAHN-doh-BOH-noos-DOR-mee-taht-hoh-MEH-roos.* (*lit.*, sometimes even great Homer dozes) even the greatest are at times not up to their best.

à l'italienne [Fr] *ah-lee-tah-LYEN.* Italian style.

aliter [Lat] *AH-lee-tehr.* otherwise.

aljamiado [Sp, from *aljamía,* corrupt Spanish as spoken by the Moors, from Ar *al- 'ajamīya,* foreign tongue] *ahl-hah-MYAH-doh.* written with Arabic characters.

Alki [Chinook] *AHL-kee.* By and by (motto of the State of Washington).

Alkoran [Ar *al-Qūrān*] *al-koh-RAHN.* the Koran.

alla [It] *AHL-lah.* to the; in the fashion or style of.

alla breve [It] *ahl-lah-BREH-veh.* (*lit.,* according to the breve; that is, using the half note as the unit of tempo) (*music*) in 2-2 or 4-2 time.

alla cacciatora [It] *ahl-lah-kah-chah-TOH-rah.* (*cookery*) huntsman's style; potted with tomato sauce.

alla marinara [It] *ahl-lah-mah-ree-NAH-rah.* (*cookery*) mariner style; prepared with a sauce of tomatoes, garlic and spices.

alla milanese [It] *ahl-lah-mee-lah-NAY-seh.* (*cookery*) Milan style; of veal cutlets, breaded and browned in oil or butter.

alla prima [It] *ahl-lah-PREE-mah.* (*lit.,* at the first) of a painting, executed spontaneously and without retouching.

alla (vostra) salute [It] *ahl-lah-(VOHS-trah)-sah-LOO-teh.* to your health!

allegretto [It] *ahl-leh-GRAYT-toh.* (*music*) light, cheerful and moderately fast.

allegro [It] *ahl-LEH-groh.* (*music*) lively; quick; cheerful; lively piece.

allemand [Fr] *ahl-MÃ.* German.

allentando [It] *ahl-len-TAHN-doh.* (*music*) slowing down gradually.

allez-vous-en [Fr] *ah-LAY-voo-ZÃ.* be off!, go away!, get out!

allgemein [Ger] *AHL-guh-myn.* general; universal.

allongé [Fr] *ah-lõ-ZHAY.* (*lit.,* lengthened) of a ballet movement, performed with arms and one leg extended in a straight line.

allons [Fr] *ah-LÕ.* let's go! come on!; nonsense!

allure [Fr] *ah-LÜR.* gait; carriage, bearing.

alma [Sp] *AHL-mah.* soul.

almacén [Sp, from Ar *al-makhzan*] *ahl-mah-SEN*. storehouse, warehouse; magazine.

Alma Mater [Lat] *AHL-mah-MAH-tehr*. (*lit*., nourishing mother) school or college from which one has graduated.

almoço [Port] *uhl-MOH-soo*. breakfast.

almuerzo [Sp] *ahl-MWEHR-soh*. lunch; luncheon.

aloha [Hawaiian] *ah-LOH-hah*. (*lit*., love) expression of greeting and farewell; —**oe** (*-OH-eh*) farewell to thee.

à l'orange [Fr] *ah-loh-RÃZH*. (*cookery*) with orange or orange sauce.

alors [Fr] *ah-LOR*. then; so; well then.

alouette [Fr] *ah-loo-ET*. lark.

Alpenhorn [Ger] *AHL-p'n-horn*. long horn used by Swiss herdsmen and mountaineers.

Alpenstock [Ger] *AHL-p'n-SHTOHK*. long climbing-staff with iron point.

Alpha and Omega [Gk] *AL-fuh-and-oh-MEE-guh*. first and last letters of the Greek alphabet; hence, beginning and end.

alpino [It] *ahl-PEE-noh*. member of Italian mountain troops.

al segno [It] *ahl-SEH-nyoh*. (*lit*., to the sign) (*music*) a direction to the performer to continue as far as the sign.

alt [Ger] *ahlt*. old.

alter ego [Lat] *AHL-tehr-EH-goh*. one's other self; a very close friend.

alter kacker [Yid] *AHL-tuh-KAH-kuh*. (*slang*) old fuddy-duddy; old curmudgeon. Also, **alter kocker**. Abbr. **A.K.**

Altertum [Ger] *AHL-tuh-toom*. antiquity, esp. classical.

altesse [Fr] *ahl-TES*. Highness.

alteza [Sp] *ahl-TEH-sah*. Highness.

altezza [It] *ahl-TAY-tsah*. Highness.

altiplano [Sp] *ahl-tee-PLAH-noh*. high plateau.

altissimo [It] *ahl-TEES-see-moh*. highest; most high.

alto [It] *AHL-toh*. (abbr. from *contralto*, counter-high or low) low female voice, ranging between soprano and tenor.

alto [Sp] *AHL-toh*. (*SW U.S.*) hill.

alto-rilievo [It] *AHL-toh-ree-LYEH-voh*. high relief.

alumnus [Lat: *fem.* **alumna;** *pl.* **alumni, alumnae**] *ah-LOOM-noos* (*-nah*) (*-nee, -ny*) graduate of an institution.

A.M. [Lat: abbr. of **ante meridiem**] *AHN-teh-meh-REE-dee-em.* before noon.

ama [Port] *AH-muh.* in India, wet nurse; nursemaid; female servant. Also, **amah.**

amabile [It] *ah-MAH-bee-leh.* (*music*) amiably; sweetly.

amant [Fr] *ah-MÃ.* lover, sweetheart.

amantes amentes [Lat] *ah-MAHN-tes-ah-MEN-tes.* lovers are crazy.

amapola [Sp] *ah-mah-POH-lah.* poppy.

amarillo [Sp] *ah-mah-REE-lyoh.* yellow.

ambiance [Fr] *ã-BYÃS.* environment; surroundings.

A.M.D.G. Abbr. of **ad majorem Dei gloriam.**

âme [Fr] *ahm.* soul.

amende honorable [Fr] *ah-MÃD-oh-noh-RAH-bluh.* honorable amends; public apology.

a mensa et toro [Lat] *ah-MEN-sah-et-TOH-roh.* from board and bed.

americano (al selz) [It] *ah-meh-ree-KAH-noh* (*-ahl-SELTS*). vermouth aperitif (with soda).

amerikanka [Russ] *uh-mee-ree-KAHN-kuh.* (*lit.,* American woman) beauty salon.

à merveille [Fr] *ah-mehr-VEH-yuh.* wonderfully.

a mezza voce [It] *ah-MED-zah-VOH-chay.* (*music*) at half voice; softly.

ami [Fr: *fem.* **amie**] *ah-MEE.* friend; —**de coeur** (*-duh-KÖR*) bosom friend; —**de cour** (*-duh-KOOR*) false friend; —**de table** (*-duh-TAH-bluh*) table companion; —**du peuple** (*-dü-PÖ-pluh*) friend of the people.

amico [It: *pl.* **amici**] *ah-MEE-koh* (*-chee*) friend.

amicus curiae [Lat] *ah-MEE-koos-KOO-ree-y* (*lit.,* friend of the court) an impartial advisor in a case at law.

amicus humani generis [Lat] *ah-MEE-koos-hoo-MAH-nee-GEH-neh-rees.* friend of the human race.

amie [Fr, fem. of **ami**] *ah-MEE.* girl friend; lady friend; mistress.

amigo [Sp: *pl.* **amigos**] *ah-MEE-goh* (*-gohs*) friend.

amir [Ar] *AH-meer.* Mohammedan ruler's title.

amitié [Fr: *pl.* **amitiés**, cordial greetings] *ah-mee-TYAY.* amity; friendship.

amo [Sp] *AH-moh.* master.

à moi [Fr] *ah-MWAH.* help (me)!, here!

à moitié [Fr] *ah-mwah-TYAY.* half; in part; halfway.

amok [Malay] *AH-mohk.* amuck; in a confused, frenzied manner; in a wild state.

à mon avis [Fr] *ah-mõ-nah-VEE.* in my opinion.

amore [It] *ah-MOH-reh.* love; —**con amor si paga** (*-koh-nah-MOR-see-PAH-gah*) love is repaid with love; one good turn deserves another.

amoretto [It] *ah-moh-RAYT-toh.* a Cupid (in painting or sculpture). Also, **amorino** (*ah-moh-REE-noh*).

amoroso [It] *ah-moh-ROH-soh.* (*music*) amorously; tenderly.

amor patriae [Lat] *AH-mor-PAH-tree-y.* love of country; patriotism.

amor proximi [Lat] *AH-mor-PROHK-see-mee.* love of one's neighbor.

amorti [Fr] *ah-mor-TEE.* (*lit.*, deadened, half dead) (*slang*) senior citizen.

amortissement [Fr] *ah-mor-tees-MÃ.* liquidation; amortization; end; (*archit.*) a pyramidal ornament at the peak of a building.

amour [Fr] *ah-MOOR.* love; love affair; —**propre** (*-PROH-pruh*) self-esteem; self-respect; self-love; vanity.

amourette [Fr] *ah-moo-RET.* trivial love affair; garnish made from spinal marrow of sheep or calves.

amparo [Sp] *ahm-PAH-roh.* (*lit.*, protection, shelter) (*SW U.S.*) a temporary land claim, good until full title is granted.

ampulla [Lat] *ahm-POOL-lah.* glass bottle or flask of globular form for holding drugs.

Amt [Ger] *ahmt.* public office.

an [Fr] *ã.* year.

ana [Gk] *ah-NAH.* up; back; again; throughout.

anabasis [Gk] *ah-NAH-bah-sees.* (*lit.*, a going up) military expedition.

analekta [Gk] *ah-nah-LEK-tah.* gleanings; literary excerpts or selections.

ananas [Fr] *ah-nah-NAH.* pineapple.

anangke [Gk] *ah-NAHNG-keh.* force; necessity; fate.

anchois [Fr] *ã-SHWAH.* anchovy.

ancien régime [Fr] *ã-SYÊ-ray-ZHEEM.* old regime; pre-Revolutionary France.

ancilla [Lat] *ahn-KEEL-lah.* handmaiden; assistant.

ancora [It] *ahn-KOH-rah.* still; yet; again; more.

andabata [Lat] *ahn-DAH-bah-tah.* Roman gladiator who fought blindfolded.

ándale [MexSp] *AHN-dah-leh.* go on!, come on!, hurry!

andante [It] *ahn-DAHN-teh.* (*music*) medium slow.

andantino [It] *ahn-dahn-TEE-noh.* (*music*) slow; a little faster than **andante**.

andén [Sp] *ahn-DEN.* sidewalk; footpath.

Andenken [Ger] *AHN-den-k'n.* commemoration.

andiamo [It] *ahn-DYAH-moh.* let's go.

andouillette [Fr] *ã-doo-YET.* forcemeat ball or patty; small pork sausage.

âne [Fr] *ahn.* ass; donkey; fool.

Anfang [Ger] *AHN-fahng.* inception; beginning.

angaria [Lat, from Gk] *ahn-GAH-ree-ah.* mandatory public service; forced duty.

angelus [Lat] *AHN-geh-loos.* angel.

anglais [Fr] *ã-GLEH.* English; Englishman.

Angleterre [Fr] *ã-gluh-TEHR.* England.

anglice [Lat] *AHN-glee-keh.* in English.

Angst [Ger] *ahnkst.* fear; anxiety; foreboding.

Anhang [Ger] *AHN-hahng.* appendix to a book; (*music*) coda.

anima [Lat] *AH-nee-mah.* soul; spirit; life; feeling.

animato [It] *ah-nee-MAH-toh.* with animation; with spirit.

animelles [Fr] *ah-nee-MEL.* (*cookery*) lamb's fries.

animis opibusque parati [Lat] *AH-nee-mees-oh-pee-BOOS-kweh-pah-RAH-tee.* Prepared in minds and resources (motto of South Carolina).

animo [Lat] *AH-nee-moh.* intentionally; wittingly; —**et fide** (*-et-FEE-deh*) by courage and faith.

animoso [It] *ah-nee-MOH-soh.* (*music*) with animation; lively.

animus [Lat] *AH-nee-moos.* will; mind; intention; hostility; enmity.

ankh [Egyptian] *ahngk.* cross with ring or loop in place of upper arm, used as life symbol in ancient Egypt.

Anlaut [Ger] *AHN-lowt.* initial sound or letter.

Anmerkung [Ger; *pl.* **Anmerkungen**] *AHN-mer-koong* (*-koon-g'n*) note; remark; annotation.

anna [Hindi] *AHN-nah.* former monetary unit of India.

année [Fr] *ah-NAY.* year.

anno [It] *AHN-noh.* year.

anno Domini [Lat: *abbr.* **A.D.**] *AHN-noh-DOH-mee-nee.* (in the) year of Our Lord.

anno regni [Lat] *AHN-noh-REG-nee.* in the year of the reign.

anno urbis conditae [Lat: *abbr.* **A.U.C.**] *AHN-noh-OOR-bees-KOHN-dee-ty.* in the year from the founding of the city (of Rome, about 753 B.C.).

annuit coeptis [Lat] *AHN-noo-eet-KOYP-tees.* (God) has favored (our) undertakings.

annulus et baculus [Lat] *AHN-noo-loos-et-BAH-koo-loos.* ring and staff (bishop's investiture symbols).

año [Sp] *AH-nyoh.* year.

anomie [Fr, from Gk *a*, without + *nomos*, law] *ah-noh-MEE.* state of lawlessness or lack of norms, with social disorganization or upheaval.

Año Nuevo [Sp] *AH-nyoh-NWEH-voh.* New Year.

An Poblacht Abu [IrGael] *un-POH-blahkht-uh-BOO.* Up with the Republic!

Anschauung [Ger] *AHN-show-oong.* insight; view; direct insight or intuition.

Anschluss [Ger] *AHN-shloos.* union; annexation (of Austria to Germany, 1938).

Ansicht [Ger] *AHN-ziçt.* opinion; viewpoint.

ante [Lat] *AHN-teh.* before.

ante-bellum [Lat] *AHN-teh-BEL-loom.* prewar; before the war.

ante Christum [Lat: *abbr.* **A.C.**] *AHN-teh-KREES-toom.* before Christ.

ante meridiem. See **A.M.**

ante mortem [Lat] *AHN-teh-MOR-tem.* before death.

anthropos [Gk] *AHN-throh-pohs.* man.

antipasto [It] *ahn-tee-PAHS-toh.* (*lit.*, before the meal) (*cookery*) a dish of appetizers, often including olives, anchovies, salami and cheese.

antiquaille [Fr] *ã-tee-KY-yuh.* worthless antiques.

Anzeige [Ger] *AHN-tsy-geh.* advertisement; announcement.

a otro perro con ese hueso [Sp] *ah-OH-troh-PER-roh-kohn-EH-seh-WEH-soh.* [*lit.*, (go) to some other dog with that bone] tell it to the Marines.

à outrance [Fr] *ah-oo-TRÃS.* to the extreme; to the death.

apache [Fr] *ah-PASH.* in Paris, a gangster or hood; wild one.

à part [Fr] *ah-PAR.* apart; aside.

apartheid [Afrikaans] *uh-PART-hayt.* separation; segregation; in Africa, the separation of blacks and coloreds from the whites.

apellido [Sp] *ah-peh-LYEE-doh.* surname.

aperçu [Fr] *ah-pehr-SÙ.* glance; quick sketch; outline; intuitive understanding.

apéritif [Fr] *ah-pay-ree-TEEF.* appetizer; mildly alcoholic before-dinner drink.

à peu près [Fr] *ah-pö-PREH.* nearly; almost.

Apfelkuchen [Ger] *AHP-f'l-koo-kh'n.* apple cake.

Apfelstrudel [Ger] *AHP-f'l-shtroo-d'l.* apple strudel.

a piacere [It] *ah-pyah-CHAY-reh.* (*music*) at (one's) pleasure; as desired.

à pied [Fr] *ah-PYAY.* on foot.

aplomb [Fr] *ah-PLŎ.* self-assurance; confidence; poise.

apo [Gk] *ah-POH.* from; away, apart.

a poco a poco [It] *ah-POH-koh-ah-POH-koh.* little by little; slowly.

à point [Fr] *ah-PWẼ.* apropos; well-timed.

a posteriori [Lat] *ah-pohs-teh-ree-OH-ree.* (*lit.*, from what is after) from effect to cause; (reasoning) from experience or inductively.

appassionato [It] *ahp-pahs-syoh-NAH-toh.* (*music*) passionately; with feeling.

appel [Fr] *ah-PEL.* (*fencing*) a call; a challenge.

appliqué [Fr] *ah-plee-KAY.* ornamentation applied directly or on a background surface; the process of direct application.

appoggiato [It] *ahp-poh-JAH-toh.* (*lit.,* supported, aided) (*music*) notes dependent on others; connecting notes to be played without a break.

appoggiatura [It] *ahp-poh-jah-TOO-rah.* (*music*) grace note.

appui [Fr] *ah-PÜEE.* prop; support.

après [Fr] *ah-PREH.* after; afterward.

après-midi [Fr] *ah-PREH-mee-DEE.* afternoon.

après moi le déluge [Fr] *ah-preh-MWAH-luh-day-LÜZH.* after me, the deluge: a distortion of Mme de Pompadour's *après nous le déluge,* a premonition of impending revolution.

a principio [Lat] *ah-preen-KEE-pee-oh.* from the beginning.

a priori [Lat] *ah-pree-OH-ree.* (*lit.,* from what is before) from cause to effect; (*reasoning*) from prior knowledge or deductively.

à propos [Fr] *ah-proh-POH.* appropriate; to the point; opportune; with regard to.

aqua [Lat] *AH-kwah.* water; —**fortis** (*-FOR-tees*) (*lit.,* strong water) nitric acid; —**pura** (*-POO-rah*) pure or distilled water; —**regia** (*REH-gee-ah*) (*lit.,* royal water) mixture of nitric and hydrochloric acids.

Aquarius [Lat, from *aqua,* water] *ah-KWAH-ree-oos.* water bearer: a sign of the Zodiac.

à quatre mains [Fr] *ah-KAH-truh-MẼ.* for four hands.

aqua vitae [Lat] *AH-kwah-VEE-ty.* (*lit.,* water of life) brandy; whiskey.

aquí [Sp] *ah-KEE.* here.

aquila [Lat] *AH-kwee-lah.* eagle.

a quo [Lat] *ah-KWOH.* from which; point of departure.

à quoi bon? [Fr] *ah-KWAH-BÕ.* to what end? what's the use?

arak [Ar] *ah-RAHK.* any of several alcoholic beverages of the East and Middle East distilled usually from fermented palm sap or molasses. Also, **arrack.**

Arbeiter [Ger] *AR-by-tuh.* worker; workers.

Arbeitsdienst [Ger] *AR-byts-deenst.* labor service or department.

arbiter bibendi [Lat] *AR-bee-tehr-bee-BEN-dee.* toastmaster.

arbiter elegantiarum [Lat] *AR-bee-tehr-eh-leh-gahn-tee-AH-room.* spokesman of elegance; authority in matters of style and good taste.

arbor vitae [Lat] *AR-bor-VEE-ty.* (*lit.,* tree of life) name of an evergreen shrub.

arcana [Lat] *ar-KAH-nah.* secrets; mysteries; ark which holds sacred objects; secluded area used for occult purposes.

arc-boutant [Fr] *ar-boo-TÃ.* flying buttress.

arc-en-ciel [Fr] *ar-kã-SYEL.* rainbow.

archon [Gk] *AR-kohn.* ruler; chief magistrate in ancient Athens.

arco [It] *AR-koh.* bow.

arena [Sp] *ah-REH-nah.* sand.

arete [Gk] *ah-reh-TEH.* virtue; excellence.

arête [Fr] *ah-RET.* (*lit.,* fishbone) sharp mountain ridge between two gorges.

argent [Fr] *ar-ZHÃ.* silver; money.

argumentum [Lat] *ahr-goo-MEN-toom.* argument; exposition; hypothesis; —**ad hominem** (see **ad hominem**); —**ad ignorantiam** (*-ahd-eeg-noh-RAHN-tee-ahm*) (*lit.,* argument to ignorance) argument directed at opponent's factual ignorance or his inability to disprove the facts presented; —**ad populum** (*-ahd-POH-poo-loom*) (*lit.,* to the populace) argument directed at the sentiments and emotions of the masses rather than at the intellect; —**ex silentio** (*-eks-see-LEN-tee-oh*) (*lit.,* from silence) verdict based on the absence of information or data.

Ar Hyd Y Nos [Welsh] *ar-HEED-ee-NOHS.* All through the night.

aria cantabile [It] *AH-ryah-kahn-TAH-bee-leh.* smooth, easily sung song.

Aries [Lat] *AH-ree-es.* ram: a sign of the Zodiac.

arietta [It] *ah-RYAYT-tah.* (*music*) brief aria.

arigatō [Jap] *ah-reeng-ah-TOH.* thank you.

arioso [It] *ah-RYOH-soh.* (*music*) gaily; melodiously; a short song, looser in form than an aria.

arista [Gk] *AH-rees-tah.* (*lit.,* the best) honors group in a high school.

a rivederci [It] *ah-ree-veh-DEHR-chee.* good-bye; till we meet again. Also, **arrivederci.**

arlecchino [It] *ar-lek-KEE-noh.* Harlequin; jester, clown; a character of the Commedia dell'Arte.

arma [Lat] *AR-mah.* arms, weapons; coat of arms.

Arma Aerea [It] *AR-mah-ah-EH-reh-ah.* the Italian air force.

arma blanca [Sp] *AR-mah-BLAHN-kah.* steel-bladed weapon, esp. a sword.

arma virumque cano [Lat] *AR-mah-vee-ROOM-kweh-KAH-noh.* arms and the man I sing: opening measures of Vergil's *Aeneid.*

arme bianca [It] *AR-meh-BYAHN-kah.* steel-bladed weapon, esp. a sword.

arme blanche [Fr] *arm-BLÃSH.* steel-bladed weapon, esp. a sword.

armoire [Fr] *ar-MWAR.* wardrobe; large cupboard or closet.

arpeggio [It] *ar-PEJ-joh.* (*music*) sounding of notes in a chord in rapid succession instead of simultaneously.

arpent [Fr] *ar-PÃ.* old French land measure, equal to about 1½ acres; in Quebec, linear measure equal to 12 rods; in Louisiana, land measure equal to about 1⅓ acres.

arrack. See **arak.**

arrayán [Sp] *ar-rah-YAHN.* myrtle.

arrectis auribus [Lat] *ar-REK-tees-OW-ree-boos.* with ears cocked.

arrêtez [Fr] *ah-reh-TAY.* stop!

arriba [Sp] *ar-REE-bah.* up; above, upstairs; (*music*) increase in tempo; faster.

arrière [Fr] *ah-RYEHR.* rear; stern; — -pensée (-*pã-SAY*) ulterior motive; afterthought; **en arrière** (*ã-nah-RYEHR*) in the rear; in arrears.

arrivé [Fr] *ah-ree-VAY.* (*lit.*, one who has arrived) a newly famous or successful person; parvenu.

arrivederci. See **a rivederci.**

arrondissement [Fr] *ah-rõ-dees-MÃ.* subdivision of French administrative department; district; section.

arroyo [Sp] *ar-ROH-yoh.* creek; small stream; gulch.

arroz [Sp] *ar-ROHS.* rice; —**con frijoles** (*-kohn-free-HOH-les*) rice with beans; —**con pollo** (*-kohn-POH-lyoh*) rice with chicken.

ars [Lat] *ars.* art; —**amandi** (*-ah-MAHN-dee*) art of loving; —**amatoria** (*-ah-mah-TOH-ree-ah*) art of lovers; amatory art; —**artium** (*-AR-tee-oom*) (*lit.*, art of arts) logic; —**(est) longa, vita brevis** (*-est-LOHN-gah-VEE-tah-BREH-vees*) art is long, life short; —**gratia artis** (*-GRAH-tee-ah-AR-tees*) art for art's sake; —**moriendi** (*-moh-ree-EN-dee*) art of dying; —**poetica** (*-poh-EH-tee-kah*) art of poetry; poetic art.

artel' [Russ] *ur-TYEL'.* unit of semi-collectivized farm in Soviet Union.

artes perditae [Lat] *AR-tes-PEHR-dee-ty.* lost arts.

Artes, Scientia, Veritas [Lat] *AR-tes-skee-EN-tee-ah-VEH-ree-tahs.* Arts, Science, Truth (motto of the University of Michigan).

artiste [Fr] *ar-TEEST.* artist.

Artium Baccalaureus [Lat] *AR-tee-oom-bahk-kah-LOW-reh-oos.* Bachelor of Arts.

Artium Magister [Lat] *AR-tee-oom-mah-GEES-ter.* Master of Arts.

art nouveau [Fr] *AR-noo-VOH.* (*lit.*, new art) style of art and architecture originating at close of 19th century, characterized by curved lines imitating natural forms.

as [Lat] *ahs.* unit, unity; copper coin.

as [Fr] *ahs.* ace (at cards or dice).

Ashkenazim [Heb] *ahsh-kuh-NAH-zeem.* central and eastern European Jews, usually Yiddish-speaking; distinguished from Ladino-speaking **Sephardim.**

así [Sp] *ah-SEE.* thus, so; such; —**es la vida** (*-es-lah-VEE-dah*) such is life.

asinus [Lat] *AH-see-noos.* ass; donkey.

asor [Heb] *ah-SOR.* stringed instrument of Biblical times.

asperges [Fr] *ahs-PEHRZH.* asparagus.

assai [It] *ahs-SAH-ee.* enough; quite; very.

assez [Fr] *ah-SAY.* enough; quite; rather; —**bien** (*-BYĒ*) well enough; quite well.

assiette [Fr] *ah-SYET.* plate; dish.

aster [Lat, from Gk] *AHS-tehr.* star.

astron [Gk] *AHS-trohn.* star.

Asunción [Sp] *ah-soon-SYOHN.* Assumption.

ataman [Russ, from Ger *Hauptmann*, head man] *uh-tuh-MAHN.* Cossack chief. Also, **hetman.**

até a vista [Port] *ah-TEH-uh-VEESH-tuh.* till we meet again; good-bye.

atelier [Fr] *ah-tuh-LYAY.* studio; workshop.

a tempo [It] *ah-TEM-poh.* (*music*) in correct time; resuming the former tempo; —**giusto** (*-JOOS-toh*) in strict time.

atento [Sp] *ah-TEN-toh.* attentive; diligent; (closing a letter) sincerely.

athlon [Gk] *AH-thlohn.* prize.

atman [Skt] *AHT-mun.* breath; soul; life principle.

à tort et à travers [Fr] *ah-TOR-ay-ah-trah-VEHR.* at random; indiscriminately.

à tort ou à raison [Fr] *ah-TOR-oo-ah-reh-ZŎ.* right(ly) or wrong(ly).

à tout prix [Fr] *ah-TOO-PREE.* at any price; whatever the cost.

à travers [Fr] *ah-trah-VEHR.* across; through.

à trois [Fr] *ah-TRWAH.* for or among three; three at a time.

attacca [It] *aht-TAHK-kah.* (*music*) attack; begin at once.

au [Fr] *oh.* with (the); in the manner or style of. See **à la.**

aubade [Fr] *oh-BAHD.* morning song; song sung at dawn.

auberge [Fr] *oh-BEHRZH.* inn; hotel; tavern.

aubergine [Fr] *oh-behr-ZHEEN.* eggplant.

au besoin [Fr] *oh-buh-ZWĒ.* in case of need; if need be.

au beurre fondu [Fr] *oh-BÖR-fŏ-DÜ*. (*cookery*) with melted butter or butter sauce.

au beurre noir [Fr] *oh-BÖR-NWAR*. (*cookery*) with browned butter.

au bout de son latin [Fr] *oh-BOO-duh-sŏ-lah-TẼ*. (*lit.*, at the end of one's Latin) at one's wit's end.

au bout du compte [Fr] *oh-BOO-dü-CŌT*. (*lit.*, at the end of the account) after all; finally.

A.U.C. See **ab urbe condita, anno urbis conditae.**

auch ich war in Arkadien geboren [Ger] *owkh-IÇ-var-in-ar-KAH-dee-'n-guh-BOR-'n*. (*lit.*, I, too, was born in Arcadia) I, too, have my ideals.

au clair de la lune [Fr] *oh-KLEHR-duh-lah-LÜ-nuh*. by the light of the moon.

au contraire [Fr] *oh-kŏ-TREHR*. on the contrary.

au courant [Fr] *oh-koo-RÃ*. well-informed; up-to-date.

audaces fortuna juvat [Lat] *ow-DAH-kes-for-TOO-nah-YOO-vaht*. fortune favors the brave.

audemus jura nostra defendere [Lat] *ow-DEH-moos-YOO-rah-NOHS-trah-deh-FEN-deh-reh*. We dare defend our rights (motto of Alabama).

audi alteram partem [Lat] *OW-dee-AHL-teh-rahm-PAR-tem*. hear the other side.

auf [Ger] *owf*. (*prep.*) on; upon; in, at; to; toward; for; (*adv.* and *prefix*) up, upward; (*interj.*) stand up! (also, **aufstehen!**).

au fait [Fr] *oh-FEH* (*lit.*, to the act or deed) expert; well versed.

Auffassung [Ger] *OWF-fahs-soong*. comprehension; interpretation; conception; view.

aufgeschoben ist nicht aufgehoben [Ger] *OWF-guh-shoh-b'n-ist-niçt-OWF-guh-hoh-b'n*. postponed is not abandoned.

Aufklärung [Ger] *OWF-klehr-oong*. solution; answer; enlightenment.

Auflage [Ger] *OWF-lah-geh*. edition; printing; circulation (of a periodical).

Auflösung [Ger] *OWF-lö-zoong*. dissolution.

au fond [Fr] *oh-FÕ*. at bottom; basically.

aufstehen. See **auf.**

auf Wiedersehen [Ger] *owf-VEE-duh-zeh-'n.* till we meet again; good-bye.

Augenblick [Ger] *OW-g'n-blik.* twinkling of an eye; instant; moment.

au gras [Fr] *oh-GRAH.* with fat; with gravy.

au gratin [Fr] *oh-grah-TÉ.* (*cookery*) having a topping of crisply baked grated cheese or crumbs.

au jus [Fr] *oh-ZHÜ.* (*cookery*) in its natural juice or gravy.

au levant [Fr] *oh-luh-VÃ.* to the east; easterly.

au mieux [Fr] *oh-MYÖ.* at best; for the best.

au naturel [Fr] *oh-nah-tü-REL.* in its natural state; in the nude; unadorned; unaffected; (*cookery*) uncooked; plainly cooked.

au pair [Fr] *oh-PEHR.* (*lit.*, at par, even) without wages; referring usually to a young girl serving as domestic or companion in return for room and board.

au pied de la lettre [Fr] *oh-PYAY-duh-lah-LEH-truh.* literally.

au plaisir(de vous revoir) [Fr] *oh-pleh-ZEER-(duh-voo-ruh-VWAR)* good-bye; until the pleasure (of seeing you again).

aurea mediocritas [Lat] *OW-reh-ah-meh-dee-OH-kree-tahs.* the golden mean.

au revoir [Fr] *oh-ruh-VWAR.* good-bye; till we meet again.

auri sacra fames [Lat] *OW-ree-SAH-krah-FAH-mes.* accursed greed for gold.

Aurora [Lat] *ow-ROH-rah.* Dawn; the goddess of the morning; —**australis** (*-ows-TRAH-lees*) the southern lights; —**borealis** (*-boh-reh-AH-lees*) the northern lights.

aurum [Lat] *OW-room.* gold.

aus den Augen, aus dem Sinn [Ger] *OWS-den-OW-g'n-OWS-dem-ZIN.* out of sight, out of mind.

Ausdruck [Ger] *OWS-drook.* expression; phrase; saying; term.

au secours [Fr] *oh-suh-KOOR.* help!

Ausgabe [Ger] *OWS-gah-beh.* issue; edition.

Ausgang [Ger] *OWS-gahng.* exit.

Ausländer [Ger] *OWS-len-duh.* foreigner; outsider.

Auslandsdeutscher [Ger] *OWS-lahnts-doy-chuh.* German national; native German living abroad.

Auslaut [Ger] *OWS-lowt.* (*ling.*) final sound or letter.

au soleil [Fr] *oh-suh-LAY.* in the sun.

auspicium [Lat] *ows-PEE-kee-oom.* divination; augury; omen; sign.

aussitôt dit, aussitôt fait [Fr] *oh-see-toh-DEE-oh-see-toh-FEH.* no sooner said than done.

Auster [Lat] *OWS-tehr.* the south wind; the south.

aut Caesar aut nullus (or **nihil**) [Lat] *owt-KY-sar-owt-NOOL-loos* (*-NEE-heel*) either Caesar or nothing; nothing but the best; all or nothing.

aut disce aut discede [Lat] *owt-DEES-keh-owt-dees-KEH-deh.* either learn or depart.

Autobahn [Ger] *OW-toh-bahn.* highway; expressway.

auto-da-fé [Port] *OW-too-dah-FEH*; [Sp] **auto de fe.** *OW-toh-deh-FEH.* act of faith; death for a religious cause; during the Inquisition, sentence of burning at the stake.

autore [It] *ow-TOH-reh.* author.

autos [Gk] *ow-TOHS.* self.

autostrada [It] *ow-toh-STRAH-dah.* highway; expressway.

autre [Fr] *OH-truh.* other.

autrefois [Fr] *oh-truh-FWAH.* formerly; at other times.

autres temps, autres moeurs [Fr] *OH-truh-TÃ-ZOH-truh-MÖRS.* other times, other customs.

aut vincere aut mori [Lat] *owt-VEEN-keh-reh-owt-MOH-ree.* either win or die.

au voleur [Fr] *oh-vuh-LÖR.* stop, thief!

aux armes [Fr] *oh-ZARM.* to arms!

aux arrêts [Fr] *oh-zah-REH.* under arrest; in confinement or detention.

aux choux [Fr] *oh-SHOO.* with cabbage.

aux confitures [Fr] *oh-kõ-fee-TÜR.* with preserved fruit.

aux cressons [Fr] *oh-kreh-SÕ.* with watercress.

aux oignons [Fr] *oh-zoh-NYÕ.* with onions.

aux petits pois [Fr] *oh-p'tee-PWAH.* with peas.

aux soins de [Fr] *oh-SWÑ-duh.* in care of.

avant [Fr] *ah-VÃ.* ahead; before.

avant-coureur [Fr] *ah-VÃ-koo-RÖR.* one who rides ahead;

forerunner; harbinger. Also, **avant-courrier** (*-koo-RYAY*).

avant-garde [Fr] *ah-VĂ-GARD*. vanguard.

avanti [It] *ah-VAHN-tee*. ahead; before; forward!; come in!

avant-propos [Fr] *ah-VĂ-proh-POH*. preface; preamble; introduction.

ave [Lat] *AH-veh*. hail!

ave atque vale [Lat] *AH-veh-AHT-kweh-VAH-leh*. hail and farewell!

avec [Fr] *ah-VEK*. with.

ave, Caesar; morituri te salutamus [Lat] *AH-veh-KY-sar-moh-ree-TOO-ree-TEH-sah-loo-TAH-moos*. Hail, Caesar! We who are about to die salute you! (the salute of the gladiators to the Roman emperor).

avec plaisir [Fr] *ah-VEK-pleh-ZEER*. with pleasure.

Ave Maria [Lat] *AH-veh-mah-REE-ah*. Hail, Mary!

avertissement [Fr] *ah-vehr-tees-MĂ*. notice; warning; advice; advertisement.

a vinculo matrimonii [Lat] *ah-VEEN-koo-loh-mah-tree-MOH-nee-ee*. from the bond of matrimony.

avion [Fr] *ah-VYŎ*. airplane; **par—** (*PAR-*) by air mail.

avis [Lat] *AH-vees*. bird.

avis [Fr] *ah-VEE*. advice; notice; point of view; opinion; **—au lecteur** (*-oh-lek-TÖR*) note to the reader; **—au public** (*-oh-pü-BLEEK*) public notice.

aviso [Sp] *ah-VEE-soh*. advice; notice; warning.

avocat [Fr] *ah-voh-KAH*. lawyer; advocate.

à volonté [Fr] *ah-voh-lõ-TAY*. at will; voluntarily; at leisure.

à votre santé [Fr] *ah-VOH-truh-sã-TAY*. to your health!

avoué [Fr] *ah-voo-AY*. lawyer; barrister; advocate.

a vuelta de correo [Sp] *ah-VWEL-tah-deh-kor-REH-oh*. by return mail.

a vuestra salud [Sp] *ah-VWES-trah-sah-LOOD*. to your health!

avviso [It] *ahv-VEE-soh*. advice; notice; warning; advertisement.

axis [Lat] *AHK-sees*. axle.

ayah [Hindi, from Port *aia*] *AH-yuh*. in India, a native nursemaid; lady's maid.

ayer [Sp] *ah-YEHR.* yesterday.

ayuntamiento [Sp] *ah-yoon-tah-MYEN-toh.* municipal council; town hall; city hall.

azafrán [Sp] *ah-sah-FRAHN.* saffron.

azotea [Sp] *ah-so-TEH-ah.* flat roof; roof patio.

azúcar [Sp] *ah-SOO-kar.* sugar.

azul [Sp] *ah-SOOL.* blue.

azzurro [It] *ah-DZOOR-roh.* blue.

B

baas [Afrikaans] *bahs.* boss; master.

bab [Ar] *bahb.* gate.

baba [Fr] *bah-BAH.* plum cake (or pudding), served with hot rum sauce. Also, **baba au rhum** (*-oh-ROHM*).

baba [Russ] *BAH-buh.* old woman, grandmother.

babbo [It] *BAHB-boh.* dad; father.

babu [Hindi: father] *BAH-boo.* Mr., Sir, Esquire; derisive term for an English-speaking native. Also, **baboo.**

babushka [Russ: grandmother] *BAH-boosh-kuh.* triangular head scarf tied under the chin, commonly worn by peasant women.

bacalao [Sp] *bah-kah-LAH-oh.* codfish; —**a la vizcaína** (*-ah-lah-vees-kah-EE-nah*) Basque-style codfish, stewed in tomato sauce.

bacalhau [Port] *buh-kuh-LYAH-oo.* codfish; —**à portuguesa** (*-ah-poor-too-GAY-zuh*) Portuguese-style codfish, stewed with tomatoes and potatoes.

baccalauréat [Fr] *bah-kah-loh-reh-AH.* in France, examination taken at completion of pre-university studies; the degree so conferred; baccalaureate.

bacchanale [Fr] *bah-kah-NAHL.* revel, orgy.

Bach [Ger] *bahkh.* brook.

bachelier [Fr] *bah-sh'-LYAY.* bachelor; in Middle Ages, a knight; in French educational system, one who has passed the **baccalauréat**; —**ès Arts** (*-eh-ZAR*) Bachelor of Arts; —**ès lettres** (*-es-LET-truh*) Bachelor of Letters (*abbr.* **B. ès L.**); —**ès sciences** (*-es-SYÃS*) Bachelor of Sciences (*abbr.* **B. ès S.**)

bacio [It] *BAH-choh.* kiss.

Backfisch [Ger] *BAHK-fish.* (*lit.*, baked fish) awkward adolescent girl; teenager; bobby-soxer.

Bad [Ger] *baht.* spring; bath; place-name denoting presence of mineral springs.

badinage [Fr] *bah-dee-NAHZH.* banter; chitchat.

Baedeker [Ger; after Karl Baedeker, original publisher] *BAY-duh-kuh.* well-known European guidebook.

bagel [Yid] *BAY-g'l.* hard, chewy roll about the size and shape of a doughnut.

bagnio [It *bagno*, bath, bathhouse] *BAH-nyoh.* brothel; prison, esp. for slaves.

baguette [Fr] *bah-GET.* rod, wand, stick, baton; gem cut in narrow, oblong shape; architectural molding of semi-cylindrical shape.

bahadur [Hindi] *BAH-hah-door.* (*lit.*, valiant, brave) hero; champion; Indian title of honor.

Baha'i [Pers] *bah-HAH-ee.* religious group of Asia which advocates unity of all religions.

Bahasa Indonesia [Skt *bhāṣā*, speech] *bah-HAH-sah-een-doh-NEH-see-ah.* official name of language of Indonesia, recently created.

bahía [Sp] *bah-EE-ah.* bay.

Bahnhof [Ger] *BAHN-hohf.* railroad station.

Bahnpostamt [Ger] *BAHN-pohst-ahmt.* railway post office.

baignoire [Fr] *beh-NYWAR.* bathtub; theater box.

bailarina [Sp] *by-lah-REE-nah.* ballerina; female dancer.

baile [Sp] *BY-leh.* dance; ball; —**flamenco** (*-flah-MEN-koh*) dance in flamenco or gypsy style.

bain [Fr] *bẽ.* bath; —**de soleil** (*-duh-soh-LAY*) sun bath; —**marie** (*-mah-REE*) a kind of double boiler.

Bairam [Turk] *by-RAHM.* Muslim holiday in Turkey, celebrated by a day of fasting and a day of sacrifice.

bairn [Scot] *behrn;* Scot *bahrn.* child, baby.

baiser [Fr] *beh-ZAY.* kiss.

baize [Fr] *behz.* woven cloth, resembling serge, usually green.

baklava [Turk] *BAH-kluh-vah.* rich many-layered pastry made with butter, nuts and honey.

bakshish [Pers] *BAHK-sheesh.* tip; gratuity. Also, **bakhshish, baksheesh.**

bal [Fr] *bahl.* dance; ball; —**masqué** (*-mahs-KAY*) masked ball.

balalaika [Russ] *buh-luh-LY-kuh.* guitarlike instrument with three strings and a triangular body.

baldacchino [It] *bahl-dahk-KEE-noh.* canopy of state; baldachin.

Ballet Russe [Fr] *bah-LAY-RÜS.* Russian Ballet.

ballo [It] *BAHL-loh.* dance; ball; —**in maschera** (*-een-MAHS-keh-rah*) masked ball.

ballon d'essai [Fr] *bah-LÕ-deh-SAY.* trial balloon; test case; probe.

balteus [Lat] *BAHL-teh-oos.* baldric; sheath for dagger or sword.

bambino [It: *fem.* **bambina**] *bahm-BEE-noh* (*-nah*) infant; baby; in art, the infant Jesus.

ban [Serbo-Croatian *bān*, lord, ruler] *bahn.* governor.

banalité [Fr] *bah-nah-lee-TAY.* commonplace; trite expression.

banat [Hung, from Serbo-Croatian] *BAH-naht.* province.

banco [It] *BAHN-koh.* seat, bench; bank.

Band [Ger: *pl.* **Bände**] *bahnt* (*BEN-deh*) volume, tome.

bandeau [Fr] *bã-DOH.* headband.

banderilla [Sp] *bahn-deh-REE-lyah.* in bullfighting, small dart or dagger, usually decorated with streamers, used to excite the bull by being thrust into its neck or shoulders.

banderillero [Sp] *bahn-deh-ree-LYEH-roh.* member of bullfighting team who hurls the **banderillas.**

bandido [Sp] *bahn-DEE-doh.* bandit.

banditti [erroneous form of It *banditi*] *bahn-DEE-tee.* bandits.

bandolero [Sp] *bahn-doh-LEH-roh.* highwayman.

bandurria [Sp] *bahn-DOOR-ryah.* stringed guitarlike instrument, but smaller, with twelve strings tuned in pairs.

banlieue [Fr] *bã-LYÖ.* suburbs; outskirts.

banquette [Fr] *bã-KET.* window seat or bench; (SW U.S.) sidewalk, raised footwalk.

banzai [Jap] *bahn-ZY.* (May you live) 10,000 years; salute to the Japanese Emperor; also, a battle cry.

bapuji [Hindi] *BAH-poo-jee.* little father: term applied to Mahatma Gandhi.

barato [Sp] *bah-RAH-toh.* cheap.

barba [Lat] *BAR-bah.* beard; whiskers.

barba a barba [Sp] *BAR-bah-ah-BAR-bah.* (*lit.*, beard to beard) face to face.

barbacoa [AmerSp] *bar-bah-KOH-ah.* barbecue rack; barbecued meat.

Barbarossa [It] *BAR-bah-ROHS-sah.* Redbeard.

Barbe-bleu [Fr] *BAR-buh-BLÖ.* Bluebeard.

barbu [Fr] *bar-BÜ.* bearded.

barbudo [Sp] *bar-BOO-doh.* bearded; applied to Fidel Castro and his followers.

Bar-le-duc [Fr] *BAR-luh-DÜK.* a currant jelly.

bar mitzvah [Heb] *bar-MITS-vah.* (*lit.*, son of the commandment) Jewish confirmation ceremony for boys attaining their 13th year.

barraca [Sp] *bar-RAH-kah.* barrack; rustic cabin.

barranco [Sp] *bar-RAHN-koh.* deep gorge or ravine.

barre [Fr] *bar.* in ballet schools, a practice bar mounted at waist height along the walls.

barrera [Sp] *bar-REH-rah.* barrier; barricade.

barrio [Sp] *BAR-ryoh.* municipal district; outlying area under city's jurisdiction.

barshchina [Russ] *BARSH-chee-nuh.* farm rent paid in form of labor on owner's estate.

baruch [Heb] *bah-ROOKH.* blessed.

bas [Fr] *bah.* low; subordinate; stocking.

bas bleu [Fr, translation of Eng *bluestocking*] *bah-BLÖ.* literary or intellectual woman.

bashi-bazouk [Turk] *BAH-shee-buh-ZOOK.* [*lit.*, the head (is) turned] Turkish irregular soldiers, famed for brutality.

basileus [Gk] *bah-see-LEH-oos.* king.

bas mitzvah [Heb] *bahs-MITS-vah.* See **bath mitzvah.**

basso [It: *pl.* **bassi**] *BAHS-soh* (*-see*) bass; low; —**buffo** (*-BOOF-foh*) comic bass; —**continuo** (*-kohn-TEE-noo-oh*) bass accompaniment to orchestral piece; —**profondo** (*-proh-FOHN-doh*) very deep bass; lowest voice range; erroneously rendered as **basso profundo**.

basso rilievo [It] *BAHS-soh-ree-LYEH-voh*. low relief; bas-relief.

basta [It] *BAHS-tah*. enough! stop!

bastante [Sp] *bahs-TAHN-teh*. enough.

Bastille [Fr] *bahs-TEE-yuh*. prison, fortress; the state prison, captured and stormed by the Paris mob on July 14, 1789; the French national holiday.

bastinado [Sp *bastonada*, from *bastón*, stick] *bahs-tee-NAH-doh*. a beating with a stick on the soles of the feet; a stick or cudgel; a blow or beating with a stick or cudgel.

bateau [Fr] *bah-TOH*. small, flat-bottomed boat; —**mouche** (*pl.* **bateaux-mouches**) (*-MOOSH*) (*lit.*, fly-boat) small passenger steamer used on the river Seine.

bateleur [Fr] *bat'LÖR*. juggler, buffoon, mountebank; rope-dancer.

bath mitzvah [Heb] *bahs-MITS-vah*. confirmation ceremony for girls, similar to the **bar mitzvah**.

bâtir des châteaux en Espagne [Fr] *bah-TEER-day-shah-TOH-ză-nes-PAH-nyuh*. to build castles in Spain (or in the air).

batiste [Fr] *bah-TEEST*. fine, sheer fabric.

bâton [Fr] *bah-TŎ*. baton; wand, stick.

Batrachomyomachia [Gk] *BAH-trah-khoh-MÜ-oh-mah-KHEE-ah*. battle of the frogs and mice.

batterie de cuisine [Fr] *baht'REE-duh-küee-ZEEN*. complete set of cooking utensils.

battue [Fr] *bah-TÜ*. the beating of game from cover toward the hunters.

battuta [It] *baht-TOO-tah*. beat; accent.

Bauer [Ger: *pl.* **Bauern**] *BOW-uh* (*-uhn*) peasant; (*cards*) knave, jack; (*chess*) pawn.

Bauhaus [Ger] *BOW-hows*. early 20th-century artistic and architectural school, founded in 1919 by Walter Gropius.

Baukunst [Ger] *BOW-koonst.* architecture.

bavaroise [Fr] *bah-vah-RWAHZ.* Bavarian-style tea, with orange juice and syrup.

bayadère [Fr, from Port *bailadera*, dancer] *bah-yah-DEHR.* Hindu dancing girl.

béarnaise [Fr, from *Béarn*, a district in SW France] *beh-ar-NEZ.* a sauce made of egg yolks, butter, vinegar, shallots, tarragon, etc.

beatae memoriae [Lat: *abbr.* **B.M.**] *beh-AH-ty-meh-MOH-ree-y.* of blessed memory.

Beata Maria [Lat: *abbr.* **B.M.**] *beh-AH-tah-mah-REE-ah.* Blessed Mary; **Beata Virgo** (*-VEER-goh*) Blessed Virgin (*abbr.* **B.V.**); **Beata Virgo Maria** Blessed Virgin Mary.

beati possidentes [Lat] *beh-AH-tee-pohs-see-DEN-tes* (*lit.*, blessed are the possessors) possession is nine points of the law.

beato [It: *fem.* **beata**] *beh-AH-toh* (*-tah*) blessed; holy man or woman.

beau [Fr: *pl.* **beaux**] *boh.* beautiful; handsome; fine; admirer, suitor

beaucoup [Fr] *boh-KOO.* much; many.

beau geste [Fr: *pl.* **beaux gestes**] *boh-ZHEST.* grand or magnanimous gesture, often insincere.

beau idéal [Fr] *boh-ee-day-AHL.* ideal beauty; perfect beauty; model of excellence.

beau monde [Fr] *boh-MŎD.* fashionable society; world of fashion; "beautiful people."

beau sabreur [Fr] *BOH-sah-BRÖR.* dashing cavalry soldier or officer; swashbuckler.

beauté du diable [Fr] *boh-TAY-dü-DYAH-bluh.* (*lit.*, beauty of the devil) the freshness of youth.

beaux arts [Fr] *boh-ZAR.* fine arts.

beaux esprits [Fr] *BOH-zes-PREE.* men of wit or spirit.

beaux yeux [Fr] *boh-ZYÖH.* (*lit.*, beautiful eyes) good looks.

bébé [Fr] *bay-BAY.* baby; infant.

béchamel [Fr] *bay-shah-MEL.* rich white sauce, often flavored with onions and nutmeg.

bêche-de-mer [Fr, from Port *bicho do mar*, sea worm]

BESH-duh-MEHR. sea slug, used for food in the Orient; a pidgin English of the South Pacific.

Bedeutung [Ger: *pl.* **Bedeutungen**] *buh-DOY-toong* (*-'n*) meaning, significance.

Befana [It, from *befania*, colloq. var. of *epifania*, Epiphany] *beh-FAH-nah.* an old woman believed by Italian children to come down the chimney with gifts at Epiphany: the Italian equivalent of Santa Claus.

Begeisterung [Ger] *buh-GYS-tuh-roong.* inspiration; rapture.

Begleitung [Ger] *buh-GLY-toong.* (*music*) accompaniment.

Begriff [Ger] *buh-GRIF.* idea; notion; concept.

béguin [Fr] *bay-GẼ.* romantic infatuation; "crush."

Béguine [Fr] *bay-GEEN.* member of a lay sisterhood, founded in 1180 in the Netherlands by Lambert le Bègue.

begum [Hindi *begam*, from Turk *beg*, Lord] *BEH-goom.* Moslem princess or woman of high rank in India.

Behauptung [Ger: *pl.* **Behauptungen**] *buh-HOWPT-oong* (*-'n*) assertion, allegation, contention.

Beiheft [Ger] *BY-heft.* supplement to a periodical.

Bei Nacht sind alle Katzen grau [Ger] *by-NAHKHT-zint-AHL-leh-KAH-ts'n-GROW.* by night (in the dark) all cats are gray.

Beitrag [Ger: *pl.* **Beiträge**] *BY-trahk* (*-tray-guh*) contribution (of an article to a journal).

Bekanntmachung [Ger] *buh-KAHNT-mahkh-oong.* proclamation; announcement; notice.

bel air [Fr] *bel-EHR.* fine carriage; striking appearance and manner.

bel canto [It] *BEL-KAHN-toh.* smooth, cantabile style of singing, in the Italian tradition.

bel esprit [Fr: *pl.* **beaux esprits**] *bel-es-PREE* (*boh-zes-PREE*) brilliant or witty person; (*ironically*) affected or foppish person.

belge [Fr] *belzh.* Belgian.

belle amie [Fr] *BEL-ah-MEE.* lady friend; mistress.

belle-fille [Fr] *bel-FEE-yuh.* daughter-in-law; stepdaughter.

belle-mère [Fr] *bel-MEHR.* mother-in-law; stepmother.

belles-lettres [Fr] *bel-LET-truh.* writing of genuine artistic and aesthetic merit; true literature and related fields; poetry, oratory, criticism, aesthetics.

belle-soeur [Fr] *bel-SÖR.* sister-in-law; stepsister.

bellum [Lat] *BEL-loom.* war.

Bel Paese [It] *BEL-pah-AY-seh.* (*lit.*, beautiful country) brand name of a semisoft Italian cheese.

beluga [Russ] *BYEH-loo-guh.* white sturgeon found in Black and Caspian Seas, a source of fine caviar.

belyi [Russ] *BYEH-lee.* white.

Bemerkung [Ger: *pl.* **Bemerkungen**] *buh-MEHR-koong* (*-'n*) comment; remark.

bémol [Fr] *bay-MOHL.* (*music*) flat; flat note.

ben [Heb: *pl.* **b'nai**] *ben.* son.

bene [Lat, It] *BEH-neh.* well; good.

Benedicite [Lat] *beh-neh-DEE-kee-teh.* bless ye, praise ye (first word of a canticle).

Benedictus [Lat] *beh-neh-DEEK-toos.* blessed (first word of section of the Mass).

bene esse [Lat] *BEH-neh-ES-seh.* prosperity; well-being.

beneficium [Lat] *beh-neh-FEE-kee-oom.* favor; benefice.

bene merenti [Lat: *pl.* **bene merentibus**] *BEH-neh-meh-REN-tee* (*-tee-boos*) to the well deserving.

bene meritus [Lat: *pl.* **bene meriti**] *BEH-neh-MEH-ree-toos* (*-tee*) having well deserved.

beneplacito [It] *BEH-neh-PLAH-chee-toh.* by your leave; if you wish; leave, consent.

benissimo [It] *beh-NEES-see-moh.* very well; very fine.

ben marcato [It] *BEN-mar-KAH-toh.* (*music*) to be played emphatically; well stressed.

ben tornato [It] *BEN-tor-NAH-toh.* welcome back; welcome home.

ben trovato [It] *BEN-troh-VAH-toh.* well-conceived; well-invented or discovered.

ben venuto [It] *BEN-veh-NOO-toh.* welcome!; (as noun) welcome; cordial reception.

berceuse [Fr, from *bercer*, to rock or cradle] *behr-SÖZ.* lullaby; cradle song.

Berg [Ger: *pl.* **Berge**] *behrk* (*BEHR-geh*) mountain.

berger [Fr] *behr-ZHAY.* shepherd.

bergère [Fr] *behr-ZHEHR.* shepherdess; large, deep armchair.

bergerette [Fr] *behr-zh'RET.* young shepherdess; country lass; liqueur of wine and honey; brief poetic composition involving a shepherdess.

Bergschrund [Ger] *BEHRK-shroont.* crevasse, esp. in a mountain glacier.

berretta [It] *behr-RAYT-tah.* stiff square cap worn by Catholic priests; biretta.

berrettina [It] *behr-rayt-TEE-nah.* small scarlet skullcap worn by Cardinals.

bersagliere [It: *pl.* -ri] *behr-sah-LYEH-reh* (*-ree*) sharpshooter; light infantryman.

bésame [Sp] *BEH-sah-meh.* kiss me.

bésigue [Fr] *bay-ZEEG.* card game resembling pinochle; bezique.

beso [SP] *BEH-soh.* kiss.

besoin [Fr] *buh-ZWẼ.* need; necessity.

besonders [Ger] *buh-ZOHN-duhs.* especially.

Besprechung [Ger: *pl.* **Besprechungen**] *buh-SHPREÇ-oong* (*-'n*) conversation; discussion; criticism; book review.

besser aufgeschoben als aufgehoben [Ger] *BES-uh-OWF-guh-shoh-b'n-ahls-OWF-guh-hoh-b'n.* better late than never.

besser was als gar nichts [Ger] *BES-uh-VAHS-ahls-gar-NIÇTS.* better something than nothing at all; half a loaf is better than none.

Bestellung [Ger] *buh-SHTEL-oong.* order; delivery.

bestiarium [Lat] *bes-tee-AH-ree-oom.* zoo; animal collection; animal stories; medieval allegorical poems using animals to portray human characters; bestiary.

bête [Fr] *bet.* beast; brute; fool; foolish, stupid.

bête noire [Fr] *bet-NWAR.* one's strongest hatred, fear or aversion; bugbear.

bêtise [Fr] *beh-TEEZ.* foolishness, stupidity; nonsense; careless mistake.

béton [Fr] *bay-TÕ.* concrete; —**armé** (*-ar-MAY*) reinforced concrete.

betreffend [Ger] *buh-TREF-'nt.* concerning; related to.

betterave [Fr] *bet'-RAHV.* beet.

beurre [Fr] *bör.* butter; —**fondu** (*-fŏ-DŬ*) melted butter; —**noir** (*-NWAR*) browned butter.

bevollmächtigt [Ger] *buh-FOHL-mehç-tiçt.* authorized, permitted.

bévue [Fr] *bay-VŬ.* blunder; oversight.

Bewährung [Ger] *buh-VEHR-oong.* verification; substantiation; proof.

bewegt [Ger] *buh-VAYÇT.* (*music*) animated; with animation.

Bewusstsein [Ger] *buh-VOOST-zyn.* consciousness; —**überhaupt** (*-Ŭ-buh-howpt*) consciousness in general.

bez goda [Russ] *byiz-guh-DAH.* without date; date unknown.

Beziehung [Ger: *pl.* -en] *buh-TSEE-oong* (*-'n*) relation; connection; reference.

beziehungsweise [Ger: *abbr.* **bzw.**] *buh-TSEE-oongs-vy-zeh.* respectively; relatively.

bezüglich [Ger] *buh-TSÜG-liç.* regarding; pertaining to; with reference to.

bhakti [Skt] *BHUK-tee.* religious devotion or worship.

Bharat [Hindi] *BHAH-rut.* Hindi name for India.

biacca [It] *BYAHK-kah.* white lead.

biadetto [It] *byah-DAYT-toh.* blue color pigment.

Bianchi e Neri [It] *BYAHN-kee-eh-NAY-ree.* Whites and Blacks: the two factions of the Guelph party in 12th-century Florence.

bianco [It: *fem.* **bianca**] *BYAHN-koh* (*-kah*) white.

bibelot [Fr] *bee-b'LOH.* bauble; knickknack; tiny book.

biblioteca [It, Sp] *bee-blyoh-TEH-kah.* library.

bibliotheca [Lat, from Gk *bibliothēkē*, from *biblion*, book + *thēkē*, case, box, storeroom] *bee-blee-oh-THEH-kah.* library; bookcase.

Bibliothek [Ger] *bee-blyoh-TEK.* library.

bibliothèque [Fr] *bee-blyoh-TEK.* library.

bicchiere [It] *beek-KYEH-reh.* drinking glass.

bicorne [Fr, from Lat *bi-*, two- + *cornu*, horn] *bee-KORN.*

two-pointed, crescent-shaped hat, usually worn by military and naval officers.

bidet [Fr] *bee-DAY.* (*lit.*, small pony) low porcelain tub on which one sits for bathing the private parts.

bien [Fr] *byē.* well; good, fine.

bien-aimé [Fr: *fem.* **bien-aimée**] *byē-neh-MAY.* well-loved; beloved; darling.

bien ama quien nunca olvida [Sp] *BYEN-ah-mah-kyen-NOON-kah-ohl-VEE-dah.* he loves well who never forgets.

bien entendu [Fr] *byē-nā-tā-DÜ.* (*lit.*, well understood) to be sure; indeed; of course.

bienes [Sp] *BYEH-nes.* property of all descriptions, both real and personal; —**comunes** (*-koh-MOO-nes*) common property.

bien fait [Fr] *BYÊ-FEH.* well done.

bien hablar no cuesta nada [Sp] *BYEN-ah-BLAR-noh-KWES-tah-NAH-dah.* kind words cost nothing.

bien mieux [Fr] *byē-MYÖ.* far better, much better.

bienséance [Fr] *byē-say-ÃS.* propriety; decorum.

bien trouvé [Fr] *BYÊ-troo-VAY.* well-conceived; well-invented or discovered.

bien vengas mal, si vienes solo [Sp] *BYEN-VEN-gahs-mahl-see-VYEH-nes-SOH-loh.* welcome, misfortune, if you come alone.

bienvenu [Fr] *byē-vuh-NÜ.* welcome; **bienvenue** (*n.*) welcome; cordial reception.

Bier [Ger] *beer.* beer.

bière [Fr] *byehr.* beer.

Bierstube [Ger] *BEER-shtoo-beh.* tavern; beer hall.

bifteck [Fr, from Eng *beefsteak*] *beef-TEK.* beefsteak, steak.

bijou [Fr: *pl.* **bijoux**] *bee-ZHOO.* jewel, gem; **bijouterie** (*-t'REE*) jewelry; jewelry shop.

Bildung [Ger] *BIL-doong.* formation; building up; education.

Bildungsroman [Ger *Bildung*, formation + *Roman* (from Fr) novel] *BIL-doongs-roh-mahn.* psychological novel, esp. one tracing the emotional development of a character from youth to maturity.

billabong [Australian *billa*, stream + *bong*, dead] *BIL-uh-bong*. branch of a river flowing away from the main-stream; backwater.

billet [Fr] *bee-YAY*. ticket; note; letter; **—doux** (*-DOO*) love letter.

billig [Ger] *BIL-iç*. cheap.

biltong [Afrikaans] *BIL-tong*. strip or strips of sun-dried meat.

bimbo [It: *fem*. **bimba**] *BEEM-boh* (*-bah*) child; babe (in-cluding slang sense).

bint [Ar: *pl*. **banat**] *beent* (*bah-NAHT*) woman, esp. loose woman; girl.

birra [It] *BEER-rah*. beer.

bis [Lat, Fr, It, Sp] *bees*. twice; a second time; repeat; (*interj*.) again! encore!; second of two, as an extra train.

bis dat qui cito dat [Lat] *BEES-daht-kwee-KEE-toh-daht*. he gives twice who gives quickly.

bise [Fr] *beez*. dry, cold north or northeast wind of SE France and Switzerland.

bismillah [Ar] *bees-meel-LAH*. in the name of Allah!

bistec [Sp, from Eng *beefsteak*] *bees-TEK*. beefsteak, steak. Also, **bisté** (*-TEH*); **bisté a la chilena** (*-ah-lah-chee-LEH-nah*) steak Chilean style, with fried egg on top.

bistecca [It, from Eng *beefsteak*] *bees-TEK-kah*. beefsteak, steak; **—alla fiorentina** (*-AHL-lah-fyoh-ren-TEE-nah*) thick charcoal-broiled sirloin.

bistre [Fr] *BEES-truh*. brownish-yellow hue; tawny; artist's drawing done in these tones.

bistro [Fr: wine merchant, tavern-keeper] *bees-TROH*. cabaret; wine shop; small restaurant or café.

bis vivit qui bene vivit [Lat] *BEES-VEE-veet-kwee-BEH-neh-VEE-veet*. he lives twice who lives well.

bitochki [Russ] *byee-TAWCH-kee*. meat croquettes or pat-ties.

bitte [Ger] *BIT-teh*. please; don't mention it; excuse me; beg pardon.

bizarrerie [Fr, from *bizarre*, bizarre] *bee-zah-ruh-REE*. bizarreness; weird whim.

bizcocho [Sp] *bees-KOH-choh*. biscuit, cookie; cake; plaster.

blad [Swed, Norw, Dan, Du] *blahd.* leaf; folio; sheet; newspaper.

blagodaryu vas [Russ] *bluh-guh-duh-RYOO-vahs.* thank you.

blague [Fr] *blahg.* (*lit.*, tobacco pouch) (*slang*) hogwash, humbug; **blaguer** (*blah-GAY*) to talk big, brag, bluff; **blagueur** (*blah-GÖR*) joker, braggart.

blanc [Fr: *fem.* **blanche**] *blã* (*blãsh*) white.

blanc-mange [Fr *blanc-manger, lit.*, white eats] *blã-MÃZH.* rich pudding dessert usually made with milk and cornstarch and flavored with vanilla or rum.

blanquette [Fr] *blã-KET.* fricassee dish served with white sauce.

bleu [Fr: *fem.* **bleue**] *blö.* blue.

blin [Russ: *pl.* **blini**] *bleen* (*-nee*) buckwheat flour pancake.

blinchik [Russ: *pl.* **blinchiki**] *BLEEN-cheek* (*-chee-kee*) pancake or fritter, served with sour cream, jam, sugar, or cottage cheese.

blintz [Yid *blintse*, from Russ *blinyets*, dim. of *blin*, pancake] *blints.* a thin pancake filled with cottage cheese, meat, sour cream or fruit.

Blitz [Ger] *blits.* (*lit.*, lightning) a sudden, violent attack.

Blitzkrieg [Ger] *BLITS-kreek.* (*lit.*, lightning war) warfare carried on in a swift, overwhelming manner, as by German forces early in World War II.

Blut und Boden [Ger] *BLOOT-oont-BOH-d'n.* blood and soil: a Nazi theory which links character with geography.

Blut und Eisen [Ger] *BLOOT-oont-Y-z'n.* blood and iron: motto of Bismarck as military leader of Prussia.

Blutwurst [Ger] *BLOOT-voorst.* black pudding: dark sausage made of dried pork, pork blood, and seasonings.

b'nai [Heb, pl. of **ben**] *b'ny.* sons.

B'nai B'rith [Heb] *b'ny-b'RITH.* Sons of the Covenant: a Jewish social and cultural organization.

boa noite [Port] *BOH-uh-NOY-tuh.* good night.

boa tarde [Port] *BOH-uh-TAR-duh.* good afternoon; good evening.

bobèche [Fr] *boh-BESH.* disc around the base of a candelabrum or chandelier that catches drippings.

boca [Sp] *BOH-kah.* mouth.

bocca [It] *BOHK-kah.* mouth.

bocce [It] *BOHT-cheh.* Italian lawn bowling game; balls used in this game.

Boche [Fr] *bohsh.* (*slang*) term of contempt for a German.

Bock [Ger] *bohk.* dark, rich beer. Also, **Bockbier** (*BOHK-beer*).

bodega [Sp] *boh-DEH-gah.* wine cellar; grocery store.

boeuf [Fr] *böf.* ox; beef; —**à la mode** (*-ah-lah-MOHD*). See **à la mode.**

Bog [Russ] *bohkh.* God.

Bogen [Ger] *BOH-g'n.* bow; arc; sheet or folio; (*music*) tie.

Bohème [Fr] *boh-EM.* Bohemia; Bohemian; artists' quarter.

boina [Sp] *BOY-nah.* beret worn by the Basques.

bois [Fr] *bwah.* wood; woods; forest.

boîte [Fr] *bwaht.* box; case; shanty, hovel; —**de nuit** (*-duh-NÜEE*) small night club, esp. one frequented by Bohemians; dive; "joint."

boiteux [Fr: *fem.* **boiteuse**] *bwah-TÖ* (*-TÖZ*) lame; lame person.

Bokmål [Norw] *BOOK-mawl.* (*lit.*, book language) one of the two official forms of Norwegian, being the more literary form based on Danish. Also called **Riksmål.** Cf. **Nynorsk.**

bolas [Sp] *BOH-lahs.* device consisting of two or more heavy balls fastened to the end of a long rope, used by gauchos to entrap cattle and other animals by hurling it at their legs and entangling them.

bolo [Sp, from a Filipino dial.] *BOH-loh.* large, heavy jungle knife; a kind of machete orig. used in the Philippines.

bolshoi [Russ] *bul-SHOY.* large; great. Also, **bolshoy.**

bolus [Lat] *BOH-loos.* large pill; horse pill.

bombe [Fr] *bõb.* (*lit.*, bomb) frozen dessert formed in round mold or pastry shell; a bombé piece of furniture; **faire la—** (*FEHR-lah-*) to go on a spree; have a wild fling; —**glacée** (*-glah-SAY*) molded dessert of ice cream, mousse, or ices.

bombé [Fr, from **bombe**] *bõ-BAY.* of furniture, having the front rounded or swelling outward.

bombilla [Sp, dim. of *bomba*, pump, bulb] *bohm-BEE-lyah.* drinking tube or straw which strains the liquid, used in drinking maté; combination of narcotics usually taken together; electric light bulb.

bom dia [Port] *bõ-DEE-uh.* good day; good morning.

bon [Fr: *fem.* **bonne**] *bõ (bun)* good; fine; —**accueil** (*bõnah-KÖY*) good reception; hearty welcome.

bonae memoriae [Lat] *BOH-ny-meh-MOH-ree-y.* of happy memory; fondly remembered.

bona fide [Lat] *BOH-nah-FEE-deh.* in good faith; genuine; authentic.

bona gratia [Lat] *BOH-nah-GRAH-tee-ah.* in all kindness; with all good grace.

bon ami [Fr] *BÕ-nah-MEE.* good friend; bosom friend.

bon appétit [Fr] *BÕ-nah-pay-TEE.* hearty appetite!

bona roba [It] *BOH-nah-ROH-bah.* (*lit.,* fine stuff) courtesan; harlot.

bonbon [Fr] *bõ-BÕ.* bonbon; candy.

bonbonnière [Fr] *bõ-buh-NYEHR.* fancy serving dish for candy; candy shop.

bon camarade [Fr] *BÕ-kah-mah-RAHD.* good friend; boon companion.

bon diable [Fr] *bõ-DYAH-bluh.* (*lit.,* good devil) good-hearted fellow.

Bon Dieu [Fr] *bõ-DYÖ.* good God!; good heavens!

bon enfant [Fr] *BÕ-nã-FÃ.* (*lit.,* good child) good fellow.

bon goût [Fr] *bõ-GOO.* good taste.

bon gré, mal gré [Fr] *BÕ-gray-MAHL-gray.* willy-nilly.

bonheur [Fr] *boh-NÖR.* happiness; good fortune; good feeling.

bonhomie [Fr] *boh-noh-MEE.* friendliness; geniality.

bonhomme [Fr] *boh-NOHM.* good man; simple, good-natured man. Cf. **Jacques Bonhomme.**

bonito [Sp: *fem.* **-a**] *boh-NEE-toh (-tah)* pretty; handsome.

bonjour [Fr] *bõ-ZHOOR.* good morning; good day; hello.

bon marché [Fr] *BÕ-mar-SHAY.* (*lit.,* good market) cheap; at a bargain.

bon mot [Fr] *bō-MOH.* witticism; clever remark.

bonne [Fr] *bun.* good (*fem.*); maid; nursemaid.

bonne amie [Fr] *BUH-nah-MEE.* girl friend; sweetheart; mistress.

bonne à tout faire [Fr] *buh-nah-TOO-FEHR.* maid-of-all-work.

bonne bouche [Fr] *bun-BOOSH.* dainty morsel; tidbit.

bonne fortune [Fr] *BUN-for-TÜN.* good luck. Also, **bonne chance** (*BUN-SHĂS*).

bonne mine [Fr] *bun-MEEN.* good appearance; good looks.

bonne nuit [Fr] *bun-NÜEE.* good night.

bonne raison [Fr] *BUN-reh-ZŌ.* good reason; good grounds.

bonnet rouge [Fr] *buh-nay-ROOZH.* red bonnet worn in French Revolution; hence, a revolutionary or extremist.

bonsai [Jap] *BOHN-sy.* dwarf tree or shrub; art of growing dwarf plants.

bonsoir [Fr] *bō-SWAHR.* good evening.

bon ton [Fr] *bō-TŌ.* good breeding; fashionable society; elegance of form or style.

bon vivant [Fr] *BŎ-vee-VĂ.* one who lives high; man-about-town; fine-food fancier.

bon voyage [Fr] *BŎ-vwah-YAHZH.* pleasant journey!; have a good trip!

bonze [Jap. *bonsi*] *BOHN-zeh.* Buddhist monk.

boobeleh [Yid, from *bube*, child] *BOO-buh-luh.* little dear; darling. Also, **bubeleh.**

bora [It] *BOH-rah.* violent east-northeast wind of the upper Adriatic.

bordelaise [Fr] *bor-duh-LEZ.* (*lit.*, of Bordeaux) brown sauce flavored with red wine and shallots.

Boreas [Gk] *boh-REH-ahs.* the north wind.

Borgen macht Sorgen [Ger] *BOR-g'n-mahkht-ZOR-g'n.* borrowing makes sorrowing.

borné [Fr] *bor-NAY.* narrow; restricted; limited; narrow-minded.

borracho [Sp] *bor-RAH-choh.* drunk, drunkard.

borrachón [Sp] *bor-rah-CHOHN.* habitual drunk; alcoholic.

borscht [Russ *borshch*] *borsht.* soup of beets and cabbage, served hot or cold, usually with sour cream. Also, **borsht.**

borzoi [Russ] *bur-ZOY*. (*lit.*, swift) Russian wolfhound.

bosan [Jap] *BOH-sahn*. Buddhist priest.

bosch [Du] *bohs*. wood; bush.

bosco [It] *BOHS-koh*. forest; woods.

bosque [Sp] *BOHS-keh*. forest; woods.

bossa nova [Port] *BOH-suh-NOH-vuh*. (*lit.*, new bump) Brazilian dance.

Botschaft [Ger] *BOHT-shahft*. message.

bottega [It: *pl.* -ghe] *boht-TEH-gah* (*-geh*) studio; art shop; small store.

bottiglia [It] *boht-TEE-lyah*. bottle.

bouche [Fr] *boosh*. mouth.

bouchée [Fr] *boo-SHAY*. mouthful; morsel.

bouclé [Fr] *boo-KLAY*. a fabric made of yarn with loops, producing a shaggy appearance.

boudin [Fr] *boo-DẼ*. sausage-shaped dish of seasoned forcemeat; black pudding.

bouffant [Fr] *boo-FÃ*. full, ballooned out, as a full skirt or coiffure.

bouffon [Fr, from It **buffone**] *boo-FŎ*. buffoon; clown.

bouillabaisse [Fr] *boo-yah-BES*. an elaborate soup of fish, vegetables and seasonings from the Provençal region.

bouilli [Fr] *boo-YEE*. boiled; boiled meat.

bouillon [Fr] *boo-YŎ*. clear broth, flavored with meat or chicken.

boulanger [Fr] *boo-lã-ZHAY*. baker.

boulangerie [Fr] *boo-lã-zh'REE*. bakery.

Boule-Miche [Fr] *bool-MEESH*. nickname for Boulevard St. Michel in Paris.

boulette [Fr] *boo-LET*. small ball of meat or dough; —s de hachis (*-duh-ah-SHEE*) balls of forcemeat.

boulevardier [Fr] *bool-var-DYAY*. pleasure-seeker; member of theater and nightclub set.

bouleversé [Fr] *bool-vehr-SAY*. overturned, overthrown; upset, agitated.

bouleversement [Fr] *bool-vehr-s'MÃ*. overthrow; agitation, confusion.

bouquet d'herbes [Fr] *boo-KAY-DEHRB*. bunch of herbs,

spices or vegetables for use in cookery. Also, **bouquet garni** (*-gar-NEE*).

bouquiniste [Fr] *boo-kee-NEEST*. used-book dealer.

bourgeois [Fr] *boor-ZHWAH*. (*lit.*, citified; city dweller) a member of the middle classes; conventional; materialistic, hedonistic; "square."

bourgeois gentilhomme [Fr] *boor-ZHWAH-zhã-tee-YUM*. a would-be gentleman; nouveau riche, parvenu; title character of play by Molière.

bourgeoisie [Fr] *boor-zhwah-ZEE*. middle class; uncultured, materialistic masses.

Bourgogne [Fr] *boor-GUN-yuh*. Burgundy.

bourrée [Fr] *boo-RAY*. a peasant dance of the Auvergne region, similar to the polka.

Bourse [Fr] *boors*. (*lit.*, purse) stock exchange, esp. that of Paris.

boustrophedon [Gk] *boo-struh-FEE-d'n*. (*lit.*, ox-turning, as in plowing) written alternately from left to right, then from right to left; inscription written in this manner.

boutade [Fr] *boo-TAHD*. whim, caprice; **par boutades** (*par-boo-TAHD*) by fits and starts.

bouteille [Fr] *boo-TAY*. bottle.

boutique [Fr] *boo-TEEK*. shop; specialty shop; **toute la—** (*TOOT-lah-*) the whole kit and caboodle.

boutonnière [Fr] *boo-tuh-NYEHR*. (*lit.*, buttonhole) flower worn in lapel of suit.

bouts-rimés [Fr] *BOO-ree-MAY*. ends of rhyming lines; verse composed to given rhymes.

bouwerye [Du, earlier form of *bouwerij*] *BOW-uh-ree*. farm.

bouzouki [Gk, from Turk] *boo-zoo-KEE*. six-stringed musical instrument resembling the mandolin.

boyar [Russ *boyarin*, lord] *buh-YAHR*. member of landed gentry in Tsarist Russia.

Bozhe moi [Russ] *BOH-zhi-MOY*. my God!; good heavens!

Brabançonne [Fr, from Brabant, region of Belgium and Holland] *bra-bã-SUN*. national anthem of Belgium.

bracero [Sp, from *brazo*, arm] *brah-SEH-roh*. Mexican laborer working in U.S.

brachys [Gk] *brah-KHŬS.* short.

brandade de morue [Fr] *brã-DAHD-duh-moh-RŬ.* codfish Provençal style, prepared with cream, oil and garlic.

branle [Fr: a shaking, from *branler,* to shake] *BRÃ-luh.* costumed pantomime dance.

Branntwein [Ger] *BRAHNT-vyn.* brandy.

brasero [Sp] *bra-SEH-roh.* brazier.

brasserie [Fr] *brah-S'REE.* brewery; alehouse; beer saloon.

Bratwurst [Ger] *BRAHT-voorst.* type of sausage.

Brauhaus [Ger] *BROW-hows.* brewery.

Braut [Ger] *browt.* bride.

bravo [It: *fem.* **brava**] *BRAH-voh* (*-vah*) hurrah!, well done!; **bravissimo** (*-VEES-see-moh*) excellent!, stupendous!, very well done!

bravura [It, lit., bravery, daring] *brah-VOO-rah.* (*music*) intricate musical style requiring confidence and virtuosity in performance.

braw [Scot, var. of *brave*] fine; excellent; dressed in loud fashion.

brasileiro [Port] *bruh-zee-LAY-roo.* Brazilian.

bref [Fr] *bref.* in brief; in short.

breloque [Fr] *bruh-LOHK.* trinket; ornament; watch-chain bauble; (*mil.*) drum signal for dismissal.

Brennschluss [Ger] *BREN-shloos.* (*skiing*) fast (*lit.,* burning) finish.

breve [It] *BREH-veh.* brief; writ.

brevet d'invention [Fr] *bruh-VAY-dē-vã-SYŎ.* patent; proof of invention.

breveté [Fr] *breh-V'TAY.* patented.

breviarium [Lat] *breh-vee-AH-ree-oom.* abridgment; abstract; collection of laws.

brevi manu [Lat] *BREH-vee-MAH-noo.* (*lit.,* with a short hand) offhandedly.

Brief [Ger] *breef.* letter; **—marke** (*-mar-keh*) postage stamp; **—träger** (*-tray-guh*) postman; letter-carrier.

brillante [It] *breel-LAHN-teh.* (*music*) brilliant; sparkling; lucid.

briller par son absence [Fr] *bree-YAY-par-sõ-nahp-SÃS.* to be conspicuous by one's absence.

brinza. See **brynza.**

brio [It] *BREE-oh.* animation; vivacity.

brioche [Fr] *bree-OHSH.* sweet roll or bun, usually served at breakfast.

briquet [Fr] *bree-KAY.* tinder box, flint; cigarette lighter; small, compressed block of coal dust or charcoal, used for fuel.

brisance [Fr] *bree-ZĂS.* a shattering, as caused by high explosives.

broccoli [It] *BROHK-koh-lee.* green vegetable resembling cauliflower.

brochette [Fr] *broh-SHET.* skewer; **en—** (*ă-*) skewered; served or cooked on a skewer.

Broederbond [Afrikaans] *BROO-duh-bohnt.* (*lit.*, band of brothers) African association which supports apartheid on grounds of Christian belief.

brouhaha [Fr] *broo-hah-HAH.* hubbub; uproar.

brouillon [Fr] *broo-YŎ.* draft; rough copy.

Brücke [Ger, lit., bridge] *BRÜ-keh.* early 20th-century German artistic school of expressionism.

bruit [Fr] *brüee.* noise; rumor.

brujo [Sp] *BROO-hoh.* magician; wizard; sorcerer; **bruja** (*-hah*) witch, sorceress.

brûler la chandelle par les deux bouts [Fr] *brü-LAY-lah-shă-DEL-par-lay-DŎ-BOO.* to burn the candle at both ends.

brûler le (feu) rouge [Fr] *brü-LAY-luh-(FŎ)-ROOZH.* to pass a red light.

brut [Fr] *brü.* crude; raw; unrefined; unfinished; (*of wine*) unadulterated; unsweetened.

brynza [Rum *brînză*] *BRIN-zuh.* cheese made from sheep's milk.

Bube [Ger] *BOO-beh.* boy; lad; child.

bubeleh. See **boobeleh.**

Buch [Ger: pl. **Bücher**] *bookh* (*BÜ-çuh*) book.

Buchbesprechung [Ger: pl. **-en**] *BOOKH-buh-shpreç-oong* (*-'n*) book review.

Bücherbesprechung [Ger] *BÜ-çuh-buh-shpreç-oong.* review of books; book review section or page in newspaper or magazine.

Bücherei [Ger] *BÜ-çuh-ry.* printing plant; library; bookshop.

Buchhandlung [Ger] *BOOKH-hahnt-loong.* bookstore; **Buchhändler** (*-hent-luh*) bookseller.

Buchstabe [Ger] *BOOKH-shtah-beh.* letter of the alphabet; metal type.

buenas tardes [Sp] *BWEH-nahs-TAR-des.* good afternoon; **buenas noches** (*-NOH-ches*) good evening; good night.

buenos días [Sp] *BWEH-nos-DEE-ahs.* good morning; good day; hello.

buffo [It] *BOOF-foh.* jester; comic; singer who plays comic roles.

buffone [It] *boof-FOH-neh.* clown; buffoon.

Bühne [Ger] *BÜ-neh.* stage.

Bühnenaussprache [Ger] *BÜ-n'n-ows-shprah-kheh.* stage diction; theatrical pronunciation.

bulla [Lat] *BOOL-lah.* seal; stamp; amulet.

bumaga [Russ] *boo-MAH-guh.* paper.

Bund [Ger] *boont.* union; league.

Bundesrat [Ger] *BOON-d's-raht.* upper house of West German Republic, also known as Federal Council; upper house of Reichstag from 1871 to 1918; executive council of Austria and Switzerland.

Bundesrepublik [Ger] *BOON-d's-ruh-poo-bleek.* Federal Republic of West Germany.

Bundestag [Ger] *BOON-d's-tahk.* lower house of Federal Republic of West Germany, also known as Federal Assembly.

Bundeswehr [Ger] *BOON-d's-vehr.* armed forces of Federal Republic of West Germany.

Bung [Malay] *boong.* leader; elder: title of respect in Indonesia.

bunraku [Jap] *BOON-rah-koo.* puppet show.

buñuelo [Sp] *boo-NYWEH-loh.* fritter; cruller.

buona notte [It] *BWOH-nah-NOHT-teh.* good night.

buon appetito [It] *BWOH-nahp-peh-TEE-toh.* hearty appetite!

buona sera [It] *BWOH-nah-SEH-rah.* good evening.

buon giorno [It] *BWOHN-JOR-noh.* good day; good morning; hello.

buon viaggio [It] *BWOHN-VYAH-joh.* pleasant journey; have a good trip!

buon vino fa buon sangue [It] *BWOHN-VEE-noh-fah-BWOHN-SAHN-gweh.* good wine makes good blood.

Burg [Ger] *boork.* castle; fortress; suffix of names of cities, orig. fortified towns.

burgemeester [Du] *BOOR-huh-mays-tuh.* mayor; burgomaster.

Bürgermeister [Ger] *BÜR-guh-mys-tuh.* mayor; burgomaster.

Burgtheater [Ger] *BOORK-tay-ah-tuh.* State Theater in Vienna.

burletta [It] *boor-LAYT-tah.* burlesque; farce.

burnoose [Fr *bournous,* from Ar *burnus,* from Gk *birros*] *BUR-noos.* hooded cape or cloak.

burro [Sp] *BOOR-roh.* donkey; ass.

burro [It] *BOOR-roh.* butter.

bursa [Lat] *BOOR-sah.* purse; pouch.

Burschenschaft [Ger] *BOOR-sh'n-shahft.* student group; fraternity.

bushido [Jap] *BOO-shee-doh.* code of the samurai: loyalty, obedience and honor.

Butter [Ger] *BOO-tuh.* butter; **Butterbrot** (*-broht*) (*lit.,* buttered bread) sandwich.

bwana [Swahili, from Ar *abuna,* our father] *BWAH-nah.* master (used by East Africans in speaking to Europeans).

bylina [Russ] *bi-LEE-nuh.* narrative folksong.

bzw. Abbr. of **beziehungsweise.**

C

ca. Abbr. of **circa.**

ça [Fr] *sah.* that. See **cela.**

cabala. See **cabbala.**

cabaletta [It, var. of *coboletta*, dim. of *cobola*, from Prov *cobla*, from Lat *copula*, strophe] *kah-bah-LAYT-tah*. (*music*) a catchy refrain at the end of an aria or duet.

cabalgata [Sp] *kah-bahl-GAH-tah*. cavalcade. Also, formerly, **cabalgada** (*-dah*).

caballería [Sp] *kah-bah-lyeh-REE-ah*. cavalry; knight-errantry, chivalry.

caballero [Sp] *kah-bah-LYEH-roh*. horseman; cavalier, knight; gentleman.

caballo [Sp] *kah-BAH-lyoh*. horse; (*chess*) knight; a— (*ah-*) on horseback.

cabaña [Sp] *kah-BAH-nyah*. hut, cabin; cabana.

cabane [Fr] *kah-BAHN*. hut, cabin; covered flat-bottomed boat.

cabbala [Heb *qabbālāh*] *kahb-bah-LAH*. (*lit.*, tradition) Hebrew occult religious philosophy. Also, **cabala, kab-(b)ala.**

cabeza [Sp] *kah-BEH-sah*. head.

cabildo [Sp, from Lat *capitulum*, chapter] *kah-BEEL-doh*. cathedral chapter; town council; town hall.

cabine [Fr] *kah-BEEN*. cabin; bathhouse; cabana.

cabinet d'aisance [Fr] *kah-bee-NAY-deh-ZÃS*. toilet; water closet.

cabo [Sp] *KAH-boh*. cape; headland, promontory; noncommissioned officer.

cabochon [Fr, from earlier *caboche*, head] *kah-boh-SHŎ*. highly polished uncut stone; unfaceted stone.

cabotage [Fr] *kah-boh-TAHZH*. coastwise trade; (*aero.*) legal limitation of domestic carrier's franchise to points within a country's own borders.

cabriole [Fr] *kah-bree-OHL*. ballet leap executed by fluttering but not crossing the feet in the air.

caccia [It] *KAH-chah*. hunt, chase; poem which celebrates the chase.

cacciatora. See **alla cacciatora.**

cacciatore [It] *kah-chah-TOH-reh*. hunter, huntsman: sometimes erroneously used for **alla cacciatora.**

cacciucco [It, from Turk *kuçuk*, small, in allusion to small pieces of fish found in it] *kah-CHOOK-koh.* fish chowder of the Italian seacoast.

cachet [Fr] *kah-SHAY.* personal seal; symbol; distinguishing mark; prestige.

cachette [Fr] *kah-SHET.* hiding place; **en—** (*ã-*) secretly; stealthily.

cachucha [Sp] *kah-CHOO-chah.* spirited Andalusian folk dance.

caciocavallo [It] *kah-choh-kah-VAHL-loh.* hard, piquant southern Italian cheese.

cacique [Sp, from Taino] *kah-SEE-keh.* Indian chief of Mexico and W Indies; local political boss.

cacoëthes [Lat, from Gk] *kah-koh-EH-thes.* propensity; compulsion; mania; **—carpendi** (*-kar-PEN-dee*) habit of faultfinding; **—loquendi** (*-loh-KWEN-dee*) compulsive talking; **—scribendi** (*-skree-BEN-dee*) compulsion to write.

cada [Sp] *KAH-dah.* each; every.

cada oveja con su pareja [Sp] *KAH-dah-oh-VEH-hah-kohn-soo-pah-REH-hah.* (*lit.,* every sheep with its mate) birds of a feather flock together.

cadeau [Fr] *kah-DOH.* gift; present.

cadenza [It] *kah-DEN-tsah.* (*music*) an elaborate solo passage introduced near the end of a vocal or instrumental piece.

cadet [Fr] *kah-DAY.* younger; younger son or brother.

cadi [Ar] *KAH-dee.* judge in a Moslem community who interprets the religious law. Also, **kadi.**

cadre [Fr] *KAH-druh.* framework; nucleus of a military or other organization.

caetera desunt [Lat] *KY-teh-rah-DEH-soont.* the rest are missing.

caeteris paribus [Lat] *KY-teh-rees-PAH-ree-boos.* other things being equal.

café [Fr] *kah-FAY.* coffee; coffee shop; restaurant; barroom; cabaret; **—au lait** (*-oh-LEH*) coffee with milk; a light brown color; **café-concert** (*-kŏ-SEHR*) music hall; vaudeville or variety theater; **—noir** (*-NWAR*) black coffee.

caffè [It] *kahf-FEH.* coffee; —**espresso** (*es-PRES-soh*) Italian-style strong black coffee, made by forcing live steam through finely ground coffee.

caftan [Turk] *KAHF-tahn.* a long tunic, usually with a sash or girdle at the waist.

cagnotte [Fr] *kah-NYOHT.* box which holds the house cut of stakes at a gambling table; the money therein.

Cagoulards [Fr] *kah-goo-LAR.* (*lit.,* hooded men) reactionary French organization of the 1930's.

cahier [Fr] *kah-YAY.* notebook; journal.

caïque [Fr, from Turk *kayik*] *kah-EEK.* long, narrow rowboat used on the Bosporus; single-masted sailing vessel of the eastern Mediterranean.

ça ira [Fr] *sah-ee-RAH.* it will go; it will succeed: refrain of a French Revolutionary song.

caisse [Fr] *kes.* caisson; chest; cashier's office or window; money box; till; treasury.

caja [Sp] *KAH-hah.* box; chest; safe; cashier's office or window.

calabaza [Sp] *kah-lah-BAH-sah.* pumpkin; gourd.

calabozo [Sp] *kah-lah-BOH-soh.* jail, prison; jail cell, dungeon.

calamar [Sp: *pl.* **calamares**] *kah-lah-MAR* (*-mah-res*) squid; **calamares en su tinta** (*-en-soo-TEEN-tah*) squid cooked in their own ink.

calamus [Lat, from Gk *kalamos*] *KAH-lah-moos.* reed; stalk.

calando [It] *kah-LAHN-doh.* (*music*) getting slower and softer.

calcio [It] *KAHL-choh.* (*lit.,* kick) soccer.

caldeirada [Port] *kuhl-day-RAH-duh.* a fish and shellfish stew.

caldo [Sp, Port] *KAHL-doh* (*-doo*) broth; juice; soup; —**gallego** (*-gah-LYEH-goh*) soup of turnip greens, potatoes and white beans, flavored with pork (Spain); —**verde** (*-VEHR-duh*) hot soup made with fresh kale and potatoes, flavored with sausages or pork (Portugal).

calèche [Fr] *kah-LESH.* two-wheeled carriage with accordion fold-down hood.

calembour [Fr] *kah-lã-BOOR.* pun.

calendae [Lat] *kah-LEN-dy.* calends; the first day of the month in the Roman calendar. Also, **kalendae.**

caliente [Sp] *kah-LYEN-teh.* hot; warm.

calix [Lat: cup] *KAH-leeks.* wine goblet with two small handles affixed to the stem; chalice; cup used for the wine of the Eucharist.

calle [Sp] *KAH-lyeh.* street.

callejón [Sp] *kah-lyeh-HOHN.* narrow lane or passageway; alley.

calmato [It] *kahl-MAH-toh.* (*music*) calm; tranquil.

caló [Sp] *kah-LOH.* Spanish Gypsy language.

calore [It] *kah-LOH-reh.* heat; ardor, passion; **con—** (*kohn-*) (*music*) passionately; in a fiery manner.

caloroso [It] *kah-loh-ROH-soh.* (*music*) warmly; with animation and ardor.

calunnia [It] *kah-LOON-nee-ah.* calumny; slander.

Calvados [Fr] *kahl-vah-DOHS.* apple brandy from French department of same name, in Normandy.

calzada [Sp] *kahl-SAH-dah.* highway; causeway.

cámara [Sp] *KAH-mah-rah.* chamber; hall.

camarade [Fr] *kah-mah-RAHD.* comrade; pal; friend; buddy.

camaraderie [Fr] *kah-mah-rah-d'REE.* comradeship; fellowship; group spirit.

camarão [Port: *pl.* **camarões**] *kuh-muh-RÃ-OO* (*-RŎ-EESH*) shrimp.

camarero [Sp] *kah-mah-REH-roh.* waiter; valet.

camarilla [Sp] *kah-mah-REE-lyah.* (*lit.,* small chamber) band of plotters; cadre; clique; group of special advisors.

camarón [Sp: *pl.* **camarones**] *kah-mah-ROHN* (*-ROH-nes*) shrimp.

cambio [Sp, It] *KAHM-byoh.* exchange; change.

camelot [Fr] *kah-m'LOH.* peddler; vendor; newsboy; **camelots du roi** (*-dü-RWAH*) Knights of the King; King's Hawkers; French royalist party, defunct since 1936.

Camembert [Fr] *kah-mã-BEHR.* a soft French cheese.

cameriere [It] *kah-meh-RYEH-reh.* waiter; valet.

Camicie Rosse [It] *kah-MEE-cheh-ROHS-seh.* Red Shirts: a name given to Garibaldi's men.

camino [Sp] *kah-MEE-noh.* road; highway; —**real** (*-reh-AHL*) royal road; main highway.

camion [Fr] *kah-MYŎ.* truck, wagon; military transport; bus.

camión [Sp] *kah-MYOHN.* truck, wagon; military transport; bus.

camion [It] *KAH-myohn.* truck, wagon; military transport, bus; **camioncino** (*-CHEE-noh*) small truck; tow car.

camisa [Sp] *kah-MEE-sah.* shirt; blouse.

camisado [Sp *camisada*, from *camisa*, shirt] *kah-mee-SAH-doh.* camouflaged attack; attack by night. Also, **camisade** [Fr] *kah-mee-SAHD.*

Camisards [Fr, from Prov *camisa*, shirt] *kah-mee-ZAR.* wearers of the Shirt: French Protestants who rebelled against the Edict of Nantes in the early 18th century.

Camorra [It] *kah-MOR-rah.* Neapolitan secret society, generally given to criminal activities.

camorrista [It: *pl.* **camorristi**] *kah-mor-REES-tah* (*-tee*) member of the Camorra.

campagna [It] *kahm-PAH-nyah.* country; countryside; —**romana** (*-roh-MAH-na*h) the low, flat region surrounding Rome.

campanile [It] *kahm-pah-NEE-leh.* belfry; bell tower; church tower.

campeador [Sp] *kahm-peh-ah-DOR.* champion; warrior; soldier; **Cid**— (*SEED-*) Spanish epic hero.

campilán [Sp, from Tagalog] *kahm-pee-LAHN.* a sword with a straight blade widened toward the tip, used by Filipino natives.

campione [It] *kahm-PYOH-neh.* champion; sample; —**senza valore** (*-SEN-tsah-vah-LOH-reh*) sample of nominal value sent by uninsured mail.

campo [It] *KAHM-poh.* field; open country.

camposanto [It] *kahm-poh-SAHN-toh.* hallowed ground; cemetery.

Campus Martius [Lat] *KAHM-poos-MAR-tee-oos.* Field of

Mars: field used by ancient Romans for military training and contests.

cañada [Sp] *kah-NYAH-dah.* glen; dale; small canyon.

canaille [Fr, from Lat *canis*, dog] *kah-NY.* (*lit.*, pack of dogs) riffraff; rabble.

canapé [Fr] *kah-nah-PAY.* a thin piece of bread or toast, or cracker, topped with savory food, served as an appetizer; large sofa or divan; (*bridge*) bidding convention by which short suits are bid before long suits.

canard [Fr] *kah-NAR.* (*lit.*, duck) hoax; rumor.

canasta [Sp] *kah-NAHS-tah.* (*lit.*, basket) card game; a variety of rummy.

cancan [Fr] *kã-KÃ.* dance originally performed in French cabarets, featuring high kicks and bumps; (*slang*) tittle-tattle; gossip.

Cancer [Lat] *KAHN-kehr.* crab: a sign of the Zodiac.

cancionero [Sp] *kahn-syoh-NEH-roh;* **cancioneiro** [Port] *kahn-syoo-NAY-roo.* collection of songs and poems.

cancrizans [Lat, pr. p. of *cancrizare*, to move backward, from *cancer*, crab] *KAHN-kree-zahns.* (*music*) using a melody or section of a musical piece in reverse.

caneton [Fr] *kah-n'TŎ.* duckling.

caniche [Fr] *kah-NEESH.* poodle.

cannelloni [It] *kahn-nel-LOH-nee.* large, hollow macaroni stuffed with meat and cheese and served with a cream or tomato sauce.

cannelon [Fr] *kah-n'LŎ.* fluted pastry mold for desserts, ices, etc; a stuffed, rolled-up meat dish.

cannoli [It: *sg.* **cannolo**] *kahn-NOH-lee (-loh)* rolled pastry shells filled with a rich mixture of custard and nuts.

cañón [Sp] *kah-NYOHN.* canyon; narrow, deep valley; cannon.

Canossa. See **nach Canossa.**

cansado [Sp] *kahn-SAH-doh.* tired.

cansó [Prov] *kahn-SOH.* Provençal love song or lyric poem of five to seven stanzas.

cantabile [It] *kahn-TAH-bee-leh.* (*lit.*, singable) in a singing, flowing style; piece performed in such style.

Cantabrigiensis [Lat, from *Cantabrigia*, Cambridge] *kahn-tah-bree-gee-EN-sees*. of Cambridge (University).

cantando [It] *kahn-TAHN-doh*. singing; in singing style.

cantar [Sp] *kahn-TAR*. song; lay; ballad; tale in verse.

cantastorie [It] *kahn-tah-STOH-ryeh*. itinerant folk singer; wandering minstrel.

cantata [It] *kahn-TAH-tah*. musical composition for solos or choruses.

cantate Domino [Lat] *kahn-TAH-teh-DOH-mee-noh*. sing unto the Lord.

cantatrice [It] *kahn-tah-TREE-cheh*. female singer; songstress.

cantilena [It] *kahn-tee-LEH-nah*. simple, lyric melody; melodious phrase.

cantina [Sp] *kahn-TEE-nah*. canteen; saloon; [It] cellar.

canto [It] *KAHN-toh*. song; lyric poem; canto.

cantus [Lat] *KAHN-toos*. song; chant; singing; —**choralis** (*-koh-RAH-lees*) choral song or chant; —**firmus** (*-FEER-moos*) (*lit.*, fixed song) simple melody to which other parts are added; —**planus** (*-PLAH-noos*) plainsong.

canzone [It] *kahn-TSOH-neh*. song.

caoutchouc [Fr] *kow-CHOO*. sticky juice of the rubber plant; India rubber.

capa [Sp] *KAH-pah*. cape; cloak; mantle.

cap-à-pied [Fr] *kah-pah-PYEH*. head to foot: usually referring to full armor.

capataz [Sp] *kah-pah-TAHS*. foreman; supervisor.

capa y espada [Sp] *KAH-pah-ee-es-PAH-dah*. cape and sword; cloak and dagger.

capeador [Sp] *kah-peh-ah-DOR*. a bullfighter who entices the bull with his cape.

capias [Lat] *KAH-pee-ahs*. (*lit.*, you shall take) warrant for arrest or seizure of property.

capilla [Sp] *kah-PEE-lyah*. chapel.

capo [It] *KAH-poh*. head; chief; beginning; **da—** (*dah-*) from the start.

capocollo [It] *kah-poh-KOHL-loh*. kind of salame made from head and neck parts of beef or pork.

capo d'anno [It] *KAH-poh-DAHN-noh*. New Year's Day.

caponatina [It] *kah-poh-nah-TEE-nah.* conserve of eggplant with capers, olive oil and spices. Also, **caponata** (*-NAH-tah*).

caporal [Fr] *kah-poh-RAHL.* [*lit.,* (tobacco of the) corporal] type of French tobacco.

capote [Fr] *kah-POHT.* cloak; cape; mantle; greatcoat; —**anglaise** (*-ā-GLEZ*) prophylactic appliance; condom.

cappuccino [It] *kahp-poo-CHEE-noh.* espresso coffee mixed with steamed milk and powdered cinnamon, topped with whipped cream; Capuchin monk.

capriccio [It] *kah-PREE-choh.* free musical composition; caprice.

capriccioso [It] *kah-pree-CHOH-soh.* (*music*) in free, whimsical style.

Capricornus [Lat, from *caper,* goat + *cornu,* horn] *kah-pree-KOR-noos.* goat: a sign of the Zodiac. Also, **Capricorn** (*KAP-ri-korn*).

capuce [Fr] *kah-PÜS.* hood; cowl. Also, **capuchon** (*kah-pü-SHŎ*).

caput [Lat] *KAH-poot.* head; —**mundi** (*-MOON-dee*) head of the world: Rome.

cara [It, fem of **caro**] *KAH-rah.* dear; beloved; [Sp] face.

carabao [Philippine Sp, from Malay *karbau*] *kah-rah-BAH-oh.* water buffalo.

carabiniere [It: *pl.* **-ri**] *kah-rah-bee-NYEH-reh* (*-ree*) rifleman; carbineer; military policeman; policeman.

caracoles. See **caramba.**

carafe [Fr, from Ar *gharrāfah*] *kah-RAHF.* bottle for water or other beverages.

caramba [Sp] *kah-RAHM-bah.* exclamation of astonishment, incredulity, appreciation, distress, annoyance, etc. Also, **caray** (*kah-RY*); **caracoles** (*cah-rah-KOH-les*).

Carbonari [It] *kar-boh-NAH-ree.* (*lit.,* charcoal burners) Italian secret society of republicans, founded in early 19th century.

carbón de leña [Sp] *kar-BOHN-deh-LEH-nyah.* charcoal; —**de piedra** (*-deh-PYEH-drah*) hard coal.

carbone bianco [It] *kar-BOH-neh-BYAHN-koh.* (*lit.,* white coal) water power.

carcajou [Fr, from Algonquian] *kar-kah-ZHOO.* badger; wolverine.

cárcel [Sp] *KAR-sel.* jail; prison.

carciofo [It: *pl.* **carciofi,** from Ar *kharshūf*] *kar-CHOH-foh* (*-fee*) artichoke.

Carême [Fr] *kah-REM.* Lent.

carilloneur [Fr] *kah-ree-yoh-NÖR.* carillon player; bell-ringer.

Carioca [Port, from Tupi *cari,* white + *oka,* house] *kah-ree-OH-kah.* native of Rio de Janeiro; Brazilian dance similar to the samba.

cariole. See **carriole.**

carissimo [It: *fem.* **-ma**] *kah-REES-see-moh* (*-mah*) dearest, beloved.

carità [It] *kah-ree-TAH.* (*lit.,* charity, kindness) (*music*) tenderness; feeling; **per—!** (*pehr-*) please!; for goodness' sake!

caritas [Lat] *KAH-ree-tahs.* charity; love.

Carmagnole [Fr, from Carmagnola, a town in Piedmont, Italy] *kar-mah-NYOHL.* song of the French Revolution; costume of the same period.

carmen [Lat] *KAR-men.* song; lay; poem.

carne [Sp, It] *KAR-neh;* [Port] *KAR-nuh.* flesh; meat.

caro [It: *fem.* **cara**] *KAH-roh* (*-rah*) dear; beloved.

caroche [Fr, from It **carroccio**] *kah-ROHSH.* stately carriage of the 17th century.

carpe diem [Lat] *KAR-peh-DEE-em.* (*lit.,* seize the day) make hay while the sun shines.

carré [Fr] *kah-RAY.* square; squared.

carreta [Sp] *kar-REH-tah.* long narrow two-wheeled cart.

carretera [Sp] *kar-reh-TEH-rah.* road; highway.

carriole [Fr] *kah-RYOHL.* small open two-wheeled vehicle; light covered cart; trap. Also, **cariole.**

carroccio [It] *kahr-ROH-choh.* medieval carriage carrying a flag as a rallying point in battle.

Carro di Tespi [It] *KAR-roh-dee-TES-pee.* theater cart or wagon; traveling show.

carte [Fr] *kart.* card; menu; map; **—blanche** (*-BLÄSH*) free hand; authorization to act as one wills; —de visite (*-duh-vee-ZEET*) visiting card.

Carthago delenda est [Lat] *kar-TAH-goh-deh-LEN-dah-EST.* Carthage must be destroyed: phrase repeated in many speeches before the Roman Senate by Cato.

carton [Fr] *kar-TŎ.* pasteboard; cardboard.

cartouche [Fr] *kar-TOOSH.* cartridge; ornamental emblem in shield or ovoid form, carved, painted, inlaid or stenciled on furniture, woodwork, etc., often used for inscriptions on heraldic devices, and to record the names of Egyptian Pharaohs wherever they occur in a hieroglyphic text.

casa [Sp, It] *KAH-sah*; [Port] *KAH-zuh.* house; home.

casa de huéspedes [Sp] *KAH-sah-deh-WES-peh-des.* guest house; inn; boardinghouse.

casbah. See **kasbah.**

cáscara sagrada [Sp] *KAHS-kah-rah-sah-GRAH-dah.* bark of the cascara plant, used as a laxative.

casetta [It] *kah-SAYT-tah.* small house; cottage.

casse-noisette [Fr] *KAHS-nwah-ZET.* nutcracker.

cassoulet [Fr] *kah-soo-LAY.* stew of white beans with slices of duck, goose, pork or lamb.

castañeta [Sp, from *castaña*, chestnut, from resemblance in shape] *kahs-tah-NYEH-tah.* castanet. Also **castañuela** (*-NYWEH-lah*).

castellano [Sp] *kahs-teh-LYAH-noh.* Castilian; Spanish.

castigat ridendo mores [Lat] *KAHS-tee-gaht-ree-DEN-doh-MOH-res.* it (comedy) chastens customs by laughing at them.

Castilla la Nueva [Sp] *kahs-TEE-lyah-lah-NWEH-vah.* New Castile; —**la Vieja** (*-VYEH-hah*) Old Castile.

castrato [It; *pl.* **-ti**] *kahs-TRAH-toh* (*-tee*) (*lit.*, castrated) male soprano, esp. in 18th-century Italy, castrated before puberty to keep voice from changing.

casus [Lat, from *cadere*, to fall] *KAH-soos.* (*lit.*, fall, falling) happening; event; case; —**belli** (*-BEL-lee*) occurrence giving rise to war; —**foederis** (*-FOY-deh-rees*) act or condition invoking the provisions of a treaty.

catabasis [Gk] *kah-TAH-bah-sees.* (*lit.*, a going down) post-climactic action in a play; retreat, esp. a military retreat.

catalogue raisonné [Fr] *kah-tah-LOHG-reh-zuh-NAY.* annotated catalogue footnoting and explaining works of art.

cathedra [Lat, from Gk *kathedra,* chair] *KAH-teh-drah.* papal throne; bishop's throne; large armchair; professorial chair.

caudillo [Sp] *kow-DEE-lyoh.* chief; dictator; title of Francisco Franco.

causa [Lat] *KOW-sah.* cause.

cause célèbre [Fr] *KOZ-say-LEH-bruh.* famous or sensational case.

causerie [Fr, from *causer,* to converse] *koh-z'REE.* chat; informal talk; chatty essay or interview.

Causeries du lundi [Fr] *koh-z'REE-dü-lü-DEE.* Monday conversations: collection of literary essays (1849-1869) by the French critic Sainte-Beuve.

causeur [Fr: *fem.* **causeuse**] *koh-ZÖR* (*-ZÖZ*) conversationalist; talkative.

ça va [Fr] *sah-VAH.* (*lit.,* it goes) all right; good; O.K.

cavaliere [It] *kah-vah-LYEH-reh.* horseman; cavalryman; knight, chevalier; gentleman; gallant, lady's escort; nonhereditary title of semi-nobility.

cavalier servente [It] *kah-vah-LYEHR-sehr-VEN-teh.* married woman's lover or escort.

cavatina [It] *kah-vah-TEE-nah.* simple song or instrumental piece.

caveat [Lat] *KAH-veh-aht.* (*lit.,* let him beware) warning, caution; (*law*) legal notice to a court to suspend proceedings until the claimant has had a hearing; **—emptor** (*-EMP-tor*) let the buyer beware.

cave canem [Lat] *KAH-veh-KAH-nem.* beware of the dog.

cave quid dicis, quando, et cui [Lat] *KAH-veh-kweed-DEE-kees-KWAHN-doh-et-KOO-ee.* beware what you say, when, and to whom.

cavo-rilievo [It] *KAH-voh-ree-LYEH-voh.* (*sculp.*) hollow relief.

cayo [Sp] *KAH-yoh.* reef; key.

ceci [Fr] *suh-SEE.* this.

ceci [It] *CHEH-chee.* chickpeas; garbanzo beans.

cedant arma togae [Lat] *KEH-dahnt-AR-mah-TOH-gy.* Let arms yield to the toga: Cicero's exhortation to subject the military to civil authority; motto of Wyoming.

cédez [Fr] *say-DAY.* yield!

cedilla [Sp] *seh-DEE-lyah.* (*lit.*, little zee) symbol usually put under *c* in Old Spanish, modern French and Portuguese, to indicate sibilant quality before back vowels (*a, o, u*).

ceinture [Fr] *sẽ-TÙR.* waist; belt, sash.

ceja [Sp] *SEH-hah.* (*lit.*, eyebrow) strip of chaparral or dense brush.

cela [Fr] *suh-LAH.* that; often contracted to ça; —**m'est égal** (*-meh-tay-GAHL*) it's all the same to me; —**m'importe peu** (*-mẽ-port-PÖ*) that matters little to me; —**ne fait rien** (*-nuh-feh-RYẼ*) that makes no difference; —**saute aux yeux** (*-soh-toh-ZYÖ*) (*lit.*, that leaps to the eyes) that's obvious; —**va sans dire** (*-vah-sã-DEER*) that goes without saying.

célèbre [Fr] *say-LEH-bruh.* celebrated; famous.

celeste [It] *cheh-LES-teh.* celestial, heavenly; sky-blue.

cembalo [It] *CHEM-bah-loh.* harpsichord; tambourine.

ce n'est que le premier pas qui coûte [Fr] *suh-NEH-kuh-luh-pruh-MYAY-pah-kee-KOOT.* it's only the first step that costs; the first move is the hardest.

centavo [Sp] *sen-TAH-voh.* unit of currency in various Latin-American countries; one hundredth of a peso or other unit.

centesimo [It] *chen-TEH-see-moh.* unit of Italian currency; one hundredth of a lira.

centime [Fr] *sã-TEEM.* unit of currency in France, Belgium, Switzerland, etc.; one hundredth of a franc.

céntimo [Sp] *SEN-tee-moh.* unit of currency in Spain and some Latin-American countries; one hundredth of a peseta, peso or other unit.

centum [Lat] *KEN-toom.* one hundred; (*ling.*) designation of those branches of the Indo-European language family that have in common the velar sound of the initial consonant of the word for hundred. See **satem.**

cerda [Sp, from *cerdo*, hog] *SEHR-dah.* horsehair; boar bristle.

cerise [Fr] *suh-REEZ.* cherry; cherry color; deep, rich pink.

certiorari [Lat] *kehr-tee-oh-RAH-ree.* (*lit.*, to be ascertained) (*law*) writ to procure records from a lower court for review by a higher court.

certum est quia impossibile est [Lat] *KEHR-toom-est-kwee-ah-eem-pohs-SEE-bee-leh-est.* it is certain because it is impossible.

cervelle [Fr] *sehr-VEL.* (*cookery*) brains.

cerveza [Sp] *sehr-VEH-sah.* beer.

cervoise [Fr] *sehr-VWAHZ.* the beer of the ancient Gauls.

cessante causa cessat effectus [Lat] *kes-SAHN-teh-KOW-sah-KES-saht-ef-FEK-toos.* the cause ceasing, the effect ceases.

cesta [Sp] *SES-tah.* basket; a wicker scoop worn strapped to the wrist in jai alai.

c'est à dire [Fr] *set-ah-DEER.* that is to say.

c'est bien [Fr] *seh-BYẼ.* that's fine; good.

c'est (si) bon [Fr] *seh-(see)-BŎ.* it's (so) good.

c'est dommage [Fr] *seh-doh-MAHZH.* it's a pity.

c'est la guerre [Fr] *seh-lah-GEHR.* that's war.

c'est la vie [Fr] *seh-lah-VEE.* that's life.

c'est le commencement de la fin [Fr] *seh-luh-koh-mãs-MÃ-duh-lah-FẼ.* it's the beginning of the end.

c'est magnifique [Fr] *seh-mah-nyee-FEEK.* it's magnificent.

c'est plus qu'un crime, c'est une faute [Fr] *seh-plü-kü-KREEM-seh-tün-FOHT.* it's worse than a crime, it's a mistake.

cestus [Lat] *KES-toos.* basket; glove worn by Roman boxers, made of leather strips, often loaded with metal.

cetera desunt [Lat] *KEH-teh-rah-DEH-soont.* See **caetera desunt.**

ceteris paribus [Lat] *KEH-teh-rees-PAH-ree-boos.* See **caeteris paribus.**

cf. Abbr. of **confer.**

cha [Chin] *chah.* tea.

chabouk [Hindi, from Pers] *CHAH-book.* a horsewhip,

often used in the Orient for inflicting corporal punishment. Also, **chabuk.**

cha-cha [Sp] *CHAH-chah.* popular Latin-American dance.

chaconne [Fr] *shah-KUN.* slow, stately dance, said to be of Spanish origin.

chacun à son goût [Fr] *shah-KŪ-nah-sō-GOO.* everyone to his taste.

chacun pour soi [Fr] *shah-KŪ-poor-SWAH.* every man for himself.

chai [Russ] *chy.* tea.

chaise longue [Fr] *shez-LŎG.* (*lit.*, long chair) reclining sofa with adjustable headrest.

chalet [Fr] *shah-LAY.* cottage; small house built in Swiss style.

challah [Yid, from Heb *khallāh*] *KHAH-lah.* a leavened bread made with eggs, usu. in a braided shape, glazed with egg white, and sprinkled with poppy seeds. Also, **hallah.**

chamade [Fr, from Port *chamada*, from *chamar*, to call, sound] *shah-MAHD.* signal of agreement to negotiate or surrender, usually made by drum or trumpet.

chambre [Fr] *SHÃ-bruh.* room; chamber.

chambré [Fr] *shã-BRAY.* chambered; (*of wine*) brought to room temperature before serving.

chameau [Fr] *shah-MOH.* camel; wench, slattern; dope, dumbbell.

chamorro [Sp: having frizzled hair] *chah-MOR-roh.* native of the Marianas Islands; the language of the Chamorros; native of Guam holding U.S. citizenship.

champ [Fr] *shã.* field; —**de Mars** (*-duh-MARS*) (*lit.*, field of Mars) large open space on the left bank of the Seine, formerly used as a drill ground.

champignon [Fr] *shã-pee-NYŎ.* mushroom.

champlevé [Fr] *shã-luh-VAY.* (*lit.*, raised field) enamel work made by fusing enamel onto an incised or hollowed design in metal.

Champs Élysées [Fr] *shã-zay-lee-ZAY* (*lit.*, Elysian Fields) a main boulevard in Paris.

chanson [Fr] *shã-SŎ*. song; lyric poem; —**de geste** (*duh-ZHEST*) any of a number of medieval French epic poems of which the most famous is the *Chanson de Roland*.

chansonnette [Fr] *shã-suh-NET*. little song; ditty.

chansonnier [Fr] *shã-suh-NYAY*. singer, esp. of satirical topical songs; collection of songs; song book; collection of troubadour lyrics; songwriter, esp. of satirical topical songs.

chant [Fr] *shã*. song; singing.

chantage [Fr] *shã-TAHZH*. extortion; blackmail.

Chantecler [Fr] *shã-t'KLEHR*. (*lit.*, sing clear) name of the rooster in medieval French fables.

chante-fable [Fr] *shãt-FAH-bluh*. medieval French tale in prose and verse.

chanteur [Fr: *fem.* **chanteuse**] *shã-TÖR* (*-TÖZ*) singer.

chapar(r)ajos [MexSp, from *chaparral*, chaparral, blended with *aparejos*, gear, equipment] *chah-pah(r)-RAH-hohs*. chaps; leather or sheepskin covering for the legs of horsemen in bushy country. Also, **chapar(r)ejos** (*-REH-hohs*); **chapar(r)eras** (*-REH-rahs*).

chapeau [Fr] *shah-POH*. hat.

chaqueta [Sp] *chah-KEH-tah*. jacket.

char-à-bancs [Fr] *shar-ah-BÃ*. (*lit.*, cart with benches) sightseeing bus with open sides and no center aisle.

charbon [Fr] *shar-BŎ*. coal.

charco [Sp] *CHAR-koh*. shallow pool; puddle.

charcuterie [Fr] *shar-kü-t'REE*. pork shop; pork cold cuts.

charcutier [Fr] *shar-kü-TYAY*. pork butcher.

chargé [Fr] *shar-ZHAY*. charged, entrusted; a sub-ambassador; lower diplomatic official; —**d'affaires** (*-dah-FEHR*) minor government official temporarily replacing a higher diplomat.

charivari [Fr, from Lat *caribaria*, headache, from Gk] *shah-ree-vah-REE*. mock serenade or raucous music for a newly married couple; shivaree.

charmante [Fr] *shar-MÃT*. charming; charming woman.

charqui [Sp] *CHAR-kee*. jerked beef.

Chartreuse [Fr, after La Grande Chartreuse, monastery

near Grenoble where the liqueur is made] *shar-TRÖZ.*
a yellow-green liqueur; a shade of yellow-green.

chassé [Fr] *shah-SAY.* (*lit.*, chased) gliding ballet step.

chassepot [Fr, from name of inventor] *shahs-POH.* breech-loading rifle used by the French army in the latter part of the 19th century.

chasseur [Fr] *shah-SÖR.* hunter; light infantryman; footman; bellhop; —**des Alpes** (*-day-ZAHLP*) member of French mountain troops.

chat [Fr] *shah.* cat.

château [Fr: *pl.* -**eaux**] *shah-TOH.* castle; palace; manor house.

châteaubriant [Fr] *shah-toh-bree-Ã.* beefsteak served lavishly, usually with mushrooms and potatoes or truffles. Also, **Chateaubriand.**

châtelaine [Fr] *shah-t'LEN.* mistress of a manor or château; clasp or chain for holding keys, charms, etc., worn at the waist by women.

chaud-froid [Fr] *shoh-FRWAH.* (*lit.*, hot-cold) jellied dish of cold fowl; ice cream with hot syrup.

chaudière [Fr] *shoh-DYEHR.* cauldron; boiler; chowder.

chaussée [Fr, from Lat *calceata* (*via*), paved road] *shoh-SAY.* causeway; highway.

chaussure [Fr] *shoh-SÜR.* footgear; boots; shoes.

chauve-souris [Fr] *shohv-soo-REE.* (*lit.*, bald mouse) bat.

chauvin [Fr, from name of a soldier in Napoleon's army] *shoh-VÊ.* fanatic patriot.

che [AmerSp] *cheh.* comrade; companion; fellow; (*interj.*) hey!, ho! Also, **ché.**

chéchia [Fr, from Ar *shāshiya*] *shay-SHYAH.* fezlike conical hat, formerly worn by native troops in French service in N Africa.

chee-chee [Anglo-Ind, from Hindi *chhī-chhī*, dirt] *CHEE-chee.* E Indian half-caste or Eurasian, in reference to their mincing English; English as spoken by Eurasians. Also, **chi-chi.**

chef [Fr, short for *chef de cuisine*, chief of the kitchen] *shef.* head cook.

chef de cabinet [Fr] *sheh-d'kah-bee-NAY.* chief aide to a minister in the French cabinet.

chef de gare [Fr] *sheh-d'GAR.* stationmaster.

chef-d'oeuvre [Fr] *sheh-DÖV-ruh.* masterpiece.

cheka [Russ, from initials of *Chresvychainaya Kommissiya,* Extraordinary Commission] *cheh-KAH.* Communist secret police from 1917 to 1922, predecessor of OGPU.

chemin de fer [Fr] *sh'MẼ-d'FEHR.* (*lit.,* iron road) railroad; (*cards*) variation of baccarat.

chemise [Fr] *sh'MEEZ.* shirt; woman's shirtlike undergarment; loose-fitting dress hanging straight down from the shoulders; shimmy.

chemisier [Fr] *sh'mee-ZYAY.* shirtmaker.

chenille [Fr] *sh'NEE-yuh.* (*lit.,* caterpillar) fabric, usually cotton, with rough, nubby pile.

cher [Fr: *fem.* **chère**] *shehr.* dear; beloved; expensive; —**ami** (*fem.* **chère amie**) *sheh-rah-MEE.* dear friend; beloved.

chercher la petite bête [Fr] *shehr-SHAY-lah-p'TEET-BET.* (*lit.,* to search for the little beast) to be excessively finicky.

cherchez la femme [Fr] *shehr-SHAY-lah-FAHM.* look for the woman (in the case): a stereotype of whodunits.

chéri [Fr: *fem.* **chérie**] *shay-REE.* dear; sweetheart.

che sarà sarà [It] *keh-sah-RAH-sah-RAH.* whatever will be, will be.

chetnik [Serbo-Croatian, from *cheta,* troop + -*nik* (suffix of appurtenance)] *CHET-neek.* Yugoslav resistance fighter against the Turks and later in the two World Wars.

cheval [Fr: *pl.* **chevaux**] *sh'VAHL* (*sh'VOH*) horse; à— (*ah-*) on horseback; — -**de-frise** (*-duh-FREEZ*) (*lit.,* Frisian horse, first used by Frisians) portable barrier resembling a sawhorse, covered with spikes or barbed wire; —**glass** full-length, freestanding mirror, framed and attached to a base.

chevalier [Fr] *sh'-vah-LYAY.* horseman; cavalier; knight; gentleman; —**d'industrie** (*-dē-düs-TREE*) (*lit.,* knight of industry) one who gets around by shrewdness and wits; con man; adventurer; —**sans peur et sans reproche** (*-sā-*

PÖR-ay-sā-ruh-PROHSH) fearless and irreproachable knight: epithet of Bayard.

chevet [Fr, from *chef*, head] *sh'VEH.* head (of a bed); pillow; bolster; eastern end of the apse of a church beyond the altar.

chez [Fr] *shay.* at the home or place of business of; among; according to.

chi ama assai parla poco [It] *kee-AH-mah-ah-SY-PAR-lah-POH-koh.* he who loves much speaks little; true love is without words.

chi ama crede [It] *kee-AH-mah-KREH-deh.* he who loves believes; there is no love without trust.

chiarezza [It] *kyah-RAY-tsah.* (*music*) clarity; purity.

chiaroscuro [It] *KYAH-roh-SKOO-roh* (*lit.*, light and dark) use of light and shade in painting to give the impression of three dimensions.

chiasmus [Lat, from Gk *chiasmos*, from *chi*, the Gk letter χ] *kee-AHS-moos.* a rhetorical figure in which the second part counterbalances the first by repeating the first part backwards.

chibook [Turk] *chee-BOOK.* elongated Turkish smoking pipe.

chic [Fr, from Ger *Schick*] *sheek.* elegant; elegance.

chicano [AmerSp] *chee-KAH-noh.* designation for people of Mexican birth or origin living on U.S. soil.

chicha [AmerSp, from native Indian name] *CHEE-chah.* beer made from fermented corn or cane sugar.

chi-chi [Fr] *shee-SHEE.* chic to the point of absurdity or ostentatiousness; [Anglo-Indian] See **chee-chee**.

chico [Sp] *CHEE-koh.* small; small boy.

chi dà presto dà due volte [It] *kee-DAH-PRES-toh-DAH-doo-eh-VOHL-teh.* he who gives promptly, gives twice.

chien [Fr] *shyē.* dog.

chienne [Fr] *shyen.* female dog; bitch.

chiesa [It, from Lat *ecclesia*, from Gk *ekklēsia*, assembly] *KYEH-sah.* church.

chiffré [Fr] *shee-FRAY.* (*music*) figured.

chignon [Fr] *shee-NYŎ.* knot or lump of hair worn at the nape of the neck.

chile con carne [Sp] *CHEE-leh-kohn-KAR-neh.* Mexican dish consisting of kidney beans, ground meat and red pepper.

chi lo sa? [It] *KEE-loh-SAH.* who knows?

chin-chin [Chin *ch'ing-ch'ing*, please-please] *cheen-CHEEN.* expression used in toasting someone or in greeting or farewell; polite or lighthearted talk; to make small talk. Also, **cin-cin.**

chi niente sa di niente dubita [It] *kee-NYEN-teh-SAH-dee-NYEN-teh-DOO-bee-tah.* he who knows nothing, doubts nothing; what you don't know won't hurt you.

chi non fa non falla [It] *kee-nohn-FAH-nohn-FAHL-lah.* he who does nothing errs not.

chi non ha non è [It] *kee-nohn-AH-nohn-EH.* he who has not is not.

chi non s'arrischia non guadagna [It] *kee-nohn-sar-REES-kyah-nohn-gwah-DAH-nyah.* he who risks nothing gains nothing; nothing ventured, nothing gained. Also, **chi non risica non rosica** (*kee-nohn-REE-see-kah-nohn-ROH-see-kah*).

chinook [AmerInd tribal name] *chi-NOOK.* warm, dry wind of the eastern slopes of the Rocky Mountains.

chi tace acconsente [It] *kee-TAH-cheh-ahk-kohn-SEN-teh.* he who is silent consents; silence is assent; sometimes followed by **ma chi sta zitto non dice niente** (*mah-kee-stah-TSEET-toh-nohn-DEE-cheh-NYEN-teh*) but he who keeps his mouth shut says nothing.

chi tardi arriva male alloggia [It] *kee-TAR-dee-ar-REE-vah-MAH-leh-ahl-LOH-jah.* he who arrives late finds bad lodgings; first come, first served.

chiton [Gk] *KEE-tohn.* garment worn beneath the toga in classical times.

chi va piano va sano e va lontano [It] *kee-vah-PYAH-noh-vah-SAH-noh-eh-vah-lohn-TAH-noh.* he who goes slowly goes safely and goes far; sometimes followed by **e non arriva mai** (*eh-nohn-ar-REE-vah-MY*) and never gets there.

chlamys [Gk] *KLAH-müs.* short, loose cloak for men, fastened at one shoulder.

choisi [Fr: *fem.* **choisie**] *shwah-ZEE.* chosen; select.

chop-chop [Pidgin Eng] quick!, quickly!

chop suey [Chin *shap sui,* mixed bits] *chahp-SOO-ee.* Chinese-American dish of meat and vegetables.

choriambus [Lat, from Gk *choriambos,* from *choreios,* trochee + *iambos,* iamb] *koh-ree-AHM-boos.* metrical foot of one long, two short and one long syllables.

chorizo [Sp] *choh-REE-soh.* pork sausage seasoned with garlic and spices.

chornaya sotnya [Russ] *CHOR-nuh-yuh-SAWT-nyuh.* (*lit.,* black hundred) Cossack squadron under the czars.

chose [Fr] *shohz.* thing.

chou [Fr: *pl.* **choux**] *shoo.* cabbage; ornamental fabric flower on dress; rosette; light pastry in this shape; darling, lambkin; —**à la crème** (*-ah-lah-KREM*) creamed cabbage.

choucroute [Fr] *shoo-KROOT.* sauerkraut; —**garnie** (*-gar-NEE*) sauerkraut garnished with sausages and pork.

chouette [Fr] *shwet.* (*lit.,* screech owl) elegant; stunning.

chou-fleur [Fr] *shoo-FLÖR.* cauliflower.

chouriço [Port] *shoo-REE-soo.* pork sausage seasoned with garlic and spices.

chow mein [Chin: fried dough] *chow-MAYN.* Chinese-American dish of meat and vegetables.

choza [Sp] *CHOH-sah.* hut; cabin; shanty.

chrestomathie [Fr] *kres-toh-mah-TEE.* anthology; chrestomathy.

chrisma [Gk] *KREES-mah.* holy oil used for baptism, confirmation, etc.

Christe eleison [Lat *Christe,* Christ + Gk *eleēson*] *KREES-teh-eh-LEH-ee-sohn.* Christ, have mercy!

chroma [Gk] *KROH-mah.* (*lit.,* color) distinctive quality, excluding brightness, that identifies any particular color: absent from white, black and gray.

chronique scandaleuse [Fr] *kroh-NEEK-skä-dah-LÖZ.* scandalous news; gossip.

Chronos [Gk] *KHROH-nohs.* God of time; (*l.c.*) time.

chrysos [Gk] *krü-SOHS.* gold.

chthon [Gk] *kthohn.* earth.

chukker [Anglo-Ind, from Hindi *chakkar*, from Skt *cakra*, wheel] *CHUK-kur.* track for exercising horses; time period in polo game.

chung [Chin] *joong.* Confucian concept of conscientiousness in human affairs.

chupatty [Anglo-Ind, from Hindi *chapātī*] *chuh-PAHT-tee.* thin unleavened cake.

chut [Fr] *shüt.* quiet!, silence!, ssh!, hush!

chutney [Anglo-Ind, from Hindi *chatnī*] *CHUT-nee.* E Indian sweet-and-sour sauce.

chutzpah [Yid] *KHOOTS-pah.* audacity; gall; nerve.

ciao [It, from Venetian form of *schiavo*, (your) slave] *chow.* hello!, good-bye!

cicerone [It] *chee-cheh-ROH-neh.* (*lit.*, a Cicero) guide, esp. one who knows the antiquities.

cicisbeo [It; prob. imitative of the finch's call] *chee-cheez-BEH-oh.* known lover of a married woman.

Cid [Sp, from Ar *sayyid*] *seed.* chieftain, leader: epithet of Rodrigo Díaz de Bivar (1040-1099), hero of the wars against the Moors.

ci-devant [Fr] *see-duh-VÃ.* former; ex-.

cigarrillo [Sp] *see-gar-REE-lyoh.* cigarette; small cigar.

ci-gît [Fr] *see-ZHEE.* here lies.

cin-cin. *cheen-CHEEN.* See **chin-chin.**

cine [Sp] *SEE-neh*; [It] *CHEE-neh.* movie theater; movie.

cinéaste [Fr] *see-nay-AHST.* moviegoer, movie fan; film producer or collaborator.

cinecittà [It] *chee-neh-cheet-TAH.* film studio; movieland.

cinéma vérité [Fr] *see-nay-MAH-vay-ree-TAY.* realistic style in film making; realistic films.

cinquecento [It] *cheen-kweh-CHEN-toh.* the 1500's; the 16th century.

cinquefoil [Fr, from Lat *quinque folia*, five leaves] *SINK-foil.* perennial rose; heraldic sign in the form of five-leaved clover; architectural decoration in the form of five lobes about a common center.

ciociara [It] *choh-CHAH-rah.* Neapolitan costumed folk dance about fickle lovers.

cippus [Lat] *KEEP-poos.* inscribed memorial pillar; stele.

circa [Lat: *abbr.* **ca.**] *KEER-kah.* about, approximately.

cire perdue [Fr] *SEER-pehr-DÜ.* (*lit.*, lost wax) a casting technique in which a mold is built around a wax original, which is burned away when hot molten metal is poured into the mold.

cité [Fr] *see-TAY.* city, town.

cithara [Lat, from Gk] *KEE-thah-rah.* See **kithara.**

citoyen [Fr: *fem.* **citoyenne**] *see-twah-YẼ (-YEN)* citizen.

città [It] *cheet-TAH.* city, town.

cittadino [It: *fem.* **-a**] *cheet-tah-DEE-noh (-nah)* citizen.

ciudad [Sp] *syoo-DAHD.* town, city.

ciudadano [Sp: *fem.* **-a**] *syoo-dah-DAH-noh (-nah)* citizen.

ciuinga [It, corrupted from Eng] *CHOO-een-gah.* chewing gum.

civet [Fr] *see-VEH.* ragout of game, heavily seasoned with wines, herbs and spices.

civetta [It] *chee-VAYT-tah.* (*lit.*, owl) flirt; coquette.

civis romanus sum [Lat] *KEE-vees-roh-MAH-noos-SOOM.* I am a Roman citizen.

Civitas Dei [Lat] *KEE-vee-tahs-DEH-ee.* The city of God.

clair de lune [Fr] *KLEHR-duh-LÜN.* moonlight.

claque [Fr, from *claquer*, to clap] *klak.* band of hired applauders.

claqueur [Fr] *klah-KÖR.* member of a **claque.**

clepsydra [Gk] *KLEP-see-drah.* water clock.

cliché [Fr] *klee-SHAY.* stereotype; hackneyed expression.

clique [Fr] *kleek.* set; group, esp. an exclusive one.

cloaca [Lat] *kloh-AH-kah.* sewer; privy; filthy or immoral place; (*zool.*) the common opening of the digestive and genitourinary tracts of an animal.

cloche [Fr] *klohsh.* bell; close-fitting bell-shaped hat.

cloisonné [Fr] *klwah-zuh-NAY.* enamel work in which the design pattern is laid out in metal strips welded to the surface and the enamel inlaid between.

clou [Fr] *kloo.* nail; peg; focal point of a story or event.

C.M.B., c.m.b. Abbr. of **cuyas manos beso.**

cobre [Sp] *KOH-breh.* copper.

coca [Sp, from Quechua] *KOH-kah.* a shrub whose juice is the base of cola drinks.

cochon [Fr] *koh-SHŎ.* pig, swine.

cocido [Sp] *koh-SEE-doh.* Spanish stew.

coco [Fr] *koh-KOH.* (*lit.*, coconut) chap, fellow; darling, lambkin.

cocoliche [Sp] *koh-koh-LEE-cheh.* jargon of Italians in Argentina; an Argentine of Italian extraction.

cocotte [Fr] *koh-KOHT.* flirtatious, loose woman; casserole.

coda [It] *KOH-dah.* tail; (*music*) concluding passage.

code civil [Fr] *KOHD-see-VEEL.* civil code; civil law.

Code Napoléon [Fr] *KOHD-nah-poh-lay-Ŏ.* Napoleonic Code; code of civil laws of France of 1804, applied with modifications in Louisiana.

codetta [It] *koh-DAYT-tah.* (*music*) a brief coda.

codex [Lat] *KOH-deks.* body of laws; manuscript on parchment.

coeur [Fr] *kör.* heart.

cofradía [Sp] *koh-frah-DEE-ah.* confraternity; brotherhood.

cogito ergo sum [Lat] *KOH-gee-toh-EHR-goh-SOOM.* I think, therefore I am: aphorism of Descartes.

cognomen [Lat] *kohg-NOH-men.* surname; family name; nickname.

cognoscenti [It, now *conoscenti*] *koh-nyoh-SHEN-tee.* experts; connoisseurs.

coiffeur [Fr: *fem.* **coiffeuse**] *kwah-FÖR* (*-FÖZ*) hairdresser; beautician.

coiffure [Fr] *kwah-FÜR.* hairdo; hair style.

Cointreau [Fr, after the distiller] *kwĕ-TROH.* a colorless, orange-flavored liqueur.

coirboully [adapted from Fr]. See **cuir-bouilli.**

colazione [It] *koh-lah-TSYOH-neh.* breakfast; lunch.

coles catalanas [Sp] *KOH-les-kah-tah-LAH-nahs.* a Catalan cabbage soup.

collage [Fr, from *colle*, paste, glue] *koh-LAHZH.* art technique which involves paste-up of various materials and textures.

colleen [Ir *caillín*] *kah-LEEN.* young Irish girl.

collegium [Lat] *kohl-LEH-gee-oom.* society or group united officially by common interest or studies; college, faculty, or department.

colocación [Sp] *koh-loh-kah-SYOHN.* job, position; employment.

colon [Fr] *koh-LÕ.* colonist, colonial; Frenchman born in French overseas territory.

colophon [Gk] *KOH-loh-fohn.* (*lit.*, summit) final touch; publisher's trademark or emblem.

colorado [Sp] *koh-loh-RAH-doh.* colored; red.

coloratura [It] *koh-loh-rah-TOO-rah.* embellishment in vocal music; lyric soprano of high range.

columbaria [Lat] *koh-loom-BAH-ree-ah.* dovecotes; wall niches for support of beams; niches for burial urns in tombs.

columna bellica [Lat] *koh-LOOM-nah-BEL-lee-kah.* war column or memorial.

coma [Gk *komē*, head of hair] *KOH-mah.* the diffuse head of a comet; an aberration of reflecting telescopes which gives off-center images a cometlike appearance.

comandante [Sp, It] *koh-mahn-DAHN-teh.* commander; commanding officer, major in the military; naval captain.

comare [It] *koh-MAH-reh.* godmother; confidante; gossip.

combien [Fr] *kõ-BYÉ.* how much?

comedia de capa y espada [Sp] *koh-MEH-dyah-deh-KAH-pah-ee-es-PAH-dah.* cloak-and-dagger play.

comédie [Fr] *koh-may-DEE.* comedy; play; —**de moeurs** (*-duh-MÖRS*) comedy of manners; —**française** (*-frã-SEZ*) State theater of France in Paris, founded in 1680; —**humaine** (*-ü-MEN*) human comedy; comedy of manners.

comédienne [Fr] *koh-may-DYEN.* female comedian; actress in comedy.

comendador [Sp] *koh-men-dah-DOR.* knight commander; prefect of certain religious orders.

come prima [It] *KOH-meh-PREE-mah.* (*music*) as before; as at first.

comerciante [Sp] *koh-mer-SYAHN-teh.* merchant; trader; businessman.

come si dice [It] *KOH-meh-see-DEE-cheh.* how do you say . . . ?

come sta [It] *KOH-meh-STAH.* how are you?, how do you do?

come va [It] *KOH-meh-VAH.* how goes it?, how are things?

comida [Sp] *koh-MEE-dah.* meal; dinner; food.

comitadji [Turk] *koh-mee-TAH-jee.* (*lit.*, committeeman) irregular Balkan soldiers of the early 20th century.

comma [Gk *komma*] *KOHM-mah.* pause; comma.

commandite [Fr] *koh-mã-DEET.* joint-stock company; limited liability company. Also, **société en—** (*soh-syay-TAY-ã-*)

comme ci, comme ça [Fr] *kum-SEE-kum-SAH.* so-so.

Commedia dell'Arte [It] *kohm-MEH-dyah-del-LAR-teh.* Italian popular comedy using masked players representing stock characters and improvising from plot outlines or stock situations.

comme il faut [Fr] *kum-eel-FOH.* proper; in good form; as it should be.

commère [Fr] *koh-MEHR.* godmother; biddy, gossip.

commodo. See **comodo.**

communiqué [Fr] *koh-mü-nee-KAY.* official statement or dispatch.

comodo [It] *KOH-moh-doh.* comfortable; (*music*) easily, quietly. Also, **commodo.**

¿cómo está? [Sp] *KOH-moh-es-TAH.* how are you?

como se vive, se muere [Sp] *KOH-moh-seh-VEE-veh-seh-MWEH-reh.* as one lives, one dies.

compagnia [It] *kohm-pah-NYEE-ah.* company.

compagnie [Fr] *kõ-pah-NYEE.* company.

compañero [Sp] *kohm-pah-NYEH-roh.* companion; comrade.

compañía [Sp] *kohm-pah-NYEE-ah.* company.

compare [It] *kohm-PAH-reh.* godfather; kinsman; confederate; companion.

compère [Fr] *kõ-PEHR.* godfather; confederate; companion.

compluvium [Lat] *kohm-PLOO-vee-oom.* rain barrel; open roof of an ancient Roman house; the open space under this.

compos mentis [Lat] *KOHM-pohs-MEN-tees.* of sound mind; in one's right mind.

compos sui [Lat] *KOHM-pohs-SOO-ee.* in control of himself; master of himself.

compote [Fr] *kŏ-POHT.* stewed fruit; dish for serving candy, nuts or fruit.

comprimario [It] *kohm-pree-MAH-ryoh.* a first among equals; co-star.

compris [Fr] *kŏ-PREE.* understood; included.

compte courant [Fr] *KŎT-koo-RÃ.* current account.

compte ouvert [Fr] *KŎT-oo-VEHR.* open account.

compte rendu [Fr] *KŎT-rã-DÜ.* (*lit.*, account rendered) critique; report; book review.

comte [Fr] *kŏt.* count.

comtesse [Fr] *kŏ-TES.* countess.

con [It, Sp] *kohn.* with.

con abbandono [It] *koh-nahb-bahn-DOH-noh.* with abandon; at will; (*music*) passionately.

con amore [It] *koh-nah-MOH-reh.* (*music*) lovingly; tenderly.

con brio [It] *kohn-BREE-oh.* (*music*) with vigor; spiritedly.

conca [It] *KOHN-kah.* hollow; hollow vessel; valley; conch; basin.

con calore [It] *kohn-kah-LOH-reh.* (*music*) with warmth; passionately.

concertino [It] *kohn-chehr-TEE-noh.* short concerto; the solo instruments or players in a concerto grosso.

Concertmeister [Ger] *kohn-TSEHRT-mys-tuh.* concertmaster.

concerto [It] *kohn-CHEHR-toh.* musical composition for solo instruments with orchestral accompaniment; **—grosso** (*-GROHS-soh*) (*lit.*, big concert) a concerto for a small group of soloists accompanied by a full orchestra.

concha [Sp] *KOHN-chah.* shell; conch; theatrical prompter's shell.

concierge [Fr] *kŏ-SYEHRZH.* janitor; superintendent; porter; doorkeeper.

conciergerie [Fr] *kŏ-syehr-zh'REE.* doorkeeper's quarters; janitor's office; (*cap.*) name of a Paris prison.

concordat [Fr, from Lat *concordatus*] *kŏ-kor-DAH.* pact, agreement; concord.

concours [Fr] *kŏ-KOOR.* concurrence, agreement; meeting; contest, competition.

conde [Sp] *KOHN-deh.* count.

condesa [Sp] *kohn-DEH-sah.* countess.

conditio sine qua non [Lat] *kohn-DEE-tee-oh-SEE-neh-kwah-NOHN.* indispensable condition.

con dolcezza [It] *kohn-dohl-CHAY-tsah.* (*music*) sweetly; tenderly.

con dolore [It] *kohn-doh-LOH-reh.* (*music*) sadly; mournfully.

condottiere [It: *pl.* -**i**] *kohn-doht-TYEH-reh* (*-ree*) Italian Renaissance leader of mercenary troops.

con espressione [It] *koh-nes-pres-SYOH-neh.* (*music*) with expression; with feeling.

confection [Fr] *kŏ-fek-SYŎ.* ready-made dress or suit.

confer [Lat: *abbr.* **cf.**] *KOHN-fehr.* compare; see; refer to.

conférence [Fr] *kŏ-fay-RÃS.* conference, meeting; lecture, speech, talk.

confezione [It] *kohn-feh-TSYOH-neh.* ready-made dress or suit.

confiture [Fr] *kŏ-fee-TÜR.* preserves; jam; sweetmeat.

con forza [It] *kohn-FOR-tsah.* (*music*) forcefully; firmly.

confrère [Fr] *kŏ-FREHR.* colleague; associate.

con fuoco [It] *kohn-FWOH-koh.* (*music*) with fire; passionately.

conga [Sp] *KOHN-gah.* popular Latin-American dance, usually performed by a group following a leader in single file.

congé [Fr] *kŏ-ZHAY.* discharge; furlough.

con grazia [It] *kohn-GRAH-tsyah.* (*music*) gracefully; fluidly.

Congregatio de Propaganda Fide [Lat] *kohn-greh-GAH-tee-oh-deh-proh-pah-GAHN-dah-FEE-deh.* Congregation for the Propagation of the Faith: a committee in charge of outgoing messages and missions, made up of Cardinals and other Roman Catholic prelates.

con gusto [It] *kohn-GOOS-toh.* (*music*) tastefully; properly.

con impeto [It] *kohn-EEM-peh-toh.* (*music*) impetuously; impulsively.

conjunctis viribus [Lat] *kohn-YOONK-tees-VEE-ree-boos.* with united forces.

con más miedo que vergüenza [Sp] *kohn-mahs-MYEH-doh-keh-vehr-GWEN-sah.* with more fear than shame.

con molta forza [It] *kohn-MOHL-tah-FOR-tsah.* (*music*) with great force; very forcefully.

con molta passione [It] *kohn-MOHL-tah-pahs-SYOH-neh.* (*music*) very passionately.

con moto [It] *kohn-MOH-toh.* (*music*) with movement; fast.

con mucho gusto [Sp] *kohn-MOO-choh-GOOS-toh.* with great pleasure; very gladly.

connaître [Fr] *koh-NEH-truh.* to know; to be acquainted with.

connu [Fr, p.p. of **connaître**, to know] *koh-NÜ.* noted; known; understood.

conocido [Sp, p.p. of *conocer*, to know] *koh-noh-SEE-doh.* noted; known; acquaintance.

con permesso [It] *kohn-pehr-MAYS-soh.* with your permission; by your leave.

con piacere [It] *kohn-pyah-CHAY-reh.* with pleasure; gladly.

con prestezza [It] *kohn-pres-TAY-tsah.* (*music*) quickly; rapidly.

conquistador [Sp] *kohn-kees-tah-DOR.* conqueror.

conseil [Fr] *kõ-SAY.* council.

con semplicità [It] *kohn-sem-plee-chee-TAH.* (*music*) simply; with simplicity.

consommé [Fr] *kõ-soh-MAY.* concentrated meat broth.

consortium [Lat] *kohn-SOR-tee-oom.* international finance control group.

con spirito [It] *kohn-SPEE-ree-toh.* (*music*) with spirit; animatedly.

consule Planco [Lat] *KOHN-soo-leh-PLAHN-koh.* during the consulship of Plancus; in my youth (Horace).

consummatum est [Lat] *kohn-soom-MAH-toom-EST.* it is finished: Christ's words on the cross.

contadino [It] *kohn-tah-DEE-noh.* peasant; rustic; farmer.

conte [Fr] *kõt.* story, tale; account.

contra [Lat] *KOHN-trah.* against.

contrabandista [Sp] *kohn-trah-bahn-DEES-tah.* smuggler; dealer in contraband.

contrabbandiere [It] *kohn-trahb-bahn-DYEH-reh.* smuggler; dealer in contraband.

contrabbasso [It] *kohn-trahb-BAHS-soh.* (*music*) bass viol; double bass.

contra bonos mores [Lat] *KOHN-trah-BOH-nohs-MOH-res.* against good morals.

contrapposto [It] *kohn-trahp-POHS-toh.* in art, representation of the human body in a curving axis, producing an appearance of asymmetry and imbalance.

contraria contrariis curantur [Lat] *kohn-TRAH-ree-ah-kohn-TRAH-ree-ees-koo-RAHN-toor.* things are cured by their opposites.

contre [Fr] *KÕ-truh.* against; counter-.

contrecoup [Fr] *kõ-truh-KOO.* repercussion; counterattack; rebound; backlash.

contredanse [Fr, as if *counter-dance,* by misinterpretation of Eng *country dance*] *kõ-truh-DÃS.* a variation of the quadrille.

contretemps [Fr] *kõ-truh-TÃ.* unexpected occurrence; accident; misfortune; misfire.

contrôlé [Fr] *kõ-troh-LAY.* controlled; registered; quality checked.

convenance [Fr] *kõ-vuh-NÃS.* convenience; conformity; propriety.

conversazione [It: *pl.* -i] *kohn-vehr-sah-TSYOH-neh* (*-nee*) conversation; conference.

cooee [native Australian] *KOO-ee.* shrill call or cry used by Australian aborigines, and adopted by Australian settlers as a long-distance hallo.

copain [Fr] *koh-PÃ.* pal, chum.

copeck. See **kopeck.**

copla [Sp] *KOH-plah.* couplet; stanza; chorus; popular song, ballad.

coppa [It] *KOHP-pah*. drinking cup, goblet; (*cards*) heart; a form of salami.

coq [Fr] *kohk*. cock, rooster; chicken; —-à-l'âne (*-ah-LAHN*) (*lit.*, from the cock to the donkey) cock-and-bull story; —au vin (*-oh-VẼ*) chicken braised in wine.

coquetterie [Fr] *koh-keh-t'REE*. flirtatiousness; coquettish wiles.

coquillage [Fr] *koh-kee-YAHZH*. shellfish; ornamental shellwork.

coquille [Fr] *koh-KEE-yuh*. shell; scallop; patty.

coquin [Fr] *koh-KẼ*. rascal; knave.

coraggio [It] *koh-RAH-joh*. courage; impudence, nerve.

coram [Lat] *KOH-rahm*. in the presence of; before; —nobis (*-NOH-bees*) before us (i.e., the sovereign); (*law*) in the court of King's Bench; —populo (*-POH-poo-loh*) before the public; publicly.

cor anglais [Fr] *koh-rã-GLEH*. English horn.

corazziere [It] *koh-rah-TSYEH-reh*. cuirassier.

corbeau [Fr] *kor-BOH*. crow; raven; (*archit.*) corbel; grappling iron.

corbeille [Fr] *kor-BAY-yuh*. basket; (*archit.*) a sculptured ornament in the shape of a basket.

corbel [MF: raven, from its shape] *kor-BEL*. (*archit.*) supporting bracket of brick or stone.

corcovado [Port] *koor-koo-VAH-doo*. hunchback(ed).

corda [It] *KOR-dah*. string; (*music*) chord; release of the soft pedal.

cordelle [Fr] *kor-DEL*. towrope.

cordillera [Sp] *kor-dee-LYEH-rah*. mountain range.

cordon [Fr] *kor-DÕ*. band, ribbon; cord, string; —bleu (*-BLÖ*) blue ribbon; master chef; distinguished person; mark of excellence, especially as awarded to a distinguished restaurant; —sanitaire (*-sah-nee-TEHR*) quarantine line; a political limit on spread of propaganda.

cornemuse [Fr] *kor-n'MÜZ*. bagpipe.

corno [It] *KOR-noh*. horn; —di bassetto (*-dee-bahs-SAYT-toh*) basset horn; —inglese (*-een-GLAY-seh*) English horn.

cornu copiae [Lat] *KOR-noo-KOH-pee-y.* horn of plenty.

cornudo [Sp] *kor-NOO-doh* (*lit.*, horned) cuckold.

cornuto [It] *kor-NOO-toh* (*lit.*, horned) cuckold.

corps [Fr] *kor.* body; group; **—à corps** (*-ah-KOR*) body to body; hand to hand; **—de ballet** (*-duh-bah-LEH*) ballet troupe; **—de garde** (*-duh-GARD*) guardhouse, guardroom; **—diplomatique** (*-dee-ploh-mah-TEEK*) diplomatic corps.

corpus [Lat] *KOR-poos.* body; corpse; collection, compilation; **—Christi** (*-KREES-tee*) (*lit.*, body of Christ) festival of the Holy Eucharist [also, **—Domini** (*DOH-mee-nee*)]; **—delicti** (*-deh-LEEK-tee*) the body, or tangible evidence of a crime; **—juris** (*-YOO-rees*) body of law; collection of laws; **—juris canonici** (*-kah-NOH-nee-kee*) body of canon law; **—juris civilis** (*-KEE-vee-lees*) body of civil law.

corregidor [Sp] *kor-reh-hee-DOR.* chief magistrate of a town.

correo [Sp] *kor-REH-oh.* mail; post office; **en lista de correos** (*en-LEES-tah-deh-kor-REH-ohs*) general delivery.

corrida [Sp] *kor-REE-dah.* bullfight. Also, **—de toros** (*-deh-TOH-rohs*).

corriente [Sp] *kor-RYEN-teh.* current; present (month, year, etc.).

corrigenda [Lat] *kor-ree-GEN-dah.* corrections; things to be corrected.

corso [It] *KOR-soh.* course; avenue.

cortège [Fr] *kor-TEZH.* procession; retinue.

Cortes [Sp] *KOR-tes.* Spanish legislative assembly; parliament.

cortigiano [It] *kor-tee-JAH-noh.* courtier.

cortile [It] *kor-TEE-leh.* courtyard; patio.

corvée [Fr] *kor-VAY.* forced labor, esp. on roads, bridges, etc.

coryphée [Fr, from Gk *koryphaios*, leader] *koh-ree-FAY.* leader of a chorus; one of the leading dancers in a ballet troupe.

cosa [Sp, It] *KOH-sah.* thing; matter.

cosa ben fatta è fatta due volte [It] *KOH-sah-ben-FAHT-tah-eh-FAHT-tah-DOO-eh-VOHL-teh.* a thing well done is twice done.

cosa fatta, capo ha [It] *KOH-sah-FAHT-tah-KAH-poh-AH.* (*lit.*, a thing done has a head) once a thing is done, it's done.

cosa mala nunca muere [Sp] *KOH-sah-MAH-lah-NOON-kah-MWEH-reh.* a bad thing never dies; the wicked never die young.

Cosa Nostra [It] *KOH-sah-NOHS-trah.* (*lit.*, our affair) a group alleged to be in control of extensive criminal organizations in the U.S.

cosecha [Sp] *koh-SEH-chah.* crop; harvest, harvest season.

così così [It] *koh-SEE-koh-SEE.* so-so.

così fan tutti (or **tutte**) [It] *koh-SEE-fahn-TOOT-tee* (*-teh*) that's the way they all do; that's the way of the world.

costumé [Fr] *kohs-tü-MAY.* costumed.

côte [Fr] *koht.* shore; coast; hillside, slope.

côté [Fr] *koh-TAY.* side; edge, corner; direction.

coteau [Fr] *koh-TOH.* slope; hill, knoll; ridge between valleys.

Côte d'Azur [Fr] *koht-dah-ZÜR.* Azure Coast; French Riviera.

côte de boeuf [Fr] *koht-duh-BÖF.* side of beef; ribs of beef.

Côte d'Ivoire [Fr] *koht-dee-VWAR.* Ivory Coast.

Côte d'Or [Fr] *koht-DOR.* Gold Coast; a sector of southern France famous for Burgundy wine.

côtelette [Fr, from *côte*, rib] *koh-t'LET.* cutlet.

coterie [Fr] *koh-t'REE.* small, intimate group or circle; clique.

cothurnus [Lat, from Gk *kothornos*] *koh-TOOR-noos.* high boot or buskin favored by actors in Greek and Roman tragedy; tragic style; tragedy.

cotoletta [It, from Fr *côtelette*] *koh-toh-LAYT-tah.* cutlet; —**alla milanese** (*-ahl-lah-mee-lah-NEH-seh*) cutlet Milan style, breaded and pan-fried.

cou-de-pied [Fr] *KOO-duh-PYAY.* (*lit.*, neck of the foot) instep.

coulée [Fr, from *couler*, to flow] *koo-LAY*. deep ravine, usually dry; small valley.

couloir [Fr, from *couler*, to flow] *koo-LWAR*. corridor, passage; deep gorge, gulley.

coup [Fr] *koo*. sharp blow; stroke; sudden act; —**d'éclat** (*-day-KLAH*) brilliant deed; dashing move; —**de grâce** (*-duh-GRAHS*) deathblow; finishing stroke; —**de main** (*-duh-MẼ*) sudden blow; slap; sneak attack; sudden revolution; —**de pied** (*-duh-PYAY*) kick; —**de soleil** (*-duh-soh-LAY*) sunstroke; —**d'essai** (*-deh-SAY*) first try; essay; —**d'état** (*-day-TAH*) sudden seizure of power; takeover of government by force; —**de tête** (*-duh-TET*) caprice; brainstorm; desperate act; —**de théâtre** (*-duh-tay-AH-truh*) theatrical act or attempt; trick performance; —**d'oeil** (*-DÖY*) quick glance; once-over.

coupé [Fr, from *couper*, to cut] *koo-PAY*. cut, cut off; (*of wines*) diluted with water; ballet step in which one foot replaces the other by a kick.

coup manqué [Fr] *KOO-mã-KAY*. aborted attempt; miss, failure.

courage sans peur [Fr] *koo-RAHZH-sã-PÖR*. fearless courage.

Cour de Cassation [Fr] *KOOR-duh-kah-sah-SYÕ*. highest court of appeal in France.

coureur [Fr, from *courir*, to run] *koo-RÖR*. runner; hunter; (*mil.*) scout, rover; stroller; rake, libertine; —**de bois** (*-duh-BWAH*) trapper, hunter; —**de nuit** (*-duh-NÜEE*) night owl.

courtisane [Fr] *koor-tee-ZAHN*. courtesan; mistress of the court.

court plaisir, long repentir [Fr] *KOOR-pleh-ZEER-LÕ-ruh-pã-TEER*. short pleasure, long repentance.

couscous [Fr, from Ar *kuskus*, from *kaskasa*, to grind] *KOOS-koos*. a N African dish consisting of a paste of wheat meal, steamed, and served with meat, vegetables or fruit. Also, **kouskous**.

coûte que coûte [Fr] *KOOT-kuh-KOOT*. at all costs; cost what it may.

couture [Fr] *koo-TÜR.* dressmaking; tailoring; art of sewing.

couturier [Fr: *fem.* **couturière**] *koo-tü-RYAY* (*-RYEHR*) dressmaker; fashion designer.

couvade [Fr, from *couver,* to brood, hatch] *koo-VAHD.* custom among primitive tribes in which the father goes to bed and simulates childbirth.

cozido [Port] *koo-ZEE-doo.* Portuguese stew of meat and vegetables.

C.P.B., c.p.b. Abbr. of **cuyos pies beso.**

crèche [Fr] *kresh.* crib, manger; public nursery; representation of the Nativity.

credenza [It] *kreh-DEN-tsah.* small table or cupboard; sideboard; buffet.

crédit foncier [Fr] *kray-DEE-fŏ-SYAY.* loan association that lends money on land collateral; **crédit mobilier** (*-moh-bee-LYAY*) loan made on personal property; organization making such loans.

credo [Lat: I believe] *KREH-doh.* belief, code of beliefs; creed; article of faith.

credo quia absurdum (*or* **impossibile**) [Lat] *KREH-doh-kwee-ah-ahb-SOOR-doom* (*-eem-pohs-SEE-bee-leh*) I believe it because it is absurd (or impossible).

creese. See **kris.**

crème [Fr] *krem.* cream; —**de cacao** (*-duh-kah-KAH-oh*) liqueur with chocolate or cocoa flavor; —**de la crème** (*-duh-lah-KREM*) cream of the cream; the very best, the élite; —**de menthe** (*-duh-MÃT*) peppermint liqueur.

créole [Fr] *kray-OHL.* West Indian; Creole; type of casserole cookery containing tomatoes, onions, peppers and seasonings.

crêpe [Fr, from Lat *crispus,* curly] *krep.* thin, crinkled fabric of silk, rayon, wool, etc.; mourning band; thin pancake; —**de Chine** (*-duh-SHEEN*) Chinese crêpe fabric; silk crêpe; —**Suzette** (*-sü-ZET*) thin pancake, rolled or folded, served with flaming liqueur sauce.

crescendo [It] *kreh-SHEN-doh.* gradual increase in loudness and intensity.

crescite et multiplicamini [Lat] *KRES-kee-teh-et-mool-tee-*

plee-KAH-mee-nee. Increase and multiply (motto of Maryland).

crescit eundo [Lat] *KRES-keet-eh-OON-doh.* It grows as it goes (motto of New Mexico).

cresson [Fr] *kreh-SÕ.* watercress.

crevasse [Fr, from *crever,* to split, crack] *kruh-VAHS.* narrow, deep gorge in a mountain or glacier.

crève-coeur [Fr] *krev-KÖR.* heartbreak; a heartbreaking event.

crevette [Fr] *kruh-VET.* shrimp; prawn.

criado [Sp: *fem* -**da**] *KRYAH-doh* (*-dah*) servant; domestic.

crimen [Lat] *KREE-men.* crime.

crochet [Fr] *kroh-SHAY.* hooked knitting needle; type of knitting; an eccentricity.

croissant [Fr] *krwah-SÃ.* crescent-shaped roll.

croix [Fr] *krwah.* cross; —**de Feu** (*-duh-FÖ*) Cross of Fire: Fascist organization in France during the 1930's; —**de Guerre** (*-duh-GEHR*) war cross: French military decoration.

cromlech [Welsh] *KROM-lekh.* prehistoric stone monument consisting of a circle of massive upright stones.

croquante [Fr] *kroh-KÃT.* tart; pie; almond cake.

croquembouche [Fr] *kroh-kã-BOOSH.* (*lit.,* crunch in the mouth) crisp, sweet cake; an exceedingly delectable work of art.

croquette [Fr, from *croquer,* to crunch] *kroh-KET.* fried fish or meatball, covered with bread crumbs.

croquis [Fr] *kroh-KEE.* sketch; pen-and-ink drawing.

croulant [Fr: *fem* -**e**] *kroo-LÃ* (*-LÃT*) (*lit.,* crumbling) (*slang*) elderly person; senior citizen.

croupier [Fr] *kroo-PYAY.* attendant at a gambling table who collects and pays out bets.

croûte [Fr] *kroot.* toast; crust.

croûton [Fr, from *croûte,* crust] *kroo-TÕ.* cube of toasted or fried bread used in soups and salads.

crudités [Fr, from *cru,* raw] *krü-dee-TAY.* raw shredded vegetables served as hors d'oeuvres.

csárdás [Hung] *CHAR-dahsh.* Hungarian folk dance (sometimes erroneously spelled **czardas**).

crux [Lat] *krooks.* cross; core, main point, gist; —**ansata** (*-ahn-SAH-tah*) T-shaped cross with top loop, signifying eternal life; —**commissa** (*-kohm-MEES-sah*) T-shaped cross; tau cross; —**criticorum** (*-kree-tee-KOH-room*) the riddle of critics; —**decussata** (*-deh-koos-SAH-tah*) X-shaped cross of St. Andrew or St. Patrick; —**spes unica** (*-SPES-OO-nee-kah*) The cross is the only hope (motto of Notre Dame University); —**stellata** (*-stel-LAH-tah*) cross with star-shaped ends.

cruz [Sp] *kroos.* cross.

cuadrilla [Sp] *kwah-DREE-lyah.* crew; bullfighting team.

¿cuánto? [Sp] *KWAHN-toh.* how much?

cuartel [Sp] *kwar-TEL.* barracks; quarters; —**general** (*-heh-neh-RAHL*) headquarters.

cuarto [Sp] *KWAR-toh.* fourth, quarter; room.

cucaracha [Sp] *koo-kah-RAH-chah.* cockroach.

cuchillo [Sp] *koo-CHEE-lyoh.* knife.

cucina [It] *koo-CHEE-nah.* kitchen; cookery.

cuenta [Sp] *KWEN-tah.* bill; account; —**abierta** (*-ah-BYEHR-tah*) open account; —**corriente** (*-kor-RYEN-teh*) current account.

cuénteselo a su abuela [Sp] *KWEN-teh-seh-loh-ah-soo-ah-BWEH-lah* (*lit.*, tell it to your grandmother) tell it to the Marines.

cuento [Sp] *KWEN-toh.* tale; story.

cuerpo [Sp] *KWEHR-poh.* body; group, force.

cuesta [Sp] *KWES-tah.* hill; slope, ridge.

cui bono? [Lat] *KOO-ee-BOH-noh.* to whose advantage? for what good?

cuidado [Sp] *kwee-DAH-doh.* care; careful! beware!

cuir-bouilli [Fr] *KÜEER-boo-YEE.* (*lit.*, boiled leather) leather molded and hardened by steeping in boiling water or molten wax, used for armor, bookbinding, etc.

cuisine [Fr] *küee-ZEEN.* kitchen; cookery, cooking; —**bourgeoise** (*-boor-ZHWAHZ*) plain, home cooking; —**canaille** (*-kah-NY*) very lower-class cooking; —**française** (*-frã-SEZ*) French cooking.

cuisinier [Fr] *küee-zee-NYAY.* cook; chef.

cuisse [Fr] *küees.* thigh; beef rump; leg of fowl.

cuivre [Fr] *KÜEE-vruh.* copper.

cul-de-sac [Fr: *pl.* **culs-de-sac**] *KÜL-duh-SAHK.* (*lit.*, bottom of a sack) blind alley; dead end.

culottes [Fr] *kü-LOHT.* breeches, pants; women's short trousers cut full so as to resemble a skirt.

culpa [Lat] *KOOL-pah.* blame; fault; guilt.

culteranismo [Sp] *kool-teh-rah-NEES-moh.* Gongorism; an affected literary style of the 17th century.

cum [Lat] *koom.* with; as far as; to the point of; —**grano salis** (*-GRAH-noh-SAH-lees*) with a grain of salt; —**laude** (*-LOW-deh*) with praise, with honor.

cummerbund [Anglo-Ind, from Hindi *kamarband*] *KUM-ur-bund.* wide sash about the waist. Also **kummerbund.**

cumpleaños [Sp] *koom-pleh-AH-nyohs.* birthday.

cumshaw [Pidgin Eng, from Amoy Chin *kam sia*, grateful thanks] *KUM-shaw.* tip, gratuity; gift.

cum tacent, clamant [Lat] *koom-TAH-kent-KLAH-mahnt.* while silent, they speak; silence is an admission.

cupolone [It] *koo-poh-LOH-neh.* large cupola: used esp. in connection with the dome of St. Peter's in Rome.

cura [Lat] *KOO-rah.* care; cure; guardianship; [Sp] priest; curate.

curandero [Sp] *koo-rahn-DEH-roh.* healer; witch doctor; quack.

curé [Fr] *kü-RAY.* parish priest; rector, vicar.

curia [Lat] *KOO-ree-ah.* court; manor; senate chamber; court of justice; the Papal entourage.

curriculum vitae [Lat] *koor-REE-koo-loom-VEE-ty.* outline of one's life; personal résumé.

cursus [Lat, from *currere*, to run, flow] *KOOR-soos.* course; way; flow; march; metrical cadence used at end of a sentence in Greek and Latin prose.

cuvée [Fr, from *cuve*, tub, vat] *kü-VAY.* tubful, vatful; kind, sort; blend of wines.

cuyas manos beso [Sp: *abbr.* **C.M.B.** or **c.m.b.**] *KOO-yahs-MAH-nohs-BEH-soh.* whose hands I kiss (formula used in very formal correspondence). Also, **cuyos pies beso**

(-*PYES*-) (*abbr.* **C.P.B.** or **c.p.b.**) whose feet I kiss (used only to women).

cygne [Fr] *SEE-nyuh.* swan; —**noir** (-*NWAR*) black swan; rare object.

cyma [Lat, from Gk *kyma*, swelling, wave] *KEE-mah.* architectural molding having an outline partly convex, partly concave; —**recta** (-*REK-tah*) curved molding having the convex part next to the wall and the concave part further away from the wall; —**reversa** (-*reh-VEHR-sah*) curved molding having the concave part next to the wall and the convex further away from the wall.

cynghanedd [Welsh] *king-HAH-neth.* symphony; Welsh verse form.

cywydd [Welsh] *KEE-with.* Welsh verse form.

czar [Russ *tsar'*] *tsahr.* ruler, emperor; title of former Russian ruler; autocratic leader; boss. Also spelled **tsar, tzar.**

czardas. See **csárdás.**

czarevna [Russ *tsarevna*] *tsuh-RYEV-nuh.* daughter of a czar. Also, **tsarevna, tzarevna.**

czarevitch [Russ *tsarevich*] *tsuh-RYEH-vich.* son of a czar; eldest son and heir apparent to the throne. Also, **tsarevitch, tzarevitch.**

czarina [*czar* + -*ina* (fem. suffix, modeled on Ger *Zarin*)] *tsuh-REE-nuh.* wife of a czar; Russian empress. Also, **tsarina, tzarina.**

czaritza [Russ *tsaritsa*] *tsuh-REE-tsuh.* czarina; empress of Russia. Also, **tsaritsa, tzaritza.**

D

da [It] *dah.* from; by; through; at the house of; since; at the value of; in the name or style of; for the purpose or use of.

da [Ger] *dah.* there; then; thereupon; since, because; whereas.

da [Russ] *dah.* yes; really?; but; oh, but; and, moreover.

da ballo [It] *dah-BAHL-loh.* (*music*) in dance tempo.

dabit Deus his quoque finem [Lat] *DAH-beet-DEH-oos-HEES-kwoh-kweh-FEE-nem.* God will put an end even to these (adversities).

dabit qui dedit [Lat] *DAH-beet-kwee-DEH-deet.* he who gave will give.

da capo [It: *abbr.* **D.C.**] *dah-KAH-poh.* (*music*) from the beginning; —**al fine** (*-ahl-FEE-neh*) from the beginning to the end; —**al segno** (*-ahl-SEH-nyoh*) from the beginning to the sign.

da cappella [It] *dah-kahp-PEL-lah.* (*music*) in church style. Also, **da chiesa** (*-KYEH-sah*).

d'accord [Fr] *dah-KOR.* agreed; granted; in agreement.

dacha [Russ] *DAH-chuh.* country house, villa.

dacoit [Anglo-Ind, from Hindi *dakait*] *duh-KOYT.* bandit, outlaw.

dada [Fr: hobbyhorse, from *da*, giddap] *dah-DAH.* movement in the arts and literature of the early 20th century which advocated the fantastic and absurd as a reaction to conventional tastes. Also, **Dadaisme** (*dah-dah-EEZ-muh*).

dado [It: die, cube, pedestal] *DAH-doh.* a single stone forming the main part of pedestal; panel at the base of a wall, usually extending up to chair height and having a chair rail along the top edge.

daemon [Lat, from Gk *daimon*] *DY-mohn.* See **daimon.**

daibutsu [Jap: great Buddha] *DY-boot-soo.* large figure of Buddha.

Dail Eireann [Gaelic] *dohl-AH-run.* lower house of the Irish legislature.

d'ailleurs [Fr] *dy-YÖR.* moreover, in addition; on the other hand; nevertheless.

daimio [Jap] *DY-myoh.* (*lit.*, great name) Japanese feudal lord. Also, **daimyo.**

daimon [Gk] *DY-mohn.* demon, spirit. Also, **daemon.**

Dalai Lama [Mongol: great priest] *DAH-ly-LAH-mah.* title of former priest-king of Tibet.

dak [Hindi] *duk.* mail or goods transported by relays of men and horses.

dal [Du] *dahl.* dale; glen; valley.

dal [Hindi] *dul.* a kind of pea. Also, **dhal.**

dalla rapa non si cava sangue [It] *dah-lah-RAH-pah-non-see-KAH-vah-SAHN-gweh.* you can't get blood out of a turnip.

dal segno [It: *abbr.* **D.S.**] *dahl-SEH-nyoh.* (*music*) (repeat) from the sign.

dama [It, Sp] *DAH-mah*; [Port, Russ] *DAH-muh.* lady.

dame [Fr, from Lat **domina,** fem. of **dominus,** lord] *dahm*; [Ger, from Fr] *DAH-muh.* lady; mistress.

dame de compagnie [Fr] *DAHM-duh-kŏ-pah-NYEE.* lady's companion; —**d'honneur** (*-duh-NÖR*) maid of honor; lady in waiting.

dames seules [Fr] *DAHM-SÖL.* ladies only; ladies' lounge; ladies' compartment.

damhsa na mairbh [Gael] *DAHV-sah-nah-MEHRV.* dance of death.

Dämmerung [Ger] *DEH-muh-roong.* twilight.

damnant quod non intellegunt [Lat] *DAHM-nahnt-kwohd-nohn-een-TEL-leh-goont.* they condemn what they do not understand.

damnum [Lat] *DAHM-noom.* damage; loss; —**absque injuria** (*-AHBS-kweh-een-YOO-ree-ah*) loss without actionable injury.

Dampfschiff [Ger] *DAHMPF-shif.* steamship.

Danelaw [AS *dena lagu*] *DAYN-law.* the body of laws of northeastern England under the Danes; the part of England governed by those laws. Also, **Danelagh.**

danke [Ger] *DAHN-keh.* thanks; —**schön** (*-shön*) thanks very much.

danse [Fr] *däs.* dance; —**du ventre** (*-dü-VÃ-truh*) belly dance; —**macabre** (*-mah-KAH-bruh*) dance of death.

danseur [Fr] *dä-SÖR.* male dancer, esp. of the ballet.

danseuse [Fr] *dä-SÖZ.* female dancer; ballerina.

danza [It] *DAHN-tsah*; [Sp] *DAHN-sah.* dance.

danza de la muerte [Sp] *DAHN-sah-deh-lah-MWEHR-teh.* dance of death.

das [Ger] *dahs.* the; that.

das Beste ist gut genug [Ger] *dahs-BES-teh-ist-GOOT-guh-NOOK.* the best is good enough.

Dasein [Ger] *DAH-zyn.* existence; presence.

das Ewig-Weibliche [Ger] *dahs-AY-viç-VYB-li-çeh.* the eternal feminine (Goethe).

das heisst [Ger: *abbr.* **d.h.**] *dahs-HYST.* that is; that is to say.

das ist [Ger] *dahs-IST.* that is.

das Kapital [Ger] *dahs-kah-pi-TAHL.* Capital: ideological work by Karl Marx.

das Leben ist die Liebe [Ger] *dahs-LAY-b'n-ist-dee-LEE-beh.* life is love.

das schöne Geschlecht [Ger] *dahs-SHÖ-neh-guh-SHLEÇT.* the fair sex.

dà tempo al tempo [It] *DAH-TEM-poh-ahl-TEM-poh.* give time to time; some things can't be rushed.

daube [Fr] *dohb.* style of braising meat or fowl; dish prepared in this style.

d'aujourd'hui en huit [Fr] (*lit.,* from today eight days) *doh-zhoor-DÜEE-ã-ÜEET.* a week from today; **d'aujourd'hui en quinze** (*-ã-KÊZ*) (*lit.,* from today fifteen days) two weeks from today.

Dauphin [Fr] *doh-FÊ.* now obsolete title given eldest son of French kings.

davai [Russ] *duh-VY.* let's go!; come on!

D.C. Abbr. of **da capo.**

D.D. Abbr. of **Divinitatis Doctor.**

de [Fr] *duh.* of; from; by; in; with; some.

de [Lat] *deh.* from; of; about, concerning.

de [Sp] *deh.* of; from; by; in; with; for.

de [Du] *duh.* the.

débâcle [Fr] *day-BAH-kluh.* disaster; collapse.

débauche [Fr] *day-BOHSH.* debauch; debauchery; lewdness; dissoluteness.

débauché [Fr] *day-boh-SHAY.* debauchee; roué; rake.

de bene esse [Lat] *deh-BEH-neh-ES-seh.* on condition; provisionally.

debitum [Lat: *pl.* **debita**] *DEH-bee-toom* (*-tah*) debt.

de bon gré [Fr] *duh-BÕ-GRAY.* willingly; with good will.

débonnaire [Fr] *day-buh-NEHR.* gracious, affable; handsome, dashing.

de bonne volonté [Fr] *duh-bun-voh-lõ-TAY*. willingly; with good will or good grace.

de bono et malo [Lat] *deh-BOH-noh-et-MAH-loh*. for good and bad; for better or worse.

de bon vouloir servir le roy [MF] *duh-BŎ-voo-LWAR-sehr-VEER-luh-RWAH*. to serve the king with good will.

début [Fr] *day-BÜ*. coming out; first public appearance; formal entrance into society.

débutante [Fr] *day-bü-TÃT*. girl making first formal social appearance.

decanus [Lat] *deh-KAH-noos*. dean; deacon.

déclassé [Fr] *day-klah-SAY*. declassed; fallen down the social ladder.

décolletage [Fr] *day-kohl-TAHZH*. low neckline; dress with a low neckline; state of being **décolleté**.

décolleté [Fr: having the neck bared, from *dé-* apart, down + *collet*, collar] *day-kohl-TAY*. low-necked, low-cut; wearing a low-cut dress; —**plongeant** (*-plõ-ZHÃ*) plunging neckline.

décor [Fr] *day-KOR*. design, furniture and finishing decoration of a room; room setting; stage setting.

décoré [Fr] *day-koh-RAY*. decorated with military or civilian honors.

decrescendo [It] *deh-kreh-SHEN-doh*. (*music*) decreasing in loudness.

dédicace [Fr] *day-dee-KAHS*. dedication; inscription.

de die in diem [Lat] *deh-DEE-eh-een-DEE-em*. from day to day.

de duobus malis, minus est semper eligendum [Lat] *deh-doo-OH-boos-MAH-lees-MEE-noos-est-SEM-pehr-eh-lee-GEN-doom*. of two evils the lesser is always to be chosen.

de facto [Lat] *deh-FAHK-toh*. in existence; in actuality; in fact.

défense d'afficher [Fr] *day-FÃS-dah-fee-SHAY*. post no bills; **défense d'entrer** (*-dã-TRAY*) no admittance; **défense de fumer** (*-duh-fü-MAY*) no smoking.

dégagé [Fr] *day-gah-ZHAY*. disengaged; uninhibited.

degollada [Sp] *deh-goh-LYAH-dah*. décolleté; having a revealing neckline.

dégoût [Fr] *day-GOO*. distaste, disgust; dislike, aversion.

de gratia [Lat] *deh-GRAH-tee-ah*. (*law*) by grace; by favor, by the good will (of).

de gustibus non est disputandum [Lat] *deh-GOOS-tee-boos-non-est-dees-poo-TAHN-doom*. there is no accounting for tastes.

de haut en bas [Fr] *duh-OH-ā-BAH*. (*lit.*, from high to low) in a condescending manner; with a patronizing attitude.

dehors [Fr] *duh-OR*. outside; out of doors; (*n.pl.*) appearances.

Dei gratia [Lat: *abbr.* **D.G.**] *DEH-ee-GRAH-tee-ah*. by the grace of God.

déjà vu [Fr] *day-zhah-VÜ*. (*lit.*, already seen) unoriginal, trite; (*psych.*) the illusion of having experienced something previously.

déjeuner [Fr] *day-zhö-NAY*. breakfast; lunch; —**à la fourchette** (*-ah-lah-foor-SHET*). light luncheon, with meat, eggs, etc.; brunch.

de jure [Lat] *deh-YOO-reh*. legal; sanctioned by law.

del credere [It] *del-KREH-deh-reh*. (*lit.*, of belief) merchant's guarantee of a buyer's solvency.

dele [Lat] *DEH-leh*. (*typog.*) delete.

delenda est Carthago. See **Carthago delenda est.**

délicat [Fr] *day-lee-KAH*. delicate, exquisite; dainty; frail, fragile.

delicato [It] *deh-lee-KAH-toh*. (*music*) delicately, tenderly.

delirium tremens [Lat] *deh-LEE-ree-oom-TREH-mens* (*lit.*, trembling deliriousness) severe physical and mental disturbance caused by alcoholic excess.

del plato a la boca se pierde la sopa [Sp] *del-PLAH-toh-ah-lah-BOH-kah-seh-PYEHR-deh-lah-SOH-pah*. there's many a slip between the cup and the lip.

de luxe [Fr] *duh-LÜKS*. luxurious; fancy, extra special.

demain [Fr] *duh-MẼ*. tomorrow.

de mal en pis [Fr] *duh-MAHL-ā-PEE*. from bad to worse.

démarche [Fr] *day-MARSH*. (*lit.*, step, gait) diplomatic approach or procedure; change in plan or course of action.

dementia [Lat] *deh-MEN-tee-ah.* insanity; **—praecox** (*-PRY-kohks*) adolescent insanity.

demi [Fr] *duh-MEE.* half; **— -mondaine** (*-mō-DEN*) woman living on the fringes of society; woman of low repute; **— -monde** (*-MŌD*) fringe of society; world of low repute; **— -tasse** (*-TAHS*) small cup of coffee; small coffee cup.

democristiano [It] *deh-moh-krees-TYAH-noh.* member of the Italian Christian Democratic party.

de mortuis nihil (or **nil**) **nisi bonum** [Lat] *deh-MOR-too-ees-NEE-heel* (*-NEEL*)-*NEE-see-BOH-noom.* (say) nothing but good about the dead.

Demotike [ModGk] *dee-moh-tee-KEE* (*lit.*, popular, plebeian) Demotic: the vernacular form of modern Greek. Cf. **Katharevousa.**

de nada [Sp] *deh-NAH-dah.* it's nothing; don't mention it; you're welcome.

denarius [Lat] *deh-NAH-ree-oos.* Roman silver coin.

denier [Fr] *duh-NYAY.* old French silver or copper coin; unit of weight for measuring fineness of silk and synthetic fabrics, esp. those used for women's hosiery.

de nihilo nihil [Lat] *deh-NEE-hee-loh-NEE-heel.* from nothing, nothing.

Denkschrift [Ger] *DENK-shrift.* memorial book; memorial; inscription.

de noche todos los gatos son pardos [Sp] *deh-NOH-cheh-TOH-dohs-lohs-GAH-tohs-sohn-PAR-dohs.* at night, all cats are gray.

dénouement [Fr, from *dénouer*, to unknot, unravel] *day-noo-MÃ.* the final resolution of the plot of a play or story; the outcome of a series of events or circumstances.

de nouveau [Fr] *duh-noo-VOH.* anew; over again.

de novo [Lat] *deh-NOH-voh.* anew; over again.

dentelle [Fr, dim. of *dent*, tooth] *dã-TEL.* lace.

deodar [Hindi, from Skt *devadaru*, wood of the gods] *DEE-uh-dar.* Himalayan tree having a fine, hard wood.

Deo favente [Lat] *DEH-oh-fah-VEN-teh.* God favoring; with God's favor.

Deo gratias [Lat] *DEH-oh-GRAH-tee-ahs.* thanks to God.

Deo Optimo Maximo [Lat: *abbr.* **D.O.M.**] *DEH-oh-OHP-tee-moh-MAHK-see-moh.* To God, the best and greatest (motto of the order of St. Benedict). Cf. **Domino Optimo Maximo.**

Deo volente [Lat] *DEH-oh-voh-LEN-teh.* God willing.

département [Fr] *deh-par-t'MÃ.* department: largest administrative division of the French government.

dépêche [Fr] *day-PESH.* dispatch; message.

de pied en cap [Fr] *duh-PYAY-ã-KAHP.* from head to foot.

de pis en pis [Fr] *duh-PEE-ã-PEE.* from bad to worse.

déplacé [Fr] *day-plah-SAY.* displaced; misplaced; ill-timed.

de plus belle [Fr] *duh-plü-BEL.* more than ever; better (or worse) than ever; with renewed desire or energy.

dépôt [Fr] *day-POH.* station; train station; military supply station; depot; dump.

de prix [Fr] *duh-PREE.* (*lit.,* of price) valuable, expensive.

de profundis [Lat] *deh-proh-FOON-dees.* out of the depths: first words of a prayer for the dead.

depuis [Fr] *duh-PÜEE.* since.

député [Fr] *day-pü-TAY.* deputy; delegate; member of lower house of parliament.

dérangement [Fr] *day-rã-zh'MÃ.* derangement; disorder; insanity.

derecha [Sp] *deh-REH-chah.* right; right side.

de règle [Fr] *duh-REH-gluh.* proper, required; according to Hoyle.

de retour [Fr] *duh-ruh-TOOR.* returned, back; on the way back; again.

der Führer [Ger] *dehr-FÜ-ruh.* the Leader: title of Hitler.

der Heiland [Ger] *dehr-HY-lahnt.* the Savior.

de rien [Fr] *duh-RYẼ.* it's nothing; you're welcome; don't mention it.

de rigueur [Fr] *duh-ree-GÖR.* indispensable; required; according to the laws of etiquette.

derma [Gk] *DEHR-mah.* skin; integument.

derma [Yid, from *darm,* intestine] *DEHR-muh.* intestine of beef or fowl used as sausage casing.

der Mensch denkt, Gott lenkt [Ger] *dehr-MENSH-DENKT-GOHT-LENKT.* man proposes, but God disposes.

dernier [Fr] *dehr-NYAY.* last; —**cri** (*-KREE*) the latest style; the last word.

derrière [Fr] *deh-RYEHR.* back part; buttocks, rump.

der Teufel ist los! [Ger] *dehr-TOY-f'l-ist-LOHS.* the devil to pay.

desayuno [Sp] *deh-sah-YOO-noh.* breakfast.

descamisados [Sp] *des-kah-mee-SAH-dohs.* shirtless ones: followers of Eva Perón.

déshabillé [Fr] *day-zah-bee-YAY.* in a state of informal undress.

desideratum [Lat: *pl.* **desiderata**] *deh-see-deh-RAH-toom* (*-tah*) what is desired or needed.

desierto [Sp] *deh-SYEHR-toh.* desert; deserted, abandoned.

désolé [Fr] *day-zoh-LAY.* desolate; disconsolate; extremely sorry.

despacho [Sp] *des-PAH-choh.* study; office.

dessein [Fr] *deh-SẼ.* design; intention; plot.

dessin [Fr] *deh-SẼ.* design; drawing; plan.

de stijl [Du, from the name of an art journal] *duh-STYL.* (*lit.,* the style) Dutch style of painting utilizing basic geometric forms and primary colors.

destra [It] *DES-trah.* right; right side.

desunt caetera. See **caetera desunt.**

détente [Fr] *day-TÄT.* release of strained relations; releasing of tension.

détenu [Fr] *day-tuh-NÜ.* one who is detained; prisoner.

détour [Fr] *day-TOOR.* change of course; detour; deviation.

de trop [Fr] *duh-TROH.* in excess; superfluous; not wanted.

deus [Lat] *DEH-oos.* god; God; —**ex machina** (*-eks-MAH-kee-nah*) in classic drama, a god who appears to solve the plot; outside intervention to solve a crisis; —**vobiscum** (*-voh-BEES-koom*) God (be) with you; —**vult** (*-VOOLT*) God wills it: cry of the Crusaders.

deutsches Reich [Ger] *DOY-ch's RYÇ.* German Empire; Germany, German Republic.

Deutschland über Alles [Ger] *DOYCH-lahnt-Ü-buh-AH-l's.* Germany above all; Germany first.

deva [Skt] *DEH-vuh.* god.

Devanagari [Skt; *lit.*, of the city of the gods] *deh-vuh-NAH-guh-ree.* the alphabet of Sanskrit, Hindi and other languages of India.

devant [Fr] *duh-VÃ.* before; in front of.

devi [Skt] *DEH-vee.* goddess; mother goddess.

devoir [Fr] *duh-VWAR.* duty; debt; task; student's homework.

dey [Fr, from Turk *dayi,* maternal uncle] *day.* title of former rulers of Algiers, Tunis and Tripoli.

D.F. Abbr. of **distrito federal.**

D.G. Abbr. of **Dei gratia.**

d.h. Abbr. of **das heisst.**

dhal. See **dal.**

Dharma [Skt] *DAR-muh.* essential quality or character; religion; religious devotion; the teachings of Buddha.

dhobi [Hindi] *DOH-bee.* washerman.

dhoti [Hindi] *DOH-tee.* loincloth; cotton fabric used for loincloths.

dhu [Ir & Gael] *doo.* black: suffix of personal and place names.

di [It] *dee.* from; of; by; for; about; some.

dì [It] *dee.* day.

día [Sp] *DEE-ah.* day.

diable [Fr] *DYAH-bluh.* devil.

diablerie [Fr] *dyah-bluh-REE.* devilry; witchcraft; malice; mischief.

diablo [Sp] *DYAH-bloh.* devil.

diabolique [Fr] *dyah-boh-LEEK.* diabolic; fiendish; dreadful.

día de Año Nuevo [Sp] *DEE-ah-deh-AH-nyoh-NWEH-voh.* New Year's Day; **Día de la Raza** (*-deh-lah-RAH-sah*) Day of the (Hispanic) Race: Columbus Day, Oct. 12; **Día de los Reyes** (*-deh-los-REH-yes*) Day of the (Three) Kings: Epiphany, Jan. 6.

diamant [Fr] *dyah-MÃ.* diamond.

diario [Sp] *DYAH-ryoh.* newspaper; daily.

diaspora [Gk] *dee-AHS-poh-rah.* dispersal, scattering, esp. of the Jews after the destruction of Jerusalem.

diavolo [It] *DYAH-voh-loh.* devil.

dibbuk. See **dybbuk.**

di bravura [It] *dee-brah-VOO-rah.* (*music*) with animation; with bravado.

dicho y hecho [Sp] *DEE-choh-ee-EH-choh.* no sooner said than done.

Dichter [Ger] *DIÇ-tuh.* poet.

Dichtung [Ger] *DIÇ-toong.* poetry; creative prose.

dictée [Fr] *deek-TAY.* dictation.

dictum [Lat: *pl.* **dicta**] *DEEK-toom* (*-tah*) saying; pronouncement.

didaktikos [Gk] *dee-dahk-tee-KOHS.* didactic; instructive.

die [Ger] *dee.* the; that.

die [Lat, abl. of **dies**] *DEE-eh.* day.

die Kunst geht nach Brot [Ger] *dee-KOONST-gayt-nahkh-BROHT.* (*lit.*, art goes after bread) the artist must first earn a living.

die lustige Witwe [Ger] *dee-LOOS-tee-geh-VIT-veh.* the merry widow.

diem [Lat, acc. of **dies**] *DEE-em.* day; —**perdidi** (*-PEHR-dee-dee*) I have lost a day.

dies [Lat] *DEE-es.* day; —**Irae** (*-EE-ry*) The Day of Wrath: 13th-century Latin hymn set to music by several famous composers, now a part of the Requiem Mass; —**non juridicus** (*-nohn-yoo-REE-dee-koos*) day when court is not in session.

die schöne Welt [Ger] *dee-SHÖ-neh-VELT.* the beautiful world; fashionable society.

Dieu [Fr] *dyö.* God; god; —**avec nous** (*-ah-vek-NOO*) God with us; —**et mon Droit** (*-ay-mö-DRWAH*) God and my right: motto of England.

die Wacht am Rhein [Ger] *dee-VAHKHT-ahm-RYN.* The Watch on the Rhine: German patriotic song.

difficile [Fr] *dee-fee-SEEL.* difficult; hard.

di fresco [It] *dee-FRES-koh.* recent(ly); fresh(ly).

difunto [Sp] *dee-FOON-toh.* dead; defunct; deceased.

di grado in grado [It] *dee-GRAH-doh-een-GRAH-doh.* step by step; gradually.

dii (or di) minores (or **inferi**) [Lat] *DEE-ee-mee-NOH-res*

(-*EEN-feh-ree*) lesser gods; —**penates** (-*peh-NAH-tes*) household gods.

dilettante [It, pr. p. of *dilettare*, to delight, take pleasure] *dee-let-TAHN-teh*. dabbler; amateur.

diligence [Fr] *dee-lee-ZHÃS*. diligence; stagecoach.

di minores (or **inferi**). See **dii**.

diminuendo [It] *dee-mee-NWEN-doh*. (*music*) diminishing in volume.

di molto [It] *dee-MOHL-toh*. much; very; by much.

dîner [Fr] *dee-NAY*. dinner; to dine.

dinero [Sp] *dee-NEH-roh*. money.

Ding an sich [Ger] *DING-ahn-ZIÇ*. (*philos.*) thing in itself; reality behind appearances.

ding hao [Chin] *DING-how*. very good; fine.

Dios se lo pague [Sp] *DYOHS-seh-loh-PAH-geh*. may God reward you.

Dios, Unión, Libertad [Sp] *DYOHS-oo-NYOHN-lee-behr-TAHD*. God, Union, Liberty (motto of El Salvador).

di penates. See **dii penates**.

diplôme [Fr] *dee-PLOHM*. diploma; document.

Directoire [Fr] *dee-rek-TWAR*. French regime, 1795-99; a style of furnishings, decoration and dress, characterized by use of classical forms.

dirigo [Lat] *DEE-ree-goh*. I guide (motto of Maine).

Dirndl [Ger: girl] *DEERN-d'l*. dress of colorful material, with tight bodice and full-cut skirt.

dis aliter visum [Lat] *DEES-AH-lee-tehr-VEE-soom*. the gods deemed otherwise.

discobolus [Lat, from Gk *diskobolos*] *dees-KOH-boh-loos*. discus thrower: Greek statue by the sculptor Myron.

discothèque [Fr] *dees-koh-TEK*. place where modern dancing goes on, usually to the music of records.

diseur [Fr: *fem.* **diseuse**] *dee-ZÖR* (-*ZÖZ*) talker; monologist; conversationalist.

disjecta membra [Lat] *dees-YEK-tah-MEM-brah*. (*lit.*, scattered limbs) sundry or disjointed parts.

dis manibus sacrum [Lat] *DEES-MAH-nee-boos-SAH-kroom*. sacred to the gods of the underworld.

distingué [Fr] *dees-tē-GAY.* distinguished; of distinguished bearing; esteemed.

distrait [Fr] *dee-STRAY.* forgetful; absentminded; distracted.

distrito federal [Sp: *abbr.* **D.F.**] *dees-TREE-toh-feh-deh-RAHL.* federal district; the federal area in which Mexico City is located.

dit [Fr, p.p. of *dire*, to say, tell; *fem.* **dite**] *dee (deet)* said; named; called.

ditat Deus [Lat] *DEE-taht-DEH-oos.* God enriches (motto of Arizona).

diva [It, from Lat: goddess] *DEE-vah.* distinguished female singer; prima donna.

divertimento [It] *dee-vehr-tee-MAYN-toh.* amusement, entertainment; diversion; (*music*) light, diverting composition.

divertissement [Fr] *dee-vehr-tees-MÃ.* amusement; entertainment; diversion; between-the-acts entertainment; (*music*) divertimento.

dives [Lat] *DEE-ves.* rich; rich man.

divide et impera [Lat] *dee-VEE-deh-et-EEM-peh-rah.* divide and rule.

Divina Commedia [It] *dee-VEE-nah-kohm-MEH-dyah.* Divine Comedy: epic poem by Dante.

Divinitatis Doctor [Lat: *abbr.* **D.D.**] *dee-vee-nee-TAH-tees-DOHK-tor.* Doctor of Divinity.

dixi [Lat, p.t. of *dicere*, to say, speak] *DEEK-see.* I have spoken.

d'occasion [Fr] *doh-kah-ZYŎ.* accidentally; secondhand.

docendo discimus [Lat] *doh-KEN-doh-DEES-kee-moos.* we learn by teaching.

docent. See **Dozent.**

doctor utriusque legis [Lat] *DOHK-tor-oo-tree-OOS-kweh-LEH-gees.* doctor of both (canon and civil) laws.

dogana [It] *doh-GAH-nah.* customs; customhouse.

dogaressa [It] *doh-gah-RAYS-sah.* wife of a doge.

doge [It, Venetian var. of *duce*, leader, from Lat *dux*] *DOH-jeh.* title of the medieval rulers of Venice and Genoa.

dolce [It] *DOHL-cheh.* sweet, sweetly; —**far niente** (*-far-NYEN-teh*) sweet idleness; it's sweet to do nothing; —**stil nuovo** (*-steel-NWOH-voh*) (*lit.*, sweet new style) Italian literary 14th-century style, based on courtly love; —**vita** (*-VEE-tah*) the sweet life; the beautiful life; hedonistic style of living.

dolcemente [It] *dohl-cheh-MAYN-teh.* (*music*) sweetly; softly.

Dolmetscher [Ger] *DOHL-met-chuh.* interpreter; translator.

doloroso [It] *doh-loh-ROH-soh.* (*music*) doleful; mournful.

Dom [Ger] *dohm.* cathedral.

dom [Port, from Lat *dominus*, lord, master) *dohm.* title of respect given to a gentleman of rank.

dom [Russ] *dohm.* house; home.

D.O.M. Abbr. of **Deo** (or **Domino**) **Optimo Maximo.**

domani [It] *doh-MAH-nee.* tomorrow.

Domei [Jap] *DOH-may.* Japanese government news agency.

domina [Lat, fem. of **dominus**] *DOH-mee-nah.* lady; mistress.

domine [Lat, voc. of **dominus**] *DOH-mee-neh.* lord!, master!; —**, dirige nos** (*-DEE-ree-geh-nohs*) Lord, guide us (motto of the city of London).

domingo [Sp] *doh-MEEN-goh.* Sunday.

Domino Optimo Maximo [Lat: *abbr.* **D.O.M.**] *DOH-mee-noh-OHP-tee-moh-MAHK-see-moh.* To the Lord, best and greatest (motto of the Benedictine Order). Cf. **Deo, Optimo, Maximo.**

Dominus [Lat] *DOH-mee-noos.* Lord, Master; —**, illuminatio mea** (*-eel-loo-mee-NAH-tee-oh-MEH-ah*) The Lord is my light (motto of Oxford U.); —**vobiscum** (*-voh-BEES-koom*) the Lord be with you.

domus [Lat] *DOH-moos.* house; —**Dei** (*-DEH-ee*) house of God; —**procerum** (*-PROH-keh-room*) House of Lords.

dona [Port, from Lat **domina**, lady, mistress] *DOH-nuh.* title of respect for a lady.

doña [Sp: see **dona**] *DOH-nyah.* title of respect given to a lady.

donde [Sp: in questions, **dónde**] *DOHN-deh.* where.

Donde está la verdad está Dios [Sp] *DOHN-deh-es-TAH-lah-ver-DAHD-es-TAH-DYOHS.* Where the truth is, there is God.

Donde hay gana hay maña [Sp] *DOHN-deh-y-GAH-na-y-MAH-nyah.* Where there's a will there's a way.

Donde las dan las toman [Sp] *DOHN-deh-lahs-DAHN-lahs-TOH-mahn.* As ye sow, so shall ye reap.

donna [It: see **dona**] *DOHN-nah.* title of respect given to a lady; woman.

donnée [Fr, p.p. of *donner*, to give] *duh-NAY.* that which is given; fact; idea; (*math.*) known quantity.

Donner [Ger] *DOHN-uh.* thunder.

Donnerwetter [Ger] *DOHN-uh-vet-uh.* thunderstorm; drat!, darn!

dopo [It] *DOH-poh.* after; afterwards.

Dopolavoro [It] *doh-poh-lah-VOH-roh.* (*lit.*, after work) Italian Fascist organization.

Doppelgänger [Ger] *DOHP-'l-gen-guh.* ghostly double; shadow-self; alter ego.

dorado [Sp] *doh-RAH-doh.* gilded; golden.

doré [Fr] *doh-RAY.* gilded; golden.

Dorf [Ger] *dorf.* village.

dorsum [Lat] *DOR-soom.* back.

Dos de Mayo [Sp] *DOHS-deh-MAH-yoh.* May 2nd; celebration of Spanish uprising against the French in 1808.

dossier [Fr] *doh-SYAY.* file; collection of documents on a single person or subject.

do svidanya [Russ] *duh-svee-DAH-nyuh.* good-bye; till we meet again.

dottore [It] *doht-TOH-reh.* doctor.

douane [Fr] *doo-AHN.* customs; customhouse.

douanier [Fr] *doo-ah-NYAY.* customs officer.

double entendre [Fr] *DOO-blä-TÄ-druh.* expression with double meaning; ambiguous saying.

douce [Fr, fem. of *doux*] *doos.* sweet; gentle; docile.

doucement [Fr] *doos-MÄ.* sweetly; gently; slowly.

douche [Fr] *doosh.* shower; internal application of a liquid.

douloureux [Fr, from *douleur*, pain, sorrow] *doo-loo-RÖ.* sad; melancholy; painful.

douzaine [Fr, from *douze*, twelve] *doo-ZEN.* dozen.

doyen [Fr] *dwah-YẼ.* dean; eldest member; patriarch.

Dozent [Ger, from Lat *docens*, pr.p. of *docere*, to teach] *doh-TSENT.* teacher; lecturer; tutor. Also, **docent.**

Drachen [Ger] *DRAH-kh'n.* dragon; dragon-kite; termagant, shrew.

dragée [Fr] *drah-ZHAY.* sugarplum; chocolate-coated candy; small beadlike bit of candy used as a top sprinkle.

dragoman [Fr, from Ar *targuman*] *DRAG-uh-m'n.* interpreter, guide.

dramatis personae [Lat] *DRAH-mah-tees-per-SOH-ny.* cast of characters.

Drang nach Osten [Ger] *DRAHNG-nahkh-OHS-t'n.* drive toward the East; Eastern expansionism.

drap d'or [Fr] *drah-DOR.* gold cloth; lamé.

drapeau [Fr, from *drap*, cloth] *drah-POH.* flag; banner; drape.

Dreck [Ger, Yid] *drek.* dung, excrement, filth; junk, refuse.

Dreibund [Ger] *DRY-boont.* triple alliance: Germany, Italy and Austria-Hungary, 1882.

Dreikönigsabend [Ger] *DRY-kö-niks-ah-b'nt.* Epiphany Eve; Twelfth Night.

dressage [Fr] *dreh-SAHZH.* intricate movements performed by show horses; method of training show horses.

droit [Fr] *drwah.* right; of or on the right side; law; legal or moral right; —**d'auteur** (*-doh-TÖR*) copyright; author's rights; —**du seigneur** (*-dü-seh-NYÖR*) right of the feudal lord (**cf. jus primae noctis**).

droite [Fr] *drwaht.* right; right side.

drôle [Fr] *drohl.* droll, odd, queer; rascal.

droshky [Russ] *DROHSH-kee.* light, open carriage used in Russia.

Druck [Ger] *drook.* print, printing; impression; type.

Druckerei [Ger] *DROOK-uh-ry.* printing press; printing shop.

Druckfehler [Ger] *DROOK-fay-luh.* misprint, typographical error.

Druse [Ar] *drooz.* religious sect originating in 11th century in northern Syria, having features of Christianity, Judaism and Islam. Also, **Druze.**

D.S. Abbr. of dal segno.

dubash [Anglo-Ind, from Hindi *dubāshī*, bilingual person] *DOO-bahsh.* in India, a native interpreter; commissionaire.

duc [Fr] *dük.* duke.

duce [It, from Lat *dux*] *DOO-cheh.* leader: title of Mussolini.

duchesse [Fr] *dü-SHES.* duchess; gondola-shaped chaise longue with rounded ends.

ducit amor patriae [Lat] *DOO-keet-AH-mor-PAH-tree-y.* love of country leads (me).

duello [It] *doo-EL-loh.* art or practice of dueling; code of dueling.

dueña [Sp, from Lat **domina**] *DWEH-nyah.* lady of the house; mistress; chaperone.

dueño [Sp, from Lat **dominus**] *DWEH-nyoh.* owner; master, man of the house.

dulce [Lat, neut. of *dulcis*] *DOOL-keh.* sweet; —est desipere in loco (*-est-deh-SEE-peh-reh-een-LOH-koh*) it's sweet to unbend from time to time; —et decorum est pro patria mori (*-et-deh-KOH-room-est-proh-PAH-tree-ah-MOH-ree*) it is sweet and proper to die for one's country.

Duma [Russ] *DOO-muh.* (*lit.*, thought, meditation) council; Russian parliament of 1905–1917.

dum spiro, spero [Lat] *doom-SPEE-roh-SPEH-roh.* while I breathe, I hope; while there's life, there's hope.

dum tacent, clamant [Lat] *doom-TAH-kent-KLAH-mahnt.* while silent, they speak; silence is admission; their silence is a shout.

dum vita est, spes est [Lat] *doom-VEE-tah-est-SPES-est.* while there's life, there's hope.

dunque [It] *DOON-kweh.* now; so; well, then; therefore.

duomo [It] *DWOH-moh.* cathedral.

dur [Fr] *dür.* hard; difficult.

durak [Russ] *doo-RAHK.* fool; oaf; moron.

dura lex, sed lex [Lat] *DOO-rah-leks-sed-LEKS.* the law is hard, but it's the law.

durante [Lat, It, Sp] *doo-RAHN-teh.* during.

Durbar [Anglo-Ind, from Urdu *darbar*, court] *DUR-bar.* in India, royal court; audience hall; royal reception; regal ceremony.

durchkomponiert [Ger] *DOORÇ-kohm-poh-neert.* (*of a musical setting*) composed for an entire poem and not repeated for each stanza.

durée [Fr] *dü-RAY.* duration.

duro [Sp] *DOO-roh.* hard; coin of Spain and Spanish America; [It] hard.

durwan [Anglo-Ind, from Hindi *darwan*] *DUR-wun.* in India, doorman, hall porter.

duvet [Fr] *dü-VAY.* eiderdown; eiderdown quilt.

dux femina facti [Lat] *DOOKS-FEH-mee-nah-FAHK-tee.* a woman is the perpetrator of the deed.

dvandva [Skt, from *dva*, two] *DVAHN-dvah.* compound of two equal and apposite elements; e.g., *Eurasia, bittersweet*.

dvorets [Russ] *dvuh-RYETS.* palace; public building.

dybbuk [Yid *dibbuk*, from Heb *dibbūq*] *DIB-book.* bewitched person; evil spirit that enters a human body. Also, **dibbuk.**

dynamis [Gk] *DEE-nah-mees.* power; potential.

E

e [It] *eh.* and; before a vowel, **ed**; [Port] *eh.* and.

eau [Fr: *pl.* **eaux**] *oh.* water; —**courante** (*-koo-RÃT*) running water; —**de cologne** (*-duh-koh-LOH-nyuh*) cologne; perfumed water; diluted perfume; —**de toilette** (*-duh-twah-LET*) toilet water; cologne; —**de vie** (*-duh-VEE*) (*lit.*, water of life) brandy.

ébauche [Fr] *ay-BOHSH.* rough draft or outline of a work of literature or art.

ecce [Lat] *EK-keh.* behold; here is, here are; —**homo** (*-HOH-moh*) behold the man.

ecclesia [Lat, from Gk *ekklēsia*] *ek-KLEH-see-ah.* church; assembly.

echando flores [Sp] *eh-CHAHN-doh-FLOH-res.* (*lit.*, throwing flowers) paying compliments; flattering.

échanson [Fr] *ay-shã-SŎ.* cupbearer.

échantillon [Fr] *ay-shã-tee-YŎ.* sample; pattern.

échelle [Fr, from Lat *scala*] *ay-SHEL.* ladder; (*music*) scale.

échelon [Fr] *ay-sh'LŎ.* steplike formation of troops; any hierarchical arrangement; one step in this arrangement.

éclair [Fr] *ay-KLEHR.* (*lit.*, lightning flash) pastry filled with cream or custard.

éclat [Fr, from *éclater*, to burst, blaze] *ay-KLAH.* success; prestige; brilliance.

école [Fr] *ay-KOHL.* school; **—normale** (*-nor-MAHL*) normal school, where teachers are trained.

écrasé [Fr] *ay-krah-ZAY.* crushed; overwhelmed; overburdened; stunned.

écrasez l'infâme [Fr] *ay-krah-ZAY-lē-FAHM.* wipe out the odious; crush the abomination: attributed to Voltaire, in reference to pre-Revolutionary France.

écrevisse [Fr] *ay-kruh-VEES.* crawfish; a type of armor formed by overlapping plates, as in a crawfish tail.

écru [Fr] *ay-KRÜ* (*lit.*, raw, unbleached) a neutral brown color characteristic of unbleached fabric; material of this color.

écu [Fr, from Lat *scutum*, shield] *ay-KÜ.* small crest or shield; any of several old French coins.

ed [It] *ed.* See **e.**

Edda [Icel] *ED-dah.* Old Scandinavian epic poetry.

edecán [Sp, from Fr **aide-de-camp**] *eh-deh-KAHN.* aide-de-camp.

Edelweiss [Ger] *AY-d'l-vys.* white Alpine flower; edelweiss.

éditeur [Fr] *ay-dee-TÖR.* publisher.

édition de luxe [Fr] *ay-dee-SYŎ-duh-LÜKS.* de luxe edition.

editio princeps [Lat] *eh-DEE-tee-oh-PREEN-keps.* first edition.

effacé [Fr, p.p. of *effacer*] *eh-fah-SAY*. effaced; erased; obliterated.

effendi [Turk, from Gk *authentēs*, master, author] *eh-FEN-dee*. master: a title of respect in the Near East.

e.g. Abbr. of **exempli gratia.**

égalité [Fr] *ay-gah-lee-TAY*. equality.

égard [Fr] *ay-GAR*. regard; respect; consideration.

égaré [Fr] *ay-gah-RAY*. wandered, straying, roving; confused.

ego [Lat, Gk] *EH-goh*. I; myself; regard for oneself; the self; self-conceit.

eguale [It] *eh-GWAH-leh*. See **uguale; egualmente** (*eh-gwahl-MAYN-teh*). See **ugualmente.**

Eheu [Lat] *eh-HEH-oo*. Oh!; Alas!

eicon. See **eikon.**

eidos [Gk: something seen, from *idein*, to see] *AY-dohs*. form; type; species; idea.

Eigenschaft [Ger] *Y-g'n-shahft*. quality, property, feature.

eikon [Gk] *AY-kohn*. icon, image; representation, esp. of religious personages. Also, **eicon.**

ein [Ger] *yn*. a, an; one.

Einfluss [Ger] *YN-floos*. influence.

Einführung [Ger] *YN-fü-roong*. introduction.

Eingang [Ger] *YN-gahng*. entrance; gate, doorway; introduction, beginning.

Einleitung [Ger] *YN-ly-toong*. preamble, introduction, preface.

Einsamkeit [Ger] *YN-zahm-kyt*. loneliness, solitude.

einschliesslich [Ger] *YN-shlees-liç*. included; including.

Einstellung [Ger] *YN-shtel-oong*. attitude; adjustment; enlistment; cessation.

Eisenbahn [Ger] *Y-z'n-bahn*. railroad.

Eisen und Blut. See **Blut und Eisen.**

eisteddfod [Welsh] *ay-STETH-vohd*. musical or poetic contest.

ejido [Sp] *eh-HEE-doh*. public land, common; land on which a town will be built.

El [Heb *Elōh*] *el*. God, Lord.

el [Sp] *el.* the; **él** (*el*). he; him; it.

élan [Fr] *ay-LÃ.* sparkle, liveliness; enthusiasm; flair.

E.L.A.S. Abbr. of **Ellenikos Laikos Apeleutherotikos Stratos.**

El Cid Campeador [Sp] *el-SEED-kahm-peh-ah-DOR.* warrior chief; epic hero of Spain.

El dinero es mal amo, pero buen criado [Sp] *el-dee-NEH-roh-es-MAHL-AH-moh-peh-roh-BWEN-KRYAH-doh.* Money is a bad master, but a good servant.

El Dorado [Sp] *el-doh-RAH-doh.* (*lit.*, the golden one) legendary land of gold in S America.

elegantemente [It] *eh-leh-gahn-teh-MAYN-teh.* (*music*) elegantly, with elegance.

élève [Fr] *ay-LEV.* pupil; student.

Eli, Eli, lama sabachthani [Heb] *EH-lee-EH-lee-LAH-mah-sah-BAHKH-thah-nee.* My God, my God, why hast thou forsaken me?

elisir [It] *eh-lee-SEER.* elixir; potion.

élite [Fr, earlier fem. p.p. of *élire*, to elect] *ay-LEET.* select few; special group.

Ellenikos Demokratikos Ethnikos Stratos [Gk] *el-lee-nee-KOHS-dee-moh-krah-tee-KOHS-eth-nee-KOHS-strah-TOHS.* Greek National Democratic Army (a right-wing party, now defunct).

Ellenikos Laikos Apeleutherotikos Stratos [Gk: *abbr.* **E.L.A.S.**] *el-lee-nee-KOHS-ly-KOHS-ah-pee-lef-thee-roh-tee-KOHS-strah-TOHS.* Greek People's Liberation Army.

Elohim [Heb, honorific pl. of *Elōh*, God] *eh-loh-HEEM.* Lord, God, Supreme Being.

el pan, pan, y el vino, vino [Sp] *el-PAHN-PAHN-ee-el-VEE-noh-VEE-noh.* (*lit.*, bread is bread, and wine is wine) to call a spade a spade.

Elysium [Lat, from Gk *ēlysion* (*pedion*), blessed (plain)] *eh-LEE-see-oom.* mythological paradise; utopia.

embarcación [Sp] *em-bar-kah-SYOHN.* embarkation; boat, craft.

embarras [Fr] *ã-bah-RAH.* embarrassment; burden; difficulty; surfeit; **—du choix** (*-dü-SHWAH*) embarrassment of choice; inability to make up one's mind among many choices; —de richesses (-duh-ree-SHES) embarrassment of riches; more than one can handle.

em boca cerrada não entra mosca [Port] ẽ-BOH-kuh-sehr-RAH-duh-nã-oh-EN-truh-MOHSH-kuh. into a closed mouth a fly does not enter; if you keep your mouth shut you don't put your foot in it.

embonpoint [Fr] ã-bõ-PWẼ. plumpness.

émeute [Fr, from émouvoir, to move, excite] ay-MÖT. popular revolt; civil uprising.

émigré [Fr] ay-mee-GRAY. emigrant; refugee, exile.

emir [Ar amir] eh-MEER. title given to a commander; leader; ruler.

empanada [Sp] em-pah-NAH-dah. meat pie.

Empfindung [Ger] em-PFIN-doong. sensation; emotion.

empressement [Fr] ã-pres-MÃ. eagerness; cordiality.

emptor [Lat] EMP-tor. buyer.

en [Fr] ã. in; for; at; by; with; [Sp] en. in; at; to; on; [Gk] en. in; at; by; [Swed] en. a, an; one; [Du] en. and.

en arrière [Fr] ã-nah-RYEHR. in arrears; behind; backward.

en avant [Fr] ã-nah-VÃ. onward; forward, ahead.

en bloc [Fr] ã-BLAWK. together; in a mass.

en brochette [Fr] ã-broh-SHET. on a skewer.

en cabochon [Fr] ã-kah-boh-SHÕ. (of a gem) set and polished uncut.

en cachette [Fr] ã-kah-SHET. cached; concealed; secretly.

encargo [Sp] en-KAR-goh. commission; charge, trust.

en casa de [Sp] en-KAH-sah-deh. in care of; at the home of.

en casserole [Fr] ã-kah-s'ROHL. served in a single deep dish.

enceinte [Fr] ã-SẼT. pregnant.

enchanté [Fr] ã-shã-TAY. enchanted; delighted; charmed.

ench(e)iridion [Gk] en-khay-REE-dee-ohn. manual, guidebook; handbook.

enchilada [Sp] en-chee-LAH-dah. Mexican tortilla, rolled and filled with highly seasoned meat and vegetables, served with a hot chile sauce.

enclave [Fr] *ã-KLAHV*. foreign territory surrounded by another country; linguistic or ethnic island.

encomium [Lat] *en-KOH-mee-oom*. speech of praise; eulogizing poem.

en congé [Fr] *ã-kõ-ZHAY*. on leave; on furlough.

en coquille [Fr] *ã-koh-KEE-yuh*. (of seafood) served in the shell.

encore [Fr] *ã-KOR*. again! repeat!

encylopédistes [Fr] *ã-see-kloh-pay-DEEST*. contributors to the 18th-century French encyclopedia edited by Diderot and D'Alembert, noted for its revolutionary views.

Ende gut, alles gut [Ger] *EN-deh-GOOT-AH-l's-GOOT*. all's well that ends well.

en deshabillé [Fr] *ã-day-zah-bee-YAY*. undressed; disheveled.

en effet [Fr] *ã-neh-FEH*. in effect; actually; in fact.

en face [Fr] *ã-FAHS*. facing; opposite.

en fait [Fr] *ã-FEH*. in fact; in truth.

en famille [Fr] *ã-fah-MEE-yuh*. in or within the family; among close friends.

enfant [Fr] *ã-FÃ*. child; infant; —**gâté** (*-gah-TAY*) spoiled child; brat; —**terrible** (*-teh-REE-bluh*) terrible child; rascal; brat; incorrigible child; overprecocious child.

enfaticamente [It] *en-fah-tee-kah-MAYN-teh*. (*music*) emphatically; firmly.

enfin [Fr] *ã-FĔ*. in fine; in summary; finally; after all.

en fin de compte [Fr] *ã-fĕ-duh-KŎT*. in the end; in the final analysis.

en flagrant [Fr] *ã-flah-GRÃ*. flagrantly; ostentatiously; in the act.

en garçon [Fr] *ã-gar-SŎ*. as a bachelor.

engobe [Fr] *ã-GOHB*. an opaque ceramic glaze, esp. one serving as a base for an outer glaze.

en grand [Fr] *ã-GRÃ*. in high style; grandly; ostentatiously.

en grande tenue [Fr] *ã-GRÃD-tuh-NÙ*. in full dress; in review form.

en grand seigneur [Fr] *ã-GRÃ-seh-NYÖR*. in grand style; in noble form.

en gros [Fr] *ã-GROH.* in all; in total; gross, wholesale.

en guerre [Fr] *ã-GEHR.* at war; in disagreement.

en haut [Fr] *ã-NOH.* at or on the top; on high; above; upstairs.

en l'air [Fr] *ã-LEHR.* in the air; in a flutter; suspended; wild(ly); up in the air.

en manège [Fr] *ã-mah-NEZH.* (of show horses) in a circular pattern.

en masse [Fr] *ã-MAHS.* all together; in a mass.

ennui [Fr] *ã-NÜEE.* boredom; world-weariness; annoyance.

ennuyé [Fr] *ã-nüee-YAY.* bored; world-weary; annoyed.

en papillotes [Fr] *ã-pah-pee-YOHT.* (of food) served wrapped in foil or oiled paper.

en passant [Fr] *ã-pah-SÃ.* in passing; incidentally; by the way; chess move in which a pawn on its first move can capture an opposing pawn in the fifth rank of its own file; by the way.

en pension [Fr] *ã-pã-SYŎ.* (living) in a boardinghouse.

en plein [Fr] *ã-PLẼ.* fully; completely; in the midst of; in the very act or state of; —**air** (*-NEHR*) in the open air; —**jour** (*-ZHOOR*) in broad daylight.

en rapport [Fr] *ã-rah-POR.* in sympathy; in agreement.

en règle [Fr] *ã-REG-luh.* in order; by the rule; according to Hoyle.

en résumé [Fr] *ã-ray-zü-MAY.* summing up; on the whole.

en revanche [Fr] *ã-ruh-VÃSH.* in retaliation; in return.

en route [Fr] *ã-ROOT.* on or along the way; move out!; start!; let's go!

ens [Lat, pr.p. of *esse,* to be] *ens.* being; thing; entity.

ensayo [Sp] *en-SAH-yoh.* essay.

en scène [Fr] *ã-SEN.* on stage.

en seguida [Sp] *en-seh-GEE-dah.* at once, immediately; forthwith, thereupon.

enseignement [Fr] *ã-seh-nyuh-MÃ.* instruction; teaching.

ensemble [Fr] *ã-SÃ-bluh.* together; group; small orchestra; theatrical group; chorus; complete costume, esp. of matching garments and accessories.

ensenada [Sp] *en-seh-NAH-dah.* cove; inlet.

Ense petit placidam sub libertate quietem [Lat] *en-seh-*

PEH-teet-PLAH-kee-dahm-soob-lee-behr-TAH-teh-kwee-EH-tem. By the sword she seeks tranquil peace under liberty (motto of Massachusetts).

ensis [Lat] *EN-sees.* sword.

en somme [Fr] *ã-SUM.* in short; in sum; to make a long story short.

ensuite [Fr] *ã-SÜEET.* after, afterward; then, thereupon.

en suite [Fr] *ã-SÜEET.* in succession; in a series or set.

en suivant la vérité [Fr] *ã-süee-VÃ-lah-vay-ree-TAY.* in following the truth.

entasis [Gk] *EN-tah-sees.* a convexity in the outline of a column or tower, for visual effect.

entendu [Fr] *ã-tã-DÜ.* understood; agreed.

entente [Fr] *ã-TÃT.* understanding; international agreement; alliance.

en tête-à-tête [Fr] *ã-TET-ah-TET.* privately; intimately; face to face.

entourage [Fr] *ã-too-RAHZH.* surrounding company; attendants; retinue; following.

en tout cas [Fr] *ã-TOO-KAH.* in any case; in all events; at any rate.

en-tout-cas [Fr] *ã-TOO-KAH.* combination umbrella-parasol.

entr'acte [Fr] *ã-TRAHKT.* between the acts; intermission; interlude.

entrada [Sp] *en-TRAH-dah.* entrance; entry; admittance; attendance; gate receipts; income.

en train [Fr] *ã-TRÊ.* in progress; on the way; in the act of.

entrata [It] *en-TRAH-tah.* entrance; entry; admittance; income; receipts; (*music*) attack.

entre [Fr] *Ã-truh.* among; between.

entrechat [Fr, from It *intrecciata*, intertwined] *ã-truh-SHAH.* ballet leap in which the heels are struck together in midair.

entre chien et loup [Fr] *Ã-truh-SHYÊ-nay-LOO* (*lit.*, between dog and wolf; i.e., when it's too dark to tell them apart) at twilight; at dusk.

entrecôte [Fr] *ã-truh-KOHT* (*lit.*, between ribs) (*cookery*) tenderloin cut.

entre deux [Fr] *ã-truh-DÖ.* between two; for two; duet.

entrée [Fr] *ã-TRAY.* entrance; main desk; entry; admission; income; main course.

entremés [Sp: *pl.* entremeses] *en-treh-MES (-MEH-ses)* short playlet during intermission; entr'acte; hors d'oeuvre, appetizers.

entremets [Fr] *ã-truh-MEH.* side dish served between courses; hors d'oeuvre.

entre nous [Fr] *ã-truh-NOO.* just between you and me; among ourselves; in confidence.

entrepôt [Fr] *ã-truh-POH.* warehouse; emporium; market.

entrepreneur [Fr] *ã-truh-pruh-NÖR.* one who undertakes or manages; impresario.

entresol [Fr] *ã-truh-SOHL.* mezzanine.

Entwicklung [Ger] *ent-VIK-loong.* development; growth.

en vérité [Fr] *ã-vay-ree-TAY.* truly; in truth.

en vigueur [Fr] *ã-vee-GÖR.* in force; in effect; in operation; enforced.

envoi [Fr] *ã-VWAH.* postscript to a poem or song.

en voiture [Fr] *ã-vwah-TÜR.* all aboard!

envoyé [Fr] *ã-vwah-YAY.* envoy; ambassador; messenger.

en wagon [Fr] *ã-vah-GÕ.* all aboard!; take your seats!

eo nomine [Lat] *EH-oh-NOH-mee-neh.* under or by that name.

épatant [Fr] *ay-pah-TÃ.* dazzling, stunning; amazing; astonishing.

épater le bourgeois [Fr] *ay-pah-TAY-luh-boor-ZHWAH.* to bedazzle or befuddle the general public.

épaule [Fr] *ay-POHL.* shoulder.

épaulement [Fr, from *épaule,* shoulder] *ay-pohl-MÃ.* ballet position in which the shoulders are aligned at right angles to the supporting leg.

épaulette [Fr] *ay-poh-LET.* shoulder decoration or insignia; epaulet.

épaulière [Fr] *ay-poh-LYEHR.* (*armor*) shoulder plate.

épée [Fr] *ay-PAY.* sword.

épi [Fr] *ay-PEE.* ear of corn; ornament or design in this shape.

épicerie [Fr] *ay-pee-s'REE.* grocery.

épicier [Fr] *ay-pee-SYAY.* grocer; uncultured person.

épinard [Fr] *ay-pee-NAR.* spinach. Also, épinards (*pl.*).

episcopus [Lat, from Gk *episkopos,* overseer] *eh-PEES-koh-poos.* bishop.

epistola [Lat, from Gk *epistolē*] *eh-PEES-toh-lah.* epistle; letter; charter.

epithalamion [Gk, from *epi,* before + *thalamos,* bedchamber] *eh-pee-thah-LAH-mee-on.* wedding song; hymeneal.

E pluribus unum [Lat] *eh-PLOO-ree-boos-OO-noom.* Out of many, one (motto of the U.S.A.)

épopée [Fr] *ay-poh-PAY.* epic; epic song or poem.

epos [Gk] *EH-pos.* folk tale; tale in song; heroic poem or lyric.

eppur si muove [It] *ehp-POOR-see-MWOH-veh.* and yet it moves: attributed to Galileo after being forced to testify before the Inquisition that the earth stands still.

È pur troppo vero [It] *EH-poor-TROHP-poh-VEH-roh.* it is all too true.

eques [Lat, from *equus,* horse] *EH-kwes.* knight; horseman.

equites [Lat, pl. of eques] *EH-kwee-tes.* mounted troops, cavalry; an ancient Roman class between the senatorial class and the commoners.

équivoque [Fr] *ay-kee-VOHK.* equivocal; ambiguous; an ambiguity.

equus [Lat] *EH-kwoos.* horse.

eretz [Heb] *eh-RETS.* earth; country; land; —Israel (*-Yiz-rah-EL*) land of Israel.

ergo [Lat] *EHR-goh.* therefore; hence.

ergon [Gk] *EHR-gohn.* work; labor; unit of work.

Erin go bragh [Ir] *EH-rin-goh-BRAH.* Ireland forever!

Erinnerung [Ger] *ehr-IN-uh-roong.* remembrance; souvenir.

eripuit caelo fulmen sceptrumque tyrannis [Lat] *eh-REE-poo-eet-KY-loh-FOOL-men-skep-TROOM-kweh-tee-RAHN-nees.* He snatched the thunder from heaven and the scepter from tyrants: inscription beneath Houdon's bust of Franklin.

Erkenntnis [Ger] *ehr-KENT-nis.* realization; insight; recognition.

Erlebnis [Ger] *ehr-LAYB-nis.* experience.

Erlkönig [Ger] *EHRL-kö-niç.* Elf King (mischievous mythical spirit).

Ernst [Ger] *ehrnst.* earnestness; seriousness.

eroico [It] *eh-ROY-koh.* (*music*) heroically.

Eros [Gk] *EH-rohs.* the god of love; love.

erotema [Gk] *eh-roh-TEH-mah.* rhetorical question.

erotica [It] *eh-ROH-tee-kah.* love song; (*music*) eroticism; [Lat] collection of erotic writings.

errare humanum est [Lat] *ehr-RAH-reh-hoo-MAH-noom-est.* to err is human.

erratum [Lat: *pl.* **errata**] *ehr-RAH-toom* (*-tah*) error; mistake.

ersatz [Ger] *EHR-zahts.* substitute; synthetic.

erythros [Gk] *eh-rü-THROHS.* red.

Erzählung [Ger] *ehr-TSAY-loong.* narration; narrative; tale.

Erzherzog [Ger] *EHRTS-hehr-tsohk.* archduke.

Erziehung [Ger] *er-TSEE-oong.* upbringing; rearing; education.

escadrille [Fr] *es-kah-DREE-yuh.* squadron.

escalier [Fr] *es-kah-LYAY.* stairway, staircase.

escargot [Fr] *es-kar-GOH.* snail.

escarpe [Fr] *es-KARP.* escarpment; slope in rear section of a trench.

esclandre [Fr] *es-KLÃ-druh.* scandal; public scene.

escritoire [Fr, earlier form of *écritoire,* from *écrire,* to write] *es-kree-TWAR.* desk, writing table.

escudo [Sp] *es-KOO-doh;* [Port] *ish-KOO-doo.* shield; blazon; any of various gold or silver coins presently used in Portugal and Chile and formerly in other Spanish countries.

escuela [Sp] *es-KWEH-lah.* school.

es decir [Sp] *es-deh-SEER.* that is to say.

Es de vidrio la mujer [Sp] *es-deh-VEE-dryoh-lah-moo-HEHR.* Woman is made of glass.

esencia [Sp] *eh-SEN-syah.* essence; liquid fuel; gasoline.

Es ist nicht alles Gold was glänzt [Ger] *es-ist-niçt-AH-l's-GOLHT-wahs-GLENTST.* All is not gold that glitters.

espada [Sp] *es-PAH-dah.* sword; (*cards*) spade; (*bullfight-*

ing) the swordsman or matador; [Port] *ish-PAH-duh*. sword; swordsman; reckless driver.

espadrille [Fr] *es-pah-DREE-yuh*. sandal with rope sole, laced about the ankle.

espagnol [Fr] *es-pah-NYOHL*. Spanish; Spaniard.

español [Sp] *es-pah-NYOHL*. Spanish; Spaniard.

esparto [Sp] *es-PAR-toh*. grass used in making paper, cordage, etc.

Esperanto [Esp] *es-peh-RAHN-toh*. (*lit.*, the hoping one) artificial language constructed in 1887 by L. L. Zamenhof, Polish philologist.

espiègle [Fr] *es-PYEH-gluh*. roguish; mischievous.

espoir [Fr] *es-PWAR*. hope.

esposa [Sp] *es-POH-sah*. wife; bride.

esposo [Sp] *es-POH-soh*. husband.

espressione [It] *es-pres-SYOH-neh*. (*music*) expression; emotion.

espressivo [It] *es-pres-SEE-voh*. (*music*) expressively.

espresso [It] See **caffè espresso**.

esprit [Fr] *es-PREE*. spirit; wit; soul; —**de corps** (*-duh-KOR*) spirit or loyalty to one's group; group spirit; —**fort** (*-FOR*) strong, free spirit; freethinker; —**gaulois** (*-goh-LWAH*) Gallic spirit; French wit.

esquisse [Fr] *es-KEES*. sketch; rough outline; draft.

essai [Fr] *es-SEH*. trial, test; attempt; essay.

essayage [Fr, from *essayer*, to try] *es-seh-YAHZH*. trying, testing; fitting (of clothes).

esse [Lat: to be] *ES-seh*. essence; being.

essence [Fr] *eh-SÃS*. essence; perfume; liquid fuel; gasoline.

esse quam videri [Lat] *ES-seh-kwahm-vee-DEH-ree*. To be rather than to seem (motto of North Carolina).

está bien [Sp] *es-TAH-BYEN*. all right! fine!

estação [Port] *ish-tah-SÃ-oo*. station; season.

estación [Sp] *es-tah-SYOHN*. station; season.

estado [Sp] *es-TAH-doh*. state.

Estados Unidos [Sp] *es-TAH-dohs-oo-NEE-dohs*. United States; [Port] *ish-TAH-doo-zoo-NEE-doosh*.

estafette [Fr, from It *staffetta*, from *staffa*, stirrup] *es-tah-FET*. courier; messenger.

estaminet [Fr] *es-tah-mee-NEH.* wine shop; café.

estancia [Sp] *es-TAHN-syah.* ranch; estate.

estanco [Sp] *es-TAHN-koh.* monopoly; store that sells government monopoly goods; **—de tabaco** (*-deh-tah-BAH-koh*) tobacco shop.

estaño [Sp] *es-TAH-nyoh.* tin.

estate [It] *es-TAH-teh.* summer.

est modus in rebus [Lat] *est-MOH-doos-een-REH-boos.* there is a medium (measure) in all things.

Esto Perpetua [Lat] *ES-toh-pehr-PEH-too-ah.* May she live forever (motto of Idaho).

estrade [Fr] *es-TRAHD.* platform; stage, viewing stand.

estrella [Sp] *es-TREH-lyah.* star.

estribillo [Sp] *es-tree-BEE-lyoh.* opening stanza of a song; refrain; chorus.

estro [It] *ES-troh.* ardor, passion; **—poetico** (*-poh-EH-tee-koh*) poetic fire.

et [Lat] *et*; [Fr] *ay.* and.

Eta [Jap] *EH-tah.* a former outcast class of Japan, subject to segregation.

étage [Fr] *ay-TAHZH.* floor; story; stage; layer, stratum.

étagère [Fr] *ay-tah-ZHEHR.* set of shelves for bric-a-brac, books, etc.

et al. Abbr. of **et alia; et alibi; et alii.**

étalage [Fr] *ay-tah-LAHZH.* ostentatious show; finery; display of goods for sale.

et alia [Lat: *abbr.* **et al.**] *et-AH-lee-ah.* and other things; et cetera.

et alibi [Lat: *abbr.* **et al.**] *et-AH-lee-bee.* and elsewhere.

et alii [Lat: *abbr.* **et al.**] *et-AH-lee-ee.* and others; and other persons.

étape [Fr] *ay-TAHP.* stage; step; interval; stopping place.

état-major [Fr] *ay-TAH-mah-ZHOR.* general staff; general staff office.

États-Généraux [Fr] *ay-TAH-zhay-nay-ROH.* States General: general assembly of France, 1392-1789.

États-Unis [Fr] *ay-TAH-zü-NEE.* United States.

et cetera [Lat: *abbr.* **etc.**] *et-KEH-teh-rah.* and other things; and so forth.

été [Fr] *ay-TAY.* summer.

ethnos [Gk] *ETH-nohs.* race; people; nation.

et hoc genus omne [Lat] *et-HOHK-GEH-noos-OHM-neh.* and all that sort of thing. Also, **et id genus omne** (-*EED*-).

ethos [Gk] *EH-thohs.* national character; spirit of a people or culture.

etiam atque etiam [Lat] *EH-tee-ahm-aht-kweh-EH-tee-ahm.* again and again.

et nunc et semper [Lat] *et-NOONK-et-SEM-pehr.* now and forever.

étoile [Fr] *ay-TWAHL.* star; point of convergence.

étonnant [Fr] *ay-tuh-NÃ.* stunning; astounding; surprising.

et passim [Lat: *abbr.* **et pass.**] *et-PAHS-seem.* and everywhere; scattered throughout.

être [Fr] *EH-truh.* to be; being, existence; a being.

et sequentes [Lat: *abbr.* **et seq.**] *et-seh-KWEN-tes.* and the following.

et sic de ceteris [Lat] *et-SEEK-deh-KEH-teh-rees.* and the same for the rest.

et sic de similibus [Lat] *et-SEEK-deh-see-MEE-lee-boos.* and so for the like.

et similia [Lat] *et-see-MEE-lee-ah.* and similar things; and the like.

étude [Fr] *ay-TÜD.* study; short musical composition.

étui [Fr] *ay-TÜEE.* small case; sheath; holder.

et tu, Brute [Lat] *et-TOO-BROO-teh.* you too, Brutus: attributed by Shakespeare to Julius Caesar in the play of that name.

et uxor [Lat: *abbr.* **et ux.**] *et-OOK-sor.* and wife.

etwas [Ger] *ET-vahs.* something; somewhat; some; rather.

etymon [Gk] *ET-ü-mohn.* basic ingredient; root; origin.

Eunmoon [Korean] *ÖN-moon.* name of the Korean alphabet.

eureka [Gk *heúrēka*] *hay-OO-reh-kah.* I have found (it)! (motto of California); hurrah!

Eurovision [Fr] *ö-roh-vee-ZYÕ.* continental European television network.

Euskara [Basque] *eh-oo-SKAH-rah.* Basque.

Evangelium [Lat, from Gk *euangelion*] *eh-vahn-GEH-lee-oom*. The New Testament; Good News; the Gospel.

événement [Fr] *ay-vay-n'MĂ*. event; emergency; result; outcome.

evviva [It] *ehv-VEE-vah*. hurrah!; long live!

ewig [Ger] *AY-viç*. eternal, everlasting; **Ewig-Weibliche** (*-vyb-li-çeh*) the eternal feminine.

Ewigkeit [Ger] *AY-viç-kyt*. eternity.

ex animo [Lat] *eks-AH-nee-moh*. from the heart; sincerely.

ex cathedra [Lat] *eks-KAH-teh-drah*. from the chair; with authority; pontifically.

Excelentísimo [Sp] *ek-seh-len-TEE-see-moh*. Excellency; Honorable.

Excellentíssimo [Port] *ek-suh-len-TEE-see-moo*. Excellency; Honorable.

Excelsior [Lat] *eks-KEL-see-or*. Ever upward (motto of New York State).

ex curia [Lat] *eks-KOO-ree-ah*. out of court.

exegi monumentum aere perennius [Lat] *ek-SEH-gee-moh-noo-MEN-toom-Y-reh-peh-REN-nee-oos*. I have raised a monument more lasting than bronze.

exemplaire [Fr] *eg-zā-PLEHR*. copy; specimen; sample.

exemple [Fr] *eg-ZĂ-pluh*. example; instance; specimen; sample; **par—** (*par-*) for example, for instance; fancy that!

exempli gratia [Lat; *abbr.* **e.g.**] *ek-SEM-plee-GRAH-tee-ah*. for example; for instance.

exequatur [Lat: let him perform] *ek-seh-KWAH-toor*. permission to perform official duties given by a state to an officer of another state; permission of a secular government to publish ecclesiastical documents; Also, **exsequatur.**

exercitus [Lat] *ek-SEHR-kee-toos*. army; militia.

exeunt [Lat] *EK-seh-oont*. they exit; they leave the stage; **—omnes** (*-OHM-nes*) all exit; they all leave the stage.

ex facie [Lat] *eks-FAH-kee-eh*. (*law*) on its face; apparently.

ex facto [Lat] *eks-FAHK-toh*. out of the fact; actually.

exit [Lat, from *exire*, to go out] *EK-sit.* he (she) leaves the stage; point of departure; exit.

exitus acta probat [Lat] *EK-see-toos-AHK-tah-PROH-baht.* the end justifies the means.

ex libris [Lat] *eks-LEE-brees.* from among the books of: used on bookplates to identify the owner.

ex more [Lat] *eks-MOH-reh.* according to custom.

ex nihilo [Lat] *eks-NEE-hee-loh.* out of nothing; —**nihil fit** (*-NEE-heel-feet*) out of nothing comes nothing.

ex officio [Lat] *eks-ohf-FEE-kee-oh.* by virtue of his office; still a member by reason of former high office.

exordium [Lat] *ek-SOR-dee-oom.* (*lit.*, the laying down of the warp on the loom) first stage; introduction; commencement.

ex parte [Lat] *eks-PAR-teh.* for one side only; partisan.

expertise [Fr] *eks-pehr-TEEZ.* expertness; skill.

exposé [Fr] *eks-poh-ZAY.* statement; explanation; revelation; exposure, esp. of private facts or situations.

ex post facto [Lat] *eks-pohst-FAHK-toh.* after the fact or occurrence.

exsequatur. See **exequatur.**

ex tempore [Lat] *eks-TEM-poh-reh.* without previous preparation; off the cuff.

extrait [Fr] *eks-TREH.* extract; abstract.

extra muros [Lat] *EKS-trah-MOO-rohs.* outside the walls (of conventions, institutions or of a political boundary).

extraneus [Lat] *eks-TRAH-neh-oos.* foreign; foreigner; alien.

extranjero [Sp] *eks-trahn-HEH-roh.* foreign; foreigner; stranger.

extremis. See **in extremis.**

ex uno disce omnes [Lat] *eks-OO-noh-DEES-keh-OHM-nes.* from one, judge all.

ex voto [Lat] *eks-VOH-toh.* (*lit.*, out of a vow) tablet or inscription recording an accomplished vow.

F

f. Abbr. of **forte.**

fabada [Sp, from *faba*, var. of *haba*, broad bean] *fah-BAH-dah.* bean stew; —**asturiana** (*-ahs-too-RYAH-nah*) bean stew Asturian style, with ham, bacon and/or sausage added.

fabliau [Fr: *pl.* **fabliaux**] *fah-BLYOH.* short medieval verse tale or fable, usu. ribald and humorous.

fábrica [Sp] *FAH-bree-kah.* factory; industrial plant.

fabula [Lat] *FAH-boo-lah.* comedy; fable; —**Atellana** (*-ah-tel-LAH-nah*) Atellan fable: farcical form originating in Atella, ancient southern Italian town.

facchino [It] *fahk-KEE-noh.* porter; bellboy.

facile [It: easy] *FAH-chee-leh.* (*music*) lightly; freely.

Facit. See **Fazit.**

façon [Fr] *fah-SŎ.* fashion, style, manner; —**de parler** (*-duh-par-LAY*) manner of speaking.

facta non verba [Lat] *FAHK-tah-nohn-VEHR-bah.* deeds, not words.

facteur [Fr] *fahk-TÖR.* agent; messenger; postman; porter.

factotum [Lat: do-all] *fahk-TOH-toom.* jack-of-all-trades; man-of-all-work.

factum [Lat] *fahk-toom.* (*lit.*, something done) fact; deed; situation; —**est** (*-est*) it is done; —**probandum** (*-proh-BAHN-doom*) fact to be proved; —**probans** (*-PROH-bahns*) proving fact; fact that proves another statement.

factura [Sp] *fahk-TOO-rah.* invoice; bill.

facture [Fr] *fahk-TÜR.* invoice; bill.

facula [Lat] *FAH-koo-lah.* (*lit.*, little torch) small spot on the sun's surface, brighter than the rest of the photosphere.

fado [Port, from Lat *fatum*, fate] *FAH-doo.* popular ballad, usu. sung with guitar accompaniment.

fagioli [It: *sg.* **fagiolo**] *fah-JOH-lee* (*-loh*) beans.

fagot [Fr] *fah-GOH.* fagot; idle tale; (*slang*) ex-convict.

faible [Fr] *FEH-bluh.* weak; weakness; weak spot, foible.

faille [Fr] *FAH-yuh.* soft, ribbed fabric of silk, rayon or taffeta.

fainéant [Fr] *fay-nay-Ã.* idle; lazy; apathetic; idler; loafer; do-nothing.

faire [Fr] *FEHR.* to do; make; act; cause; —école (*-ay-KOHL*) to found a school or cult; —feu (*-FÖ*) to fire, shoot; —la bombe (*-lah-BÕB*) to go on a spree, have a ball; —l'amant (*-lah-MÃ*) to play the lover; —l'amende honorable (*-lah-MÃ-doh-noh-RAH-bluh*) to make honorable amends, apologize; —la noce (*-lah-NOHS*) (*lit.*, to have a wedding) to go on a lark; —la sourde oreille (*-lah-SOOR-doh-REH-yuh*) to play deaf; to turn a deaf ear; —l'école buissonnière (*-lay-KOHL-büee-suh-NYEHR*) to play hooky; —le plein (*-luh-PLÊ*) to fill up, esp. a gas tank; —le salon (*-luh-sah-LÕ*) to review an art exhibit; —le savant (*-luh-sah-VÃ*) to play the sage; —les quatre-cents (400) coups (*lit.*, to strike the 400 blows) (*-lay-KAH-truh-SÃ-KOO*) to go on a spree; to do everything; —l'ingénu (*-lẽ-zhay-NÜ*) to play the innocent; —sans dire (*-sã-DEER*) to act without speaking; to get things done quietly.

fais ce que dois, advienne que pourra [Fr] *FEH-suh-kuh-DWAH-ahd-VYEN-kuh-poo-RAH.* do your duty, come what may.

fait [Fr] *feh.* done, finished, accomplished; thing, fact; —accompli (*FEH-tah-kõ-PLEE*) accomplished fact; a thing done.

faja [Sp] *FAH-hah.* band, strip; girdle, sash; highway lane.

fakir [Ar *faqīr*, poor] *fah-KEER.* Mohammedan or Hindu religious mendicant or ascetic.

Falange [Sp] *fah-LAHN-heh.* (*lit.*, phalanx) the Fascist party of Spain.

falangista [Sp] *fah-lahn-HEES-tah.* member of the Falange.

falsetto [It, from *falso*, false] *fahl-SAYT-toh.* strained, high-pitched; speaking or singing in this manner.

fama [Lat, It, Sp] *FAH-mah.* fame; reputation; common opinion.

fameux [Fr: *fem.* **fameuse**] *fah-MÖ* (*-MÖZ*) famous.

fanciulla [It] *fahn-CHOOL-lah.* girl, lass.

fandango [Sp] *fahn-DAHN-goh.* lively Spanish dance; any wild, spirited dance.

fanfaronnade [Fr] *fã-fah-ruh-NAHD.* fanfare; boasting.

fantaisie [Fr] *fã-teh-ZEE.* fantasy; fancy, imagination; (*music*) fantasia.

fantaisiste [Fr] *fã-teh-ZEEST.* whimsical, fanciful; a whimsical painter, writer, composer, etc.

fan tan [Chin *fan t'an*, repeated divisions] *FAHN-TAHN.* card game in which the object is to dispose of one's cards before the other players; Chinese game in which a number of counters are placed under a bowl and bets are made on what the remainder will be after they are counted out in fours.

fantasia [It] *fahn-tah-SEE-ah.* (*lit.*, fantasy) a musical composition in free, fanciful form; group of variations on one or more familiar themes.

fantasque [Fr] *fã-TAHSK.* fantastic, bizarre, whimsical.

fantoccino [It: *pl.* **-ni**] *fahn-toh-CHEE-noh* (*-nee*) doll, puppet; (*pl.*) puppet show.

farallón [Sp: *pl.* **farallones**] *fah-rah-LYOHN* (*-LYOH-nes*) small, rocky island, usually found in clusters or groups.

farandole [Fr] *fah-rã-DOHL.* lively Provençal group dance.

farash [Ar] *fah-RAHSH.* servant who sweeps floors, takes care of carpets, etc.

Farbe [Ger] *FAR-beh.* dye; pigment; color.

farce [Fr] *fars.* stuffing; forcemeat; farce, low comedy.

farceur [Fr] *far-SÖR.* jester; practical joker, clown; writer or teller of jokes.

farfel [Yid] *FAR-f'l.* small dumpling made of noodles or matzo crumbs, usu. served in soups.

farina [Lat, It] *fah-REE-nah.* flour; meal.

farinha [Port] *fuh-REE-nyuh.* flour, meal.

far niente [It] *far-NYEN-teh.* (*lit.*, do nothing) idleness; inactivity.

farol [Sp] *fah-ROHL.* lantern; headlight; street lamp.

farruca [Sp] *far-ROO-kah.* flamenco dance.

fasces [Lat] *FAHS-kes.* ax bundled with twigs, emblem of

authority of Roman magistrates: used as symbol of
authority of the state by Fascists.

Fascio (di Combattimento) [It; *pl.* **Fasci**] *FAH-shoh* (*-shee*)
(*-dee-kohm-baht-tee-MAYN-toh*) (*lit.*, bundle) local
Fascist groups, armed for combat duty.

Fascismo [It] *fah-SHEEZ-moh*. Fascism.

fascista [It: *pl.* **fascisti**] *fah-SHEES-tah* (*-tee*) Fascist.

fasti et nefasti dies [Lat] *FAHS-tee-et-neh-FAHS-tee-DEE-es*. lucky and unlucky days.

Fastnachtsspiel [Ger, from *Fastnacht*, Shrove Tuesday]
FAHST-nahkhts-shpeel. carnival games and merriment;
carnival play.

Fata obstant [Lat] *FAH-tah-OHB-stahnt.* the fates oppose;
it is impossible.

fatti maschi, parole femmine [It] *FAHT-tee-MAHS-kee-pah-ROH-leh-FAYM-mee-neh.* Deeds (are) manly, words
womanly (motto of Maryland).

faubourg [Fr] *foh-BOOR.* suburb.

fauna [Lat *Fauna*, sister of Faunus, a woodland deity]
FOW-nah. the animals of a given region or period, taken
collectively. Cf. **flora.**

faute [Fr] *foht.* fault; lack; mistake, error; —**de mieux**
(*-duh-MYÖ*) for lack of anything better.

fauteuil [Fr] *foh-TÖY.* armchair; theater box; box seat;
speaker's chair.

faux [Fr: *fem.* **fausse**] *foh* (*fohs*) false, sham, counterfeit;
—**pas** (*-PAH*) false step; blunder.

fava [It: *pl.* **fave**] *FAH-vah* (*-veh*) broad bean.

favela [Port] *fuh-VEH-luh.* in Brazil, a shantytown or slum.

favete linguis [Lat] *fah-VEH-teh-LEEN-gwees.* (*lit.*, favor
with your tongues) be silent.

Fazit [Ger, from Lat *facit*, it makes] *FAH-tseet.* (*arith.*)
result; sum; product. Also, **Facit.**

fazzoletto [It] *fah-tsoh-LAYT-toh.* handkerchief.

fe [Sp]; **fé** [Port] *feh.* faith.

Februa [Lat] *FEH-broo-ah.* Roman festival of purification
and expiation, celebrated in February.

fecha [Sp] *FEH-chah.* date; day of the month.

fecit [Lat] *FEH-keet.* he made (it): often affixed to an artist's work.

Feiertag [Ger: *pl.* **Feiertage**] *FY-uh-tak* (*-tah-guh*) holiday.

feijoada [Port] *fay-ZHWAH-duh.* dish of beans and pork.

feis [Gael] *fesh.* Irish song festival.

Feld [Ger] *felt.* field.

Feldherr [Ger] *FELT-hehr.* (*mil.*) general.

feliciter [Lat] *feh-LEE-kee-tehr.* happily, fortunately.

felis [Lat] *FEH-lees.* cat; member of the feline family.

felix [Lat: *pl.* **felices**] *FEH-leeks* (*-LEE-kes*) happy, fortunate; —**culpa** (*-KOOL-pah*) O fault most fortunate!: St. Augustine's reference to original sin, which made possible the redemption in Christ.

fellah [Ar: *pl.* **fellahīn**] *fel-LAH* (*-lah-HEEN*) peasant; farmer.

Fels [Ger: *pl.* **Felsen**] *fels* (*FEL-s'n*) rock; cliff.

felucca [Sp *faluca,* from Ar *fulūk,* pl. of *fulk,* ship] kind of sailing vessel used in the Mediterranean and on the Spanish and Portuguese coasts.

femme [Fr] *fahm.* woman, wife; —**couverte** (*-koo-VEHRT*) (*law*) married woman; —**C.** (*FEM-SEE*) mistress of ceremonies (after M.C., master of ceremonies); —**de chambre** (*-duh-SHÃ-bruh*) chambermaid; —**fatale** (*-fah-TAHL*) enchantress; vamp; seductive woman; —**incomprise** (*-ē-kō-PREEZ*) unappreciated, misunderstood woman; —**savante** (*-sah-VÃT*) intellectual woman; bluestocking; —**sole** (*-SOHL*) (*law*) unmarried woman.

fer [Fr, from Lat **ferrum**] *fehr.* iron.

feria [Sp] *FEH-ryah.* fair; fiesta; festival.

Feringhi [Pers *Farangī,* Ar *Faranjī; lit.,* Frank] *feh-REEN-gee.* in the Near and Middle East, a European or person of European descent.

Feringhistan [Pers *Farangistan; lit.,* country of the Franks] *feh-REEN-gee-stahn.* Europe.

fermata [It, from *fermare,* to stop] *fehr-MAH-tah.* (*music*) hold; pause.

ferme [Fr] *fehrm.* farm.

fermé [Fr: *fem.* **fermée**] *fehr-MAY.* closed; shut.

fermez [Fr] *fehr-MAY.* close; shut; —**la bouche** (*-lah-*

BOOSH) close your mouth; shut up; —**la porte** (*-PORT*) close the door.

ferro [It, from Lat **ferrum**] *FEHR-roh.* iron.

ferrocarril [Sp] *fehr-roh-kar-REEL.* railroad.

ferrovia [It] *fehr-roh-VEE-ah.* railroad.

ferrum [Lat] *FEHR-room.* iron; horseshoe.

fertig [Ger] *FEHR-tiç.* ready; prepared; skilled.

Fertigkeit [Ger] *FEHR-tiç-kyt.* dexterity, skill; (*music*) technical virtuosity.

fervet opus [Lat] *FEHR-vet-OH-poos.* the work goes on apace.

festa [It] *FES-tah.* festival, feast, holiday; —**del Grillo** (*-del-GREEL-loh*) Feast of the Cricket, an annual Florentine festival; —**del Lavoro** (*-del-lah-VOH-roh*) Italian Labor Day, April 21; —**dello Statuto** (*-del-loh-stah-TOO-toh*) Constitution Day, celebrating the granting of the Italian constitution; —**del Redentore** (*-del-reh-den-TOH-reh*) feast of the Redeemer, annual Venetian festival.

festina lente [Lat] *fes-TEE-nah-LEN-teh.* make haste slowly.

festivamente [It] *fes-tee-vah-MAYN-teh.* (*music*) festively, gaily.

Festschrift [Ger] *FEST-shrift.* memorial or commemorative volume, often published upon recipient's retirement.

Festspielhaus [Ger] *FEST-shpeel-hows.* carnival playhouse; theater, esp. a theater in Bayreuth, Germany, built in 1876 for performing Wagner's operas.

Festung Europa [Ger] *FEST-oong-ö-ROH-pah.* Fortress Europe: German-occupied Europe of World War II.

fête [Fr] *fet.* festival, feast; celebration; (in English, as a verb) to celebrate, give a party in honor of; —**champêtre** (*-shã-PEH-truh*) outdoor festival; —**nationale** (*-nah-syoh-NAHL*) national holiday.

fettuccine [It, dim. pl. of *fetta*, slice, strip] *fet-too-CHEE-neh.* noodles in long, thin strips, usu. served with butter and grated cheese.

feu [Fr: *pl.* **feux**] *fö.* fire; deceased (preceding the name of a dead person); —**d'artifice** (*-dar-tee-FEES*) fireworks;

—de joie (*-duh-ZHWAH*) (*lit.*, fire of joy) bonfire; salute of firearms in celebration of a victory or joyous event.

Feuer [Ger] *FOY-uh*. fire; passion.

feuille [Fr] *FÖ-yuh*. leaf; sheet; folio.

feuilleton [Fr] *fö-yuh-TÕ*. regularly published literary column in a newspaper; serially published novel; literary review.

fève [Fr] *fev*. broad bean.

ff. Abbr. of **fortissimo.**

fiacre [Fr] *FYAH-kruh*. cab; hackney.

fiancé [Fr: *fem.* **fiancée**] *fyā-SAY*. betrothed; engaged.

Fianna Fail [Ir] *FEE-uh-nuh-FOYL*. (*lit.*, Fenians of the sod) Irish political party founded in 1927 by Eamon de Valera.

fiasco [It] *FYAHS-koh*. (*lit.*, flask, wine bottle) failure; flop; ruin.

fiat [Lat: let it be done] *FEE-aht*. authoritative decree or order, esp. one given by an individual or group holding absolute power; **—lux** (*-looks*) let there be light; **—voluntas tua** (*-voh-LOON-tahs-TOO-ah*) thy will be done.

fichu [Fr] *fee-SHÜ*. triangular scarf; neckerchief.

fidalgo [Port] *fee-DAHL-goo*. noble; gentleman. Cf. **hidalgo.**

fide [Lat, abl. of *fides*, faith] *FEE-deh*. by faith; **—et amore** (*-et-ah-MOH-reh*) by faith and love; **—et fiducia** (*-et-fee-DOO-kee-ah*) by faith and trust.

fidei commissum [Lat] *fee-DEH-ee-kohm-MEES-soom*. bequeathed in trust.

Fidei defensor [Lat] *fee-DEH-ee-deh-FEN-sor*. defender of the faith.

fidelismo [Sp] *fee-deh-LEES-moh*. beliefs of Fidel Castro's Cuban followers; Castroism.

fides punica [Lat] *FEE-des-POO-nee-kah*. Punic faith, i.e., treachery.

fi donc [Fr] *FEE-dõk*. for shame!, fie!

fiducia [Lat: confidence, trust] *fee-DOO-kee-ah*. mortgage; pledge, vow.

fidus Achates [Lat] *FEE-doos-ah-KAH-tes*. faithful Achates; faithful, trustworthy friend.

Fiera del Levante [It] *FYEH-rah-del-leh-VAHN-teh.* Fair of the Orient: annual fair of Eastern nations held in Bari, Italy.

fieramente [It] *fyeh-rah-MAYN-teh.* (*music*) with fire; fiercely; proudly.

fieri facias [It] *FEE-eh-ree-FAH-kee-ahs.* (*lit.*, make it be done) (*law*) a writ ordering execution of a judgment against a debtor.

fiesta [Sp] *FYES-tah.* feast; festival; celebration; holiday.

Figaro [Fr] *fee-gah-ROH.* shrewd, clever manservant, as typified in Beaumarchais' *The Barber of Seville*; a major Paris newspaper.

figlia [It: *pl.* **figlie**] *FEE-lyah* (*-lyeh*) daughter; child.

figlio [It: *pl.* **figli**] *FEE-lyoh* (*-lyee*) son; child; —**di papà** (*dee-pah-PAH*) (*lit.*, papa's boy) mama's boy; playboy; wealthy man's do-nothing son.

figurant [Fr: *fem.* **figurante**] *fee-gü-RĂ* (*-RĂT*) ballet dancer who appears only in a group or ensemble; supernumerary.

fijo de algo [Sp] *FEE-hoh-deh-AHL-goh.* older form of **hidalgo**.

filar la voce [It] *fee-LAR-lah-VOH-cheh.* (*music*) to "wind out" the voice, sustaining and gradually decreasing the volume of a note.

filet [Fr] *fee-LAY.* strip of boneless fish or meat; steak, fillet; —**mignon** (*-mee-NYŎ*) (*lit.*, dainty or delicate steak) tenderloin steak.

filius [Lat: *pl.* **filii** or **fili**] *FEE-lee-oos* (*-ee*) son; —**est pars patris** (*-est-pars-PAH-trees*) the son is part of the father; —**nullius** (*-nool-LEE-oos*) (*lit.*, the son of no one) a bastard.

fille [Fr] *FEE-yuh.* daughter; young girl; maiden; —**de joie** (*-duh-ZHWAH*) (*lit.*, daughter of joy) woman of pleasure; courtesan; prostitute; —**d'honneur** (*-duh-NÖR*) maid of honor.

filon [Fr] *fee-LŎ.* metallic vein; lode.

fils [Fr: *pl.* **fils**] *fees.* son; —**à papa** (*-ah-pah-PAH*) (*lit.*, papa's boy) mama's boy; playboy; wealthy man's do-nothing son; —**naturel** (*-nah-tü-REL*) natural son.

fin [Fr] *fẽ.* end; finish; closing.

financière [Fr, fem. from *financier,* financier] *fee-nã-SYEHR.* spicy stew.

finca [Sp] *FEEN-kah.* farm; plantation; ranch.

fin de siècle [Fr] *FẼ-duh-SYEH-kluh.* (*lit.,* end of the century) decadent era; era of relaxed morality and customs.

fine [It] *FEE-neh.* (*fem.*) end; finish; closing; (*masc.*) purpose.

fine champagne [Fr] *FEEN-shã-PAH-nyuh.* brandy; cognac.

fine épice [Fr] *FEEN-ay-PEES.* (*lit.,* fine spice) sharp fellow; wit.

fines herbes [Fr] *feen-ZEHRB.* (*lit.,* fine herbs) minced chives, parsley, etc.

finis [Lat] *FEE-nees.* end; finish.

finocchio [It] *fee-NOHK-kyoh.* fennel.

fioco [It] *FYOH-koh.* (*music*) faint, low.

fiord. See **fjord.**

fiore [It: *pl.* **fiori**] *FYOH-reh* (*-ree*) flower.

fioreggiante [It] *fyoh-reh-JAHN-teh.* (*music*) floridly, vividly.

fiorito [Lat] *fyoh-REE-toh.* (*music*) florid; flowery.

firma [Sp, It] *FEER-mah.* signature.

firman [Turk *ferman,* from Pers] *feer-MAHN.* passport; special decree of a sovereign, esp., formerly, of a sultan of the Ottoman Empire.

firme [Sp] *FEER-meh.* pavement; roadbed.

fiscus [Lat] *FEES-koos.* (*lit.,* basket) treasury.

Fitz [Anglo-Fr *filz,* son] *fits.* son of: patronymic particle prefixed to family names.

fiumara [It, from *fiume,* river] *fyoo-MAH-rah.* gushing river; torrent; crowd. Also, in last meaning, **fiumana** (*-nah*).

fiume [It] *FYOO-meh.* river; stream.

fjord [Norw] *fyord.* long, narrow inlet banked by high cliffs. Also, **fiord.**

fl. Abbr. of **floruit.**

flacon [Fr] *flah-KÕ.* vial; flask; flagon.

flagellum [Lat] *flah-GEL-loom*. whip; whiplike tail.

flagrante delicto [Lat] *flah-GRAHN-teh-deh-LEEK-toh*. in the act of the crime; red-handed.

Flak [Ger, abbr. of *Fl(ieger)-a(bwehr)-k(annone)*, antiaircraft gun] *flak*. antiaircraft fire.

flambé [Fr] *flä-BAY*. flaming; singed; a dish served with flaming rum or brandy.

flamen [Lat] *FLAH-men*. in ancient Rome, a priest serving a particular deity.

flamenco [Sp, orig. Fleming] *flah-MEN-koh*. Gypsy style; of Gypsy origin, esp. a style of music and dancing of Andalusia.

Flammenwerfer [Ger] *FLAH-m'n-vehr-fuh*. flamethrower.

flan [Fr] *flä*. rich custard tart; [Sp] *flahn*. sweetened egg custard.

Flasche [Ger] *FLAH-shuh*. flask; bottle; vial.

flebile [It] *FLEH-bee-leh*. (*music*) mournful; plaintive.

flebilmente [It] *fleh-beel-MAYN-teh*. mournfully; feebly.

flèche [Fr] *flesh*. arrow; spire.

fléchette [Fr] *flay-SHET*. dart.

Fledermaus [Ger] *FLAY-duh-mows*. bat.

fleur [Fr] *flör*. flower; — -de-lis (*-duh-LEE*) (*pl.* **fleurs-de-lis**) lily flower: royal emblem of France. Also, **fleur-de-lys.**

fleuret [Fr] *flö-REH*. fencing foil.

fleuve [Fr] *flöv*. river; stream.

flocculus [Lat, dim. of *floccus*, tuft of wool] *FLOHK-koo-loos*. a bright or dark spot on the sun's surface.

flora [Lat, from *flos*, flower] *FLOH-rah*. the plants of a given region or period, taken collectively. Cf. **fauna.**

flores [Lat, pl. of *flos*] *FLOH-res*. flowers.

florido [Sp: *fem.* **florida**] *floh-REE-doh* (*-dah*) flowery; blooming.

florilegium [Lat] *floh-ree-LEH-gee-oom*. collection of flowers; anthology.

floruit [Lat: *abbr.* **fl.**] *FLOH-roo-eet*. (he) flourished.

Flugschrift [Ger] *FLOOK-shrift*. pamphlet; brochure; broadside.

flûte [Fr] *flüt*. (*lit.*, flute) damn!

fluvius [Lat] *FLOO-vee-oos.* river; flood; of or pertaining to a river.

foedus [Lat] *FOY-doos.* league; pact.

Foehn [Ger] *fön.* warm, dry wind of Alpine regions. Also, **Föhn.**

foetus [Lat] *FOY-toos.* embryo; fetus.

foi [Fr] *fwah.* faith; **ma—!** goodness! heavens!

foie [Fr] *fwah.* liver; **—gras** (*-grah*) livers of fattened geese.

Folketing [Dan, from *folk*, people + *t(h)ing*, assembly] *FOHL-kuh-ting.* the parliament of Denmark. Also, **Folkething.**

folle. See **fou.**

fonda [Sp] *FOHN-dah.* hotel; restaurant; inn.

fondant [Fr, pr.p. of *fondre*, to melt] *fõ-DÃ.* creamy, rich candy made with melted sugar; sugar base used in making fondant.

fondu [Fr, p.p. of *fondre*, to melt] *fõ-DÜ.* ballet movement executed by standing on one leg and slowly bending the supporting leg.

fondue [Fr, fem. p.p. of *fondre*, to melt] *fõ-DÜ.* melted cheese or dip dish.

fontein [Du] *FOHN-tayn.* spring; fountain.

force de frappe [Fr] *FORS-duh-FRAHP.* nuclear striking force; **force de dissuasion** (*-duh-dee-süah-ZYŎ*) deterrent force; **force majeure** (*-mah-ZHÖR*) superior force; compelling circumstance; **force ouvrière** (*-oo-VRYEHR*) working force; labor unions.

Forelle [Ger] *foh-REL-leh.* trout.

forensis [Lat] *foh-REN-sees.* pertaining to the court or forum; public; forensic.

forfait [Fr] *for-FEH.* crime, transgression; contract under penalty of forfeit.

forlana [It] *for-LAH-nah.* pantomime dance performed by a trio.

forma [Lat] *FOR-mah.* form, shape; appearance; beauty.

formaggio [It] *for-MAHJ-joh.* cheese.

Formenlehre [Ger] *FOR-m'n-leh-reh.* (*ling.*) morphology.

formid [Fr, abbr. of *formidable*] *for-MEED.* (*slang*) splendid! great!

Foro Romano [It] *FOH-roh-roh-MAH-noh.* Roman Forum.

Forsan et haec olim meminisse juvabit [Lat] *FOR-sahn-et-HYK-OH-leem-meh-mee-NEES-seh-yoo-VAH-beet.* Perhaps it will be a joy later to remember these things.

Forschung [Ger] *FOR-shoong.* investigation; research; probe.

fort [Fr] *for.* strong; loud; strong point or feature; talent; ability.

forte [It: *abbr.* **f.**] *FOR-teh.* (*music*) loud; strong point or feature; talent; ability.

forte-piano [It: *abbr.* **fp.**] *FOR-teh-PYAH-noh.* (*music*) loud followed by soft.

fortes fortuna juvat [Lat] *FOR-tes-for-TOO-nah-YOO-vaht.* fortune favors the brave.

fortiori. *See* **a fortiori.**

fortissimo [It: *abbr.* **ff.**] *for-TEES-see-moh.* (*music*) very loud.

fortiter, fideliter, feliciter [Lat] *FOR-tee-tehr-fee-DEH-lee-tehr-feh-LEE-kee-tehr.* bravely, faithfully, happily.

fortiter in re, sed suaviter in modo [Lat] *FOR-tee-tehr-een-REH-sed-SWAH-vee-tehr-een-MOH-doh.* strong in action, but gentle in manner.

fortuna caeca est [Lat] *for-TOO-nah-KY-kah-est.* luck is blind.

fortuna fortes juvat. See **fortes fortuna juvat.**

forza [It] *FOR-tsah.* (*music*) force; power.

forzando [It] *for-TSAHN-doh.* (*music*) forced; accented.

fou [Fr: *fem.* **folle**] *foo* (*fohl*) fool; crazy, mad.

fouetté [Fr] *fweh-TAY.* ballet step in which one leg is swung and snapped at the finish.

foulard [Fr] *foo-LAR.* soft, printed silk, cotton or rayon fabric used for neckties, neckerchiefs, etc.

foule [Fr] *fool.* crowd; mob, rabble.

four [Fr] *foor.* oven.

fourchette [Fr] *foor-SHET.* fork.

fourreau [Fr] *foo-ROH.* sheath; scabbard; cover.

foyer [Fr] *fwah-YAY*. hearth; fire, fireside; home, family; entrance hall, lobby, foyer.

fp. Abbr. of **forte-piano**.

fra [It] *frah*. between; among; within; brother: title of a priest or friar. Cf. **frate**.

Fra Diavolo [It] *frah-DYAH-voh-loh*. (*lit.*, Brother Devil) nickname of a famous bandit leader; a spicy sauce with tomatoes, garlic, oregano, etc., often used for lobster and other seafood.

fraise [Fr] *frez*. strawberry.

Fraktur [Ger: *lit.*, fracture, with reference to the curlicues that break up the continuous line of type] *frahk-TOOR*. Gothic letters; older German alphabet.

framboise [Fr] *frã-BWAHZ*. raspberry.

France d'Outremer [Fr] *FRÃS-doo-truh-MEHR*. Overseas France: the loose union that binds former French colonial possessions together and with France.

franc-tireur [Fr: *pl.* **francs-tireurs**] *FRÃ-tee-RÖR*. sharpshooter; sniper, guerrilla fighter, esp. in the Franco-Prussian War of 1870.

Franglais [Fr *français*, French + *anglais*, English] *frã-GLEH*. a jargon of mixed French and English, with copious Anglo-American borrowings superimposed on a French base.

fra poco [It] *frah-POH-koh*. in a little while; soon.

frappé [Fr] *frah-PAY*. whipped; frozen; iced; a dessert prepared in this manner.

frate [It] *FRAH-teh*. brother; friar, monk; padre.

frater [Lat: *pl.* **fratres**] *FRAH-tehr* (*-tres*) brother.

Frau [Ger: *pl.* **Frauen**] *frow* (*FROW'n*) woman; lady; madam, Mrs.; wife.

Fräulein [Ger] *FROY-lyn*. young lady; miss.

frei [Ger] *fry*. free.

Freiheit [Ger] *FRY-hyt*. freedom, liberty; **—ist nur in dem Reich der Träume** (*-ist-NOOR-in-dem-RYÇ-dehr-TROY-muh*) freedom exists only in the world of dreams.

Freiherr [Ger: *pl.* **Freiherren**] *FRY-hehr* (*-'n*) (*lit.*, free man) a baron in Germany or Austria.

Freischütz [Ger] *FRY-shüts*. hunter; marksman.

fremd [Ger: *pl.* **Fremde**] *fremt* (*FREM-deh*) foreign; alien, strange; stranger, foreigner; guest.

frère [Fr] *frehr.* brother; friar, monk.

fresco [It] *FRAYS-koh.* (*lit.*, fresh) painting done on a wet-lime plaster surface. Also, **affresco**.

Freude [Ger] *FROY-deh.* joy; gladness.

friandise [Fr] *free-ä-DEEZ.* sweetmeat; delicacy; taste for delicacies; epicurean taste.

fricandeau [Fr] *free-kä-DOH.* veal stew.

fricassé [Fr, from *frire,* to fry] *free-kah-SAY.* meat or fowl sautéed and stewed, and served in a sauce.

frijol [Sp: *pl.* **frijoles**] *free-HOHL* (*-HOH-les*) kidney bean.

frisch [Ger] *frish.* (*music*) fresh; lively; —**gewagt ist halb gewonnen** (*-guh-VAHKHT-ist-hahlp-guh-VOHN'n*) a good beginning is half the battle.

friseur [Fr, from *friser,* to curl; *fem.* **friseuse**] *free-ZÖR* (*-ZÖZ*) hairdresser.

frisson [Fr] *free-SÕ.* shiver; thrill.

frit [Fr: *fem.* **frite**] (*free, freet*) fried; ruined, done for.

fritos [Sp] *FREE-tohs.* fried potatoes; potato flakes or chips.

fritto misto [It] *FREET-toh-MEES-toh.* (*lit.,* mixed fry) dish of meat, fowl, fish or vegetables, diced, dipped in batter and deep-fried.

friture [Fr] *free-TÜR.* fried food; fry.

fromage [Fr] *froh-MAHZH.* cheese.

Fronde [Fr] *frõd.* (*lit.,* sling) during the minority of Louis XIV, a party of French nobles and members of the Paris parliament that unsuccessfully revolted against the authority of the Prime Minister, Cardinal Mazarin.

frontón [Sp] *frohn-TOHN.* court for playing jai alai.

Front Populaire [Fr] *FRÕ-poh-pü-LEHR.* Popular Front: merger of French left-wing parties.

frottola [It] *FROHT-toh-lah.* popular ballad; humbug, nonsense.

froufrou [Fr] *froo-FROO.* swishing or rustling of a full skirt or silk fabric; elaborate decoration of ribbons, ruffles, etc.

fructus [Lat] *FROOK-toos.* fruit; profit; harvest.

früh [Ger] *frü.* early.

Frühlingslied [Ger] *FRÜ-links-leet.* spring song.

Frühstück [Ger] *FRÜ-shtük.* breakfast.

frustra [Lat] *FROOS-trah.* in vain.

frutta [It] *FROOT-tah.* fruit; fruits.

fuego [Sp] *FWEH-goh.* fire.

Fuehrer. See **Führer.**

fuente [Sp] *FWEN-teh.* fountain, spring; source.

fuero [Sp, from Lat *forum*] *FWEH-roh.* statute; body of laws; jurisdiction, authority; exemption, privilege.

fuerza [Sp] *FWER-sah.* force; power; strength.

fuése por lana, y volvió trasquilada [Sp] *FWEH-seh-por-LAH-nah-ee-vohl-VYOH-trahs-kee-LAH-dah.* she went for wool, and came back shorn.

fuga [It] *FOO-gah.* (*lit.*, flight) fugue.

fugaces labuntur anni [Lat] *foo-GAH-kes-lah-BOON-toor-AHN-nee.* the years glide swiftly on.

fugato [It] *foo-GAH-toh.* (*music*) like a fugue; in fugue style.

fughetta [It, dim. of *fuga*, fugue] *foo-GAYT-tah.* (*music*) brief fugue.

fugit hora [Lat] *FOO-geet-HOH-rah.* the hour flies; time flies.

Führer [Ger] *FÜ-ruh.* leader: title of Adolf Hitler. Also, **Fuehrer.**

Führerprinzip [Ger] *FÜ-ruh-prin-tseep.* principles of the Leader; belief that the Leader's will is the will of the people.

fulano [Sp, from Ar *fulān*, such] *foo-LAH-noh.* John Doe; so-and-so. Also, **—de tal** (*-deh-TAHL*); **—, zutano y mengano** (*-soo-TAH-noh-ee-men-GAH-noh*) Tom, Dick and Harry.

funicolare [It, from *fune*, rope, cable] *foo-nee-koh-LAH-reh.* funicular; cable railway.

fuoco [It] *FWOH-koh.* fire; (*music*) passion; fire.

furiosamente [It] *foo-ryoh-sah-MAYN-teh.* furiously; passionately.

furioso [It] *foo-RYOH-soh.* (*music*) furious; passionate.

furlana [It, from *friulana*, Friulian] *foor-LAH-nah.* lively Friulian and Venetian dance.

Fürst [Ger] *fürst*. prince.
fusil [Fr] *fü-ZEE*. gun; rifle.

G

gabelle [Fr] *gah-BEL*. tax; excise; in pre-Revolutionary France, a tax on salt.

gabinetto [It] *gah-bee-NAYT-toh*. cabinet; small room or office; toilet, water closet.

gaffe [Fr] *gahf*. blunder; faux pas; boathook.

gaga [Fr] *gah-GAH*. senile; out-of-date.

gaieté [Fr] *gay-TAY*. gaiety. Also, gaîté.

gaita [Sp] *GY-tah*. bagpipe.

gaku [Jap] *GAH-koo*. picture on a stretched frame.

galant [Fr] *gah-LÃ*. gallant; gentleman; sweetheart, suitor.

galantuomo [It: *pl.* galantuomini] *gah-lahn-TWOH-moh* (*-mee-nee*) gallant, gentleman; dandy, fop; honest man, square dealer.

galeón [Sp] *gah-leh-OHN*. ship; galleon.

galette [Fr] *gah-LET*. light cake; biscuit; pancake.

galinha [Port] *guh-LEE-nyuh*. hen; chicken.

gallego [Sp] *gah-LYEH-goh*. Galician; language of Galicia, northwestern Spanish province, closely related to Portuguese; native or inhabitant of Galicia.

gallicum [Lat, from *Gallia*, Gaul] *GAHL-lee-koom*. the Gaulish language; the French language; gallice (*GAHL-lee-keh*) in Gaulish; in French.

gallo [Sp] *GAH-lyoh*. cock, rooster; cockfight.

gamin [Fr: *fem.* gamine] *gah-MÃ* (*-MEEN*) urchin; pert child.

ganado [Sp] *gah-NAH-doh*. cattle; livestock.

ganef [Yid, from Heb *gannābh*] *GAH-nuf*. thief, swindler. Also, ganev, ganof, ganov, gonif(f), gonoph.

gant [Fr] *gã*. glove.

garaje [Sp] *gah-RAH-heh*. garage.

garbanzo [Sp] *gar-BAHN-soh*. chickpea; ceci bean.

garbure [Fr] *gar-BÜR*. Gascon soup made of cabbage and other vegetables, slices of various meats, and bread.

garçon [Fr] *gar-SŎ*. boy; waiter.

garde [Fr] *gard*. guard; —**champêtre** (*-shã-PEH-truh*) gamekeeper; game warden; —**de nuit** (*-duh-NÜEE*) night watchman; —**du corps** (*-dü-KOR*) bodyguard; —**nationale** (*-nah-syoh-NAHL*) national guard; militia.

gare [Fr] *gar*. railroad station; (*interj.*) look out! beware!; **chef de—** (*SHEH-duh-*) stationmaster.

garni [Fr] *gar-NEE*. furnished; garnished.

garrafa [Sp] *gar-RAH-fah*. bottle; decanter; carafe; [Port] *gur-RAH-fuh*.

garrafón [Sp] *gar-rah-FOHN*. demijohn.

garrote [Sp] *gar-ROH-teh*. club; big stick; death by strangulation or hanging.

gasconnade [Fr, from *Gascon*, Gascon, allegedly noted for bragging] *gahs-kuh-NAHD*. boasting; braggadocio.

Gasse [Ger] *GAH-seh*. street; lane; alley.

Gasthaus [Ger] *GAHST-hows*. guest house; inn; tavern.

Gasthof [Ger] *GAHST-hohf*. hotel; guest house.

gâteau [Fr] *gah-TOH*. cake; cookie.

gato [Sp: *fem.* **gata**] *GAH-toh* (*-tah*) cat.

gato escaldado da água fria tem medo [Port] *GAH-too-'shkuhl-DAH-doo-DAH-gwuh-FREE-uh-tê-MEH-doo*. a scalded cat fears even cold water; a burnt child dreads the fire.

Gau [Ger] *gow*. district; administrative division of the Nazi party.

gauche [Fr] *gohsh*. (*lit.*, left) clumsy, maladroit; **la—** (*lah-*) the political Left.

gaucherie [Fr] *goh-sh'REE*. clumsiness; tactlessness; awkward or tasteless action.

gaucho [AmerSp, perh. from Arawak *cachu*, comrade] *GOW-choh*. cowboy of the pampas of southern S America.

gaudeamus igitur [Lat] *gow-deh-AH-moos-EE-gee-toor*. let us therefore rejoice: first words and title of a popular international student song.

Gauleiter [Ger] *GOW-ly-tuh.* head of a Nazi district or administrative division.

Gautama [Skt *gautama, gotama*] *GOW-tuh-muh.* epithet of Buddha. Also, **Gotama** (*GOH-*).

gavotte [Fr, from *gavot,* mountaineer, hillbilly] *gah-VOHT.* old French dance in moderately fast tempo.

gavroche [Fr] *gah-VROHSH.* street urchin; gamin.

gazpacho [Sp] *gahs-PAH-choh.* cold vegetable soup.

gazzetta [It, from the name of a Venetian coin, orig. the price of the newspaper] *gah-DZAYT-tah.* gazette; journal; newspaper.

Gebet [Ger] *guh-BAYT.* prayer.

Gebirg [Ger, *usu. pl.* **Gebirge**] *guh-BEERK* (*-BEER-geh*) mountain; mountain range.

geboren [Ger] *guh-BOR'n.* born.

Gebrauchsmusik [Ger] *guh-BROWKHS-moo-zeek.* (*lit.,* music for use) music intended for nonprofessional performance.

Gebrüder [Ger] *guh-BRÜ-duh.* brothers.

Geburt [Ger] *guh-BOORT.* birth.

Geburtstag [Ger] *guh-BOORTS-tak.* birthday.

gedämpft [Ger] *guh-DEMPFT.* (*music*) muted; damped.

Gedicht [Ger] *guh-DIÇT.* poem.

gefilte fish [Yid, from Ger *gefüllte Fische,* stuffed fish] *guh-FIL-tuh-fish.* minced fish blended with eggs, matzoth meal and seasoning, shaped into balls or sticks, and cooked in vegetable broth.

Gefühl [Ger] *guh-FÜL.* feeling; sensation; expression in song or theatrical performance.

Gegenreformation [Ger] *GAY-g'n-reh-for-mah-tsyohn.* Counter-Reformation.

Gegenstand [Ger: *pl.* **Gegenstände**] *GAY-g'n-shtahnt* (*-shten-duh*) object; subject; item.

Gegenwart [Ger] *GAY-g'n-vart.* now; present time.

Gehalt [Ger] *guh-HAHLT.* contents; wages.

Geheime Staatspolizei [Ger] *guh-HY-meh-SHTAHTS-poh-li-tsy.* secret police; Gestapo.

gehend [Ger, pr.p. of *gehen,* to go, walk] *GAY'nt.* (*music*) at walking speed; andante.

Gehenna [Heb] *geh-HEN-nah.* biblical place of misery or hell.

geisha [Jap] *GAY-shah.* Japanese professional girl entertainer.

Geist [Ger] *gyst.* soul; spirit; sensibilities.

Geisteswissenschaften [Ger] *GYST's-vis'n-shahf-t'n.* the social or historical sciences.

gelato [It] *jeh-LAH-toh.* ice cream; ice-sherbet.

Geld [Ger] *gelt.* money.

gelée [Fr, from *geler*, to freeze] *zhuh-LAY.* jellied; jelly.

Gelehrter [Ger] *guh-LEHR-tuh.* learned man, savant; scholar.

Gemeinschaft [Ger] *guh-MYN-shahft.* community; partnership, association.

Gemini [Lat] *GEH-mee-nee.* the twins: a sign of the Zodiac.

gemütlich [Ger] *guh-MÜT-liç.* good-natured, congenial; **Gemütlichkeit** (*-kyt*) congeniality, coziness.

gendarme [Fr] *zhã-DARM.* policeman, constable.

gendarmerie [Fr] *zhã-dar-muh-REE.* police; police force.

generalísimo [Sp] *heh-neh-rah-LEE-see-moh*; **generalissimo** [It] *jeh-neh-rah-LEES-see-moh.* supreme commander.

genitor [Lat] *GEH-nee-tor.* progenitor; father.

genius loci [Lat] *GEH-nee-oos-LOH-kee.* guardian deity of a place; local god; the particular character of a place.

genre [Fr] *ZHÃ-ruh.* kind, sort, species; paintings in realistic style depicting scenes of everyday life.

gens [Lat] *gens.* clan, tribe; people; [Fr] *zhã.* people, persons.

gentil [Fr: *fem.* **gentille**] *zha-TEE* (*-yuh*) noble, gentle; pretty, graceful; amiable.

gentile [It] *jen-TEE-leh.* noble, gentle; well-bred, polite; elegant, graceful; amiable, kind.

gentilhomme [Fr] *zhã-tee-YOHM.* gentleman; nobleman.

genus homo [Lat] *GEH-noos-HOH-moh.* genus of man: the human race.

Geopolitik [Gk] *geh-oh-poh-lee-TEEK.* geopolitics, the study of the relationship of politics to geography; a national policy based on geopolitics.

georgette [Fr] *jor-JET.* light silk or rayon fabric having a dull finish.

gepanzerte Faust [Ger] *guh-PAHN-tsur-teh-FOWST.* mailed fist.

gerade aus [Ger] *guh-RAH-deh-OWS.* onward! straight ahead!

gérant [Fr] *zhay-RÃ.* manager; editor.

geräuchert [Ger: *pl.* **geräucherte**] *guh-ROY-çurt* (*-teh*) smoked; cured by smoking; **geräucherte Heringe** (*-HEH-reen-geh*) smoked herring.

Germania [Lat] *gehr-MAH-nee-ah.* Germany; feminine figure symbolical of Germany.

germen [Lat] *GEHR-men.* germ; seed; bud; offshoot.

gerousia [Gk, from *gerōn*, old man] *geh-roo-SEE-ah.* senate; council of elders, esp. at Sparta.

gesammelt [Ger] *guh-ZAH-m'lt.* gathered; compiled, collected.

Gesang [Ger] *guh-ZAHNG.* singing; song.

Geschichte [Ger] *guh-SHIÇ-tuh.* history.

geschichtlich [Ger] *guh-SHIÇT-liç.* historical.

Geschlecht [Ger] *guh-SHLEÇT.* sex; gender; race; kind, genus.

Geschwister [Ger] *guh-SHVIS-tuh.* brothers and sisters; siblings.

Gesellschaft [Ger] *guh-ZEL-shahft.* association; company.

gesso [It] *JES-soh.* chalk; plaster; prepared ground for canvases for painting.

Gestalt [Ger] *guh-SHTAHLT.* configuration; unified whole not derivable from the sum of the parts.

Gestapo [Ger] *guh-SHTAH-poh.* Abbr. of **geheime Staatspolizei.**

Gesta Romanorum [Lat] *GES-tah-roh-mah-NOH-room.* Deeds of the Romans: a collection of stories about the period of the Roman Emperors.

gestern [Ger] *GES-turn.* yesterday.

gestorben [Ger, p.p. of *sterben*, to die] *guh-SHTOR-b'n.* deceased; dead.

Gesundheit [Ger] *guh-ZOONT-hyt.* health; God bless you!; here's how!

get [Yid, from Aramaic] *get.* divorce; bill of divorcement.

geta [Jap] *GEH-tah.* wooden sandal mounted on two cross-pieces.

Gewehr [Ger] *guh-VEHR.* weapon; gun, rifle.

ghat [Hindi *ghāṭ*] *gawt.* stairway or passage leading down to a river bank; landing; mountain range. Also, **ghaut.**

ghazal [Ar] *guh-ZAHL.* Persian lyric poem.

ghazi [Ar] *GAH-zee.* soldier; champion, conqueror: title of Mustapha Kemal.

ghee [Hindi *ghī*] *gee.* clarified liquid butter from milk of cows or buffaloes.

ghetto [It, perh. from Heb *get*, divorcement, or from It *borghetto*, small city section or borough] *GET-toh.* crowded slum quarter where a minority group is forced to live; any disadvantaged area.

ghibellino [It, from *Waiblingen*, princely estate in Germany] *gee-bel-LEE-noh.* Ghibelline: member of the imperial party in medieval Italy, opposed to the Guelphs. Cf. **guelfo.**

ghiribizzoso [It] *gee-ree-bee-TSOH-soh.* (*music*) capricious; whimsical.

giaour [Turk *giaur*, from Pers *gaur*] *jowr.* infidel; non-Moslem; Christian.

gibier [Fr] *zhee-BYAY.* game; animals hunted as game.

gigolo [Fr slang: fancy man] *zhee-goh-LOH.* a man paid to be a dancing partner or companion.

gigot [Fr] *zhee-GOH.* leg of lamb or mutton; leg-o'-mutton sleeve.

gigue [Fr, from It *giga*, fiddle] *zheeg.* high-pitched viol used by French minstrels; lively dance, jig.

Gilgamesh [Sumerian] *GEEL-gah-mesh.* Sumerian epic, about 2000 B.C.; mythical king of Babylon.

gillie [Scot, from Gael *gille*, lad, servant] *GIL-ee.* attendant; hunting or fishing guide; shoe or slipper laced at the ankle.

ginkgo [Jap *ginkyo*: *gin*, silver + *kyo*, apricot] *GINK-goh.* large Oriental tree with fan-shaped leaves, producing edible nuts. Also, **gingko.**

ginnasio [It, orig. gymnasium] *jeen-NAH-syoh.* academic high school.

ginseng [Chin *jên shen*: *jên*, man + *shen* (of obscure meaning)] *JIN-seng.* Oriental plant having a medicinal root.

gioconda [It] *joh-KOHN-dah.* merry, smiling: epithet of the Monna Lisa.

giornale [It] *jor-NAH-leh.* daily; newspaper, journal.

giorno [It] *JOR-noh.* day.

gioviale [It] *joh-VYAH-leh.* (*music*) jovially.

giovinezza [It] *joh-vee-NAY-tsah.* youth; title of a Fascist anthem.

Giralda [Sp] *hee-RAHL-dah.* (*lit.*, weathervane) Moorish tower in Seville, Spain.

girandole [Fr, from It *girandola*, from *girare*, to turn] *zhee-rã-DOHL.* bracket for a candelabrum; pendant consisting of a large jewel surrounded by smaller jewels; rotating fireworks display.

Girondins [Fr, from *Gironde*, department in SW France] *zhee-rõ-DẼ.* 18th-century political party of moderate republican beliefs, the leaders of which came from the Gironde.

girouette [Fr] *zhee-RWET.* weathervane; whirligig.

gitano [Sp: *fem.* **gitana**] *hee-TAH-noh* (*-nah*) (*lit.*, Egyptian) Gypsy.

giusto [It] *JOOS-toh.* just, exact; appropriate; (*music*) in moderate tempo.

glace [Fr] *glahs.* ice; ice cream.

glacé [Fr] *glah-SAY.* iced; sugared, glazed.

gladius [Lat] *GLAH-dee-oos.* sword, esp. of type used by gladiators.

Gleichschaltung [Ger] *GLYÇ-shahl-toong.* coordination, assimilation; in politics, elimination of opposition.

glissade [Fr, from *glisser*, to slip, glide] *glee-SAHD.* glide; (*dancing*) sliding or gliding step.

glissando [pseudo-It, from Fr *glisser*, to slide] *glee-SAHN-doh.* (*music*) gliding, smoothly.

gli Stati Uniti [It] *lyee-STAH-tee-oo-NEE-tee.* the United States.

Glocke [Ger] *GLOH-keh*. bell.

Glockenspiel [Ger] *GLOH-k'n-shpeel*. set of bells; carillon; marching-band instrument consisting of steel bars mounted in a frame and struck by hammers.

glögg [Norw] *glög*. beverage used by mountain-climbers and skiers.

Gloria [Lat] *GLOH-ree-ah*. glory; passage in the Mass; —**in excelsis Deo** (*-een-ex-KEL-sees-DEH-oh*) Glory to God on high; —**Patri** (*-PAH-tree*) Glory be to the Father; —**tibi, Domine** (*-TEE-bee-DOH-mee-neh*) Glory be to Thee, O Lord.

Glück [Ger] *glük*. fortune; luck.

glückliche Reise [Ger] *GLÜK-liç-eh-RY-zeh*. happy journey!, bon voyage!

gnädige Frau [Ger] *GNAY-di-geh-FROW*. (*lit.*, gracious lady) Madame: a form of address.

gnädiges Fräulein [Ger] *GNAY-di-g's-FROY-lyn*. Miss: a form of address.

gnocchi [It: *sing*. **gnocco**] *NYOHK-kee* (*-koh*) small flour, potato or rice dumplings.

gnosis [Gk] *GNOH-sees*. knowledge, esp. mystical knowledge.

gnothi seauton [Gk] *GNOH-thee-seh-ow-TOHN*. know thyself.

goban [Jap *go*, name of the game + *ban*, board] *GOH-bahn*. Japanese game played on a board with counters.

Gobelins [Fr] *goh-b'LẼ*. valuable tapestries produced by a Parisian factory of that name during the reign of Louis XIV.

gobemouches [Fr] *gohb-MOOSH*. (*lit.*, fly-swallower) simpleton; ninny.

godet [Fr] *goh-DEH*. drinking cup, mug; triangular piece of cloth inserted in a garment for filling out; gore.

gogo [Fr slang] *goh-GOH*. easy mark; sucker. See **à gogo**.

goi. See **goy**.

golem [Heb: monster] *GOH-lem*. automaton; robot created for an evil purpose.

Golgotha [Aramaic: skull] *GOHL-goh-thah*. Calvary; place of suffering; burial place.

golondrina [Sp] *goh-lohn-DREE-nah.* swallow.

golubets [Russ: *pl.* **golubtsy**] *guh-loo-BYETS* (*-loob-TSEE*) stuffed cabbage roll.

goma [Sp] *GOH-mah.* gum; rubber; rubber tire.

gomei kaisha [Jap] *GOH-may-KY-shah.* continuing partnership; association.

gondola [It (Venetian)] *GOHN-doh-lah.* long, narrow boat, having a high stem and stern, rowed by a single oarsman standing at the stern, used on Venetian canals.

gondoliere [It] *gohn-doh-LYEH-reh.* oarsman of a gondola; gondolier.

gonfalon [Fr, from Germanic] *gõ-fah-LÕ.* banner; battle flag; standard.

gongorismo [Sp, from Gongora, 16th-century poet] *gohn-goh-REES-moh.* very elaborate and intricate literary style; Gongorism.

goniff, gonoph. See **ganef.**

gopak [Russ] *goh-PAHK.* Ukrainian folk dance. Also, **hopak** (Ukrainian var.).

gora [Russ] *gah-RAH.* mountain; hill.

gorgheggio [It] *gor-GEJ-joh.* (*music*) trill; melodious passage.

Gorgio [Romany] *GOR-joh.* non-Gypsy.

gorgonzola [It, from name of locality where made] *gor-gohn-DZOH-lah.* semisoft Italian cheese, veined with green mold.

gorod [Russ] *GOH-rut.* town; city.

gospod' [Russ] *gahs-PAWD'.* God; Lord.

gospodin [Russ: *pl.* **gospoda**] *gus-pah-DYEEN* (*-DAH*) gentleman; master; sir, mister.

gospozha [Russ] *gus-pah-ZHAH.* lady, dame; mistress; madam, Mrs.; miss.

gosse [Fr] *gohs.* urchin, rascal; boy; kid.

gostinnitsa [Russ] *gahs-TEEN-nyee-tsuh.* hotel; inn.

Gotama. See **Gautama.**

Gott [Ger] *goht.* God; —**mit uns** (*-mit-OONS*) God with us; —**sei dank** (*-zy-DAHNK*) thank God; —**will es** (*-VIL-es*) God wills it.

gouache [Fr, from It *guazzo*, puddle, pool] *gwahsh.* opaque painting method which uses a water and gum base; painting so made.

goulash [Hung *gulyás hús*, herdsman's meat] *GOO-lahsh*. Hungarian meat stew.

goum [Fr, from Ar] *goom*. family, tribe; formerly in Algeria, contingent of native military scouts under French command.

goumier [Fr] *goo-MYAY*. soldier serving in a **goum**.

gourmand [Fr] *goor-MÃ*. glutton.

gourmandise [Fr] *goor-mã-DEEZ*. gluttony.

gourmet [Fr] *goor-MEH*. epicure; lover of good food; food connoisseur.

goût [Fr] *goo*. taste; preference; style.

goûter [Fr] *goo-TAY*. (*lit.*, to taste) lunch; snack.

gouverneur [Fr] *goo-vehr-NÖR*. governor.

goy [Yid, from Heb; *pl.* **goyim**] *GOY* (*-yim*) Gentile; non-Jew. Also, **goi**.

G. P. U. [Russ, abbr. of *Gosudarstvennoye Politicheskoye Upravleniye*, State Political Department] *gay-pay-OO*. Soviet secret police, known as NKVD since 1934. Also, **Ogpu**.

grâce à Dieu [Fr] *GRAHS-ah-DYÖ*. thank God.

gracias [Sp] *GRAH-syahs*. thanks; thank you.

gracioso [Sp, from *gracia*, grace, charm] *grah-SYOH-soh*. gracious, charming; funny, witty.

gradatim [Lat, from *gradus*, step, degree] *grah-DAH-teem*. gradually; by degrees.

Graf [Ger: *pl.* **Grafen**] *grahf* (*-'n*) count, earl.

Gräfin [Ger: pl. unchanged] *GRAY-fin*. countess.

graffiti [It, pl. of *graffito*, scratch made by a stylus] *grahf-FEE-tee*. scratched inscriptions on stone and plaster; words or phrases written on walls in public places, often humorous or ribald.

grammaticus [Lat] *grahm-MAH-tee-koos*. grammarian; grammar teacher.

gramme [Fr] *grahm*. gram.

granada [Sp, from *grano*, grain, seed] *grah-NAH-dah*. pomegranate.

grancassa [It] *grahn-KAHS-sah.* (*lit.*, big case) bass drum. Also, **gran cassa.**

grand [Fr: *fem.* **grande**] *grã (GRÃ-duh)* large, great; tall, high; **grande dame** (*-DAHM*) great lady; aristocratic lady; **grande passion** (*-pah-SYŎ*) great passion; overpowering love; **grand Guignol** (*-gee-NYOHL*) Paris theater famous for its horror plays.

grande [It, Sp] *GRAHN-deh.* large, great; in Spain, nobleman, grandee.

grandioso [It] *grahn-DYOH-soh.* grandiose; (*music*) in grand style.

grand-mère [Fr] *grã-MEHR.* grandmother.

grand-messe [Fr] *grã-MES.* High Mass.

grand monde [Fr] *grã-MŎD.* high society.

grand-père [Fr] *grã-PEHR.* grandfather.

grand prix [Fr] *grã-PREE.* grand or first prize; international auto race; orig. a horse race held in Paris.

grand seigneur [Fr] *grã-seh-NYÖR.* great gentleman; nobleman.

granita [It] *grah-NEE-tah.* ice pudding; crushed ice drink; frappé.

gras [Fr: *fem.* **grasse**] *grah (grahs)* fat; thick; dense.

grasseyé [Fr] *grah-say-YAY.* (*lit.*, fattened, thickened) pronounced by rolling in the throat, as the French uvular *r*.

gratia Dei [Lat] *GRAH-tee-ah-DEH-ee.* thanks to God; by the grace of God.

gratias agere [Lat] *GRAH-tee-ahs-AH-geh-reh.* to give thanks; —**tibi ago** (*-TEE-bee-AH-goh*) I thank you.

gratin [Fr] *grah-TẼ.* topping of browned crumbs or grated cheese; dish so prepared.

gratiné [Fr: *fem.* **gratinée**] *grah-tee-NAY.* grated; covered with grated cheese, crumbs or other garnish.

gratis [Lat] *GRAH-tees.* free; without charge.

grau [Ger] *grow.* gray.

Graupel [Ger] *GROW-p'l.* sleet; hail.

grave [It] *GRAH-veh.* (*music*) grave; solemn; in very slow tempo.

gravis ira regum est semper [Lat] *GRAH-vees-EE-rah-*

REH-goom-est-SEM-pehr. the wrath of kings is always severe.

gravure [Fr] *grah-VÜR.* engraving; engraved plate.

grazhdanin [Russ: *fem.* **grazhdanka**] *gruzh-dah-NYEEN (-DAHN-kuh)* citizen.

grazia [It] *GRAH-tsyah.* grace; elegance; mercy; favor.

grazie [It] *GRAH-tsyeh.* thanks, thank you.

grazioso [It] *grah-TSYOH-soh.* (*music*) graceful(ly). Also, **graziosamente** (*-sah-MAYN-teh*).

gré [Fr] *gray.* will; wish; liking, pleasure; accord, consent; **bon—, mal—** (*BŎ-gray-MAHL-gray*) willy-nilly; **de bon—** (*duh-bŏ-GRAY*) willingly, with pleasure; **de—à—** (*duh-GRAY-ah-GRAY*) by mutual agreement; by private contract.

greffier [Fr] *greh-FYAY.* recorder; registrar; court or town clerk.

Grenze [Ger: *pl.* **Grenzen**] *GREN-tseh* (*-ts'n*) boundary; limit; border; frontier.

grève [Fr] *grev.* strike; work stoppage.

griffe [Fr] *greef* (*lit.,* claw) clawlike or leaflike ornament at the base of a column.

grillé [Fr] *gree-YAY.* broiled; grilled.

gringo [MexSp, of disputed origin] *GREEN-goh.* disparaging term applied by Spanish-Americans to foreigners, esp. from the U.S.

grisette [Fr, from *gris*, gray, typical color of their clothes] *gree-ZET.* working-class girl.

grissini [It (Piedmontese)] *grees-SEE-nee.* long, thin, crisp breadsticks, typically used in northern Italy.

gros [Fr: *fem.* **grosse**] *groh* (*grohs*) fat, large; pregnant; gross, in bulk; **en—** (*ã-*) wholesale.

gros rouge [Fr] *groh-ROOZH.* ordinary red wine; table wine.

grosso [It] *GROHS-soh.* big; great; heavy; (*music*) full, grand.

grosso modo [Lat] *GROHS-soh-MOH-doh.* more or less; approximately.

Grundriss [Ger] *GROONT-ris.* outline, plan, groundwork.

Gruss [Ger: *pl.* **Grüsse**] *groos* (*GRÜ-seh*) greeting; salute.

gruyère [Fr, from name of Swiss district] *grü-YEHR.* a mild Swiss cheese.

guagua [WIndSp] *GWAH-gwah.* bus, omnibus.

guajiro [AmerSp] *gwah-HEE-roh.* in Cuba, a rustic, yokel.

guanaco [AmerSp, from Quechua] *gwah-NAH-koh.* wild S American animal, related to the llama and alpaca; the fur of this animal.

guano [AmerSp, from Quechua] *GWAH-noh.* natural fertilizer, rich in nitrates, composed mainly of bird droppings.

guapo [Sp: *fem.* **guapa**] *GWAH-poh* (*-pah*) handsome, good-looking; brave, courageous.

guarapo [Sp] *gwah-RAH-poh.* sugarcane juice; alcoholic beverage made from cane.

guardia [Sp, It] *GWAR-dyah.* guard; policeman; —**Civil** [Sp] (*-see-VEEL*) state police; constabulary.

guaso [AmerSp] *GWAH-soh.* rustic, yokel; In S America, gaucho.

guayaba [AmerSp, from Arawak] *gwah-YAH-bah.* tropical plant having berrylike fruit used in making jams and jellies; guava; —**con queso** (*-kohn-KEH-soh*) guava paste with cheese, served as dessert.

guazzo [It] *GWAH-tsoh.* (*lit.,* pool, puddle) method of watercolor painting; gouache.

guberniya [Russ] *goo-BYER-nee-yuh.* territorial subdivision in former Russian Empire; province; in the Soviet Union, a division of a volost'.

guelfo [It, from MHG *Welf*, name of a princely family] *GWEL-foh.* Guelph or Guelf: member of the papal party in medieval Italy. Cf. **Ghibellino.**

guerra [Sp, from Germanic] *GEHR-rah*; [It] *GWEHR-rah.* war.

guerra cominciata, inferno scatenato [It] *GWEHR-rah-koh-meen-CHAH-tah-een-FEHR-noh-skah-teh-NAH-toh.* when war begins, all hell breaks loose.

guerre [Fr, from Germanic] *gehr.* war.

guerrilla [Sp, dim. of *guerra*, war] *gehr-REE-lyah.* (*lit.,* little war) warfare by irregulars; guerrilla warfare; guerrilla fighter. Also, **guerilla** (*guh-RIL-uh*).

guerrillero [Sp] *gehr-ree-LYEH-roh.* guerrilla fighter.

guía [Sp] *GEE-ah.* (*masc.*) guide; (*fem.*) guidebook, directry.

guichet [Fr] *gee-SHEH.* box-office window; teller's window; wicket; wicket gate.

Guignol [Fr] *gee-NYOL.* puppet show; standard character of French puppet shows.

guillemet [Fr] *gee-yuh-MEH.* quotation mark.

guimpe [Fr] *gēp.* frock or jumper worn under low-cut dress; stiff starched collar extending over neck and shoulders worn by certain orders of nuns.

güiro [AmerSp, from Arawak] *GWEE-roh.* musical instrument made from ridged gourd over which wires are wrapped; bottle gourd.

guitarra [Sp] *gee-TAR-rah.* guitar.

Gulasch [Ger] *GOO-lahsh.* See **goulash**; — -**suppe** (*-zoo-puh*) strained goulash.

G.U.M. [Russ, abbr. of *Gosudarstvennyi Universal'nyi Magazin*, Government Universal Store] *gay-oo-EM.* state department store in Moscow.

gumbo [Louisiana Fr *gombo*, from Bantu *kingombo*, from *ngumbo*, okra] *GUM-boh.* okra; okra pods; stew or soup made with okra and chicken or seafood.

gung ho [Chin: work together] *gung-HOH.* slogan of Carlson's Raiders, a U.S. Marine detachment in World War II; (*adj.*) wholehearted, enthusiastically loyal.

Gurkha [Hindi] *GOOR-khuh.* Himalayan tribe; member of that tribe in service of the British Army.

guru [Hindi, from Skt: weighty, venerable] *GOO-roo.* Hindu teacher or preceptor.

gusto [It] *GOOS-toh.* enjoyment; taste.

gustoso [It] *goos-TOH-soh.* (*music*) tasteful; **gustosamente** (*-sah-MAYN-teh*) tastefully.

guten Abend [Ger] *GOO-t'n-AH-b'nt.* good evening; **guten Morgen** (*-MOR-g'n*) good morning; **guten Tag** (*-TAHK*) good day; **gute Nacht** (*GOO-teh-NAHKHT*) good night.

gutta cavat lapidem, non vi, sed saepe cadendo [Lat] *GOOT-tah-KAH-vaht-LAH-pee-dem-nohn-VEE-sed-SY-peh-kah-DEN-doh.* the drop wears away the stone, not by force, but by constant dripping.

gutta-percha [Malay *getah*, gum + *percha*, the tree that produces it] *GUT-tuh-PUR-chuh*. heavy, sticky gum used in dentistry, and in making golf balls and electrical insulation.

guzla [Serbo-Croatian] *GOOZ-lah*. Yugoslavian musical instrument.

Gymnasium [Ger: *pl.* **Gymnasien**] *gim-NAH-see-oom* (*-'n*) in Germany, an academic high school.

H

habanera [Sp, from *Habana*, Havana] *ah-bah-NEH-rah*. Cuban dance in slow rhythm, similar to the tango.

habeas corpus [Lat] *HAH-beh-ahs-KOR-poos*. (*lit.*, thou shalt have the body) a writ ordering an accused person to be brought into court.

Habimah [Heb] *hah-bee-MAH*. platform; viewing stand; stage; troupe of Hebrew actors.

habitant [Fr] *ah-bee-TÃ*. inhabitant; resident; Canadian or Louisianan of French descent, esp. of the laboring or farming class.

habitat [Lat] *HAH-bee-taht*. (*lit.*, it inhabits) geographic region where a person or group carries on its activities; native home of an animal or plant species.

habitué [Fr] *ah-bee-tü-AY*. steady customer; frequent visitor.

hace calor [Sp] *AH-seh-kah-LOR*. it is warm (weather); **hace frío** (*-FREE-oh*) it is cold.

hacendado [Sp] *ah-sen-DAH-doh*. master of a hacienda; property owner.

hachis [Fr, from *hacher*, to chop up] *ah-SHEE*. minced meat; hash.

hacienda [Sp] *ah-SYEN-dah*. estate; plantation; farm; ranch.

Hadassah [Heb] *hah-dahs-SAH*. Jewish women's Zionist organization.

hadj [Ar] *hahj*. pilgrimage; Moslem pilgrimage to Mecca. Also, **hajj**.

hadji [Ar] *HAH-jee.* Moslem who has made the pilgrimage to Mecca; title of respect. Also, **hajji.**

haec olim meminisse juvabit [Lat] *HYK-OH-leem-meh-mee-NEES-seh-yoo-VAH-beet.* it will be a joy to remember these things at a later time.

hafiz [Ar] *HAH-feez.* Moslem who knows the Koran by heart; title of respect.

hágame el favor [Sp] *AH-gah-meh-el-fah-VOR.* please; do me the favor.

Haganah [Heb] *hahg-gah-NAH.* defense; Palestinian Hebrew military force.

Haggadah [Heb] *hahg-gah-DAH.* a book containing the Jewish Passover service, or Seder; Aggadah.

Haiduk [Hung] *HY-dook.* brigand mountaineer; Hungarian mercenary soldier; outrider of France or Germany in Hungarian costume. Also, **Heyduck.**

haik [Ar] *hyk.* strip of cloth wound over head and body.

haiku [Jap] *HY-koo.* Japanese verse form of 17 syllables, employing elaborate imagery, simile and metaphor.

hajj, hajji. See **hadj, hadji.**

Hakenkreuz [Ger] *HAH-k'n-kroyts.* (*lit.*, hooked cross) swastika; Nazi symbol.

hakim [Ar] *hah-KEEM.* Moslem ruler or judge; also, **hakeem** (*HAH-keem*) Moslem wise man or physician.

Halachah [Heb] *hah-lah-KHAH.* entire body of Jewish law and tradition. Also, **Halakah.**

halavah [Turk] *HAH-lah-vah.* See **halvah.**

hallah. See **challah.**

hallelujah [Heb] *hahl-leh-LOO-yah.* praise the Lord.

halte-là [Fr] *AHLT-lah.* halt!, stop where you are!

halvah [Yid or Romanian, from Turk, from Ar *halwa*] *HAHL-vah.* sweet paste of ground sesame. Also, **halva, halavah.**

hamal [Ar] *huh-MAHL.* an Oriental porter or bearer; in India, a male servant who does the work of a housemaid. Also, **hammal.**

hamartia [Gk] *hah-mar-TEE-ah.* failure; error; sin.

hametz [Heb] *KHAH-mets.* in Jewish law, food forbidden for Passover use; dishes and utensils likewise forbidden.

Hammerklavier [Ger] *HAH-muh-klah-veer.* pianoforte; piano.

Handbuch [Ger: *pl.* **Handbücher**] *HAHNT-bookh* (*-bü-çuh*) handbook, manual; guide.

Hände hoch [Ger] *HEN-deh-HOHKH.* hands up!

Handel [Ger] *HAHN-d'l.* trade; business; commerce.

Händler [Ger] *HENT-luh.* dealer; trader.

Handschrift [Ger: *pl.* **Handschriften**] *HAHNT-shrift* (*-'n*) manuscript; handwriting; signature.

Hannibal ad portas [Lat] *HAHN-nee-bahl-ahd-POR-tahs.* Hannibal is at the gates; the enemy is near.

Hanse [Ger] *HAHN-zuh.* Hanseatic league: medieval coalition of German seaport cities for commercial purposes.

Hanukkah [Heb] *hah-nuk-KAH.* dedication; feast of lights: major Jewish holiday. Also, **chanukkah.**

hanum. See **khanum.**

haole [Hawaiian] *hah-OH-leh.* white man; any non-Polynesian.

haori [Jap] *HAH-oh-ree.* short, loose coat.

hapax legomenon [Gk] *HAH-pahks-leh-GOH-meh-nohn.* something said only once; nonce-word.

hara kiri [Jap] *HAH-rah-KEE-ree.* (*lit.,* belly-cutting) ceremonial suicide by disembowelment with a knife or sword. Also, erroneously, **hari-kari** (*HAH-ree-KAH-ree*).

hareng [Fr] *ah-RẮ.* herring.

haricot [Fr] *ah-ree-KOH.* bean; kidney bean; —**vert** (*-VEHR*) green bean, string bean.

hari-kari. See **hara kiri.**

hartebeest [Afrikaans] *HAR-tuh-behst.* large S African antelope.

haruspex [Lat, from *haru-*, entrails + *specere*, to look] *HAH-roos-peks.* in ancient Rome, a priest who read omens from the entrails of animals killed in sacrifice.

hasard [Fr] *ah-ZAR.* risk; hazard; **par—** (*par-*) by chance, accidentally.

Hasenpfeffer [Ger, from *Hase*, hare + *Pfeffer*, pepper] *HAH-z'n-pfef-fuh.* marinated hare, stewed and often served with sour cream.

hashish [Ar] *HAH-sheesh.* Indian hemp fiber smoked or eaten as a narcotic.

Hasidim [Heb, *pl.* of **Hasid**] *khah-see-DEEM* (*-SEED*) Jewish sect characterized by mysticism and religious zeal. Also, **Chasidim.**

hasta [Sp] *AHS-tah.* to; until; up to; as far as; —**la muerte todo es vida** (*-lah-MWEHR-teh-TOH-doh-es-VEE-dah*) until death, all is life; while there's life there's hope; —**la vista** (*-lah-VEES-tah*) see you later; au revoir; —**luego** (*-LWEH-goh*) until later; so long; —**mañana** (*-mah-NYAH-nah*) see you tomorrow.

hat der Bauer Geld, hat's die ganze Welt [Ger] *HAHT-dehr-BOW-uh-GELT-HAHTS-dee-GAHN-tseh-VELT.* (*lit.*, if a farmer has money, the whole world has it) a fool and his money are soon parted.

Hatikvah [Heb] *hah-TEEK-vah.* hope: national anthem of Israel.

haud ignota loquor [Lat] *HOWD-eeg-NOH-tah-LOH-kwor.* I speak of things scarcely unknown; what I'm speaking of is well known.

Hauptmann [Ger] *HOWPT-mahn.* headman, leader; captain; local government official.

Hauptstadt [Ger] *HOWPT-shtaht.* metropolis; capital city.

Hausfrau [Ger: *pl.* **Hausfrauen**] *HOWS-frow* (*-'n*) housewife; lady of the house; landlady.

Hausherr [Ger: *pl.* **Hausherren**] *HOWS-hehr* (*-'n*) master of the house; landlord.

haut [Fr: *fem.* **haute**] *oh* (*oht*) high; tall; **haute bourgeoisie** (*-boor-zhwah-ZEE*) upper middle class; gentry; **haute couture** (*-koo-TÜR*) high fashion; **haute cuisine** (*-küee-ZEEN*) fine cooking; the high art of cooking; **haut monde** (*-MŎD*) high society; **haut relief** (*-ruh-LYEF*) high relief.

hauteur [Fr, from *haut*, high] *oh-TÖR.* height; loftiness; haughtiness.

hay que bailar al son que se toca [Sp] *Y-keh-by-LAR-ahl-sohn-keh-seh-TOH-kah.* one must dance to the tune that is being played; when in Rome do as the Romans do.

hay sol [Sp] *y-SOHL.* it is sunny.

haz bien y no mires a quién [Sp] *ahs-BYEN-ee-noh-MEE-res-ah-KYEN*. do good and don't look at who (it is); let your conscience be your guide.

hectare [Fr] *ek-TAR*. land measure equal to 10,000 square meters (2.5 acres).

hedone [Gk] *heh-doh-NEH*. pleasure; enjoyment.

Heft [Ger: *pl.* **Hefte**] *heft* (*-eh*) volume of a serial; issue of a periodical; fascicle.

hegira [Ar *hijrah*] *heh-JY-ruh*. flight, escape; Mohammed's flight to Mecca; moving day.

heil [Ger] *hyl*. hail! long live!

Heiland [Ger] *HY-lahnt*. the Savior.

heilig [Ger: *fem.* **heilige**] *HY-liç* (*-li-geh*) holy, sacred; saint; **heilige Nacht** (*-NAHKHT*) Holy Night; night of Jesus' birth.

Heimat [Ger] *HY-maht*. homeland.

Heimweh [Ger] *HYM-veh*. homesickness, nostalgia.

Heimwehr [Ger] *HYM-vehr*. home guard; militia.

hekaton [Gk] *heh-kah-TOHN*. one hundred.

helados [Sp, from *helar*, to freeze] *eh-LAH-dos*. ices; ice cream.

hélas [Fr] *ay-LAHS*. alas!

Held [Ger: *pl. and gen.sing.* **Helden**] *helt* (*HEL-d'n*) hero; **Heldenleben** (*-lay-b'n*) hero's life; **Heldentod** (*-toht*) hero's death.

helios [Gk] *HEH-lee-ohs*. sun.

Hellas [Gk] *HEL-lahs*. (ModGk *EL-lahs*) Greece.

Helvetia [Lat] *hel-VEH-tee-ah*. Switzerland.

hemi [Gk] *HEH-mee*. half.

henna [Ar *ḥinnā'*] *HEN-nah*. reddish-brown dye derived from the leaves of an Asiatic tree.

hennin [Fr] *ã-NẼ*. conical headdress with long veil, worn by women in the 15th century.

heraa Suomi [Finn] *HEH-rah-SOO-oh-mee*. awaken, Finland!

Herausgeber [Ger] *heh-ROWS-gay-buh*. (*lit.,* one who gives out) editor, publisher.

Herbst [Ger] *hehrbst*. harvest season; autumn, fall.

heri [Lat] *HEH-ree*. yesterday.

hermandad [Sp] *ehr-mahn-DAHD.* brotherhood; fraternity; sisterhood; sorority.

hermano [Sp] *ehr-MAH-noh.* brother; **hermana** (*-nah*) sister.

hermoso [Sp: *fem.* **-a**] *er-MOH-soh* (*-sah*) beautiful.

Herr [Ger: *pl.* **Herren**] *hehr* (*HEHR-'n*) Mr.; sir; gentleman; master; **Herrenhaus** (*-hows*) manor house, mansion; **Herrenvolk** (*-fohlk*) master race; **Herr Ober** (*-OH-buh*) waiter!

Herz [Ger: *pl.* **Herzen**] *hehrts* (*-'n*) heart.

Herzog [Ger] *HEHR-tsohk.* count, earl.

hesternus [Lat] *hes-TEHR-noos.* of yesterday, yesterday's.

hetaira [Gk] *heh-TY-rah.* in ancient Greece, a courtesan, prostitute or concubine. Latinized to **hetaera.**

heteros [Gk] *HEH-teh-rohs.* other; various.

hetman [Pol, from Ger *Hauptmann*, headman, captain] *HET-mahn.* Cossack chief. Cf. **ataman.**

heure [Fr] *ör.* hour; time.

heute [Ger] *HOY-tuh.* today; —**mir, morgen dir** (*-MEER-MOR-g'n-DEER*) today to me, tomorrow to you.

hex [Gk] *heks.* six.

Hexe [Ger: *pl.* **Hexen**] *HEK-suh* (*-s'n*) witch, sorceress.

Hexerei [Ger] *HEK-suh-ry.* witchcraft; sorcery.

Heyduck. See **Haiduk.**

hibachi [Jap] *HEE-bah-chee.* small cook stove; brazier.

hic jacet [Lat] *HEEK-YAH-ket.* here lies.

hidalgo [Sp, contr. of *hijo de algo*, son of something, man of wealth] *ee-DAHL-goh.* nobleman; gentleman. Formerly, **fidalgo.**

hidalguía [Sp] *ee-dahl-GEE-ah.* nobility; aristocracy.

hier [Fr] *yehr.* yesterday.

hier [Ger] *HEE-uh.* here; —**spricht man Deutsch** (*-SHPRIÇT-mahn-DOYCH*) German spoken here.

hierba maté [Sp *hierba*, grass + *mate*, from Quechuan *mati*, calabash] *YEHR-bah-MAH-teh.* Paraguayan tea, made from the leaves of a S American shrub, usually drunk from a gourd with a reed or straw.

hieros [Gk] *hee-eh-ROHS.* holy; sacred.

hijo [Sp] *EE-hoh.* son; child; **hija** (*-hah*) daughter; **hijo varón** (*-vah-ROHN*) male child, boy.

himation [Gk: *pl.* **himatia**] *hee-MAH-tee-ohn* (*-ah*) square garment, like a mantle, worn by ancient Greeks.

hiragana [Jap] *HEE-rah-GAH-nah.* cursive, more common form of Japanese syllabary. Cf. **katakana.**

Hispania [Lat] *hees-PAH-nee-ah.* ancient name of Spain or the Iberian peninsula.

Histadrut [Heb] *hees-tah-DROOT.* labor federation in Israel.

histrio [Lat: *pl.* **histriones**] *HEES-tree-oh* (*-OH-nes*) actor.

Hitlerjugend [Ger] *HIT-luh-yoo-g'nt.* Hitler Youth: Nazi youth organization.

hlaford [AS] *HLAH-ford.* lord, master.

hoc [Lat] *hohk.* this; this thing; —**anno** (*-AHN-noh*) in this year; —**est** (*-est*) this is; that is; —**loco** (*-LOH-koh*) in this place; here.

hoch [Ger] *hohkh.* high; tall, lofty; noble; hurrah!

hock a chainik [Yid, lit., to bang on a teapot] *HAHK-uh-CHY-nik.* (*slang*) to prattle; gossip.

Hochamt [Ger] *HOHKH-ahmt.* High Mass.

Hochdeutsch [Ger] *HOHKH-doych.* High German; standard German.

hochet [Fr, from *hocher,* to shake] *oh-SHEH.* toy, plaything; baby's rattle.

Hochzeit [Ger] *HOHKH-tsyt.* wedding.

hodie [Lat] *HOH-dee-eh.* today; —**mihi, cras tibi** (*-MEE-hee-KRAHS-TEE-bee*) today to me, tomorrow to you.

Hof [Ger] *hohf.* court; hotel; courtyard.

Hofdichter [Ger] *HOHF-diç-tuh.* court poet; poet-in-residence.

Hoffnung [Ger, from *hoffen,* to hope] *HOHF-noong.* hope.

hogan [Navajo] *HOH-g'n.* conical shelter covered with bark and clay.

hoi polloi [Gk] *hoy-pohl-LOY.* the many; rabble.

hollandaise [Fr] *oh-lā-DEZ.* (*lit.,* Dutch) sauce made with egg yolks, butter and lemon juice; dish served with this sauce.

holos [Gk] *HOH-lohs.* whole, entire.

homagium reddere [Lat] *hoh-MAH-gee-oom-RED-deh-reh.* to renounce homage; to scorn praise.

homard [Fr] *oh-MAR.* lobster.

hombre [Sp] *OHM-breh.* man.

hominidae [New Lat, from *homo,* man] *hoh-MEE-nee-dy.* a family name for all species of the primate order, including man and all extinct manlike species.

hommage [Fr] *oh-MAHZH.* homage; reverence, respect.

hommages de l'auteur [Fr] *oh-MAHZH-duh-loh-TÖR.* (with the) compliments of the author.

homme [Fr] *ohm.* man; —**d'affaires** (*-dah-FEHR*) businessman; —**de plume** (*-duh-PLÜM*) writer; —**d'esprit** (*-des-PREE*) intellectual; man of wit.

homo [Lat: *pl.* **homines**] *HOH-moh* (*-mee-nes*) man; —**erectus** (*-eh-REK-toos*) extinct form of man of Middle Pleistocene age, also known as Pithecanthropus or Java Man; —**homini lupus** (*-HOH-mee-nee-LOO-poos*) man is a wolf to (his fellow) man; —**sapiens** (*-SAH-pee-ens*) (*lit.,* thinking man) the species of modern man and some closely related extinct species, such as Neanderthal and Cro-Magnon man.

homo sum; humani nihil a me alienum puto [Lat] *HOH-moh-soom-hoo-MAH-nee-NEE-heel-ah-MEH-ah-lee-EH-noom-POO-toh.* I am a man; I consider nothing that pertains to man alien to me.

homunculi quanti sunt [Lat] *hoh-MOON-koo-lee-KWAHN-tee-soont.* what little creatures men are!, how many small men there are!

honcho [Jap] *HOHN-choh.* person in charge.

honnête [Fr] *oh-NET.* honest; civil; upright.

honneur [Fr] *oh-NÖR.* honor; respect.

Honi soit qui mal y pense [Fr] *oh-NEE-SWAH-kee-mahl-ee-PÃS.* Evil to him that evil thinks (motto of the Order of the Garter).

honoris causa [Lat] *hoh-NOH-rees-KOW-sah.* honorary; bestowed in recognition of merit.

honte [Fr, from Germanic] *ōt.* shame, disgrace.

honteux [Fr: *fem.* **honteuse**] *õ-TÖ* (*-TÖZ*) shameful; disgraceful.

hoodoo [var. of **voodoo**] *HOO-doo.* bad luck; person that brings bad luck; voodoo.

hookah [Ar] *HOO-kah.* a smoking pipe with a long, flexible tube through which the smoke is drawn after being passed through water in a glass jar.

hopak. hoh-PAHK. See **gopak.**

hôpital [Fr] *oh-pee-TAHL.* charity hospital; hospice where free food and lodging are available.

hora [Lat] *HOH-rah.* hour; time; —**fugit** (*-FOO-geet*) the hour flies; time waits for no man.

hora [Heb & Romanian, from Turk] *HOH-ruh.* traditional Romanian and Israeli round dance.

horchata [Sp, orig. barley water] *or-CHAH-tah.* crushed almond drink.

horribile dictu [Lat] *hor-REE-bee-leh-DEEK-too.* horrible to relate; —**visu** (*-VEE-soo*) horrible to behold.

hors [Fr] *or.* out; out of; besides; without; except; —**de concours** (*-duh-kõ-KOOR*) (*lit.,* out of the competition) pertaining to an exhibit or work presented along with others in a competition, but not eligible for a prize; also applied to an artist whose work is so exhibited; —**de combat** (*-duh-kõ-BAH*) disabled; out of the fighting; —**de saison** (*-duh-seh-ZÕ*) out of season; — **-d'oeuvre** (*-DÖ-vruh*) (*lit.,* outside of the work) appetizer; relish; side dish.

Horst Wessel Lied [Ger] *HORST-VES-s'l-LEET.* official song of the German Nazi Party, commemorating an early National Socialist hero.

hosanna [Heb *hōshi'āh nnā,* save, we pray] *hoh-ZAN-uh.* shout of praise to God; orig. an appeal to God for deliverance.

hospes [Lat: *pl.* **hospites**] *HOHS-pes* (*-pee-tes*) host; stranger, foreigner, guest.

hospice [Fr] *oh-SPEES.* almshouse; refuge; asylum.

hospodar [Romanian, from Ukrainian, from *hospod',* master] *hohs-poh-DAR.* master; lord; governor; formerly, title of princes or governors of Walachia and Moldavia.

hostia [Lat] *HOHS-tee-ah.* bread of the Host; consecrated wafer.

hôte [Fr: *fem.* **hôtesse**] *oht* (*oh-TES*) host; hostess; innkeeper; guest, visitor.

hôtel [Fr] *oh-TEL.* hotel, inn; mansion, manor house; town hall; **—des Invalides** (*-day-zē-vah-LEED*) famous military hospital in Paris: resting place of Napoleon; **—de ville** (*-duh-VEEL*) town hall, city hall; **—Dieu** (*-DYÖ*) (*lit.*, God's house) hospital in Paris; any hospital; **—garni** (or **meublé**) (*-gar-NEE*; *-mö-BLAY*) furnished rooms; boardinghouse; rooming house.

houngan [Haitian Fr, of Afr origin] *oon-GÃ.* voodoo priest or witch doctor.

houppelande [Fr] *oop-LÃD.* fitted waistcoat or dress, with full long sleeves and skirt, used in medieval times.

houri [Fr, from Pers *hūrī*, from Ar *ḥūrīyah*, gazelle-eyed] *HOO-ree.* Mohammedan nymph of paradise.

howdah [Hindi *haudah*, from Ar *haudaj*] *HOW-dah.* seat or litter carried on the back of an elephant.

hoy [Sp] *oy.* today.

huarache [MexSp] *wah-RAH-cheh.* laced leather sandal.

hubba hubba [origin unknown; perh. Turk *merhaba*, word of greeting] World War II military slang word: wow!; quickly!

hubris. See **hybris.**

huerta [Sp] *WER-tah.* orchard; vegetable garden.

huevo [Sp] *WEH-voh.* egg; (*pl.*) **huevos** *WEH-vohs*; **—duros** (*-DOO-rohs*) hard-boiled eggs; **— escalfados** (*es-kahl-FAH-dohs*) poached eggs; **—estrellados** (*-es-treh-LYAH-dohs*) eggs sunny-side up; **—fritos** (*-FREE-tohs*) fried eggs; **—pasados (por agua)** (*-pah-SAH-dohs-por-AH-gwah*) soft-boiled eggs; **—revueltos** (*-reh-VWEL-tohs*) scrambled eggs; also, **revoltillo de huevos** (*reh-vohl-TEE-lyoh-deh-*).

Hügel [Ger] *HÜ-g'l.* hill, hillock; knoll.

huile [Fr] *üeel.* oil.

huître [Fr] *ÜEE-truh.* oyster; **huîtres en coquille** (*-ã-koh-KEE-yuh*) scalloped oysters.

Huk(balahap) [Tagalog] *HOOK-bah-lah-hahp.* Filipino group originally organized against Japanese occupation of World War II; later, a communist guerrilla group.

hukilau [Hawaiian] *HOO-kee-low.* feast.

hula-hula [Hawaiian] *HOO-lah-HOO-lah.* graceful Hawaiian dance with intricate arm and hip motions that tell a story in pantomime.

humanum est errare [Lat] *hoo-MAH-noom-est-ehr-RAH-reh.* to err is human.

humuhumunukunukuapuaa [Hawaiian] *HOO-moo-HOO-moo-NOO-koo-NOO-koo-AH-poo-AH-ah.* trigger fish of the South Seas.

hybris [Gk] *HÜ-brees.* transgression of moral law; act of defiance; excessive pride.

hygeia [Gk] *hü-GAY-ah.* health.

hyper [Gk] *HÜ-pehr.* over; excessive.

hypnos [Gk] *HÜP-nohs.* sleep.

hypo [Gk] *HÜ-poh.* under, below.

hysteron proteron [Gk] *HÜS-teh-rohn-PROH-teh-rohn.* (*lit.,* the last first) putting the cart before the horse; begging the question; in logic, a fallacious proof that proceeds from the assumption of that which has to be proved.

I

i [It] *ee.* the (*masc. pl.*).

iacta alea est [Lat] *YAHK-tah-AH-leh-ah-est.* the die is cast; a decision has been reached.

ibidem [Lat: *abbr.* **ibid**] *EE-bee-dem.* in the same place; in the same work.

ibis et redibis non (morieris in bello) [Lat] *EE-bees-et-reh-DEE-bees-nohn-moh-ree-EH-rees-een-BEL-loh)* thou shalt go and not return (thou shalt die in war): said to be the ambiguous response of the Sibyl to departing soldiers; ambiguous by reason of lack of punctuation and the equal applicability of *non* to *redibis* and *morieris,* with the alternative reading "thou shalt go and return; thou shalt not die in war."

ich [Ger] *iç.* I.

ich dien' [Ger] *iç-DEEN.* I serve (motto of the Prince of Wales).

ichiban [Jap] *EE-chee-BAHN.* (*lit.*, number one) very good; fine.

I Ching [Chin] *EE-JING.* The Book of Changes: an ancient Chinese book of divination.

Ich-Laut [Ger] *IÇ-lowt.* the palatal sound of *ch* in German when it follows *e, i, ä, ö, ü* or consonants: opposed to **Ach-Laut.**

ich liebe dich [Ger] *iç-LEE-beh-diç.* I love you.

Ichthyophagoi [Gk] *ikh-thee-oh-FAH-goy.* the Fish-Eaters, an ancient tribe.

ichthys [Gk] *eekh-THÜS.* fish: early symbol of Christianity.

ici [Fr] *ee-SEE.* here; **—on parle français** (*-ŏ-PARL-frä-SEH*) French spoken here.

ictus [Lat, from p.p. of *icere*, to strike] *EEK-toos.* blow; emphasis; metrical accent; in medicine, a fit or stroke.

id [Lat: it] *eed.* in psychoanalysis, the unconscious source of impulses and energy.

id. Abbr. of **idem.**

idanta [Skt] *ee-DAHN-tuh.* condition of being an object or thing; an object of knowledge.

idée fixe [Fr] *ee-DAY-FEEKS.* fixed idea; singular preoccupation or obsession.

idem [Lat: *abbr.* **id.**] *EE-dem.* the same; **—quod** (*-kwohd*) the same as (*abbr.* **i.q.**).

id est [Lat: *abbr.* **i.e.**] *EED-est.* it is; that is.

id genus omne [Lat] *EED-GEH-noos-OHM-neh.* all of that kind.

idiot savant [Fr] *ee-DYOH-sa-VÄ.* idiot with one mental aptitude (mathematics, music, etc.) highly developed.

Ido [Esperanto, abbr. of *Esperantido*, lit., offspring of Esperanto] *EE-doh.* a modification of Esperanto, suggested in 1907.

i.e. Abbr. of **id est.**

ieri [It] *YEH-ree.* yesterday.

Iesous Hemeteros Soter [Gk] *ee-eh-SOOS-heh-MEH-teh-rohs-soh-TEHR.* Jesus our Savior.

Iesus Hominum Salvator [Lat: *abbr.* **I.H.S.**] *YEH-soos-HOH-mee-noom-sahl-VAH-tor.* Jesus Savior of Mankind.

Iesus Nazarenus, Rex Iudaeorum [Lat: *abbr.* **I.N.R.I.**] *YEH-soos-nah-zah-REH-noos-REKS-yoo-dy-OH-room.* Jesus of Nazareth, King of the Jews.

i frutti proibiti sono i più dolci [It] *ee-FROOT-tee-proh-ee-BEE-tee-SOH-noh-ee-PYOO-DOHL-chee.* forbidden fruits are the sweetest.

igloo [Eskimo] *EE-gloo.* the dome-shaped ice house of the Eskimos.

ignis fatuus [Lat] *EEG-nees-FAH-too-oos.* (*lit.*, foolish fire) will-o'-the-wisp; delusion.

ignobile vulgus [Lat] *eeg-NOH-bee-leh-VOOL-goos.* the ignoble masses; the lowborn populace.

ignoramus [Lat: we do not know] *eeg-noh-RAH-moos.* ignorant person; simpleton.

ignorantia juris non excusat [Lat] *eeg-noh-RAHN-tee-ah-YOO-rees-nohn-eks-KOO-saht.* ignorance of the law is no excuse.

ignorantia legis neminem excusat [Lat] *eeg-noh-RAHN-tee-ah-LEH-gees-NEH-mee-nem-eks-KOO-saht.* ignorance of the law excuses no one.

i gran dolori sono muti [It] *ee-GRAHN-doh-LOH-ree-SOH-noh-MOO-tee.* great sorrows are silent.

I.H.S. Abbr. of **Iesus Hominum Salvator; In Hoc Signo.**

ikra [Russ] *ee-KRAH.* fish roe; caviar.

il [Fr] *eel.* he; it; [It] *eel.* the (*masc. sing.*).

Île de la Cité [Fr] *EEL-duh-lah-see-TAY.* island in the Seine River, in the center of Paris.

il faut [Fr] *eel-FOH.* it is necessary; one must; **comme—** (*kohm-*) the right or proper way, the right kind of; as one should.

il fuoco non s'estingue col fuoco [It] *eel-FWOH-koh-nohn-ses-TEEN-gweh-kohl-FWOH-koh.* you don't put out fire with fire.

illuminati [Lat] *eel-loo-mee-NAH-tee.* the enlightened ones; scholars; deep thinkers.

illustrissimo [It: *pl.* -**mi**] *eel-loos-TREES-see-moh* (*-mee*) most illustrious.

il meglio è nemico del bene [It] *eel-MEH-lyoh-eh-neh-MEE-koh-del-BEH-neh*. better is the enemy of good; leave well enough alone.

il n'est sauce que d'appétit [Fr] *eel-neh-SOHS-kuh-dah-pay-TEE*. hunger is the best sauce.

il n'y a pas de quoi [Fr] *eel-nyah-PAH-duh-KWAH*. don't mention it; you're welcome.

il n'y a que le premier pas qui coûte [Fr] *eel-nyah-kuh-luh-pruh-MYAY-PAH-kee-KOOT*. it is only the first step that costs; the first step is the hardest.

il n'y en a plus [Fr] *eel-nyã-nah-PLÜ*. there is (are) no more.

il penseroso [It, earlier form of *pensieroso*] *eel-pen-seh-ROH-soh*. the pensive one; the brooding man.

ils ne passeront pas [Fr] *eel-nuh-pah-s'RÕ-PAH*. they shall not pass: French rallying cry at Verdun in World War I.

il va sans dire [Fr] *eel-VAH-sã-DEER*. it goes without saying.

il y a [Fr] *eel-YAH*. there is; there are.

imam [Ar: leader, guide] *ee-MAHM*. Moslem priest; religious leader.

imbroglio [It] *eem-BROH-lyoh*. mix-up; mess; confusion; swindle.

im Gegenteil [Ger] *im-GAY-g'n-tyl*. on the contrary.

I Mille [It] *ee-MEEL-leh*. the thousand: Garibaldi's army in the fight to liberate Sicily.

im Jahre [Ger] *im-YAH-reh*. in the year . . .

immer schlimmer [Ger] *IM-uh-SHLIM-uh*. worse and worse; from bad to worse.

imo pectore [Lat] *EE-moh-PEK-toh-reh*. from the bottom of one's heart.

impasse [Fr] *ē-PAHS*. impassable obstacle; dilemma.

impasto [It] *eem-PAHS-toh*. layers of pigment in painting; application of paint in a thick paste.

impazientemente [It] *eem-pah-tsyen-teh-MAYN-teh*. (*music*) hurriedly; impatiently.

impedimenta [Lat] *eem-peh-dee-MEN-tah.* baggage; hindrances, impediments.

imperator [Lat] *eem-peh-RAH-tor.* commander; emperor.

imperioso [It] *eem-peh-RYOH-soh.* (*music*) imperious; commanding.

imperium [Lat] *eem-PEH-ree-oom.* absolute power; empire.

imperméable [Fr] *ē-pehr-may-AH-bluh.* raincoat; slicker.

impeto [It] *EEM-peh-toh.* impetuosity; impetus; con— (*kohn-*) (*music*) impetuously.

impetuoso [It] *eem-peh-TWOH-soh.* (*music*) impetuously.

impi [Zulu] *EEM-pee.* band of Kaffir warriors; army.

impluvium [Lat] *eem-PLOO-vee-oom.* cistern; rain barrel.

imprenta [Sp] *eem-PREN-tah.* print; printing; print shop; press; publication.

impresario [It, from *impresa*, undertaking] *eem-preh-SAH-ryoh.* producer or manager, esp. of a theatrical or musical group or production.

impresos [Sp] *eem-PREH-sohs.* printed matter.

imprimatur [Lat: let it be printed] *eem-pree-MAH-toor.* license to print or publish; sanction, approval.

imprimerie [Fr] *ē-pree-m'REE.* printing shop or plant.

imprimeur [Fr] *ē-pree-MÖR.* printer.

imprimis [Lat, contr. of in primis, among the first] *eem-PREE-mees.* first in line; in the first place.

improvvisata [It] *eem-prohv-vee-SAH-tah.* (*music*) improvisation.

im Rausche [Ger] *im-ROW-sheh.* in one's cups; drunk.

in absentia [Lat] *een-ahb-SEN-tee-ah.* in (one's) absence.

in aeternum [Lat] *een-y-TEHR-noom.* eternally, forever.

in alt [Prov, from Lat *altus*, high] *een-AHLT.* (*music*) in the first octave above the treble staff.

in articulo mortis [Lat] *een-ar-TEE-koo-loh-MOR-tees.* on the brink of death.

in bello parvis momentis magni casus intercedunt [Lat] *een-BEL-loh-PAR-vees-moh-MEN-tees-MAHG-nee-KAH-soos-een-tehr-KEH-doont.* in war great events are brought about by small causes.

in camera [Lat] *een-KAH-meh-rah.* in chambers; in private.

in casa [It] *een-KAH-sah.* at home.

incipit [Lat] *EEN-kee-peet.* (here) begins.

incognito [It: unknown] *een-KOH-nyee-toh.* in disguise; not revealing one's identity.

incomunicado [Sp] *een-koh-moo-nee-KAH-doh.* cut off from communication with the outside; isolated.

inconnu [Fr] *ē-koh-NÜ.* unknown; unknown person; stranger.

in corpore [Lat] *een-KOR-poh-reh.* in the body or substance; in the flesh.

incunabula [Lat: swaddling clothes, beginnings; from *cuna*, cradle] *een-koo-NAH-boo-lah.* books printed prior to the 16th century; earliest printed books.

index [Lat: pointer, index finger] *EEN-deks.* indicator; index; list, catalogue; **—expurgatorius** (*-eks-poor-gah-TOH-ree-oos*) list of books to be censored before reading by Roman Catholics; formerly listed separately, but now included in **—librorum prohibitorum** (*-lee-BROH-room-pro-hee-bee-TOH-room*) list of books forbidden save by special permission, or unless censored.

indiano [Sp, lit., Indian, from *las Indias*, the Indies, America] *een-DYAH-noh.* a Spaniard returning to Spain after making his fortune in America.

induna [Zulu] *een-DOO-nah.* Zulu leader; warrior chief.

inédit [Fr: *fem.* **inédite**] *ee-nay-DEE* (*-DEET*) unpublished.

in esse [Lat] *een-ES-seh.* in existence; in being.

in extenso [Lat] *een-eks-TEN-soh.* in full; extensively.

in extremis [Lat] *een-eks-TREH-mees.* in the last extreme; near death.

infanta [Sp, Port, from Lat *infans*, child, infant] *een-FAHN-tah.* Spanish or Portuguese princess.

infante [Sp, Port] *een-FAHN-teh.* Spanish or Portuguese prince who is not heir to the throne.

infera [Lat, neut. pl. of *inferus*, lower] *EEN-feh-rah.* things (mentioned) below; things below ground; the underworld, the nether regions.

inferno [It, from Lat *infernus*, nether, hellish] *een-FEHR-noh.* hell; nether regions.

in fieri [Lat *in*, in + *fieri*, to be done] *een-FEE-eh-ree.* (*law*) in waiting; pending; in process.

in fine [Lat] *een-FEE-neh.* in conclusion; in summary.

in flagrante delicto [Lat] *een-flah-GRAHN-teh-deh-LEEK--toh.* red-handed; in the very act of committing a crime.

influenza [It: influence, influx] *een-floo-EN-tsah.* respiratory disease; flu, once thought to be due to the evil influx of the stars.

in folio [Lat] *een-FOH-lee-oh.* once-folded sheet of printed matter.

in forma pauperis [Lat] *een-FOR-mah-POW-peh-rees.* (*law*) in the status of a pauper; not liable for costs.

infra [Lat] *EEN-frah.* below.

ingénue [Fr, lit., ingenuous] *ē-zhay-NÜ.* actress who plays a supporting role, esp. that of an ingenuous young girl.

ingle [Yid] *EEN-gluh.* boy.

Inhalt [Ger] *IN-hahlt.* contents.

Inhaltsverzeichnis [Ger] *IN-hahlts-fehr-tsyç-nis.* index; table of contents.

in hoc [Lat] *een-HOHK.* in this; in regard to this.

in hoc signo [Lat: *abbr.* **I.H.S.**] *een-HOHK-SEEG-noh.* in this sign (i.e., the cross); —**spes mea** (*-SPES-MEH-ah*) in this sign is my hope; —**vinces** (*-VEEN-kes*) In this sign thou shalt conquer (motto of Constantine the Great).

initio [Lat: *abbr.* **init.**] *ee-NEE-tee-oh.* in the beginning: used esp. in referring to a citation to be found at the beginning of a work, or a part of a work.

in jure [Lat] *een-YOO-reh.* in law; according to law.

inkos, inkoos [Zulu] *EEN-kohs, EEN-koos.* Zulu chief; title of respect; used by white South Africans with the meaning "thanks."

inkosikazi [Zulu] *een-koh-see-KAH-zee.* chieftainess; female leader; queen.

in loco [Lat] *een-LOH-koh.* in the place; in place of; —**citato** (*-kee-TAH-toh*) (*abbr.* **loc. cit.**) in the place cited; —**parentis** (*-pah-REN-tees*) in the place of a parent; bearing a parent's responsibility.

in lumine tuo videbimus lumen [Lat] *een-LOO-mee-neh-TOO-oh-vee-DEH-bee-moos-LOO-men*. In thy light we shall see the light (motto of Columbia University).

in manus tuas commendo spiritum meum [Lat] *een-MAH-noos-TOO-ahs-kohm-MEN-doh-SPEE-ree-toom-MEH-oom*. into thy hands I commend my spirit.

in medias res [Lat] *een-MEH-dee-ahs-RES*. into the thick of things; without introduction.

in medio [Lat] *een-MEH-dee-oh*. in the middle; in the midst; in between.

in memoriam [Lat] *een-meh-MOH-ree-ahm*. in memory (of).

innamorato [It: *fem.* **-ta,** *pl.* **-ti**] *een-nah-moh-RAH-toh* (*-tah, -tee*) lover; sweetheart.

innig [Ger] *IN-niç.* (*music*) sincere; fervent.

in nomine [Lat] *een-NOH-mee-neh*. in the name (of); —**Dei** (*-DEH-ee*) in God's name; —**Patris et Filii et Spiritus Sancti** (*-PAH-trees-et-FEE-lee-ee-et-SPEE-ree-toos-SAHNK-tee*) in the name of the Father, and of the Son, and of the Holy Ghost.

in omnia paratus [Lat] *een-OHM-nee-ah-pah-RAH-toos*. prepared for all things.

in omnibus [Lat] *een-OHM-nee-boos*. in all things; in all ways.

in ovo [Lat] *een-OH-voh*. in the egg; undeveloped; immature.

in pace [Lat] *een-PAH-keh*. in peace.

in pectore [Lat] *een-PEK-toh-reh*. in the breast; in confidence; secretly.

in perpetuo [Lat] *een-pehr-PEH-too-oh*. eternally; forever. Also, **in perpetuum** (*-oom*).

in persona [Lat] *een-pehr-SOH-nah*. in person.

in personam [Lat] *een-pehr-SOH-nahm*. (*law*) against a person: applied to legal proceedings. Cf. **in rem.**

in pleno [Lat] *een-PLEH-noh*. in full.

in posse [Lat] *een-POHS-seh*. possibly; potentially.

in primis [Lat] *een-PREE-mees*. among the first.

in principio [Lat: *abbr.* **in pr.**] *een-preen-KEE-pee-oh*. in the beginning.

in promptu [Lat] *een-PROHMP-too.* in readiness; at hand; on the spot; without preparation.

in re [Lat] *een-REH.* in the matter (of); regarding.

in rem [Lat] *een-REM.* (*law*) against a thing (rather than a person). Cf. **in personam.**

I.N.R.I. Abbr. of **Iesus Nazarenus, Rex Iudaeorum.**

in saecula saeculorum [Lat] *een-SY-koo-lah-sy-koo-LOH-room.* for ever and ever.

insalata [It, from *insalare*, to salt, from *sale*, salt] *een-sah-LAH-tah.* salad.

insalutato hospite [Lat] *een-sah-loo-TAH-toh-HOHS-pee-teh.* without salutation to the host; without saying good-bye; taking French leave.

insanus omnis furere credit ceteros [Lat] *een-SAH-noos-OHM-nees-FOO-reh-reh-KREH-deet-KEH-teh-ros.* every madman believes everybody else to be mad.

insbesondere [Ger] *ins-buh-ZOHN-duh-reh.* especially.

in se [Lat] *een-SEH.* in itself.

in situ [Lat] *een-SEE-too.* in (its original) place.

insouciant [Fr] *ē-soo-SYẴ.* indifferent; unconcerned; **in-souciance** (*-SYẴS*) indifference; unconcern.

in specie [Lat] *een-SPEH-kee-eh.* in kind; in the same form.

instanter [Lat] *een-STAHN-tehr.* instantly; urgently.

instar omnium [Lat] *EEN-star-OHM-nee-oom.* worth all of them; the equal of all of them.

in statu quo [Lat] *een-STAH-too-kwoh.* in the same state as before.

insula [Lat] *EEN-soo-lah.* island.

intaglio [It, from *intagliare*, to cut in, engrave] *een-TAH-lyoh.* incised carving; a gem, stone, plate, etc., so incised; a method of engraving printing plates by cutting into the surface of the plate.

integer vitae scelerisque purus [Lat] *EEN-teh-gehr-VEE-ty-skeh-leh-REES-kweh-POO-roos.* upright in life and free of guilt.

intelligentsia [Russ, lit., intelligence] *in-tel-i-GEN-tsee-uh.* the cultured class; the intellectuals.

in tenebris [Lat] *een-TEH-neh-brees.* in darkness; obscure.

inter [Lat] *EEN-tehr.* among; between; —**alia** (*-AH-lee-ah*) among other things; —**alios** (-*AH-lee-ohs*) among others; —**nos** (-*NOHS*) between or among us.

interim [Lat] *EEN-teh-reem.* meanwhile; pause; intermission.

Interlingua [NL] *een-tehr-LEEN-gwah.* a constructed language used by scientists for international communications.

intermezzo [It] *een-tehr-MEH-dzoh.* short musical piece played between longer compositions or between parts of a long work; short independent musical composition.

Internationale [Fr, for *Chanson Internationale,* international song] *ē-tehr-nah-syoh-NAHL.* a 19th-century song of the French working class, later adopted by the Communist movement.

internuncio [It] *een-tehr-NOON-choh.* papal minister ranking below a nuncio.

inter pares [Lat] *EEN-tehr-PAH-res.* between equals; among peers.

interregnum [Lat] *een-tehr-REG-noom.* period between rulers, or in which there is no ruling authority.

inter se [Lat] *EEN-tehr-SEH.* between or among themselves.

inter vivos [Lat] *EEN-tehr-VEE-vohs.* among the living: referring to donations made during the life of the benefactor.

intime [Fr] *ē-TEEM.* intimate; private.

in toto [Lat] *een-TOH-toh.* in all; completely, entirely.

intra [Lat] *EEN-trah.* in, within; —**muros** (-*MOO-rohs*) inside the walls.

intransigeant [Fr] *ē-trā-see-ZHĂ.* intransigent, uncompromising; ultraradical; unwavering believer; **intransigeance** (-*ZHĂS*) intransigence; uncompromising stance.

intra vires [Lat] *EEN-trah-VEE-res.* (*law*) within the power or authority (of). Cf. **ultra vires.**

intrigant [Fr: *fem.* **intrigante**] *ē-tree-GĂ* (-*GĂT*) intriguer; plotter.

introit [Lat *introitus,* entrance, p.p. of *introire,* to enter] *IN-troh-it.* music or choral response; entrance; beginning of a church service.

in utrumque paratus [Lat] *een-oo-TROOM-kweh-pah-RAH-toos.* prepared for either (outcome).

in vacuo [Lat] *een-VAH-koo-oh.* in a vacuum; outside reality; isolated.

Invalides. See **Hôtel des Invalides.**

invidia [Lat] *een-VEE-dee-ah.* envy.

in vino veritas [Lat] *een-VEE-noh-VEH-ree-tahs.* in wine (there is) the truth.

io Triumphe [Lat] *EE-oh-tree-OOM-feh.* Hail, God of Triumph!: salutation in honor of a victorious Roman general.

ipse dixit [Lat] *EEP-seh-DEEK-seet.* (he) himself said (it); the master has spoken.

ipsissima verba [Lat] *eep-SEES-see-mah-VEHR-bah.* the very same words; exactly quoted.

ipso facto [Lat] *EEP-soh-FAHK-toh.* by the very fact; in the very nature of it.

ipso jure [Lat] *EEP-soh-YOO-reh.* by the law itself.

i.q. Abbr. of **idem quod.**

irato [It] *ee-RAH-toh.* (*music*) irate; angry.

Irgun Zvai Leumi [Heb] *eer-GOON-ZVY-leh-OO-mee.* organization of Zionist extremists in Palestine during the period of British rule.

ir por lana y volver trasquilado [Sp] *eer-por-LAH-nah-ee-vohl-VEHR-trahs-kee-LAH-doh.* to go for wool and come back shorn.

iskra [Russ] *EES-kruh.* spark: name of Lenin's revolutionary newspaper.

iskusstvo [Russ] *ees-KOOST-vuh.* art.

Islam [Ar, lit., submission (to Allah's will)] *ees-LAHM.* the Moslem collectivity; the Mohammedan world.

isomelos [Gk, from *isos*, same + *melos*, melody] *ee-SOH-meh-lohs.* compositional technique using repetition of a melody to create unity, and rhythm changes for variety.

isos [Gk] *EE-sohs.* equal, same.

Issei [Jap *i*, first + *sei*, generation] *EES-say.* Japanese-born resident of the U.S. Cf. **Nisei, Sansei.**

Istiqlal [Ar: independence party] *ees-teek-LAHL.* Moroccan political party founded in 1944 to promote independence from France and restoration of Moroccan sovereignty.

ita est [Lat] *EE-tah-EST.* so it is.

Italia Irredenta [It] *ee-TAH-lee-ah-eer-reh-DEN-tah.* unredeemed Italy: that part of Italy (Trieste, the Trentino, etc.) still held by Austria-Hungary at the outbreak of World War I.

italien [Fr: *fem.* **italienne**] *ee-tah-LYẼ (-LYEN)* Italian; Italian style.

item [Lat] *EE-tem.* likewise; also.

ite, missa est [Lat] *EE-teh-MEES-sah-est.* go, it has been sent on its way (the Mass is finished).

iter [Lat: *pl.* **itinera**] *EE-tehr (ee-TEE-neh-rah)* path; way; route; road.

iterum [Lat] *EE-teh-room.* over again, anew.

Ivan [Russ] *ee-VAHN.* Russian form of John: stereotype name for a Russian.

Ivrit [Heb] *ee-VREET.* modern Hebrew language.

izba [Russ] *eez-BAH.* cottage; hut.

izdanie [Russ] *eez-DAH-nee-yeh.* issue; edition.

izdatel' [Russ] *eez-DAH-tyel'.* publisher.

izdatelstvo [Russ] *eez-DAH-tyel'st-vuh.* publishing house.

izquierda [Sp, of pre-Roman origin] *ees-KYEHR-dah.* left; left hand; left side; the political left.

izvestiya [Russ] *eez-VYES-tee-yuh.* news; reports; information; name of official USSR newspaper (often spelled **Izvestia**).

J

ja [Ger] *yah.* yes.

jabot [Fr] *zhah-BOH.* ruffle or frill worn at the neckline or front of the waist.

jaçana [Port, from Tupi-Guarani] *zhuh-suh-NAH.* tropical aquatic bird having very long legs and claws that enable it to walk on floating water plants.

Jacobins [Fr, from name of the Dominican convent where they originally met] *zhah-koh-BÊ.* French Revolutionary group led by Marat: promoted the Reign of Terror from 1789 to 1794; any political or radical extremists.

jacquard [Fr, from name of inventor] *zhah-KAR.* type of loom; woven fabric with large figured patterns.

Jacquerie [Fr] *zhah-k'REE.* peasant revolt against the nobles in northern France in the 14th century. See **Jacques Bonhomme.**

Jacques Bonhomme [Fr] *ZHAHK-boh-NOHM.* (*lit.,* James Good-man) contemptuous name given by the nobles to the French peasants who took part in the Jacquerie; symbol of the French common man.

jacta est alea. See **alea jacta est.**

Jagannatha [Skt] *juh-gun-NAH-tuh.* (*lit.,* lord of the world) a name of Krishna or Vishnu; a colossal figure of Krishna, drawn on a massive cart in a Hindu festival, under the wheels of which devotees are said to have thrown themselves to be crushed; any powerful, over-whelming machine or force, juggernaut.

Jäger [Ger: *pl. unchanged*] *YAY-guh.* hunter; sharpshooter in German or Austrian army. Also, **Jaeger.**

Jahrbuch [Ger] *YAHR-bookh.* yearbook; annual report; annual.

Jahresbericht [Ger] *YAH-R's-buh-riçt.* annual report.

Jahweh [Heb] *YAH-veh* (or *-weh*) Jehovah; the Lord God. Also, **Yahweh.**

jai alai [Sp, from Basque *jai,* game + *alai,* merry] *HY-ah-LY.* a fast-moving Basque ball game resembling handball, but played with a basketlike racket (**cesta**) strapped to the hand and wrist.

jaleo [Sp] *hah-LEH-oh.* popular Andalusian dance.

Jalousie [Fr] *zhah-loo-ZEE.* (*lit.,* jealousy) Venetian blind; louvered window.

jamadar. See **jemadar.**

jamais [Fr] *zhah-MEH.* ever; never; —**de ma vie** (*-duh-mah-VEE*) never in my life; —**vu** (*-VÜ*) never seen.

jamás [Sp] *hah-MAHS.* ever; never.

jambe [Fr] *zhãb.* leg.

jambon [Fr] *zhā-BŎ.* ham.

jamón [Sp] *hah-MOHN.* ham.

jam satis [Lat] *YAHM-SAH-tees.* enough already.

jantar [Port] *zhun-TAR.* dinner; to dine.

januis clausis [Lat] *YAH-noo-ees-KLOW-sees.* (behind) closed doors; privately.

ja, prosit [Ger] *YAH-PROH-sit.* (*lit.,* yes! to your health!) you can whistle for it! you won't get it!

jarabe tapatío [Sp] *hah-RAH-beh-tah-pah-TEE-oh.* Mexican hat dance.

jardin [Fr] *zhar-DẼ.* garden; **—des plantes** (*-day-PLÃT*) botanical gardens.

jardinière [Fr] *zhar-dee-NYEHR.* garnishes used for salads and mixed vegetables; ornamental flower pot.

jaune [Fr] *zhohn.* yellow.

ja wohl [Ger] *yah-VOHL.* yes, indeed; certainly.

je [Fr] *zhuh.* I.

jefe [Sp] *HEH-feh.* chief; leader.

jehad. See **jihad.**

jehovah [an erroneous rendering of the letters JHVH or YHVH, transcribing the Hebrew letters representing the ineffable name of God] *yeh-HOH-vah.* God of the Old Testament. Cf. **Jahweh.**

jemadar [Hindi-Urdu] *JEH-muh-dar.* under the British, a native officer, equal to a lieutenant; head of a staff of messengers or attendants. Also, **jamadar** (*JAH-*).

je maintiendrai [Fr] *zhuh-mẽ-tyẽ-DRAY.* I shall maintain (motto of the Netherlands).

jen [Chin] *zhun.* man; manhood; virtue; love of man; human.

je ne sais quoi [Fr] *zhuh-n'seh-KWAH.* I don't know what; an indescribable thing or feeling.

Jerez [Sp, from a town in SW Spain noted for sherry] *heh-RES.* sherry.

je suis prêt [Fr] *zhuh-süee-PREH.* I am ready.

Jesus, Hominum Salvator. See **Iesus Hominum Salvator.**

Jesus Nazarenus Rex Judaeorum. See **Iesus Nazarenus Rex Iudaeorum.**

jet d'eau [Fr: *pl.* jets d'eau] *zheh-DOH.* water jet; fountain.

jeté [Fr, p.p. of *jeter*, to throw, hurl] *zhuh-TAY.* ballet leap in which both feet leave the floor together and descent is made on one foot.

jetée [Fr] *zhuh-TAY.* jetty; wharf.

jeter de la poudre aux yeux [Fr] *zhuh-TAY-duh-lah-POO-droh-ZYÖ.* to throw dust into the eyes; to mislead deliberately.

jeton [Fr, from *jeter*, to throw, toss] *zhuh-TÕ.* chip, counter; token.

jeu [Fr: *pl.* **jeux**] *zhö.* game; play; maneuver, ploy; —**d'esprit** (*-des-PREE*) play of wit; witticism; —**de hasard** (*-duh-ah-ZAR*) game of chance; —**de mots** (*-duh-MOH*) play on words; pun; —**de théâtre** (*-duh-tay-AH-truh*) stage trick; dramatic air or gesture.

jeune [Fr] *zhön.* young; young person; —**fille** (*-FEE-yuh*) young girl; maiden; —**premier** (*fem.* **jeune première**) (*-pruh-MYAY, -MYEHR*) young lead player.

jeunesse [Fr] *zhö-NES.* youth; young people; —**dorée** (*-doh-RAY*) gilded youth; elegant young people.

jeu parti [Fr] *zhö-par-TEE.* (*lit.,* divided game) debate in verse, usually on a theme of courtly love, popular in the Middle Ages.

jezebel [Heb, name of the wife of Ahab, king of Israel] *JEZ-uh-bel.* wicked, immoral woman.

jícara [Sp] *HEE-kah-rah.* mug; chocolate cup.

jihad [Ar] *jee-HAHD.* holy war; crusade. Also, **jehad.**

jinete [Sp] *hee-NEH-teh.* horseman; cavalier.

jinni [Ar: *pl.* **jinn**] *JIN-nee* (*jin*) supernatural being that can take human or animal shape; genie.

jinrikisha [Jap *jin*, man + *riki*, power + *sha*, vehicle] *jin-RIK-shah.* two-wheeled cab pulled by a coolie; rickshaw.

jipijapa [AmerSp, from the name of a town in Ecuador] *hee-pee-HAH-pah.* fiber used in making panama hats; a panama hat.

jiujitsu. See **jujutsu.**

Joannes est nomen ejus [Lat] *yo-AHN-nes-est-NOH-men-EH-yoos.* John is his name (motto of Puerto Rico).

jobelin [Fr] *zhoh-b'LĒ.* thieves' argot used in the days of François Villon.

Joch [Ger] *yohkh.* yoke; burden, load; mountain ridge; land measure of Austria and Hungary.

jocrisse [Fr] *zhoh-KREES.* dolt; simpleton; ninny.

Jocs Florals [Cat] *ZHOHKS-floh-RAHLS.* floral games: a Catalonian song-and-dance festival.

jodhpurs [after Jodhpur, a city and state in NW India] *JOD-purz.* riding breeches fitting loosely about the hips and tight below the knee; ankle boots worn with such breeches.

Johannisberger [Ger] *yoh-HAH-nis-behr-guh.* a type of Rhine wine.

Johannistag [Ger] *yoh-HAH-nis-tak.* St. John's Day; Midsummer Day.

joie [Fr] *zhwah.* joy; pleasure; —**de vivre** (*-duh-VEE-vruh*) joy of being alive; joy of living.

joli [Fr: *fem.* **jolie**] *zhoh-LEE.* pretty; lovely.

jongleur [Fr] *zhō-GLÖR.* minstrel; juggler.

jonkheer [Du *jonk*, young + *heer*, master, gentleman] *YOHNK-hayr.* Dutch nobleman.

jornada [Sp] *hor-NAH-dah.* journey; day's journey; measure equal to the amount of land that can be plowed in a day; in early Spanish theater, an act.

jota [Sp] *HOH-tah.* an Aragonese dance.

jotunn [Icel *jötunn*, giant] *YOH-toon.* one of a race of giants in Scandinavian mythology that often fought against the gods.

jour [Fr] *zhoor.* day; daylight; —**de fête** (*-duh-FET*) feast day, festival, holiday; —**de l'an** (*-duh-LÃ*) New Year's Day; —**des morts** (*-day-MOR*) Day of the Dead; All Souls' Day; —**J** (*-ZHEE*) D-Day; —**maigre** (*-MEH-gruh*) (*lit.*, lean day) meatless day; Friday; fast day.

journal [Fr: *pl.* **journaux**] *zhoor-NAHL* (*-NOH*) newspaper; journal; diary.

joven [Sp: *pl.* **jóvenes**] *HOH-ven* (*-veh-nes*) young; young person.

jubbah [Ar] *JOOB-bah.* long everday robe worn in Moslem countries. Also, **jubba**.

Jude [Ger: *pl.* **Juden**] *YOO-duh* (*-d'n*) Jew.

Judendeutsch [Ger] *YOO-d'n-doych*. Jewish German; Yiddish.

Judenhetze [Ger] *YOO-d'n-het-suh*. persecution of Jews.

judex [Lat: *pl.* **judices**] *YOO-deks* (*-dee-kes*) judge; juryman.

judicium [Lat] *yoo-DEE-kee-oom*. judgment; —**Dei** (*-DEH-ee*) judgment of God.

judo [Jap *jū*, soft + *dō*, art] *JOO-doh*. Japanese system of wrestling and self-defense: a milder form of jujutsu.

Jueves Santo [Sp] *HWEH-ves-SAHN-toh*. Holy Thursday; Maundy Thursday.

Jugend [Ger] *YOO-g'nt*. youth; young people.

Jugendstil [Ger] *YOO-g'nt-shteel*. Art Nouveau in German-speaking countries.

Juif [Fr: *fem.* **Juive**] *zhweef* (*zhweev*) Jew; Jewish; Jewess.

juju [Fr, from Hausa *djudju*, fetish] *JOO-joo*. fetish or amulet worn by W African natives; supernatural power exercised by such a fetish.

jujube [Fr, from Lat *zizyphum*, from Gk *zizyphon*] *joo-JOOB*. Old World tree bearing an edible plumlike fruit; the fruit of this tree; small chewy candy made of gum arabic, gelatin and fruit flavoring.

jujutsu [Jap *jū*, soft + *jutsu*, art] *joo-JOO-tsoo*. Japanese method of hand-to-hand fighting that makes use of an opponent's own weight as leverage in throwing and disabling him. Also, **jiujitsu, jujitsu.**

julienne [Fr, from a girl's name] *zhü-LYEN*. fried potatoes cut in very thin strips; soup with vegetables cut in this manner.

jumelle [Fr, fem. of *jumeau*, twin] *zhü-MEL*. twin, pair; (*pl.*) binoculars, opera glasses.

jung [Ger] *yoong*. young; new, fresh, recent.

Jungfrau [Ger] *YOONG-frow*. maiden, young girl; virgin.

Junker [Ger] *YOON-kuh*. member of the landed gentry, esp. in E Prussia, noted for militarism and authoritarianism; German military officer devoted to loyalty and discipline.

Junkers [Ger, after Hugo Junkers, aircraft designer and builder] *YOON-kurs*. type of transport or bomber plane.

junta [Sp, lit., something joined] *HOON-tah*. administrative council or committee, usu. with military power, often serving as an interim government; in Spanish countries, any council or committee.

junto [alteration of **junta**] *JUN-toh*. political group, usu. one seeking to obtain or extend power; cabal.

jupe [Fr, from Ar *jubbah*, blouse] *zhüp*. skirt; crinoline; petticoat.

jupon [Fr, from *jupe*, skirt] *zhü-PŎ*. petticoat.

jura [Lat, pl. of **jus**] *YOO-rah*. laws; rights.

jure [Lat, abl. of **jus**] *YOO-reh*. by law; by right; —**belli** (*-BEL-lee*) by the law of war; by martial law; —**divino** (*-dee-VEE-noh*) by divine law or right; —**gentium** (*-GEN-tee-oom*) by the law of nations or peoples; —**humano** (*-hoo-MAH-noh*) by human law; by the people's will.

Juris Utriusque Doctor [Lat] *YOO-rees-oo-tree-OOS-kweh-DOHK-tor*. doctor of both laws (canon and civil law).

jus [Lat: pl. **jura**] *yoos* (*YOO-rah*) law; right; —**belli** (*-BEL-lee*) law of war; —**canonicum** (*-kah-NOH-nee-koom*) canon law; —**civile** (*-kee-VEE-leh*) civil law; —**commune** (*-kohm-MOO-neh*) common law; —**divinum** (*-dee-VEE-noom*) divine law; —**et norma loquendi** (*-et-NOR-mah-loh-KWEN-dee*) law and norms of speaking; common language usage; vernacular; —**e injuria non oritur** (*-eh-een-YOO-ree-ah-non-OH-ree-toor*) right does not arise from wrong; —**gentium** (*-GEN-tee-oom*) law of nations; international law.

jus [Fr] *zhü*. juice; gravy.

jus jurandum [Lat] *YOOS-yoo-RAHN-doom*. sworn oath.

jus primae noctis [Lat] *YOOS-PREE-my-NOHK-tees*. law of the first night: a feudal master's right to spend the wedding night with his vassal's bride.

jusqu'à [Fr] *ZHÜS-kah*. until; up to.

jus regium [Lat] *YOOS-REH-gee-oom*. royal law; law of the realm.

jus sanguinis [Lat] *YOOS-SAHN-gwee-nees.* blood law: law of parentage determining the nationality of a child.

juste milieu [Fr] *zhüst-mee-LYÖ.* golden mean.

justitia [Lat] *yoos-TEE-tee-ah.* justice; judge's office.

Justitia Omnibus [Lat] *yoos-TEE-tee-ah-OHM-nee-boos.* Justice to all (motto of the District of Columbia).

juxta [Lat] *YOOKS-tah.* near; next to.

juzgado [Sp, p.p. of *juzgar,* to judge] *hoos-GAH-doh.* judged, convicted; a convict, prisoner; a court, tribunal; (*slang*) jail.

j'y suis, j'y reste [Fr] *zhee-SÜEE-zhee-REST.* here I am, here I stay: attributed to Marshal MacMahon after taking the Malakoff fortifications in the Crimean War (1855).

K

ka [Egyptian] *kah.* the soul; the spirit.

kabala, kabbala. See **cabala.**

kabab [Turk *kebab,* roast meat] *kuh-BAHB.* small cubes of meat broiled on a skewer together with pieces of various vegetables. Also, **kabob, kebab, kebob.** Cf. **shish kebab.**

kabuki [Jap *kabu,* music and dancing + *ki,* style] *KAH-boo-kee.* popular Japanese play form, including music and dancing.

kabushiki kaisha [Jap] *KAH-boo-sh'-kee-KY-shah.* joint stock company; **kabushiki goshi kaisha** (*-GOH-shee-*) limited joint stock company.

Kabyle [Ar *qabīlah,* tribe] *kah-BEEL.* member of a Berber tribe in Algeria and Tunisia; the language of this tribe.

kaddish [Heb *qaddīsh,* holy (one)] *KAHD-deesh.* daily prayer; prayer for the dead.

kadi. See **cadi.**

Kaffee [Ger] *KAH-fay.* coffee; —**mit Schlagobers** (*-mit-SHLAH-goh-buz*) coffee with whipped cream.

Kaffeeklatsch [Ger] *KAH-fay-klahch.* gathering for coffee and chatter, usu. for women.

kaffir [Ar *kāfir*, unbeliever] *KAH-feer.* non-Moslem; infidel. Also, **kafir.**

kai [Gk] *ky.* and.

kai [Maori] *ky.* food.

Kaiser [Ger, from Lat *Caesar*, Caesar, emperor] *KY-zuh.* German or Austrian emperor.

Kaiserjäger [Ger] *KY-zuh-yay-guh.* member of Alpine sharpshooter corps.

kaiserlich [Ger] *KY-zuh-liç.* imperial.

kaisha [Jap] *KY-shah.* company, association.

kai ta loipa [Gk] *ky-tah-loy-PAH.* and so forth, et cetera.

kakemono [Jap] *KAH-keh-MOH-noh.* hanging picture or scroll which unrolls from a rod at the lower end.

kala [Hindi] *KAH-lah.* black.

kala-azar [Hindi: black disease] *KAH-lah-ah-ZAR.* chronic, often fatal disease prevalent in India, somewhat similar to malaria.

Kalb [Ger: *pl.* **Kälber**] *kahlp* (*KEL-buh*) calf.

Kalbfleisch [Ger] *KAHLP-flysh.* veal.

Kalbsbraten [Ger] *KAHLPS-brah-t'n.* roast veal.

kalendae. See **calendae.**

Kalevala [Finn] *KAH-leh-vah-lah.* Finnish national epic.

kalos [Gk: *fem.* **kalē**] *kah-LOHS* (*-LEH*) beautiful; fine.

Kamarinskaya [Russ] *kuh-MAH-reen-skuh-yuh.* men's folk dance.

Kamerad [Ger] *KAH-muh-raht.* comrade; typically, the cry of a surrendering soldier.

kami [Jap] *KAH-mee.* a Shinto god; divinity; Japanese title of nobility.

kamikaze [Jap] *KAH-mee-kah-zeh.* (*lit.*, divine wind) a suicide plane or its pilot.

Kampf [Ger: *pl.* **Kämpfe**] *kahmpf* (*KEMP-feh*) struggle; conflict.

kanaka [Hawaiian] *kah-NAH-kah* (*lit.*, man) native Hawaiian or South Sea islander.

kang [Chin] *kahng.* brick sleeping platform, heated from below by a fire.

kaolin [Chin, from Kaoling, the name of a mountain in

China where it was first extracted] *KOW-lin.* fine-grained white clay used in making porcelain.

ka pai [Maori] *KAH-PY.* it is good; O.K.

Kapellmeister [Ger] *kah-PEL-mys-tuh.* conductor of an orchestra or choir.

kaput [Ger, from Fr *capot,* scoring no tricks in the game of *piquet*] *kah-POOT.* finished, done for; dead.

karakul [orig. a place-name in Asia, from Turk *kara,* black + *kul,* lake] *kah-rah-KOOL.* short, curly-haired Asian lamb; its fur; Persian lamb.

karate [Jap] *KAH-rah-teh.* (*lit.,* empty hands) Japanese method of fighting without weapons, by striking sensitive areas of opponent's body with hands or feet.

kardia [Gk] *kar-DEE-ah.* heart.

kari [Tamil: sauce] *KAH-ree.* spicy E Indian dish of vegetables with meat or fish, flavored with curry and usu. served with rice; curry.

karma [Skt] *KAR-muh.* the sum total of a person's life and deeds, the determining factor in ascertaining the person's next life; fate, destiny.

Kartell [Ger] *kar-TEL.* cartel; written agreement between enemy nations about exchanging prisoners; trade agreement, with monopolistic features; written challenge to a duel.

Kartoffel [Ger: *pl.* **Kartoffeln**] *KAR-tohf-f'l* (*-'ln*) potato.

Kartoffelklösse [Ger] *KAR-tohf-f'l-klö-seh.* potato dumplings.

kasbah [Ar] *KAHS-bah.* citadel, fortress; quarter of a city; (*cap.*) the older, native quarter of Algiers. Also, **casbah.**

kasha [Russ] *KAH-shuh.* buckwheat groats: a food staple of Russia and other E European countries.

Kasten [Ger] *KAHS-t'n.* coffer; box, chest.

katakana [Jap *kata,* form, formal + *kana,* syllabary] *KAH-tah-kah-nah.* the angular, less common form of the Japanese syllabary. Cf. **hiragana.**

katana [Jap] *KAH-tah-nah.* a Japanese samurai sword.

Katharevousa [Gk] *kah-thah-REH-voo-sah.* (*lit.,* pure, purified) the puristic literary form of modern Greek, modeled after the ancient classical Greek. Cf. **Demotike.**

katharsis [Gk] *kah-THAR-sees.* purging; purification, esp. of the emotions or conscience; catharsis.

Katzenjammer [Ger] *KAH-ts'n-yah-muh.* (*lit.*, cat's misery) hangover.

Kauderwelsch [Ger] *KOW-duh-velsh.* gibberish; jargon; nonsense.

kayak [Eskimo] *KY-ahk.* swift, light boat made by stretching skins over a wooden frame.

kazatski [Russ] *kuh-ZAHT-skee.* Cossack; a Cossack dance. Also, **kozatski.**

kebab, kebob. See **kabab.**

keddah. See **kheda.**

Kellner [Ger] *KEL-nuh.* waiter; manservant; **Kellnerin** (*-rin*) waitress.

kenning [Icel] *KEN-ing.* (*lit.*, a knowing) a fanciful and poetic name used in addition to or instead of the name of a person or thing, common in Anglo-Saxon and Old Norse poetry.

kephalē [Gk] *keh-fah-LEH.* head.

képi [Fr, from Swiss Ger *käppi,* cap] *kay-PEE.* French military cap, round with a flat top and a nearly horizontal visor.

Kerl [Ger: *pl.* **Kerle** or **Kerls**] *kehrl* (*KEHR-leh, kehrls*) fellow, chap.

kermis [Du, contr. of *kercmisse,* church Mass] *KEHR-mis.* in the Low Countries, a joyous religious festival; a charity church bazaar.

KGB [Russ, abbr. of *komitet gosudarstvennoi bezopasnosti,* Committee of State Security] *kah-gay-bay.* Soviet secret police attached to the Council of Ministers of the USSR, replacing earlier **Cheka, GPU, NKVD, MVD.**

khan [Turkic] *khahn.* ruler; chief; supreme ruler of the Tatars and, in the Middle Ages, emperor of China; lord, master; title of respect used in some Asian countries.

khan [Ar, from Pers] *khahn.* wayside inn; caravansary.

khana [Hindi] *KAH-nah.* food; meal.

khanum [Turk] *KHAH-noom.* ranking Oriental woman; first lady of a harem. Also, **hanum.**

kheda [Hindi] *KEH-dah.* enclosure for ensnaring wild elephants. Also, **keddah.**

khedive [Fr *khédive*, from Turk *hidiv*, from Pers *khidīw*, prince] *keh-DEEV.* leader; viceroy; title of the Turkish viceroys in Egypt from 1867 to 1914.

khleb [Russ] *khlyep.* bread; food.

khozyaika [Russ] *khah-ZYAH-ee-kuh.* mistress; proprietress; lady of the house; landlady; hostess.

khozyain [Russ] *khah-ZYAH-een.* master; proprietor, master of the house; landlord; host.

khushi [Hindi, from Pers] *KOO-shee.* pleasure; happiness; contentment.

kiang [Chin] *kyahng.* river.

kia ora [Maori] *KEE-ah-OH-rah.* be happy! be healthy! (in toasting someone).

kibbutz [Mod Heb: *pl.* **kibbutzim**] *keeb-BOOTS* (*keeb-boots-EEM*) Israeli collective farm settlement.

kibitzer [Yid, from Ger *Kiebitz*, busybody, lit., lapwing, plover] *KIB-it-suh.* onlooker at a game who offers unwanted comment or advice; meddler; heckler.

kielbasa [Pol] *kyel-BAH-sah.* a kind of sausage made of beef or pork, flavored with garlic and spices.

kimchi [Korean] *KIM-chee.* pickled cabbage or other vegetables, often containing also fish, seasoned with garlic and spices.

kimono [Jap] *KEE-moh-noh.* Japanese outer robe with sash and loose sleeves; woman's loose dressing gown.

Kind [Ger: *pl.* **Kinder**] *kint* (*KIN-duh*) child.

Kinder, Küche, und Kirche [Ger] *KIN-duh-KÜ-çeh-oont-KEER-çeh.* children, kitchen and church: German nationalist doctrine describing the place of women in society.

Kino [Ger, contr. of *Kinematograph*] *KEE-noh.* in Europe, motion picture theater; cinema.

kiosk [Fr *kiosque*, from Turk *kösk*, from Pers *kūshk*, pavilion] *kee-OHSK.* small stand, usually cylindrical and topped by a dome, where newspapers, magazines, or theater and lottery tickets are sold; any similar structure, such as a covered subway entrance or a small park pavilion.

Kipfel [Ger] *KIP-f'l.* crescent-shaped roll; croissant.

királj [Hung] *KEE-rahly.* prince; king; ruler.

Kirche [Ger] *KEER-çeh.* church.

Kirchhof [Ger] *KEERÇ-hohf.* churchyard; cemetery, graveyard.

Kirschwasser [Ger] *KEERSH-vah-suh.* (*lit.*, cherry water) cherry brandy.

kishke [Yid, of Slavic origin] *KISH-kuh.* in Jewish cookery, an animal intestine stuffed with a mixture of flour, fat, onion and seasonings, and roasted or boiled.

kismet [Turk, from Ar *qismat*] *KIS-met.* fate; lot; will of Allah.

Kiswahili [Swahili] *kee-swah-HEE-lee.* the Swahili language.

kitab [Ar: *pl.* **kutub**] *kee-TAHB* (*koo-TOOB*) book; religious book.

kithara [Gk] *KEE-thah-rah.* ancient Greek stringed instrument resembling a lyre; cithara.

kitsch [Ger] *kich.* vulgar art or literature, produced to satisfy popular taste.

kiwi [Maori] *KEE-wee.* flightless bird of New Zealand; (*slang*) a New Zealander.

Kladderadatsch [Ger] *KLAH-duh-rah-dahch.* mess, muddle, mixture; name of a Berlin weekly humor magazine.

Klagelied [Ger] *KLAH-guh-leet.* lament; dirge, elegy.

Klang [Ger] *klahng.* clang; sound; timbre.

Klavier [Ger] *klah-VEER.* piano.

kleftes [Mod Gk] *KLEF-tees.* irregular guerrilla fighter.

kloof [Afrikaans] *klohf.* in S Africa, gorge, glen, ravine.

Kloss [Ger: *pl.* **Klösse**] *klohs* (*KLÖ-seh*) dumpling.

klotz [Yid & Ger] *klohts.* log; block; lump; lout, clod.

Knesset [Heb: gathering] *KNES-set.* unicameral Israeli parliament.

knish [Yid, from Pol] *knish.* a thin roll of dough filled with meat, cheese or mashed potato, and fried or baked.

Knödel [Ger] *KNÖ-d'l.* dumpling.

knout [Russ *knut*] *knoot.* whip.

Kobold [Ger] *KOH-bohlt.* elf; gnome; brownie.

Kohinoor [Pers: mountain of light] *KOH-hee-noor.* famous Indian diamond, weighing 106 carats, now belonging to the British crown jewels.

kohl [Ar: antimony] *kohl.* black charcoallike powder of antimony sulfide, used as eye liner or eyeshadow.

kohlrabi [Ger, adapted from It *cavoli rape,* cabbage-turnips] *KOHL-rah-bee.* plant of the cabbage family, having a bulblike stem.

koine [Gk, from fem. of *koinos,* common] *koy-NEH.* language common to a large area; standard language of common intercourse.

koinos topos [Gk] *koy-NOHS-TOH-pohs.* commonplace; cliché.

kola [WAfrican] *KOH-lah.* extract prepared from the nuts of a tropical tree of W Africa, Brazil, and the W Indies, containing caffein, and sometimes used as a stimulant in soft drinks.

kolbasa [Russ] *kul-buh-SAH.* a type of sausage similar to Polish **kielbasa.**

kolinsky [Russ *kolinskii,* of Kola, a district in NW Russia] *kuh-LYEEN-skee.* an Asian mink; its fur.

kolkhoz [Russ, abbr. of *kollektivnoye khozyaistvo*] *kul-KHOHS.* collective farm in the USSR.

Kol Nidre [Aramaic: *kōl,* all + *nidhre,* vows, promises] *kohl-NEE-dreh.* all (my) vows: prayer of atonement offered at Yom Kippur.

kolo [Serbo-Croatian, from Old Slavic: wheel] *KOH-loh.* Serbian round dance.

kolokol [Russ] *KOH-luh-kul.* bell.

Kommandatura [Ger] *koh-mahn-dah-TOO-ruh.* military occupation headquarters; the Allied military government in Berlin after World War II. Also, **Kommandantur** (*-dahn-*).

Komsomol [Russ, abbr. of *Kommunisticheskyi Soyuz Molodezhi*] *kum-suh-MAWL.* Communist youth organization; a member of this organization.

Komsomol'skaya Pravda [Russ] *kum-suh-MAWL'-skuh-yuh-PRAHV-duh.* a Communist youth newspaper.

Konditorei [Ger] *kohn-dit-uh-RY*. bakery; sweet shop, pastry shop.

König [Ger: *pl.* **Könige**] *KÖ-niç* (*-ni-geh*) king.

Königin [Ger] *KÖ-ni-gin*. queen.

Kontrabass [Ger] *KOHN-truh-bahs*. double bass; bass viol.

Konzertmeister [Ger] *kohn-TSEHRT-mys-tuh*. first violinist; concertmaster.

kopeck [Russ *kopeika*] *KOH-pek*. a coin of the Soviet Union, 100th of a ruble. Also, **copeck**.

Koran [Ar *qur'ān*] *koo-RAHN*. (*lit*., book) book of Moslem laws as given by Mohammed.

kosher [Yid, from Heb *kāshēr*, right] *KOH-shur*. correctly prepared in accordance with Jewish dietary laws; (*slang*) legitimate; proper; correct.

kosmos [Gk] *KOHS-mohs*. order; world, universe.

kouphē gē touton kalyptoi [Gk] *KOO-feh-geh-TOO-tohn-kah-LOOP-toy*. may the earth lie light upon him: formula used in epitaphs.

kouskous. See **couscous.**

kowtow [Chin *k'o-t'ou*, knock (the) head] *KOH-tow*. to bow low, touching the forehead to the ground; show respect; fawn; be subservient.

ko wu [Chin] *KOH-WOO*. investigation; probe.

kozatski. See **kazatski.**

kraal [Afrikaans, from Port *curral*, pen, corral] *krahl*. S African native village built around an enclosure for livestock; an enclosure, corral.

Kraft durch Freude [Ger] *KRAHFT-durç-FROY-deh*. Strength through Joy: name of a Nazi recreational organization.

krakowiak [Pol, from Krakow, city in Poland] *krah-KOO-vyahk*. Polish folk dance.

Krasnaya Zvezda [Russ] *KRAHS-nuh-yuh-svyiz-DAH*. Red Star: a Soviet army publication.

Kraut [Ger] *krowt*. (*lit*., herb, weed, cabbage) American soldiers' term for a German during World War II (with allusion to German fondness for sauerkraut).

krees. See **kris.**

Kreis [Ger] *krys.* (*lit.*, circle) area of Allied occupation after World War II.

Kremlin [Russ *kreml'*, fortress] *KREM-lin.* the citadel of Moscow, seat of Soviet government; the Soviet government itself.

kreplach [Yid, pl. of *krepel*, fritter] *KREP-lahkh.* small rolls of noodle dough filled with chopped meat or chicken liver, served boiled in soups.

Kreuz [Ger: pl. **Kreuze**] *kroyts* (*KROY-tseh*) cross.

Krieg [Ger: pl. **Kriege**] *kreek* (*KREE-geh*) war.

Kriegsgefangener [Ger] *KREEKS-guh-fahn-guh-nuh.* prisoner of war.

Kriegspiel [Ger] *KREEK-shpeel.* war game, usu. played with miniature pieces on a map or table representing a battlefield, used for teaching military tactics; chess game in which each opponent sees only his own side of the board, the opponent's moves being told to him by a referee.

kris [Malay] *krees.* short sword or dagger with a wavy blade, used by Malays. Also, **creese, krees.**

Kshatriya [Skt: ruling, ruler] *KSHAH-tree-yuh.* the military and ruling caste, one of the four divisions of the Hindu caste system.

Kuchen [Ger] *KOO-kh'n.* cake; tart, pastry.

kudos [Gk] *KOO-dohs.* fame; honors; approval.

kulak [Russ] *koo-LAHK.* (*lit.*, fist, tightwad) a well-to-do peasant or merchant in pre-Revolutionary Russia.

Kultur [Ger] *kool-TOOR.* civilization; culture.

Kulturkampf [Ger] *kool-TOOR-kahmpf.* Prussia's struggle to dominate the Roman Catholic Church in the latter part of the 19th century, chiefly in matters of educational and ecclesiastical appointments.

kumiss [Russ *kumys*, from Tatar] *KOO-miss.* fermented mare's or camel's milk.

Kümmel [Ger] *KÜM-'l.* caraway or cumin seed; a clear liqueur flavored with these.

kummerbund. See **cummerbund.**

Kunst [Ger: pl. **Künste**] *koonst* (*KÜNS-teh*) art.

Künstler [Ger] *KÜNST-luh.* artist.

Künstlerroman [Ger] *KÜNST-luh-roh-mahn.* novel about an artist.

Kunstlied [Ger] *KOONST-leet.* art song; poem set to continuous, nonrepeated music.

Kuomintang [Chin *kuo,* nation + *min,* people + *tang,* party] *GWOH-min-TAHNG.* National People's Party, founded by Sun Yat-Sen in 1911, and led since 1925 by Chiang Kai-Shek; the chief political party in China until the Communist victory of 1948.

Kuo-yü [Chin] *GWOH-YÜ.* national tongue of China, based on North Mandarin dialect, and officially used throughout both Mainland China and Taiwan.

Kursaal [Ger *Kur,* treatment, cure + *Saal,* salon] *KOOR-zahl.* public room or lodge at a health resort.

kushti [Hindi] *KUSH-tee.* E Indian wrestling, similar to jujutsu.

kuskus [Anglo-Ind, from Hindi *khaskhas*] *KUS-kus.* an E Indian grass, the roots of which are used for making mats and screens. Also, **kuskos.**

kutub. See **kitab.**

kvass [Russ *kvas*] *kvahs.* a fermenting agent used in soups and beverages; a beverage so made; a Russian beer made from malt, rye and barley. Also, **quass.**

kvetch [Yid] *kvech.* to complain, gripe; a complainer, nag.

Kyrie Eleison [Gk *Kyrie,* Lord + *eleēson,* have mercy] *KEE-ree-eh-eh-LEH-ee-sohn.* Lord, have mercy (upon us): petition used in the ritual of the Roman Catholic, Greek Orthodox and Anglican Churches.

L

L. Abbr. of **liber.**

la [Fr, Sp, It] *lah.* the (*fem. sing.*).

laager [Afrikaans] *LAH-gur.* circle of wagons in defensive disposition; encampment. Also, **lager.**

la almohada es buen consejo [Sp] *lah-ahl-moh-AH-dah-es-*

BWEN-kohn-SEH-hoh. (*lit.*, the pillow is good counsel) it pays to sleep on it.

la belle dame sans merci [Fr] *lah-BEL-dahm-sã-mehr-SEE.* the beautiful (but) merciless lady.

labium [Lat: *pl.* **labia**] *LAH-bee-oom* (*-ah*) lip; liplike part or structure.

la bohème [Fr] *lah-boh-EM.* Bohemian life; unconventional mores.

Labor Omnia Vincit [Lat] *LAH-bor-OHM-nee-ah-VEEN-keet.* Work conquers all (motto of Oklahoma).

labrador [Sp] *lah-brah-DOR.* farmer; plowman; laborer.

lac [Fr] *lahk.* lake.

lac [Hindi] See **lakh.**

lâche [Fr] *lahsh.* slack; loose; coward(ly).

la commedia è finita [It] *lah-kohm-MEH-dyah-eh-fee-NEE-tah.* the comedy is ended.

Lacrima Christi [Lat] *LAH-kree-mah-KREES-tee.* [*lit.*, tear(s) of Christ] name of two Italian wines: a red wine from Naples and a sparkling dry wine from Piedmont. Also, **Lachryma Christi.**

lacrimae rerum. See **sunt lacrimae rerum.**

Laden [Ger: *pl.* **Läden**] *LAH-d'n* (*LAY-d'n*) store, shop.

Ladino [Sp, from Lat *latinus,* Latin] *lah-DEE-noh.* a Sephardic Jew; a dialect of Spanish spoken by Sephardic Jews; in Spanish America, a mestizo.

ladrón [Sp: *pl.* **ladrones**] *lah-DROHN* (*-DROH-nes*) thief; robber.

la fame non vuol leggi [It] *lah-FAH-meh-nohn-VWOHL-LAY-jee.* hunger knows no law.

la Garde meurt et ne se rend pas [Fr] *lah-GARD-MÖR-ay-nuh-suh-RÃ-PAH.* the Guard dies and does not surrender: attributed to General Cambronne at Waterloo.

lagarto [Sp] *lah-GAR-toh.* lizard; alligator.

Lager [Ger] *LAH-guh.* camp; storehouse, store; a light beer; [Afrikaans] See **laager.**

La Gioconda [It] *lah-joh-KOHN-dah.* the Monna Lisa, a painting by Da Vinci.

La Giovine Italia [It] *lah-JOH-vee-neh-ee-TAH-lyah.* Young Italy: secret liberation group under Mazzini.

lagniappe [Louisiana Fr, from AmerSp *la ñapa*, the addition, from Quechua] *lah-NYAHP*. small present given to a purchaser by way of good measure; nominal gift, token; extra bonus; tip, gratuity.

lago [It, Sp] *LAH-goh*; [Port] *LAH-goo*. lake.

lagosta [Port] *luh-GOHSH-tuh*. lobster.

lagrimoso [It] *lah-gree-MOH-soh*. (*music*) tearfully, mournfully.

lai [Fr] *leh*. lay; love poem; romantic tale.

laid [Fr: *fem.* **laide**] *leh* (*led*) ugly.

laisser-aller [Fr] *leh-SAY-ah-LAY*. (*lit.*, to let go) looseness; lack of restraint in speech or manner.

laissez donc [Fr] *leh-SAY-dõ*. (*lit.*, leave off, then) nonsense!

laissez faire [Fr] *leh-SAY-FEHR*. (*lit.*, let do) policy of noninterference, esp. by government in economic affairs; permissiveness.

lait [Fr] *leh*. milk.

laitue [Fr] *leh-TÜ*. lettuce.

lakh [Hindi *lākh*, from Skt *lākhshā*] *lahk*. in India, 100,000, esp. of rupees. Also, **lac**.

l'allegro [It] *lahl-LEH-groh*. the happy (or merry) man.

lama [Tibetan] *LAH-mah*. Buddhist priest or monk in Tibet.

La Mancha [Sp] *lah-MAHN-chah*. a plateau region in central Spain.

La Manche [Fr] *lah-MÃSH*. (*lit.*, the sleeve, from its shape) the French name of the English Channel.

La Mano Nera [It] *lah-MAH-noh-NEH-rah*. the Black Hand: an alleged former criminal secret society of Italians in the U.S.

lamé [Fr, from *lame*, thin plate or strip, from Lat *lamina*] *lah-MAY*. trimmed in gold or silver leaf; fabric of woven metal threads.

lamentando [It] *lah-men-TAHN-doh*. (*music*) lamenting; sad.

lamentevole [It] *lah-men-TAY-voh-leh*. sorrowful; sad.

Lammergeier [Ger] *LAHM-uh-gy-uh*. (*lit.*, lambs' vulture, from its habit of preying on lambs) a large European vulture. Also, **Lammergeyer**.

lanai [Hawaiian] *lah-NAH-ee.* veranda, open porch.

Land [Ger: *pl.* **Länder**] *lahnt (LEN-duh)* land, country; province, state.

landau [Ger, from the name of the town where it was first made] *LAN-dow.* car or carriage with a divided top, of which either or both sections fold down.

lande [Fr, from Germanic] *lăd.* wasteland; moor; lowlands.

Landsknecht [Ger, from *Land*, land + *Knecht*, servant, vassal] *LAHNTS-kneçt.* a mercenary foot-soldier, usu. a pikeman or halberdier in 16th-century Europe. Also, in Fr adaptation, **lansquenet**: in It, **lanzichenecco.**

Landsmål [Norw] *LAHNTS-mawl. (lit.,* country speech) **Nynorsk,** q.v.

Landsmann [Ger] *LAHNTS-mahn.* countryman; compatriot.

Landsturm [Ger] *LAHNT-shtoorm.* home guard; reserve troops (of men over 45); a general draft of all able-bodied men in wartime.

Landtag [Ger] *LAHNT-tahk.* legislature of a German state.

Landwehr [Ger] *LAHNT-vehr.* home guard; reserve troops (of men between 35 and 45).

langage [Fr] *lă-GAHZH.* language; speech; tongue.

Langlauf [Ger, from *lang*, long + *laufen*, to run] *LAHNG-lowf.* long-distance or cross-country skiing.

langooty [Anglo-Ind, from Hindi] *lahn-GOO-tee.* loincloth. Also, **langoti.**

langosta [Sp] *lahn-GOHS-tah.* lobster.

langostín [Sp] *lahn-gohs-TEEN.* crawfish. Also, **langostino** (*-TEE-noh*).

langouste [Fr] *lă-GOOST.* lobster.

langue [Fr] *lăg.* language; tongue; —**d'oc** (*-DOHK*) (*lit.,* yes-language) the medieval tongue of southern France, in which *oc* was the word for yes; —**d'oïl** (*-doh-EEL*) (*lit.,* yes-language) the medieval tongue of northern France, in which *oïl* was the word for yes; —**verte** (*-VEHRT*) (*lit.,* green language) slang.

languidamente [It] *lahn-gwee-dah-MAYN-teh.* (*music*) languidly.

lansquenet. *lăs-kuh-NEH.* See **Landsknecht.**

lantzman [Yid] *LAHNTS-m'n.* countryman; compatriot.

la nuit tous les chats sont gris [Fr] *lah-NÜEE-TOO-lay-shah-sŏ-GREE.* at night all cats are gray.

lanzichenecco. *lahn-tsee-keh-NAYK-koh.* See **Landsknecht.**

lapin [Fr] *lah-PÊ.* rabbit; rabbit fur.

lapis [Lat: *pl.* **lapides**] *LAH-pees* (*-pee-des*) stone; —**lazuli** (*-LAH-zoo-lee*) (*lit.*, stone of azure) an opaque deep-blue mineral used as a gem and a pigment; a sky-blue color, azure.

lap-lap [Melanesian Pidgin] *LAHP-lahp.* loincloth worn by natives in New Guinea.

la povertà è la madre di tutte le arti [It] *lah-poh-vehr-TAH-eh-lah-MAH-dreh-dee-TOOT-teh-leh-AR-tee.* poverty is the mother of all arts; necessity is the mother of invention.

l'appétit vient en mangeant [Fr] *lah-pay-TEE-VYÊ-tä-mä-ZHÃ.* appetite comes with eating.

La Prensa [Sp] *lah-PREN-sah.* (*lit.*, the press) Spanish-language newspaper published in New York City; the same name appears for many newspapers in the Spanish-speaking world.

lapsus [Lat, p.p. of *labi*, to fall] *LAHP-soos.* slip; blunder, lapse; —**calami** (*-KAH-lah-mee*) slip of the pen; —**linguae** (*-LEEN-gwy*) slip of the tongue; —**mentis** (*-MEN-tees*) slip of the mind.

lar [Lat: *pl.* **lares**] *lar* (*LAH-res*) god, deity; ancestral god.

lard [Fr] *lar.* bacon; animal fat, lard.

la reata [Sp] *lah-reh-AH-tah.* lariat; lasso.

lares et penates [Lat] *LAH-res-et-peh-NAH-tes.* gods of the household; spirit gods of deceased members of the family, that protected the Roman home.

l'argent [Fr] *lar-ZHÃ.* money.

larghetto [It] *lar-GAYT-toh.* (*music*) somewhat slow, not so slow as **largo.**

larghissimo [It] *lar-GEES-see-moh.* (*music*) very slow.

largo [It] *LAR-goh.* (*music*) slow; a slow, stately movement; wide, broad; (*interj.*) make way!

l'art pour l'art [Fr] *LAR-poor-LAR.* art for art's sake.

larva [Lat: *pl.* **larvae**] *LAR-vah* (*-vy*) ghost, specter; larva (from its spectral appearance).

las [Sp] *lahs.* the (*fem. pl.*).

lasagne [It] *lah-SAH-nyeh.* broad, flat macaroni; a dish made of this with cheese, meat and tomato sauce, baked in a flat pan.

lascar [Port, from Hindi *lashkarī*, soldier] *LAS-kur.* an E Indian sailor; in Anglo-Indian use, an artilleryman.

lasciate ogni speranza, voi ch'entrate [It] *lah-SHAH-teh-OH-nyee-speh-RAHN-tsah-voy-ken-TRAH-teh.* abandon all hope, ye who enter: the sign at the entrance of Dante's hell.

laticlavium [Lat] *lah-tee-KLAH-vee-oom.* a broad purple stripe on the tunic, worn by Romans as a mark of distinction or a badge of the senatorial office. Also, **laticlavus** (*-voos*).

latifondo [It] *lah-tee-FOHN-doh*; **latifundio** [Sp] *lah-tee-FOON-dyoh*; **latifúndio** [Port] *luh-tee-FOON-dee-oo.* large landed estate.

látigo [Sp] *LAH-tee-goh.* whip; strap used for tightening the cinch of a saddle.

latin de cuisine [Fr] *lah-TĔ-duh-küee-ZEEN.* (*lit.*, kitchen Latin) dog Latin; pig Latin.

latine [Lat] *lah-TEE-neh.* (translated or expressed) in Latin.

latino [Sp] *lah-TEE-noh.* Latin; a person of Latin race or tongue; (in some Spanish-American countries) Spanish; Hispanic.

Latino sine flexione [Lat] *lah-TEE-noh-SEE-neh-flek-SYOH-neh.* Latin without inflectional endings: a constructed language devised in 1903 by the Italian mathematician Giuseppe Peano.

lauda [It, from Lat *laus*, praise] *LOW-dah.* medieval Italian verse form in praise of God or the Virgin.

laudator temporis acti [Lat] *low-DAH-tor-TEM-poh-rees-AHK-tee.* one who praises the good old days.

lau lau [Hawaiian] *LOW-low.* a dish of beef, fish and pork.

Lausbube [Ger *Laus*, louse + *Bube*, boy] *LOWS-boo-beh.* rascal; mischievous person.

laus Deo [Lat] *LOWS-DEH-oh.* praise (be) to God.

laut [Ger] *lowt.* loud; loudly; in accordance with.

Laut [Ger: *pl.* **Laute**] *lowt* (*LOW-teh*) sound; tone.

Lautgesetz [Ger: *pl.* **-gesetze**] *LOWT-guh-zets* (*-zet-seh*) phonetic law; sound law.

Lautlehre [Ger] *LOWT-leh-reh.* phonetics; phonology.

lavabo [It, Sp] *lah-VAH-boh*; [Fr] *lah-vah-BOH.* (all from Lat: I shall wash) washroom; washbasin; lavatory.

lava-lava [Samoan] *LAH-vah-LAH-vah.* garment worn by both men and women in Polynesia, consisting of a piece of printed cloth fastened at the lower half of the body.

lavallière [Fr, after the Duchesse de La Vallière, one of Louis XIV's mistresses] *lah-vah-LYEHR.* pendant on a chain worn about the neck.

lavandera [Sp] *lah-vahn-DEH-rah.* washwoman.

lavasse [Fr, from *laver*, to wash] *lah-VAHS.* sudden rain shower; slops, wish-wash.

l'avenir [Fr] *lah-v'NEER.* the future.

la vérité [Fr] *lah-vay-ree-TAY.* the truth.

la vida es sueño [Sp] *lah-VEE-dah-es-SWEH-nyoh.* life is a dream.

la vie [Fr] *lah-VEE.* life.

lazzarone [It, from *lazzaro*, Lazarus, a beggar in the Bible] *lah-dzah-ROH-neh.* Neapolitan beggar; street beggar; urchin.

lb. Abbr. of **libra.**

le [Fr] *luh.* the (*masc. sing.*); [It] *leh.* the (*fem. pl.*).

le beau monde [Fr] *luh-BOH-MŎD.* (*lit.*, the beautiful world) high society; fashionable people.

Leben Sie wohl [Ger] *LAY-b'n-zee-VOHL.* good-bye; be well.

Lebensraum [Ger] *LAY-b'nz-rowm.* living space; elbow room.

Leberwurst [Ger] *LAY-buh-voorst.* liver sausage; liverwurst.

lebhaft [Ger] *LAYB-hahft.* lively, spirited.

Le Bourgeois Gentilhomme [Fr] *luh-boor-ZHWAH-zhã-tee-YUM.* the commoner turned gentleman: title of a play by Molière.

le chant du cygne [Fr] *luh-SHÃ-dü-SEE-nyuh.* swan song.

leche [Sp] *LEH-cheh.* milk.

lechón [Sp, from **leche,** milk] *leh-CHOHN.* suckling; young pig; pork.

lecture [Fr] *lek-TÜR.* reading.

Leder [Ger] *LAY-duh.* leather; **Lederhosen** (*-hoh-z'n*) short pants of leather, commonly worn in Bavaria.

le droit du plus fort [Fr] *luh-DRWAH-dü-plü-FOR.* the right of the stronger; might makes right.

legadero [AmerSp] *leh-gah-DEH-roh.* stirrup strap on a Mexican saddle.

legalis homo [Lat] *leh-GAH-lees-HOH-moh.* man with full legal rights.

legatissimo [It] *leh-gah-TEES-see-moh.* (*music*) very smoothly; lightly.

legato [It, from *legare,* to bind together] *leh-GAH-toh.* (*music*) smoothly; without pause between notes.

legatura [It] *leh-gah-TOO-rah.* (*music*) tie; brace.

legenda [Lat, from *legere,* to read] *leh-GEN-dah.* things to be read.

leges. See **lex.**

legge [It: *pl.* **leggi**] *LAY-jeh* (*-jee*) law; rule; standard, norm.

leggero [It] *leh-JEH-roh.* (*music*) light(ly), delicate(ly). Also, **leggiero.**

Légion d'Honneur [Fr] *lay-ZHŎ-duh-NÖR.* Legion of Honor: a military and civil honorary order founded by Napoleon in 1802.

légionnaire [Fr] *lay-zhuh-NEHR.* member of a legion, esp. the French **Légion d'Honneur.**

Legum Baccalaureus [Lat: *abbr.* **LL.B.**] *LEH-goom-bahk-kah-LOW-reh-oos.* Bachelor of Laws; **Legum Magister** (*-mah-GEES-tehr*) (*abbr.* **LL.M.**) Master of Laws; **Legum Doctor** (*-DOHK-tor*) (*abbr.* **LL.D.**) Doctor of Laws.

légume [Fr] *lay-GÜM.* vegetable.

legume [It: *pl.* **legumi**] *leh-GOO-meh* (*-mee*) vegetable.

lehayim [Heb] *leh-HAH-yim.* (*lit.,* to life) Jewish drinking toast.

lei [Hawaiian] *lay.* wreath of flowers worn around the neck.

Leid [Ger: *pl.* **Leiden**] *lyt* (*LY-d'n*) sorrow; suffering; wrong, injury.

Leidenschaft [Ger] *LY-d'n-shahft.* suffering; passion, ardor.

leitão [Port, from *leite*, milk] *lay-TÃ-oo.* suckling; young pig.

Leitmotif [Ger, from *leiten*, to lead + *Motiv*, theme, motif, from Fr] *LYT-moh-teef.* leading theme; central idea; recurrent theme. Also, **Leitmotiv.**

le juste milieu [Fr] *luh-ZHÜST-mee-LYÖ.* the golden mean.

le mieux est l'ennemi du bien [Fr] *luh-MYÖ-eh-len-MEE-du-BYÊ.* the better is the enemy of the good; let well enough alone.

le monde [Fr] *luh-MŌD.* the world; people, society.

lengua [Sp] *LEN-gwah.* tongue; language.

lentamente [It] *len-tah-MAYN-teh.* slowly.

lentando [It] *len-TAHN-doh.* slowing down; becoming slower.

lentissimo [It] *len-TEES-see-moh.* very slowly.

lento [It] *LEN-toh.* (*music*) slow(ly).

l'envoi [Fr] *lã-VWAH.* (*lit., envoy*) short postscript or final stanza.

leo [Lat] *LEH-oh.* lion; (*cap.*) a sign of the Zodiac.

leotard [Fr, after J. Léotard, French gymnast] *lay-oh-TAR.* skin-tight garment worn by acrobats and dancers.

le petit caporal [Fr] *luh-p'TEE-kah-poh-RAHL.* the little corporal: nickname for Napoleon.

leprechaun [Ir *leipreachãn*, from Old Ir *luchorpãn*, from *lu*, small + *corp*, body] *LEP-ruh-khahn.* in Irish folklore, an elf or sprite.

le premier pas [Fr] *luh-pruh-MYAY-PAH.* the first step.

le roi est mort, vive le roi [Fr] *luh-RWAH-eh-MOR-VEEV-luh-RWAH.* the king is dead, long live the king.

le roi le veut [Fr] *luh-RWAH-luh-VÖ.* the king wills it.

le rouge et le noir [Fr] *luh-ROOZH-eh-luh-NWAR.* the red and the black.

les [Fr] *lay.* the (*pl.*)

les [Fr, from Lat *latus*, side] *leh.* near, by: used in place-names, as *Plessis-les-Tours.*

les absents ont toujours tort [Fr] *lay-zahp-SÃ-zō-too-ZHOOR-TOR.* the absent are always in the wrong.

les aristocrates à la lanterne [Fr] See **à la lanterne.**

les convenances [Fr, from *convenir*, to agree] *lay-kō-v'NÃS.* good manners; the proprieties; conventions.

les doux yeux [Fr] *lay-DOO-ZYÖ.* tender looks; tender glances.

lèse-majesté [Fr, from Lat *laesa majestas*, offended majesty] *LEZ-mah-zhes-TAY.* treason; offense against the sovereign.

les larmes aux yeux [Fr] *lay-LARM-oh-ZYÖ.* tears in the eyes; with eyes full of tears.

les murailles ont des oreilles [Fr] *lay-mü-RY-zō-day-zoh-REH-yuh.* the walls have ears.

les petites gens [Fr] *lay-p'TEET-ZHÃ.* little people; humble people.

le style c'est l'homme [Fr] *luh-STEEL-seh-LUM.* style makes the man.

l'état c'est moi [Fr] *lay-TAH-seh-MWAH. I* am the State: attributed to Louis XIV.

L'Étoile du Nord [Fr] *lay-TWAHL-dü-NOR.* The North Star (motto of Minnesota).

lettre [Fr] *LEH-truh.* letter; **lettres** (*pl.*) letters; literature; —**de cachet** (*-duh-kah-SHEH*) letter authorizing imprisonment without due legal process.

leveche [Sp] *leh-VEH-cheh.* a warm, dry wind from Africa; sirocco.

levée [Fr, from *se lever*, to rise] *luh-VAY.* reception of visitors by a king or noble, held in the early morning; any morning or afternoon reception by a king, president or the like; —**en masse** (*-ã-MAHS*) mass uprising; general mobilization.

lévrier [Fr] *lay-vree-AY.* greyhound.

lex [Lat: *pl.* **leges**] *leks* (*LEH-ges*) law; rule; standard, norm; —**salica** (*-SAH-lee-kah*) Salic law, the legal code of the Salian Franks, later incorporated into French law; any provision of this law, esp. those excluding women from inheritance of land or succession to the throne; —**talionis** (*-tah-lee-OH-nees*) law of retaliation; an eye for an eye.

ley [Sp: *pl.* **leyes**] *lay* (*LEH-yes*) law; rule; standard, norm.

lez. Old form of **les,** q.v.

L. H. D. Abbr. of **Litterarum Humaniorum Doctor.**

l'homme [Fr] *lum.* man (in general); mankind; the man.

l'homme propose et Dieu dispose [Fr] *LUM-proh-POHZ-ay-DYÖ-dees-POHZ.* man proposes, God disposes.

liaison [Fr, from *lier,* to bind, link] *lyeh-ZŎ.* amorous attachment; linking, connection; go-between, intermediary; in French pronunciation, the carrying over of a consonant sound from the end of one word to a following word beginning with a vowel sound.

lib. Abbr. of **liber.**

libeccio [It, from Ar *lebeg,* western] *lee-BAY-choh.* hot southwest wind from Africa.

liber [Lat: *abbr.* **L.** or **lib.**; *pl.* **libri**] *LEE-behr* (*-bree*) book; chapter; volume; *adj.* (*pl.* **liberi;** *LEE-beh-ree*) free.

libera arbitria [Lat] *LEE-beh-rah-ar-BEE-tree-ah.* free choices; free decision.

liberamente [It] *lee-beh-rah-MAYN-teh.* (*music*) liberally; freely.

libertad [Sp] *lee-behr-TAHD.* liberty; freedom.

libertas [Lat] *lee-BEHR-tahs.* liberty; freedom.

liberté, égalité, fraternité [Fr] *lee-behr-TAY-ay-gah-lee-TAY-frah-tehr-nee-TAY.* liberty, equality, brotherhood: slogan of the French Revolution.

liberum arbitrium [Lat] *LEE-beh-room-ar-BEE-tree-oom.* free will; free choice.

libido [Lat] *lee-BEE-doh.* in psychoanalysis, the instinctual drives of human beings; the sexual urge.

libra [Lat: *abbr.* **lb.**] *LEE-brah.* scale, balance; pound; (*cap.*) a sign of the Zodiac.

librairie [Fr] *lee-breh-REE.* bookstore.

libre [Fr] *LEE-bruh;* [Sp] *LEE-breh.* free.

libre-service [Fr] *LEE-bruh-sehr-VEES.* self-service; self-service restaurant; cafeteria.

libretto [It, dim. of *libro,* book; *pl.* **libretti**] *lee-BRAYT-toh* (*-tee*) book containing the words of an opera or play.

licenciado [Sp] *lee-sen-SYAH-doh.* lawyer; licentiate.

licenza [It] *lee-CHEN-tsah.* permission; license; freedom of interpretation.

Licht, Liebe, Leben [Ger] *LIÇT-LEE-beh-LAY-b'n.* light, love, life.

lictor [Lat: *pl.* **lictores**] *LEEK-tor* (*-TOH-res*) in ancient Rome, bearer of the fasces; petty judicial officer or bailiff.

lido [It] *LEE-doh.* seashore, seacoast; (*cap.*) beach resort near Venice.

Liebchen [Ger] *LEEP-ç'n.* beloved; sweetheart.

Liebe [Ger] *LEE-beh.* love.

Liebeslied [Ger] *LEE-b's-leet.* love song.

Lieb und Leid [Ger] *LEEP-oont-LYT.* joy and sorrow; for better or worse.

Lied [Ger: *pl.* **Lieder**] *leet* (*LEE-duh*) song; lyric; ballad.

Liederkranz [Ger] *LEE-duh-krahnts.* (*lit.*, garland of songs) singing society; name of a type of cheese, usu. in small blocks with a creamy center.

Lieferung [Ger: *pl.* **Lieferungen**] *LEE-fuh-roong* (*-'n*) delivery; consignment, lot, parcel; issue, number, fascicle (of a work published in installments).

lieu [Fr: *pl.* **lieux**] *lyö.* place; stead; —**d'aisance** (*-deh-ZÃS*) rest room, lavatory, toilet.

lièvre [Fr] *LYEH-vruh.* hare.

Limburger [Ger, after the city of Limburg] *LIM-boor-guh.* a type of soft cheese having a sharp taste and odor.

limoges [Fr, after the French city where it is made] *lee-MOHZH.* type of fine porcelain.

limousine [Fr, from *Limousin,* former province in central France] *lee-moo-ZEEN.* automobile, usu. with closed-off passenger section, designed to be chauffeur-driven.

lingerie [Fr, from *linge,* linen] *lẽ-zh'REE.* light garments worn by women, as underwear or sleepwear.

lingo [Lingua Franca, combining It *lin(gua)* and Prov *(len)go,* tongue] *LEEN-goh.* jargon; specialized language or terminology of a given class or profession; any language, esp. if strange or foreign.

lingua [It] *LEEN-gwah.* tongue; language; —**franca**

(*-FRAHN-kah*) (*lit.*, Frankish tongue) jargon based on Italian and Provençal, formerly used in eastern Mediterranean ports; any international or common tongue used in a multilingual area; —**toscana in bocca romana** (*-tohs-KAH-nah-een-BOHK-kah-roh-MAH-nah*) Tuscan tongue in Roman mouth: characterization of the eclectic nature of modern standard Italian.

Lingua Geral [Port] *LEEN-gwuh-zhuh-RAHL.* (*lit.*, general language) jargon based on Tupi (a S American Indian language), spoken in the Amazon region.

lingüiça [Port] *leen-GWEE-suh.* a kind of thin sausage.

links [Ger] *leenks.* left; on or to the left.

Linzertorte [Ger, from Linz, a city in Austria + *Torte*, pastry] *LIN-tsuh-tor-teh.* sweet pastry filled with a mixture of crushed nuts and jam.

liqueur [Fr] *lee-KÖR.* sweet, syrupy alcoholic drink.

lis pendens [Lat] *LEES-PEN-dens.* pending lawsuit.

lit [Fr] *lee.* bed.

literati [Lat] *lee-teh-RAH-tee.* educated or cultured people; literary persons.

literatim [Lat] *lee-teh-RAH-teem.* literally; letter by letter.

Literaturnaya Gazeta [Russ] *lee-tee-ruh-TOOR-nuh-yuh-guh-ZYEH-tuh.* Literary Gazette: a Russian journal of literature and criticism.

lithos [Gk] *LEE-thohs.* stone.

litotes [Gk] *lee-TOH-tes.* rhetorical understatement, esp. affirming something by denying its opposite; e.g., not a little.

litre [Fr] *LEE-truh.* liter, a measure of capacity equal to about 1.06 quarts.

Litt.D. Abbr. of **Litterarum Doctor.**

litterae humaniores [Lat] *LEET-teh-ry-hoo-mah-nee-OH-res.* humane letters; humanities; classics.

litterae scriptae manent [Lat] *LEET-teh-ry-SKREEP-ty-MAH-nent.* written words endure.

Litterarum Doctor [Lat: *abbr.* **Litt. D.**] *leet-teh-RAH-room-DOHK-tor.* Doctor of Letters or Literature; **Litterarum Humaniorum Doctor** (*-hoo-mah-nee-OH-room-*); (*abbr.*

L.H.D.) Doctor of Humane Letters; Doctor of Humanities.

littérateur [Fr] *lee-tay-rah-TÖR.* man of letters; literary man; writer.

livraison [Fr, from *livrer,* to deliver] *lee-vreh-ZŎ.* delivery; part, number, issue (of a work printed serially).

livre [Fr] *LEE-vruh.* book; pound; old coin and monetary unit of France; —à clef (*-ah-KLAY*) book in which real persons appear under other names.

llama [AmerSp, from Quechua] *LYAH-mah.* long-haired mammal found in several Spanish-American countries.

llano [Sp] *LYAH-noh.* in S America, a large, grassy plain.

llanura [Sp] *lyah-NOO-rah.* a plain.

LL.B. Abbr. of **Legum Baccalaureus.**

LL.D. Abbr. of **Legum Doctor.**

LL.M. Abbr. of **Legum Magister.**

lluvia [Sp] *LYOO-vyah.* rain.

lobo [Sp, from Lat **lupus**] *LOH-boh.* wolf.

locale [Fr *local*] *loh-KAL.* place, locality; scene, setting.

locandiera [It, from *locare,* to let, rent] *loh-kahn-DYEH-rah.* landlady; innkeeper; hostess; **locandiere** (*-reh*) landlord; innkeeper; host.

loc. cit. Abbr. of **in loco citato.**

loch [Scot] *lohkh.* lake, pond.

loco [Lat, abl. of **locus,** place] *LOH-koh.* in the place; [It, var. of **luogo,** place] (*music*) an indication to return to the notes as printed on the staff after an ottava transposition; [Sp] crazy, mad, insane.

locos y niños dicen la verdad [Sp] *LOH-kohs-ee-NEE-nyohs-DEE-sen-lah-vehr-DAHD.* fools and children tell the truth.

locum tenens [Lat] *LOH-koom-TEH-nens.* holding the place (of); substituting for; deputy; lieutenant, second in command.

locus [Lat: *pl.* **loci**] *LOH-koos* (*-kee*) place; passage; (*geom.*) figure traced by the path of a moving point; —**classicus** (*-KLAHS-see-koos*) classical source; passage frequently cited; —**delicti** (*-deh-LEEK-tee*) scene of the crime; —**in quo** (*-een-KWOH*) place in which (a passage occurs); **—sigilli** (*-see-GEEL-lee*) (*abbr.* **L.S.**) place of the seal.

lo dicho, dicho [Sp] *loh-DEE-choh-DEE-choh.* what is said, is said.

loge [Fr] *lohzh.* theater box; balcony section.

loggia [It: *pl.* **logge** or **loggie**] *LOH-jah* (*-jeh*) gallery or portico open to the air; porch.

logos [Gk] *LOH-gohs.* word, esp. divine word; reason, rational principle.

loi [Fr] *lwah.* law; rule; standard, norm.

loin [Fr] *lwē.* far, distant; **—des yeux, loin du coeur** (*-day-ZYÖ-lwē-dü-KÖR*) far from the eyes, far from the heart; out of sight, out of mind.

loma [Sp] *LOH-mah.* hill, esp. a flat-topped hill.

longueur [Fr] *lŏ-GÖR.* length.

lo pasado, pasado [Sp] *loh-pah-SAH-doh-pah-SAH-doh.* what is past is past.

loquitur [Lat: *abbr.* **loq.**] *LOH-kwee-toor.* he (she) speaks: a stage direction.

Lorelei [Ger] *LOH-reh-ly.* siren; seductive woman; a small wildflower.

lorgnette [Fr, from *lorgner*, to leer, squint] *lor-NYET.* a pair of eyeglasses held with a handle or attached to a chain.

lorgnon [Fr] *lor-NYŎ.* pince-nez; opera glasses.

los [Sp] *lohs.* the (*masc. pl.*).

los montes ven, y las paredes oyen [Sp] *lohs-MOHN-tes-VEN-ee-lahs-pah-REH-des-OH-yen.* the mountains have eyes and the walls have ears.

lotería [Sp] *loh-teh-REE-ah.* lottery.

lotto [It: chance, lot, from Germanic] *LOHT-toh.* game of chance somewhat like bingo.

louis-d'or [Fr, from *Louis*, name of several French kings + *or*, gold] *loo-EE-DOR.* gold louis: an obsolete French gold coin.

Louis Quatorze [Fr] *loo-EE-kah-TORZ.* Louis XIV; in the style popular during his reign (1643-1715); **—Quinze** (*-KĒZ*); Louis XV; in the style popular during his reign (1715-1774); **—Seize** (*-SEZ*) Louis XVI; in the style popular during his reign (1774-1792); —**Treize** (-*TREZ*) Louis XIII; in the style popular during his reign (1610-1643).

loup [Fr: *fem*. **louve**] *loo* (*loov*) wolf; —**garou** (-*gah-ROO*) werewolf.

lox [Yid *laks*, from Ger *Lachs*, salmon] *lahks*. a kind of smoked salmon.

L.S. Abbr. of **locus sigilli.**

luau [Hawaiian] *loo-OW*. Hawaiian banquet.

luce [Lat, abl. of **lux**] *LOO-keh*; [It: *pl*. **luci**] *LOO-cheh* (-*chee*) light.

luces [Lat, pl. of **lux**] *LOO-kes*; [Sp, pl. of **luz**] *LOO-ses*. lights.

lucri causa [Lat] *LOO-kree-KOW-sah*. for the sake of lucre; for monetary gain.

lucus a non lucendo [Lat] *LOO-koos-ah-nohn-loo-KEN-doh*. (called) a grove because it excludes the light: an absurd etymology attributed to Quintilian, often quoted as an example of a non sequitur.

ludus [Lat: *pl*. **ludi**] *LOO-doos* (-*dee*) game; drama, play.

lues [Lat] *LOO-es*. plague; quarantine disease; syphilis.

Luft [Ger] *looft*. air; **Lufthansa** (-*hahn-sah*) civil air service of Germany; **Luftwaffe** (-*vah-feh*) (*lit*., air weapon) the Nazi German air force.

luganica [It, from *Lucania*, a province of southern Italy] *loo-GAH-nee-kah*. a kind of ground meat in a sausage casing. Also, **lucanica** (-*KAH-nee-kah*).

Luger [Ger, from name of inventor] *LOO-guh*. automatic pistol of 9 mm. caliber, made in Germany.

l'ultima che si perde è la speranza [It] *LOOL-tee-mah-keh-see-PEHR-deh-eh-lah-speh-RAHN-tsah*. the last thing to be lost is hope.

lumière [Fr] *lü-MYEHR*. light; luminary; prominent person in a given group.

luna [Lat, Sp, It] *LOO-nah*. moon.

lune [Fr] *lün*. moon.

lunette [Fr, dim. of *lune*, moon] *lü-NET*. small semicircular window above a larger window; anything semicircular or crescent-shaped; (*pl*.) eyeglasses.

lunik [Russ, from *luna*, moon] *LOO-nyik.* one of several rocket probes launched toward the moon by the Soviet Union.

l'union fait la force [Fr] *lü-NYŎ-FEH-lah-FORS.* Unity makes strength (motto of Belgium).

luogo [It: *pl.* **luoghi**] *LWOH-goh* (-*gee*) place; stead.

lupanar [Lat, from *lupa*, she-wolf, prostitute] *LOO-pah-nar.* brothel.

Lupercalia [Lat] *loo-pehr-KAH-lee-ah.* Roman festival in honor of Lupercus, a fertility god.

lupus [Lat: *fem.* **lupa**] *LOO-poos* (-*pah*) wolf; —**est homo homini** (-*est-HOH-moh-HOH-mee-nee*) man is a wolf to his fellowman; —**in fabula** (-*een-FAH-boo-lah*) (behold) the wolf in the fable.

Lusitania [Lat] *loo-see-TAH-nee-ah.* ancient name of Portugal.

Lust [Ger: *pl.* **Lüste**] *loost* (*LÜS-teh*) desire, drive; pleasure.

lustig [Ger] *LOOS-tiç.* jovial; lusty; amusing.

lustrum [Lat, from *luere*, to atone, expiate; *pl.* **lustra**] *LOOS-troom* (-*trah*) a five-year period; an ancient Roman ceremony of purification and atonement performed every five years.

Lustspiel [Ger] *LOOST-shpeel.* comedy.

lux [Lat: *pl.* **luces**] *looks* (*LOO-kes*) light; —**et veritas** (-*et-VEH-ree-tahs*) Light and truth (motto of Yale University); —**in tenebris** (-*een-TEH-neh-brees*) light in the darkness; —**mundi** (-*MOON-dee*) light of the world.

luxe [Fr] *lüks.* luxury.

luz [Sp: *pl.* **luces**] *loos* (*LOO-ses*) light.

lycée [Fr] *lee-SAY.* lyceum; high school; secondary school.

M

M. Abbr. of **mille** or **monsieur.**

M.A. Abbr. of **Magister Artium.**

maatschapij [Du] *MAHT-skhah-pay.* joint stock company.

maboule [Fr] *mah-BOOL.* (*slang*) fool, simpleton.

macabre [Fr] *mah-KAH-bruh.* gruesome; deathly.

maccheroni [It] *mahk-keh-ROH-nee.* macaroni; noodles.

macchinetta [It, dim. of *macchina*, machine] *mahk-kee-NAYT-tah.* small Italian coffee maker.

macédoine [Fr, from *Macédoine*, Macedonia] *mah-say-DWAHN.* mixture of fruits or vegetables served as a salad.

Mach [Ger, after Ernst Mach, Austrian physicist] *mahkh.* the speed of sound (761 mph) used as a unit of measurement, esp. for flying vehicles.

ma chère [Fr] *mah-SHEHR.* my dear (girl or woman).

machete [Sp] *mah-CHEH-teh.* large, wide-bladed knife used esp. for cutting a path through heavy undergrowth, or to cut sugarcane.

machismo [Sp, from *macho*, male] *mah-CHEES-moh.* maleness; masculinity; virility.

Macht [Ger] *mahkht.* might, power, strength, force.

macushla [Ir *mo chuisle*, my pulse] *mah-KOOSH-lah.* my darling.

madame [Fr: *pl.* **mesdames**; *abbr.* **Mme**] *mah-DAHM* (*may-DAHM*) (*lit.*, my lady) madam; Mrs.

Mädchen [Ger: *pl.* unchanged] *MAYT-ç'n.* girl; maiden.

madeira [Port] *muh-DAY-ruh.* white wine resembling sherry, from Madeira Islands.

madeleine [Fr] *mah-d'LEN.* a sweet cake or bun.

Madelon [Fr] *mah-d'LÕ.* French World War I song.

mademoiselle [Fr: *pl.* **mesdemoiselles**; *abbr.* **Mlle**] *mah-d'mwah-ZEL* (*may-d'mwah-ZEL*) young lady; Miss.

madère [Fr] *mah-DEHR.* Madeira wine.

madonna [It] *mah-DOHN-nah.* lady; my lady; the Virgin Mary; representation or painting of the Virgin.

madonnina [It] *mah-dohn-NEE-nah.* little madonna; small painting or figure of the Virgin; beautiful young woman; smug, sanctimonious woman.

madras [Hindi] *muh-DRAHS.* nonfast dark plaid cotton fabric originally from Madras, India.

madre [Sp, It] *MAH-dreh.* mother.

madrugada [Sp] *mah-droo-GAH-dah.* morning; morning song.

maestoso [It] *mah-es-TOH-soh.* (*music*) majestic; dignified; **maestosamente** (*-sah-MAYN-teh*) majestically.

maestrale [It] *mah-es-TRAH-leh.* strong northwest wind.

maestro [It] *mah-ES-troh.* master; teacher; orchestra conductor.

Mafia [It] *MAH-fyah.* secret Sicilian organization, allegedly engaged in criminal activities. Also, **Maffia.**

ma foi [Fr] *mah-FWAH.* (by) my faith; indeed.

magasin [Fr] *mah-gah-ZẼ.* shop; store; department store.

Magen David [Heb] *mah-GEN-dah-VEED.* Star of David.

maggiore [It] *mah-JOH-reh.* larger, major; elder.

Magi. See **Magus.**

magillah. See **megillah.**

Maginot Line [after André Maginot, French minister of war] *mah-zhee-NOH.* system of fortifications erected along the French-German border before World War II; blind conservatism (in the case of Maginot, to insist on fixed fortifications in an air and mobile war).

magister [Lat] *mah-GEES-tehr.* helmsman, steersman; master; teacher; —**Artium** (*-AR-tee-oom*) (*abbr.* **M.A.**) Master of Arts.

magma [Gk] *MAHG-mah.* lava; molten igneous rock; any thick paste or mixture.

magna [Lat, fem. of *magnus*] *MAHG-nah.* great; large; —**Charta** (*-KAR-tah*) the Great Charter, signed by King John and the English barons at Runnymede in 1215, guaranteeing certain fundamental legal rights; any bill of rights; —**culpa** (*-KOOL-pah*) great error; gross mistake; negligence; —**cum laude** (*-koom-LOW-deh*) with great distinction; with high honors: a distinction conferred with a diploma (cf. **cum laude, summa cum laude**); —**est veritas, et praevalebit** (*-est-VEH-ree-tahs-et-pry-vah-LEH-beet*) truth is great, and it will prevail.

Magnificat [Lat, from *magnificare*, to glorify, make great] *mahg-NEE-fee-kaht.* (my soul) doth glorify (the Lord): first word of hymn of the Virgin Mary.

magnifico [It] *mah-NYEE-fee-koh.* magnificent; a great man; a standard character of the Commedia dell'Arte.

magnifique [Fr] *mah-nyee-FEEK.* magnificent; terrific, wonderful.

magnum [Lat, neut. of *magnus*, great] *MAHG-noom.* a large bottle, usually of champagne or brandy; a unit of measurement; —**bonum** (-*BOH-noom*) a great good; great benefit; —**opus** (-*OH-poos*) great work; masterpiece.

magot [Fr] *mah-GOH.* grotesque figure; inferior genre painting.

maguey [Sp, from Taino] *mah-GAY.* tropical plant yielding a fiber used in making cloth.

Magus [Lat, from Pers; *pl.* **Magi**] *MAH-goos* (-*gee*) a priest-king of ancient Persia; one of the wise men who traveled to Nazareth to visit the Infant Jesus.

Magyar [Hung] *MUH-dyur.* Hungarian; a Hungarian.

Mahabharata [Skt] *muh-HAH-BAH-ruh-tuh.* The Great War of the Bharatas: a Hindu epic.

maharajah [Hindi, from Skt] *muh-HAH-RAH-jah.* great king; Indian prince. Also, **maharaja.**

maharani [Hindi, from Skt] *muh-HAH-RAH-nee.* great queen; a maharajah's wife. Also, **maharanee.**

Mahdi [Arab] *MAH-dee.* (*lit.*, he who is guided) Messiah; title of very high-ranking Moslem leaders.

mah jong [Chin] *MAH-johng.* popular Chinese gambling game, played with tiles marked in suits, counters and dice.

Mahlzeit [Ger] *MAHL-tsyt.* meal; mealtime; greeting on sitting at the table.

mahout [Hindi] *muh-HOWT.* elephant keeper or driver.

Mahratta [Hindi] *muh-RAHT-tuh.* member of a Hindu people of central and western India.

mai [It] *my.* ever; never.

maigre [Fr] *MEH-gruh.* thin, meager; (*cookery*) meatless; Lenten, fasting.

maiko [Jap] *MY-koh.* girl in training to become a geisha.

maillot [Fr] *mah-YOH.* close-fitting one-piece bathing suit; jersey shirt or sweater.

maintenant [Fr] *mē-t'NÃ*. now.

maire [Fr] *mehr*. mayor.

mairie [Fr] *meh-REE*. mayoralty; town hall.

maison [Fr] *meh-ZŎ*. house; business firm; —**de santé** (*-duh-sã-TAY*) private hospital or sanitarium; —**meublée** (*-mö-BLAY*) furnished house.

mais òu sont les neiges d'antan? [Fr] *meh-ZOO-sõ-lay-NEZH-dã-TÃ*. but where are the snows of yesteryear?

maître [Fr] *MEH-truh*. master; teacher; proprietor, landlord; —**de cuisine** (*-duh-küee-ZEEN*) master cook, chef; —**d'hôtel** (*-doh-TEL*) chief steward, head waiter. Also, **maître d'** (*-DEE*).

maîtresse [Fr] *meh-TRES*. mistress; teacher; proprietress, landlady; sweetheart.

maîtrise [Fr] *meh-TREEZ*. mastery; skill.

Majlis [Iranian] *MAHJ-lees*. the Iranian parliament.

majolica [It *maiolica*, from *Maiorica*, Majorca] *mah-YOH-lee-kah*. brightly glazed and richly decorated pottery.

major-domo [Sp *mayordomo*, from MedL *majordomus*, head of the house] *mah-yor-DOH-moh*. chief steward, head servant; in medieval France, the prime minister.

makanan [Malay] *mah-KAH-nahn*. dinner.

makimono [Jap] *MAH-kee-MOH-noh*. horizontal picture scroll.

makros [Gk] *mah-KROHS*. large; long.

mal [Fr: *pl.* **maux**] *mahl* (*moh*) bad; badly, ill; evil; illness; misfortune; —**à propos** (*-ah-proh-POH*) inappropriate-(ly), inopportune(ly); —**de mer** (*-duh-MEHR*) seasickness; —**du pays** (*-dü-pay-EE*) homesickness; —**du siècle** (*-dü-SYEH-kluh*) (*lit.*, malady of the century) weariness of life; moral disillusionment; —**entendu** (*-ã-tã-DÜ*) misunderstood; misapprehended.

malacca [Malay, from Malacca, a state in Malaysia] *mah-LAHK-kah*. walking stick made from the stem of an E Indian palm.

malade [Fr] *mah-LAHD*. sick; sick person, patient; invalid; —**imaginaire** (*-ee-mah-zhee-NEHR*) imaginary invalid; hypochondriac.

maladie [Fr] *mah-lah-DEE.* sickness; malady; —**d'amour** (*-dah-MOOR*) lovesickness.

maladresse [Fr] *mah-lah-DRES.* awkwardness; clumsiness; blunder.

maladroit [Fr] *mah-lah-DRWAH.* awkward; tactless; clumsy.

mala fide [Lat] *MAH-lah-FEE-deh.* in bad faith; dishonestly.

málaga [Sp] *MAH-lah-gah.* a sweet wine, made in the Spanish province of Málaga.

malagueña [Sp] *mah-lah-GEH-nyah.* Spanish dance, originating in Málaga, similar to the fandango.

mala in se [Lat] *MAH-lah-een-SEH.* bad in themselves; things that are basically wrong. Cf. **malum in se.**

malaise [Fr] *mah-LEZ.* vague, uneasy feeling of discomfort; restlessness.

malapropos [Fr *mal à propos,* ill(-suited) to the purpose] *mah-lah-proh-POH.* inappropriate(ly); out of place; inopportune(ly).

malentendu [Fr] *mah-lā-tā-DÜ.* misunderstanding; misconception.

malerisch [Ger, from *Maler,* painter, from *malen,* to paint] *MAH-luh-rish.* picturesque; pictorial; graphic.

malgré [Fr] *mahl-GRAY.* in spite of; despite.

malheur [Fr] *mah-LÖR.* misfortune; bad luck; unhappiness, misery.

malihini [Hawaiian] *MAH-lee-HEE-nee.* newcomer; stranger.

malik [Ar] *MAH-leek.* chief, leader.

malinconia [It] *mah-leen-koh-NEE-ah.* melancholy; sadness.

malo animo [Lat] *MAH-loh-AH-nee-moh.* with evil spirit or intent; with malice aforethought.

malocchio [It *malo,* bad, evil + *occhio,* eye] *mah-LOHK-kyoh.* evil eye.

malo modo [Lat] *MAH-loh-MOH-doh.* in an evil way.

malpropre [Fr] *mahl-PROH-pruh.* dirty; slovenly.

malum in se [Lat] *MAH-loom-een-SEH.* bad in itself; basically wrong. Cf. **mala in se.**

mamie [Fr, contr. of **mon amie**] *mah-MEE.* my (girl) friend; my sweetheart.

mamzer [Yid, from Heb] *MAHM-zuh.* child born of a marriage forbidden by the Jewish faith; (*slang*) bastard. Also, **momzer, momser.**

mana [Polynesian] *MAH-nah.* impersonal supernatural force to which Polynesians and Melanesians attribute good fortune or magical powers.

manada [Sp] *mah-NAH-dah.* herd of horses, cattle or sheep.

mañana [Sp] *mah-NYAH-nah.* morning; tomorrow.

manas [Skt] *MAH-nus.* (in Hinduism and Buddhism) mind; reason; judgment.

mancando [It] *mahn-KAHN-doh.* (*music*) failing; ebbing, fading away.

Manche. See La Manche.

manchette [Fr, dim. of *manche*, sleeve] *mã-SHET.* cuff; ruffle (at the wrist); wristband; arm pad.

mancia [It] *MAHN-chah.* tip, gratuity.

mandala [Skt: circle] *MUN-duh-luh.* in Oriental art, a cosmic representation of deities arranged in concentric shapes; in psychology, a symbol of the reunified self, invented by Carl Jung.

mandamus [Lat: we order] *mahn-DAH-moos.* legal writ ordering a specific thing to be done.

mandat-poste [Fr] *mã-DAH-POHST.* postal money order. Also, **mandat de** (or **sur**) **la poste** (*-duh-lah-*; *-sür-lah-*).

manducus [Lat, perh. from *manducare*, to chew] *mahn-DOO-koos.* grotesque mask worn by comic actors in the Roman theater.

manège [Fr, from It *maneggio*, from *maneggiare*, to handle, manage] *mah-NEZH.* horsemanship; training of horses.

manicotti [It, pl. of *manicotto*, muff, dim. of *manica*, sleeve] *mah-nee-KOHT-tee.* large tubes of pasta stuffed with soft cheese and baked in tomato sauce.

maniéré [Fr: *fem.* **maniérée**] *mah-nyay-RAY.* affected; overly mannered.

manifesto [It] *mah-nee-FES-toh.* declaration; proclamation; manifest.

manna [Lat, Gk, from Heb *mān*] *MAHN-nah.* the food

miraculously supplied to the Israelites in the wilderness; desired thing which miraculously appears; heaven-sent gift.

mannequin [Fr] *mah-n'KĔ.* manikin; model; dummy.

mano [Sp]; [It: *pl.* **mani**] *MAH-noh (-nee)* hand.

mano a mano [It] *MAH-noh-ah-MAH-noh.* little by little; as we go along.

Mano Nera. See **La Mano Nera.**

manqué [Fr, from p.p. of *manquer,* to fail, miss] *mā-KAY.* unsuccessful; failed: often said of one who misses his vocation.

mansarde [Fr, after N.F. Mansart, architect] *mā-SARD.* type of roof having two slopes of different lengths, the lower slope often containing dormers.

mantilla [Sp] *mahn-TEE-lyah.* shawl; head scarf.

mantis kakōn [Gk] *MAHN-tees-kah-KOHN.* prophet of evil.

mantra [Skt] *MUN-truh (lit.,* speech) religious thought or maxim; poetic section of the Vedas.

manu propria [Lat] *MAH-noo-PROH-pree-ah.* with one's own hand.

manus [Lat] *MAH-noos.* hand; band, group; **manu militari** (*-mee-lee-TAH-ree*) with armed force.

manzanilla [Sp, dim. of *manzana,* apple] *mahn-sah-NEE-lyah.* a type of sherry.

Mapai [Heb] *mah-PY.* Israeli Socialist Party.

Mapam [Heb] *mah-PAHM.* Israeli leftist party.

maquereau [Fr] *mah-k'ROH.* (*lit.,* mackerel) procurer, pimp.

maquillage [Fr, from *maquiller,* to make up] *mah-kee-YAHZH.* make-up; cosmetics.

máquina [Sp] *MAH-kee-nah.* machine; motor.

maquis [Fr] *mah-KEE.* French freedom fighters in World War II.

marabou [Fr *marabout,* from Ar] *mah-rah-BOO.* large bird of the stork family, having flowing feathers used in trimming women's clothing and in millinery.

marabout [Fr, from Ar *murābiṭ*] *mah-rah-BOO.* Moslem hermit or holy man.

maraca [Port, from Tupi] *muh-RAH-kuh.* gourd loosely filled with seeds, used as a musical instrument.

marais [Fr] *mah-REH.* marsh, swamp.

maraschino [It, from *marasca*, wild cherry] *mah-rahs-KEE-noh.* cherry; cherry liqueur.

marcato [It] *mar-KAH-toh.* (*music*) marked; accented.

marché [Fr] *mar-SHAY.* market; —**aux fleurs** (*-oh-FLÖR*) flower market; —**aux puces** (*-oh-PÜS*) flea market; secondhand market.

Märchen [Ger] *MEHR-ç'n.* tale; legend; fairy tale.

marchese [It] *mar-KEH-seh.* marquis; **marchesa** (*-sah*) marchioness.

Mardi Gras [Fr] *mar-DEE-GRAH.* (*lit.*, fat Tuesday) Shrove Tuesday; pre-Lenten festival.

mare [Lat: *pl.* **maria**] *MAH-reh* (*-ree-ah*) sea; large, dark, comparatively smooth area on the moon's surface; —**clausum** (*-KLOW-soom*) (*lit.*, closed sea) territorial sea of a country; —**nostrum** (*-NOHS-troom*) (*lit.*, our sea) the Mediterranean.

maréchal [Fr: *pl.* **maréchaux**] *mah-ray-SHAHL* (*-SHOH*) field marshal.

maremma [It, from Lat *maritima*, maritime] *mah-REM-mah.* marshy region near the coast.

marginalia [Lat] *mar-gee-NAH-lee-ah.* marginal notes; peripheral things.

marguerite [Fr, from Lat *margarita*, pearl] *mar-guh-REET.* daisy.

mari [Fr] *mah-REE.* husband.

mariache [MexSp, said to be from Fr **mariage**, wedding] *mah-RYAH-cheh.* Mexican dance similar to the fandango; music for this dance; ensemble that plays this music. Also, **mariachi** (*-chee*).

mariage [Fr] *mah-RYAHZH.* marriage; wedding; —**de convenance** (*-duh-kō-v'NÃS*) marriage of convenience.

Marianne [Fr] *mah-RYAHN.* female symbol of France.

marido [Sp] *mah-REE-doh.* husband.

marijuana [MexSp] *mah-ree-HWAH-nah.* Indian hemp, the dried leaves and flowers of which are smoked as a narcotic.

marimba [WAfr] *mah-REEM-bah*. wooden instrument resembling the xylophone, used in Latin-American music.

marina [It, Sp, fem. of *marino*, marine] *mah-REE-nah*. settled and landscaped seacoast; boat basin.

marine [Fr] *mah-REEN*. navy; admiralty; shipping; (*art*) seascape.

mariné [Fr] *mah-ree-NAY*. marinated, pickled.

marinierter Hering [Ger] *mah-ri-NEER-tuh-HEH-ring*. marinated herring.

mariscos [Sp, lit., marine, from *mar*, sea] *mah-REES-kohs*. shellfish; seafood.

Mark [Ger: *pl.* **Marken** in first sense; unchanged in second] *mark* (-*'n*) march, border region, frontier; unit of currency, mark.

Markgraf [Ger: *pl.* **Markgrafen**] *MARK-grahf* (-*'n*) Margrave: obsolete title of nobility.

markka [Finn] *MARK-kah*. Finnish monetary unit, equiv. to about 31 cents.

marmelo [Port] *mur-MEH-loo*. quince.

marmite [Fr] *mar-MEET*. pot, pan; soup pot; (*slang*) gun shell, bombshell.

marmot [Fr] *mar-MOH*. (*lit.*, little monkey) small, grotesque person.

marque [Fr, of Germanic origin] *mark*. brand; mark; —**de fabrique** (-*duh-fah-BREEK*) trademark.

marqueta [AmerSp, from Eng *market*] *mar-KEH-tah*. market, esp. the public market in the Latin quarter of New York City.

marquis [Fr] *mar-KEE*. marquis; **marquise** (-*KEEZ*) marchioness; marquee.

marquisette [Fr, dim. of **marquise**] *mar-kee-ZET*. fabric with square-patterned weave.

Marrano [Sp, lit., pig (with reference to the Jewish faith forbidding the eating of pork), from Ar *mahram*, prohibited thing] *mar-RAH-noh*. a Portuguese or Spaniard converted to Christianity in the late Middle Ages, often under duress, and often adhering to Jewish beliefs in secret.

marron [Fr] *mah-RŎ*. chestnut; —**glacé** (*-glah-SAY*) glazed chestnut.

Marsala [It, from Marsala, city in Sicily] *mar-SAH-lah*. dark, sweet Sicilian wine.

Marseillaise [Fr, from Marseille, southern French city] *mar-seh-YEZ*. the national anthem of France, written by Rouget de Lisle in 1792.

martellato [It, from *martello*, hammer] *mar-tel-LAH-toh*. (*music*) hammered; strongly accented.

martello [It] *mar-TEL-loh*. hammer; mallet; knocker.

marziale [It] *mar-TSYAH-leh*. (*music*) martial; warlike.

Marzipan [Ger, from It *marzapane*] *MAR-tsi-pahn*. candy made of sugar and almond paste; marchpane.

mas [Prov, from Vulgar Lat *mansus*, from p.p. of *manere*, to dwell] *mahs*. in southern France, farm, farmhouse.

maschera [It] *MAHS-keh-rah*. mask.

Maschinenbaukunst [Ger] *mah-SHEE-n'n-bow-koonst*. mechanical engineering.

mashallah [Ar] *mah-shahl-LAH*. Allah has willed it.

masjid [Ar, from *ma-*, prefix of place + *sajada*, to worship] *MAHS-jeed*. mosque.

Masorah [Heb] *mah-soh-RAH*. (lit., tradition) a book of critical and explanatory notes on the Old Testament.

massepain [Fr, from It *marzapane*] *mahs-PẼ*. candy made of sugar and almond paste; marchpane. Cf. **Marzipan.**

masseur [Fr, from *masser*, to massage, from Ar *massa*, to handle] *mah-SÖR*. male massage expert; **masseuse** (*-SÖZ*) female massage expert.

mässig [Ger] *MES-iç*. (*music*) moderate(ly).

mastaba [Ar: bench] *mahs-tah-BAH*. type of ancient Egyptian tomb with flat top and sloping sides, over the death chamber. Also, **mastabah.**

más vale tarde que nunca [Sp] *MAHS-VAH-leh-TAR-deh-keh-NOON-kah*. better late than never.

matador [Sp, from *matar*, to kill] *mah-tah-DOR*. bullfighter who kills the bull with a sword.

maté [Sp *mate*] *MAH-teh*. See **hierba maté.**

matelassé [Fr, from *matelas*, mattress, quilt] *mah-t'lah-SAY*. quilted; quilted fabric.

matelot [Fr] *mah-t'LOH*. sailor.

matelote [Fr, from **matelot**] *mah-t'LOHT*. fish stew seasoned with wine.

mater [Lat: *pl.* **matres**] *MAH-tehr* (*-tres*) mother; —**dolorosa** (*-doh-loh-ROH-sah*) Sorrowing Mother, referring to the Virgin Mary mourning Christ's death on the Cross; **materfamilias** (*-fah-MEE-lee-ahs*) the mother of the family; matriarch.

materia [Lat] *mah-TEH-ree-ah*. material; matter; —**medica** (*-MEH-dee-kah*) medical material; drugs; pharmacology.

matériel [Fr] *mah-tay-RYEL*. materials; supplies and equipment, esp. military.

matin [Fr] *mah-TẼ*. morning.

matinée [Fr, from **matin**] *mah-tee-NAY*. morning, forenoon; morning (or afternoon) performance.

matins [Fr] *mah-TẼ*. morning songs or prayers.

matte [Fr, from Ger *matt*, from MedL *mattus*, dull] *maht*. a dull, nonglossy finish; having such a finish.

mattina [It] *maht-TEE-nah*. morning. Also, **mattino** (*-noh*).

mattinata [It] *maht-tee-NAH-tah*. morning; morning song.

matzo [Yid *matse*, from Heb *maṣṣah*; *pl.* **matzoth**] *MAHT-soh* (*-soht*) unleavened bread, traditionally eaten during Jewish Passover.

maugré [MF, earlier form of **malgré**] See **malgré**.

Mau-Mau [Kikuyu] *MOW-mow*. terrorist native liberation movement in Kenya in the 1950's.

mauvais [Fr: *fem.* **mauvaise**] *moh-VEH* (*-VEZ*) bad, ill; mischievous; —**goût** (*-GOO*) bad taste; —**sujet** (*-sü-ZHEH*) bad character; no-good; black sheep.

mauve [Fr, lit., mallow, from Lat *malva*] *mohv*. pale purplish-gray color; a purple dye obtained from aniline.

maux. See **mal**.

mavin [Yid, from Heb] *MAY-v'n*. specialist; expert; know-it-all. Also, **maven**.

mavourneen [Ir] *muh-VOOR-neen*. my darling.

mawr [Welsh] *mowr*. black.

maxima cum laude [Lat] *MAHK-see-mah-koom-LOW-deh*. with highest honors.

maxixe [Port] *muh-SHEE-shuh*. Brazilian round dance.

Maya [Skt] *MAH-yah.* in Hinduism, illusion, confusion of reality and fantasy; the power of a god to produce illusions.

mazagran [Fr, after General Mazagran, who invented it during the Crimean War] *mah-zah-GRÃ.* black iced coffee; coffee mixed with water.

mazel-tov [Yid, from Heb] *MAH-z'l-tohv.* congratulations; good luck. Also, **mazal tov.**

mazuma [Yid *mezumen*, from Heb *mezūmān*, set, fixed] *muh-ZOO-muh.* (*slang*) money.

mazurka [Pol, from *Mazur*, Mazovia, district in N Poland] *mah-ZOOR-kah.* lively Polish dance.

M.D. Abbr. of **Medicinae Doctor.**

mea culpa [Lat] *MEH-ah-KOOL-pah.* my fault; the guilt is mine; I am to blame.

medice, cura te ipsum [Lat] *MEH-dee-keh-KOO-rah-teh-EEP-soom.* physician, heal thyself.

Medicinae Doctor [Lat: *abbr.* **M.D.**] *meh-dee-KEE-ny-DOHK-tor.* Doctor of Medicine.

medii aevi [Lat, gen. of *medius aevus*] *MEH-dee-ee-Y-vee.* of the Middle Ages, medieval.

Médoc [Fr] *may-DAWK.* a claret wine produced in Médoc, a region in SW France.

Meer [Ger] *mayr.* sea; lake.

Meerschaum [Ger] *MAYR-showm.* (*lit.*, sea foam) a hard white mineral used for making tobacco pipes; a pipe made of this mineral.

megalopolis [Gk] *meh-gah-loh-POH-lees.* a very large city; a continuously populated area, such as that which runs from Washington to Boston.

megas [Gk: *fem.* **megalē**; *neut.* **mega**] *MEH-gahs* (*meh-GAH-leh*; *MEH-gah*) large; great.

megillah [Yid, from Heb] *muh-GIL-uh.* a scroll containing portions of Jewish scripture; any long, tedious account. Also, **magillah.**

meglio tardi che mai [It] *MEH-lyoh-TAR-dee-keh-MY.* better late than never.

méhariste [Fr, from *méhari*, dromedary, from Ar] *may-ah-*

REEST. member of the French colonial camel corps in N Africa.

mein Herr [Ger: *pl.* **meine Herren**] *myn-HEHR* (*my-neh-HEHR-'n*) sir; mister.

Mein Kampf [Ger] *myn-KAHMPF.* My Battle: title of Adolph Hitler's autobiography.

Meistersinger [Ger] *MYS-tuh-zing-uh.* [*lit.*, Master Singer(s)] member of a guild of musicians and poets in Germany during the later Middle Ages.

Meisterstück [Ger: *pl.* **Meisterstücke**] *MYS-tuh-shtük* (*-eh*) masterpiece.

mélange [Fr, from *mêler*, to mix] *may-LÃZH.* mixture; miscellany; assemblage.

mêlée [Fr, from *mêler*, to mix] *meh-LAY.* brawl; free-for-all; skirmish.

melior [Lat: *pl.* **meliores**] *MEH-lee-or* (*meh-lee-OH-res*) better.

melisma [Gk: song, chant] *MEH-lees-mah.* (*music*) succession of notes sung to a single syllable.

membrum virile [Lat] *MEM-broom-vee-REE-leh.* male member, penis.

même [Fr] *mem.* same; self; even; although.

memento mori [Lat] *meh-MEN-toh-MOH-ree.* remember that you must die.

mémoire [Fr] *may-MWAR.* memory; written recollections; note; **—de lièvre** (*-duh-LYEH-vruh*) (*lit.*, hare's memory) bad memory; absentmindedness.

memorabilia [Lat] *meh-moh-rah-BEE-lee-ah.* collection of mementos or remembrances; things to be remembered.

memorandum [Lat] *meh-moh-RAHN-doom.* (*lit.*, to be remembered) memo; note.

memoriter [Lat] *meh-MOH-ree-tehr.* by memory; by heart; by rote.

mem-sahib [Anglo-Ind *mem*, from Eng *ma'am* + Hindi *sāhib*, master] *MEM-sah-heeb.* European lady, in India; wife of a **sahib.**

ménage [Fr] *may-NAHZH.* household; housekeeping; **—à trois** (*-ah-TRWAH*) household consisting of a husband and wife living together with the lover of one of them.

Mene, Mene, Tekel Upharsin [Aramaic] *MEH-neh-MEH-neh-TEH-kel-oo-far-SEEN*. (*lit*., numbered, numbered, weighed, divided) lighter and lighter with each weighing; found wanting when measured; the writing on the wall at Belshazzar's Feast.

menhir [Breton *men*, stone + *hir*, long] *MEN-heer*. huge monolithic Celtic monument.

menina [Port] *muh-NEE-nuh*. young girl; miss.

Menorah [Heb] *meh-NOH-rah*. Jewish candelabrum, usu. having seven or nine arms.

mens [Lat: *pl*. **mentes**] *mens* (*MEN-tes*) mind; meaning; understanding; —**sana in corpore sano** (*-SAH-nah-een-KOR-poh-reh-SAH-noh*) a sound mind in a sound body.

mensa [Lat] *MEN-sah*. table; (*cap*.) name of a small, strictly selected group of super-intellectuals; —**et thoro** (*-et-TOH-roh*) (*law*) from bed and board.

Mensch [Ger: *pl*. **Menschen**] *mensh* (*-'n*) man; human being; a virile man; (*pl*.) people; mankind.

Mensheviki [Russ] *men-shi-vee-KEE*. (*lit*., minority) the minority party that opposed the Bolsheviks in the Russian Revolution of 1917-18.

Mensur [Ger] *men-SOOR*. measure; distance (between duelists); student duel.

menteur [Fr: *fem*. **menteuse**, from *mentir*, to lie] *mã-TÖR* (*-TÖZ*) liar; lying, deceitful.

menthe [Fr] *mãt*. mint.

menuet [Fr, from *menu*, small, with reference to the small steps taken in the dance] *muh-nü-AY*. minuet.

mer [Fr] *mehr*. sea.

mercato [It] *mehr-KAH-toh*. market.

merci [Fr] *mehr-SEE*. thank you; mercy, grace.

merde [Fr] *mehrd*. (*vulgar*) excrement; (*interj*.) nuts!

merdeka [Indonesian] *mer-DEH-kah*. freedom, liberty, independence.

mère [Fr] *mehr*. mother.

merengue [AmerSp] *meh-REN-geh*. Dominican and Haitian dance characterized by limping and sidewise steps.

meridie [Lat, abl. of *meridies*, midday] *meh-REE-dee-eh.* at noon, at midday.

meringue [Fr] *muh-RĒG.* stiffly beaten egg whites and sugar, used as topping for cakes, pies, desserts, etc.

merino [Sp] *meh-REE-noh.* Spanish breed of sheep yielding a high-grade wool.

merlan [Fr] *mer-LÃ.* whiting (fish).

mesa [Sp, from Lat *mensa*] *MEH-sah.* table; tableland or plateau.

mésalliance [Fr] *may-zah-LYÃS.* misalliance; marriage to one of lower class or social standing.

mescal [MexSp, from Nahuatl *mexcalli*] *mes-KAHL.* cactus of northern Mexico and Texas; an intoxicating drink distilled from its fermented juice.

mesdames [Fr, pl. of **madame**; *abbr.* **Mmes**] *may-DAHM.* ladies; Mrs. (more than one).

mesdemoiselles [Fr, pl. of **mademoiselle**; *abbr.* **Mlles**] *may-d'mwah-ZEL.* young ladies; Misses.

meshuggah [Yid, from Heb] *muh-SHOO-guh.* (*slang*) crazy; insane. Also, **mishuggah.**

mesos [Gk] *MEH-sohs.* middle; mean.

mesquite [AmerSp *mezquite*, from Nahuatl *mizquitl*] *mes-KEE-teh.* dry prairie shrub the pods of which are used for fodder.

messa [It] *MAYS-sah.* Mass.

messa di voce [It] *MAYS-sah-dee-VOH-cheh.* (*music*) gradual rise and fall in the volume of the voice on a sustained note.

messe [Fr] *mes.* Mass.

messeigneurs. See **monseigneur.**

messere [It, from Prov *meser*] *mes-SEH-reh.* my lord; former Italian title of respect. Also, **messer** (*-SEHR*).

messieurs [Fr, pl. of **monsieur**; *abbr.* **MM**] *may-SYÖ.* Messrs; sirs; gentlemen.

mestizo [Sp, from Lat. *mixticius*, mixed] *mes-TEE-soh.* person of mixed Spanish and Indian blood; half-breed.

metabasis [Gk] *meh-TAH-bah-sees.* transition; transformation.

métier [Fr, from Lat *ministerium*, service] *may-TYAY.* trade; specialty; profession; skill.

métis [Fr, from Lat *mixticius*, mixed] *may-TEE.* person of mixed French and Indian blood; half-breed. Cf. **mestizo.**

mètre [Fr, from Gk *metron*, measure] *MEH-truh.* measure of length, meter; poetic measure.

Métro [Fr, abbr. of *chemin de fer métropolitain*, metropolitan railway] *may-TROH.* subway system, esp. of Paris.

meubles [Fr, from Lat *mobilis*, movable] *MÖ-bluh.* furniture; movable property.

mezhdunarodnyi [Russ, from *mezhdu*, between, among + *narod*, nation] *myizh-doo-nuh-RAWD-nyee.* international.

mezquita [Sp, from Ar **masjid**] *mes-KEE-tah.* mosque.

mezuzah [Heb: *pl.* **mezuzoth**] *meh-ZOO-zah (-zoht)* (*lit.,* doorpost) a scroll, usu. encased in a metal tube, on which are inscribed verses from the Book of Deuteronomy, attached to the doorposts of Jewish homes.

mezzanotte [It] *MED-zah-NOHT-teh.* midnight.

mezza voce [It] *MED-zah-VOH-cheh.* (*music*) with medium fulness of the voice.

mezzo [It] *MED-zoh.* middle; half; medium, moderate; **—forte** (*-FOR-teh*) (*music*) medium loud; **mezzogiorno** (*-JOR-noh*) noon, midday; south; **—piano** (*-PYAH-noh*) (*music*) medium soft; **—rilievo** (*-ree-LYEH-voh*) medium relief; sculpture in which approximately half the figure projects from the background.

mi-carême [Fr] *mee-kah-REM.* mid-Lenten season.

midi [Fr] *mee-DEE.* noon; south, esp. of France.

midinette [Fr, from *midi*, noon + *dînette*, snack] *mee-dee-NET.* French working girl, with a noon lunch hour.

miel [Fr] *myel.* honey.

mieux vaut tard que jamais [Fr] *MYÖ-voh-TAR-kuh-zhah-MEH.* better late than never.

mignon [Fr: *fem.* **mignonne**] *mee-NYÖ (-NYUN)* small and delicate; petite person; favorite; darling.

mijnheer [Du] *myn-HEHR.* mister; sir. Also, **mynheer.**

mikado [Jap *mi*, honorable + *kado*, gate (of the imperial palace)] *MEE-kah-doh.* title of the emperors of Japan.

mikros [Gk] *mee-KROHS.* small; short.

mila [It, pl. of **mille**] *MEE-lah.* thousands.

miles gloriosus [Lat] *MEE-les-gloh-ree-OH-soos.* (*lit.,* glorious soldier) bragging soldier; braggart.

milia [Lat, pl. of **mille**; *abbr.* **mm.**] *MEE-lee-ah.* thousands.

miliciano [Sp, from *milicia,* militia] *mee-lee-SYAH-noh.* militiaman.

milieu [Fr] *mee-LYÖ.* environment; sphere; center; medium; middle.

mille [Lat: *pl.* **milia**; *abbr.* **M**] *MEEL-leh* (*MEE-lee-ah*); [It: *pl.* **mila**] *MEEL-leh* (*MEE-lah*); [Fr: *pl. unchanged, but with var.* **mil** *used in dates*] *meel.* thousand.

millefiori [It] *meel-leh-FYOH-ree.* (*lit.,* a thousand flowers) type of Venetian mosaic glass.

millefoglie [It] *meel-leh-FAW-lyeh.* (*lit.,* a thousand leaves) type of pastry of many thin layers.

Mille Miglia [It] *meel-leh-MEE-lyah.* (*lit.,* a thousand miles) annual Italian auto racing event.

milreis [Port] *meel-RAYSH.* a former monetary unit of Portugal and Brazil, equal to 1000 reis.

mime parodiste [Fr] *MEEM-pah-roh-DEEST.* mime who plays parodies.

mimesis [Gk] *MEE-meh-sees.* imitation, mimicry.

mina [Lat, from Gk **mna**; *pl.* **minae**] *MEE-nah* (*-ny*). See **mna.**

minaccevolmente [It] *mee-nah-cheh-vohl-MAYN-teh.* (*music*) threateningly, menacingly. Also, **minacciando** (*mee-nah-CHAHN-doh*).

minauderie [Fr, from *minauder,* to mince, simper] *mee-noh-d'REE.* simpering; affectedness.

Minenwerfer [Ger] *MEE-n'n-vehr-fuh.* mine launcher; grenade launcher.

minestra [It, from Lat *ministrare,* to serve] *mee-NES-trah.* soup, often of rice or pasta with vegetables.

minestrone [It, lit., big soup] *mee-nes-TROH-neh.* thick soup.

ming [Chin] *ming.* type of art done during the Ming dynasty (1369-1644) in China, esp. in porcelain and painting.

minifundio [Sp] *mee-nee-FOON-dyoh.* a poor, small farm. Cf. **latifundio.**

ministerium [Lat] *mee-nees-TEH-ree-oom.* ministry; service; vocation.

Minnesang [Ger *Minne*, love + *Sang*, song] *MIN-uh-zahng.* medieval German love poetry of the 12th–14th centuries.

Minnesinger [Ger] *MIN-uh-zing-uh.* poet(s) of the Minnesang period. Also, **Minnesänger** (*-zeng-uh*).

Minseito [Jap] *MEEN-say-toh.* major Japanese political party before World War II.

minusculae [Lat] *mee-NOOS-koo-ly.* (*lit.*, tiny things) small cursive Roman letters; lower case characters.

minutiae [Lat] *mee-NOO-tee-y.* small details; trifles.

minyan [Heb] *mee-NYAHN.* (*lit.*, number, reckoning) quorum of ten men necessary for public worship in the Jewish faith.

mir [Russ] *meer.* village; world; peace.

mirabile [Lat, from *mirari*, to wonder] *mee-RAH-bee-leh.* wonderful, marvelous; —**dictu** (*-DEEK-too*) wonderful to tell; —**visu** (*-VEE-soo*) wonderful to behold.

mirabilia [Lat] *mee-rah-BEE-lee-ah.* wonders; marvels.

misa [Sp] *MEE-sah.* Mass.

mise-en-plis [Fr] *mee-zã-PLEE.* (*lit.*, a putting in curls) style of hairsetting.

mise en scène [Fr] *mee-zã-SEN.* (*lit.*, a putting on stage) theatrical production; stage setting; surroundings of a thing or event.

miserabile [Lat] *mee-seh-RAH-bee-leh.* terrible; miserable; sad; —**dictu** (*-DEEK-too*) sad to relate; —**vulgus** (*-VOOL-goos*) wretched mass; rabble.

misère [Fr] *mee-ZEHR.* misery; want; poverty; wretchedness.

miserere [Lat] *mee-seh-REH-reh.* have mercy; have pity; —**mei** (*-MEH-ee*) have mercy upon me; —**nobis** (*-NOH-bees*) have mercy upon us.

miséricorde [Fr, from Lat *misericordia*, from *miserari*, to pity + *cor*, heart] *mee-zay-ree-KORD.* mercy; pardon;

small medieval dagger, used for giving the deathblow to a wounded enemy; small bar or rail on the underside of a movable church seat which helps to support a person standing in the stall when the seat is raised.

Mishnah [Heb] *mish-NAH.* (*lit.*, oral teaching) the old section of the Talmud, consisting of oral laws collected about 200 A.D.

mishuggah. *mi-SHOO-guh.* See **meshuggah.**

misra [Ar] *mees-RAH.* metrical unit of Arabic poetry.

Missa [Lat] *MEES-sah.* Mass.

mistral [Prov, from Lat *magistralis*, masterly] *mees-TRAHL.* cold, dry wind of southern France blowing down the Rhône to the Mediterranean.

misurato [It] *mee-soo-RAH-toh.* (*music*) measured; in accurate time.

mit [Ger] *mit.* with; —**Ausdruck** (*-OWS-drook*) (*music*) expressively, with expression; —**Gewalt** (*-guh-VAHLT*) forceful; with strength; with violence.

Mitarbeiter [Ger, from *mit*, with + *arbeiten*, to work] *MIT-ar-by-tuh.* co-worker, colleague; assistant; collaborator.

mitrailleur [Fr, from *mitraille*, scrap metal, grapeshot] *mee-try-YÖR* machine gunner; **mitrailleuse** (*-YÖZ*) machine gun.

Mittag [Ger] *MIT-tahk.* midday, noon; **Mittagessen** (*-es-s'n*) midday meal; lunch.

Mitteilung [Ger] *MIT-ty-loong.* communication; announcement; notice; report.

Mittelalter [Ger] *MIT-t'l-ahl-tuh.* Middle Ages.

Mittelamerika [Ger] *MIT-t'l-ah-MEH-ree-kah.* Central America.

Mitteleuropa [Ger] *MIT-t'l-oy-ROH-pah.* Middle (Central) Europe; a World War I theory of a united Central Europe dominated by Germany.

mitzvah [Yid, from Heb] *MITS-vuh.* religious or moral commandment; good deed; fortunate event.

miya [Jap] *MEE-yah.* Shinto temple.

Mlle Abbr. of **mademoiselle; Mlles** Abbr. of **mesdemoiselles.**

MM. Abbr. of **messieurs.**

mm. Abbr. of Lat **milia**, thousands.

Mme Abbr. of **madame**; **Mmes** Abbr. of **mesdames**.

mna [Gk, from Semitic; *pl.* **mnai**] *mnah* (*mny*) ancient unit of weight equal to 100 drachmas, or about 16 oz.; sum of money equal to 1/60 of a talent. Also, **mina.**

mobile perpetuum [Lat] *MOH-bee-leh-pehr-PEH-too-oom.* something in perpetual motion; **mobile vulgus** (*-VOOL-goos*) the fickle crowd.

mode nouvelle [Fr] *MOHD-noo-VEL.* new style; the latest fashion; **mode stricte** (*-STREEKT*) conservative style; no extremes; can be worn next year.

moderato [It] *moh-deh-RAH-toh.* (*music*) moderate in speed.

modicum [Lat, from *modus*, measure] *MOH-dee-koom.* moderate measure or quantity; correct amount.

modiste [Fr, from *mode*, style, fashion] *moh-DEEST.* dress-maker; designer; milliner.

modus [Lat] *MOH-doos.* mode; method; measure; **—operandi** (*-oh-peh-RAHN-dee*) method of working; work plan; **—vivendi** (*-vee-VEN-dee*) way of living; temporary agreement pending settlement of dispute or difficulties.

Moerae [Lat, from Gk *Moirai*] *MOY-ry.* the Fates; fate. See **Moira.**

moeurs [Fr, from Lat **mores**] *mörs.* manners; customs; mores.

moglie [It: *pl.* **mogli**] *MOH-lyeh* (*-lyee*) wife.

Moharram. See **Muharram.**

moinho de vento [Port] *moh-EE-nyuh-duh-VEN-too.* wind-mill.

Moira [Gk: *pl.* **Moirai**] *MOY-rah* (*-ry*) the goddess of Fate; (*pl.*) the Fates.

moiré [Fr] *mwah-RAY.* watered; watered silk; the wavy effect of some silk, rayon and cotton fabrics.

molino de viento [Sp] *moh-LEE-noh-deh-VYEN-toh.* windmill.

Moloch [Heb, var. of *melekh*, king] *MOH-lohkh.* a pagan god mentioned in the Old Testament; something requiring compromise or sacrifice of ideals or principles.

molto [It: *pl.* **molti**] *MOHL-toh* (*-tee*) much; very; (*pl.*) many; —**allegro** (*-ahl-LEH-groh*) (*music*) very fast.

momzer, momser. See **mamzer.**

mon ami [Fr: *fem.* **mon amie**] *mõ-nah-MEE.* my friend; **mon cher** (*-SHEHR*) my dear fellow; **mon chou** (*-SHOO*) (*lit.*, my cabbage) my darling; **mon Dieu** (*-DYÖ*) my God! good heavens! **mon lapin** (*-lah-PÉ̃*) (*lit.*, my rabbit) my dear; **mon petit chou** (*-p'tee-SHOO*) (*lit.*, my little cabbage) my darling; **mon vieux** (*-VYÖ*) old man; old fellow; old pal.

Monatsbericht [Ger] *MOH-nahts-buh-riçt.* monthly report.

Mond [Ger] *mohnt.* moon.

mondain [Fr: *fem.* **mondaine**] *mõ-DÉ̃* (*-DEN*) worldly; mundane.

monde [Fr] *mõd.* world; people.

mondo cane [It] *MOHN-doh-KAH-neh.* dog's world; cruel world.

Monégasque [Fr] *moh-nay-GAHSK.* of Monaco; native or inhabitant of Monaco.

moneta [Lat] *moh-NEH-tah.* mint; coin; money.

mono [Sp] *MOH-noh.* monkey; suit of coveralls; (*pl.*) jeans; **mona** (*-nah*) (*fem.*) cute, pretty.

monocoque [Fr *mono*, single + *coque*, shell] *moh-noh-KOHK.* airplane fuselage of ovoid shape, molded in one piece; airplane with such a fuselage; boat hull or auto body molded in one piece, esp. of fiber glass or plastic.

monos [Gk] *MOH-nohs.* alone; single; one.

monos sabios [Sp] *MOH-nohs-SAH-byohs.* (*lit.*, wise monkeys) in bullfighting, the men who sand the ring between fights.

mons [Lat: *pl.* **montes**] *mohns* (*MOHN-tes*) mountain; hill; mound; —**Veneris** (*-VEH-neh-rees*) mound of Venus: rounded protuberance of fatty tissue in the pubic region of the human female.

monseigneur [Fr: *pl.* **messeigneurs**] *mõ-seh-NYÖR* (*may-*) title of princes and bishops.

monsieur [Fr: *pl.* **messieurs**; *abbr.* **M.**] *muh-SYÖ* (*may-SYÖ*) mister; sir; gentleman.

monsignor(e) [It: *pl.* **monsignori**] *mohn-see-NYOH-reh*

(-*ree*) monsignor: title conferred upon certain Roman Catholic prelates.

montage [Fr, from *monter*, to mount, set up] *mō-TAHZH.* technique of superimposing or combining photographs or motion pictures for special effects; pictures produced in this way; any combination of different elements.

montagnard [Fr] *mō-tah-NYAR.* mountaineer; member of the Montagne; member of a dark-skinned Vietnamese people of mixed ethnic origins; member of an American Indian tribe inhabiting the Canadian Rockies.

montagne [Fr] *mō-TAH-nyuh.* mountain; (cap.) a radical group that occupied the highest seats in the National Convention at the time of the French Revolution.

montaña [Sp] *mohn-TAH-nyah.* mountain.

Montani semper liberi [Lat] *mohn-TAH-nee-SEM-pehr-LEE-beh-ree.* Mountaineers are always free (motto of West Virginia.)

montant [Fr, pr.p. of *monter*, to rise] *mō-TĂ* (of a neckline) high in front.

mont-de-piété [Fr] *MŎ-duh-pyay-TAY*; **monte de piedad** [Sp] *MOHN-teh-deh-pyeh-DAHD*; **monte di pietà** [It] *MOHN-teh-dee-pyeh-TAH.* (*lit.*, mount of pity) pawnshop.

monumentum aere perennius [Lat] *moh-noo-MEN-toom-Y-reh-peh-REN-nee-oos.* monument more enduring than bronze.

mór [Gael] *mor.* large; big.

mora [Lat: *pl.* morae] *MOH-rah* (-*ry*) the time equivalent of a short syllable in classical verse; delay; pause.

morbidezza [It, from *morbido*, soft, delicate] *mor-bee-DAY-tsah.* delicacy; delicate treatment of an art or musical form.

morceau [Fr: *pl.* morceaux] *mor-SOH.* piece; morsel; extract.

more [Lat, abl. of *mos*, custom] *MOH-reh.* in the way or manner of; —**Anglico** (-*AHN-glee-koh*) in English style; —**Hibernico** (-*hee-BEHR-nee-koh*) in Irish style; —**majorum** (-*mah-YOH-room*) in the style of our ancestors; —**meo** (-*MEH-oh*) in my own style; —**Socratico** (-*soh-*

KRAH-tee-koh) in the Socratic manner; —**solito** (*-SOH-lee-toh*) in the customary manner.

more [Russ: *pl.* **morya**] *MOH-ryeh* (*muh-RYAH*) sea.

morendo [It, from *morire*, to die] *moh-REN-doh*. (*music*) dying away.

mores [Lat, pl. of *mos*, custom] *MOH-res*. folkways, habits and traditions characteristic of a group.

Morgen [Ger] *MOR-g'n*. morning; tomorrow; measure of land, orig. the amount that could be plowed in one morning; **Morgengabe** (*-gah-beh*) gift that the bridegroom gives the bride on the morning after the wedding; **Morgengruss** (*-groos*) morning greeting.

morgue [Fr] *morg*. haughty look; haughtiness; arrogance; mortuary, morgue.

morisco [Sp, from **Moro**] *moh-REES-koh*. Moorish; Moor.

morituri te salutamus [Lat] *moh-ree-TOO-ree-teh-sah-loo-TAH-moos*. we who are about to die salute you: the salutation of the gladiators to the Roman emperor.

mormorando [It] *mor-moh-RAHN-doh*. (*music*) murmuring; whispering.

Moro [Sp] *MOH-roh*. Moor; Moorish.

morphe [Gk] *mor-FEH*. form, shape, figure; appearance.

morra [It] *MOR-rah*. game in which the object is to guess the sum of the fingers quickly raised by self and opponent, similar to "odds and evens."

mors [Lat] *mors*. death; —**tua, vita mea** (*-TOO-ah-VEE-tah-MEH-ah*) your death is my life; you must die that I may live.

mort [Fr] *mor*. death; dead (*masc. adj.*); **morte** (*mort*) dead (*fem. adj.*).

mortis causa [Lat] *MOR-tees-KOW-sah*. by reason or in anticipation of death.

morue [Fr] *moh-RÜ*. codfish.

mosca [It] *MOHS-kah*. fly.

moscato [It, from Lat *muscus*, musk, with reference to the aroma] *mohs-KAH-toh*. deep purple grape; wine made from this grape.

mosso [It, p.p. of *muovere*, to move] *MOHS-soh*. moved; in motion; (*music*) rapid, fast.

mot [Fr] *moh.* word; saying; expression; aphorism; —**d'ordre** (*-DOR-druh*) watchword, password; —**juste** (*-ZHÙST*) appropriate, exact word.

motif [Fr, from Lat *motivus,* motive, moving] *moh-TEEF.* theme; design; pattern; recurrent theme in art, literature or music.

moto [It] *MOH-toh.* movement; motion; **con**— (*kohn-*) (*music*) with movement; lively; expressively; —**perpetuo** (*-pehr-PEH-too-oh*) perpetual motion.

mouche [Fr] *moosh.* fly; speck; beauty mark.

mouchoir [Fr] *moo-SHWAR.* handkerchief.

moue [Fr, from Germanic] *moo.* pout; grimace.

mouflon [Fr] *moo-FLÕ.* wild sheep of Sardinia and Corsica.

mouillé [Fr, p.p. of *mouiller,* to wet] *moo-YAY.* wet; mulled; softened.

moule [Fr] *mool.* mussel.

moulin [Fr] *moo-LÈ.* mill, windmill; —**à vent** (*-ah-VÃ*) windmill.

mousse [Fr] *moos.* moss; dessert made with frozen whipped cream and, usually, fruit; cabin boy.

mousseline [Fr] *moo-s'LEEN.* muslin.

mousseux [Fr] *moo-SÖ.* sparkling; carbonated.

moutarde [Fr] *moo-TARD.* mustard.

mouton [Fr] *moo-TÕ.* sheep; mutton.

moyen âge [Fr] *mwah-yē-NAHZH.* Middle Ages.

mozarabe [Sp, from Ar *musta'rib,* would-be Arab] *moh-SAH-rah-beh.* Mozarab; a Christian in a country, esp. Spain, under Moorish domination; dialect of the Mozarabs.

mozzarella [It] *moh-tsah-REL-lah.* mild white semisoft Italian cheese.

muchacho [Sp] *moo-CHAH-choh.* boy; **muchacha** (*-chah*) girl.

mucho [Sp: *pl.* **muchos**] *MOO-choh* (*-chohs*) much; very; (*pl.*) many; **muchas gracias** (*MOO-chahs-GRAH-syahs*) many thanks; thank you very much.

mudéjar [Sp, from Ar *muddajjar,* permitted to stay] *moo-DEH-har.* a Moslem in Spain, esp. a Christianized Moor; Spanish architectural style with strong Moorish influence.

muelle [Sp] *MWEH-lyeh*. wharf; station platform.

muet [Fr: *fem*. **muette**] *müeh* (*müet*) dumb, mute; silent.

muezzin [Ar *mu'adhdhin*] *moo-EZ-zin*. Moslem prayer crier.

mufti [Ar] *MOOF-tee*. teacher; Moslem religious leader or legal advisor; civilian clothing, as opposed to military garb.

Muharram [Ar] *moo-hah-RAHM*. (*lit.*, holy) first month of the Islamic calendar; name of a festival day.

mujer [Sp] *moo-HEHR*. woman; wife.

mulino [It] *moo-LEE-noh*. mill; —a vento (*-ah-VAYN-toh*) windmill.

mullah [Ar *mawlā*] *moo-LAH*. Moslem religious teacher or theologian; in Turkey, a provincial judge.

mulligatawny [Tamil *milagu-tanni*, pepper water] *mul-i-guh-TAW-nee*. thick, heavily curried soup.

multum in parvo [Lat] *MOOL-toom-een-PAR-voh*. much in little.

Münchener [Ger, from *München*, Munich] *MÜN-çuh-nuh*. of or pertaining to Munich; Munich beer.

mundus vult decipi [Lat] *MOON-doos-VOOLT-DEH-kee-pee*. the world wants to be deceived.

muni [Skt] *MOO-nee*. philosopher; wise one; silent one; one who has taken the vow of silence.

musette [Fr, dim. of *muse*, bagpipe] *mü-ZET*. small bagpipe; shoulder bag.

Muslim [Ar] *MUZ-lim*. (*lit.*, one who submits) Moslem, Mohammedan.

mussaka [Gk] *moo-sah-KAH*. eggplant; eggplant and lamb dish.

mutatis mutandis [Lat] *moo-TAH-tees-moo-TAHN-dees*. with changes being made; with alterations to fit a new set of circumstances.

mutato nomine, de te fabula narratur [Lat] *moo-TAH-toh-NOH-mee-neh-deh-teh-FAH-boo-lah-nar-RAH-toor*. with the name changed, the story is about you.

Mutter [Ger: *pl*. **Mütter**] *MOOT-uh* (*MÜT-uh*) mother.

Mütterchen [Ger] *MÜT-uh-ç'n*. little mother; mommy; little old woman.

muu-muu [Hawaiian] *MOO-oo-MOO-oo*. loose, brightly colored dress worn by Hawaiian women.

muzhik [Russ, dim. of *muzh*, man] *moo-ZHEEK*. Russian peasant.

MVD [Russ, abbr. of *Ministerstvo Vnutrennikh Dyel*, Ministry of Home Affairs] name of Soviet secret police since 1943. Cf. **Cheka, GPU, NKVD**.

mynheer. See **mijnheer**.

mystique [Fr] *mees-TEEK*. mystic; mystical; set of beliefs or assumptions relating to a given subject or personage; hero legend.

N

nabob [Hindi *nawwāb*] *NAY-bahb*. person of riches and power; big shot. See **nawab**.

nach Canossa [Ger] *nahkh-kah-NOHS-sah*. to Canossa: referring to the journey made to the site of a castle in northern Italy by Emperor Henry IV of the Holy Roman Empire to do penance before Pope Gregory VII in 1077; hence, an act of humility.

Nachdruck [Ger] *NAHKH-drook*. reprint; reproduction; (*music*) accent; emphasis.

Nachmittag [Ger] *NAHKH-mit-tahk*. afternoon.

Nachrichten [Ger] *NAHKH-riç-t'n*. news.

Nachtigall [Ger] *NAHKHT-i-gahl*. nightingale.

Nachtmusik [Ger] *NAHKHT-moo-zeek*. serenade; nocturne.

Nachtrag [Ger: *pl.* **Nachträge**] *NAHKH-trahk* (*-tray-guh*) supplement; addendum.

nada [Sp] *NAH-dah*. nothing; not at all.

nadie [Sp] *NAH-dyeh*. no one; nobody.

naïf [Fr: *fem.* **naïve**] *nah-EEF* (*-EEV*) innocent; naïve; naïve person.

naissance [Fr] *neh-SÃS*. birth; dawn.

naïve [Fr, fem. of **naïf**] *nah-EEV*. See **naïf**.

naïveté [Fr] *nah-eev-TAY*. innocence; artlessness.

nano [It, from Gk *nanos*] *NAH-noh*. dwarf; midget; small.

naos [Gk] *nah-OHS*. in a Greek temple, the inner part or shrine.

Napoléon [Fr, after Napoleon I, French Emperor, 1804-15] *nah-poh-leh-Õ*. pastry of many paper-thin layers with cream filling between; —**d'or** (-*DOR*) French gold coin.

narghile [Pers, from *nargil*, coconut; formerly used for the bowl of the pipe] *NAR-gee-leh*. pipe in which the smoke is drawn through a hose after passing through water; waterpipe; hookah.

narod [Russ] *nuh-RAWT*. people; nation.

narodnyi [Russ] *nuh-RAWD-nee*. of the people; popular; national.

narwhal [Dan *narhval*, from *nar-* (perh. meaning corpse, with reference to the white underside) + *hval*, whale] *NAR-wahl*. Arctic tusk whale.

natale [It] *nah-TAH-leh*. natal; native; birthday; (*cap.*) Christmas.

Nationalsozialistische Deutsche Arbeiterpartei [Ger] *nah-tsyoh-NAHL-soh-tsyah-LIS-ti-sheh-DOY-cheh-AR-by-tuh-par-ty*. National Socialist German Workers' Party; the Nazi Party (1920-45).

nature [Fr] *nah-TÜR*. (*lit.*, nature) natural, plain; (*cookery*) plainly cooked.

naturel [Fr] *nah-tü-REL*. natural; native; plain; nature, disposition; plainness, naturalness.

naufrage [Fr] *noh-FRAHZH*. shipwreck.

nauka [Russ: *pl.* **nauki**] *nuh-OO-kuh* (-*kee*) science.

naumachia [Gk] *now-mah-KEE-ah*. battle at sea; theater for staged sea spectacles.

nausia [Gk] *now-SEE-ah*. seasickness; nausea.

nautch [Anglo-Ind, from Hindi *nāch*] *nawch*. Oriental dance; performance by professional Hindu dancers.

navaja [Sp] *nah-VAH-hah*. razor; sharp knife; razor clam.

Navidad [Sp] *nah-vee-DAHD*. nativity; birth; Christmas; **Feliz Navidad** (*feh-LEES-*); also, **Felices Navidades** (*feh-LEE-ses-nah-vee-DAH-des*) Merry Christmas.

nawab [Hindi *nawwāb*, from Ar, pl. of *nā'ib*, deputy, governor] *nuh-WAWB*. governor; Moslem prince; honorary title bestowed upon distinguished Moslems in India and Pakistan. Cf. **nabob.**

Nazi [Ger, abbr. of **Nationalsozialistische Deutsche Arbeiterpartei**] *NAH-tsee.* member of the National Socialist Workers' Party; the Nazi party.

nazir [Hindi, from Pers and Ar] *nah-ZEER.* inspector; civil court official; mosque warden.

N.B. Abbr. of **nota bene.** Also, **NB**

nebbish [Yid] *NEB-ish.* colorless, insignificant person; a nobody, nonentity. Also, **nebach** (*NEB-ukh*).

necrophilia [NL, from Gk *nekros,* dead body + *philia,* love] *neh-kroh-FEE-lee-ah.* love of corpses and of things connected with the dead.

necropolis [Gk *nekropolis,* from *nekros,* dead, dead body + *polis,* city] *neh-KROH-poh-lees.* cemetery; burial ground; city of the dead.

née [Fr, fem. of *né,* born] *nay.* born; indicating maiden name of a woman.

nefasti dies [Lat] *neh-FAHS-tee-DEE-es.* in ancient Rome, days when court was not held, or general meetings of the people; unlucky days.

négligée [Fr *négligé*] *nay-glee-ZHAY.* (*lit.,* neglected) casual; a loose, sheer robe worn by women.

negro [Sp] *NEH-groh;* [Port] *NEH-groo.* black; Negro.

Negus [Amharic: king] *NEH-goos.* title of the Emperor of Ethiopia.

neige [Fr] *nezh.* snow; **neiges d'antan** (*NEZH-dā-TĀ*) snows of yesteryear.

nein [Ger] *nyn.* no.

nel mezzo del cammin di nostra vita [It] *nel-MED-zoh-del-kahm-MEEN-dee-NOHS-trah-VEE-tah.* in the middle of the journey of our life: opening line of Dante's *Divina Commedia.*

nemo [Lat] *NEH-moh.* no one; no man; **—me impune lacessit** (*-meh-eem-POO-neh-lah-KES-seet*) No one attacks me with impunity (motto of Scotland).

neos [Gk] *NEH-ohs.* new; recent.

ne plus ultra [Lat] *neh-ploos-OOL-trah.* no further; the furthest possible point; acme; limit.

nesos [Gk] *NEH-sohs.* island.

n'est-ce pas? [Fr] *nes-PAH.* is it not so?; right?

neue Sachlichkeit [Ger] *NOY-eh-ZAHKH-liç-kyt.* new Realism: an artistic and literary movement of the 1920's in Germany, a reaction against Impressionism.

Neufchâtel [Fr, from the name of a town in N France] *nö-shah-TEL.* a kind of soft, creamy white cheese.

Neustria [Vulgar Lat] *neh-OOS-tree-ah.* the western part of the Frankish kingdom in the 8th and 9th centuries.

nevada [Sp] *neh-VAH-dah.* snowfall; snowy, snow-covered.

névé [Fr] *nay-VAY.* compressed glacial snow, not quite as hard as ice.

n'è vero? [It] *neh-VAY-roh.* See **non è vero?**

nexus [Lat] *NEK-soos.* bond; joint; connection.

Nez Percés [Fr] *NAY-pehr-SAY.* (*lit.*, pierced noses) AmerInd tribe of NW U.S.

nez retroussé [Fr] *NAY-ruh-troo-SAY.* turned-up nose; pug nose.

N.F. Abbr. of **nouveau(x) franc(s).**

niaiserie [Fr, from *niais*, foolish] *nyeh-z'-REE.* foolishness; silliness; trifle; piece of nonsense.

Nibelungenlied [Ger] *ni-buh-LOONG'n-leet.* Song of the Nibelungs: old mythological German epic.

nicht wahr? [Ger] *niçt-VAR.* is it not so?; right?

niello [It, from Lat *nigellus*, blackish] *NYEL-loh.* 15th-century method of decorative metal engraving; work done in this fashion; mixture of copper, silver, lead, and sulfur, used to fill in an engraved design in such work.

niente [It] *NYEN-teh.* nothing; don't mention it; —**affatto** (*-ahf-FAHT-toh*) not at all; nothing at all.

nigaud [Fr] *nee-GOH.* simpleton; boob.

niger [Lat] *NEE-gehr.* black.

nihil [Lat] *NEE-heel.* nothing; —**obstat** (*-OHB-staht*) nothing stands in the way: formula used in the Roman Catholic Church for granting permission to publish a work that has passed censorship; —**sine Deo** (*-SEE-neh-DEH-oh*) (there is) nothing without God; —**sub sole novi** (or **novum**) (*-soob-SOH-leh-NOH-vee* or *-voom*) nothing new under the sun.

nihilisme [Fr, from Lat *nihil*, nothing] *nee-ee-LEEZ-muh.* nothingness; ennui, indifference; Nihilism.

nikak nyet [Russ] *nee-KAHK-NYET.* not at all; by no means.

nike [Gk] *NEE-keh.* victory; goddess of victory; symbol of victory.

nil [Lat, contr. of *nihilum*: *ni*, not + *hilum*, trifle] *neel.* nothing; naught; —**admirari** (*-ahd-mee-RAH-ree*) be astonished at nothing; —**desperandum** (*-des-peh-RAHN-doom*) no reason to despair; —**dicit** (*-DEE-keet*) (*law*) he says nothing; no defense; —**sine numine** (*-SEE-neh-NOO-mee-neh*) Nothing without divine will (motto of Colorado).

n'importe [Fr] *nē-PORT.* it doesn't matter; it's not important; no matter.

niño [Sp: *fem.* **niña**] *NEE-nyoh* (*-nyah*) child; little one.

Nippon [Jap] *NEEP-pohn.* Japan.

Nirvana [Skt] *neer-VAH-nah.* (*lit.*, blown out) in Buddhism, complete sublimation of individuality to a perfect state of happiness in which all pain has ceased and the individual is reabsorbed into the godhead.

Nisei [Jap *ni*, two, second + *sei*, generation] *NEE-say.* second generation of Japanese born outside Japan; Japanese-Americans. Cf. **Issei, Sansei.**

nisi [Lat] *NEE-see.* unless.

Nivôse [Fr, from Lat *nivosus*, snowy] *nee-VOHZ.* fourth month of the French Revolutionary calendar.

Nizam [Ar: order, rule] *nee-ZAHM.* title of the ruler of Hyderabad; (*l.c.*) soldier of the regular Turkish army.

N.K.V.D. [Russ, abbr. of *Narodnii Kommissariat Vnutrennikh Dyel*, People's Commissariat for Internal Affairs] Soviet Secret Police from 1935-43. Cf. **Cheka, G.P.U., M.V.D.**

Nō [Jap] *noh.* (*lit.*, ability, capacity) classical, stylized lyric drama form. Also, **Noh.**

noblesse [Fr] *noh-BLES.* nobility; —**oblige** (*-oh-BLEEZH*) (*lit.*, nobility obligates) rank imposes responsibility and obligations.

Nochebuena [Sp] *noh-cheh-BWEH-nah.* (*lit.,* good night) Christmas Eve.

Noël [Fr] *noh-EL.* Christmas; Christmas carol.

¿No es verdad? [Sp] *noh-es-vehr-DAHD.* is it not true?; right?

Noh. See **Nō.**

noir [Fr] *nwar.* black.

noli me tangere [Lat] *NOH-lee-meh-TAHN-geh-reh.* Don't touch me.

nolle prosequi [Lat: *abbr.* **nol. pros.**] *NOHL-leh-PROH-seh-kwee.* (*lit.,* to be unwilling to prosecute) discontinuance or cancellation of court proceedings.

nolo [Lat] *NOH-loh.* I am unwilling; I don't want; I will not; —**contendere** (*-kohn-TEN-deh-reh*) (*law*) I will not contest: plea of no defense; equivalent to plea of guilty.

nom [Fr] *nō.* name; noun; —**de famille** (*-duh-fah-MEE-yuh*) family name, surname; —**de guerre** (*-duh-GEHR*) (*lit.,* war name) pseudonym; —**de plume** (*-duh-PLÜM*) pen name; pseudonym; professional name.

nomen [Lat] *NOH-men.* name; noun.

nomos [Gk] *NOH-mohs.* law; custom.

non capisco [It] *nohn-kah-PEES-koh.* I don't understand.

non causa pro causa [Lat] *nohn-KOW-sah-proh-KOW-sah.* (*lit.,* no cause for cause) the logical fallacy of a false cause.

non compos mentis [Lat] *nohn-KOHM-pohs-MEN-tees.* not of sound mind; insane.

non constat [Lat] *nohn-KOHNS-taht.* it does not appear (so); it is not evident.

non è così [It] *nohn-EH-koh-SEE.* it is not so.

non est [Lat] *nohn-EST.* he (it) is not; he (it) does not exist.

non è vero? [It] *nohn-eh-VAY-roh.* is it not true?; right?

non importa [It] *nohn-eem-POR-tah.* it doesn't matter; it's not important.

non mi ricordo [It] *nohn-mee-ree-KOR-doh.* I don't remember.

non nobis, Domine [Lat] *nohn-NOH-bees-DOH-mee-neh.* not to us, Lord.

non obstante [Lat] *nohn-ohbs-TAHN-teh.* notwithstanding; in spite of; nevertheless.

non omnis moriar [Lat] *nohn-OHM-nees-MOH-ree-ar.* I shall not die completely.

non placet [Lat] *nohn-PLAH-ket.* (*lit.*, it does not please) nay; negative vote.

non possumus [Lat] *nohn-POHS-soo-moos.* we cannot: plea of inability.

non quis sed quid [Lat] *nohn-KWEES-sed-KWEED.* not who, but what.

non ragioniam di lor, ma guarda e passa [It] *nohn-rah-joh-NYAHM-dee-LOR-mah-GWAR-dah-eh-PAHS-sah.* let us not speak of them, but look and pass on.

non sequitur [Lat: *abbr.* **non seq.**] *nohn-SEH-kwee-toor.* (*lit.*, it does not follow) illogical conclusion; unconnected, irrelevant remark.

non so che [It] *nohn-soh-KEH.* (*lit.*, I don't know what) an undefinable or inexpressible something.

noodnik. See **nudnik.**

nor da hor? [Basque] *NOR-dah-HOR.* who goes there? who is there?

noria [Sp, from Ar] *NOH-ryah.* water wheel.

nosce te ipsum [Lat] *NOHS-keh-teh-EEP-soom.* know thyself.

nosh [Yid] *nahsh.* to nibble; eat between meals; a snack eaten between meals.

nosilshchik [Russ] *nah-SEEL-shcheek.* porter, bearer.

nostrum [Lat] *NOHS-troom.* (*lit.*, ours) fake panacea; quack medicine, cure-all.

nota [It] *NOH-tah.* note.

nota bene [Lat: *abbr.* **N.B.**] *NOH-tah-BEH-neh.* note well; observe this.

nota buona [It] *NOH-tah-BWOH-nah.* (*music*) accented note; —**sensibile** (*-sen-SEE-bee-leh*) lead note; —**sostenuta** (*-sohs-teh-NOO-tah*) sustained note.

Not bricht Eisen [Ger] *NOHT-briçt-Y-z'n.* (*lit.*, need breaks iron) necessity is the mother of invention.

note verbale [Fr] *noht-vehr-BAHL.* verbal communication on a diplomatic matter.

noticias [Sp] *noh-TEE-syahs.* news; word.

Notre Dame [Fr] *NOH-truh-DAHM.* Our Lady; the Virgin Mary; a Paris cathedral; a university in the U.S.

notturno [It] *noht-TOOR-noh.* of the night, nocturnal; nocturne.

n'oubliez pas [Fr] *noo-BLYAY-PAH.* don't forget.

noumenon [Gk] *NOO-meh-nohn.* the thing in itself, beyond man's grasp, as opposed to phenomenon, that which appears to the senses.

nous [Fr] *noo.* we; us.

nous [Gk] *noos.* mind; intellectual and mental faculties.

nouveau [Fr: *pl.* **nouveaux**; *fem.* **nouvelle**] *noo-VOH (-VEL)* new; —**franc** (*-FRÃ*) (*abbr.* **N.F.**) new franc; French monetary unit since 1959; —**riche** (*-REESH*) (*lit.*, new rich) person recently become wealthy; upstart.

nouveauté [Fr] *noo-voh-TAY.* novelty.

nouvelle [Fr] *noo-VEL.* news; novelette.

Nova [Lat] *NOH-vah.* (*lit.*, new) star that increases its luminosity by many thousandfold in a few hours and ejects material from its surface into space.

novela picaresca [Sp] *noh-VEH-lah-pee-kah-RES-kah.* picaresque novel.

novella [It] *noh-VEL-lah.* short prose narrative; tale; novelette.

novena [Lat: nine each] *noh-VEH-nah.* a devotion made on nine consecutive days in the Roman Catholic Church.

novia [Sp] *NOH-vyah.* fiancée; new bride; girl friend.

Novial. *NOH-vee-ahl.* an auxiliary language constructed by Otto Jespersen in 1928.

novio [Sp] *NOH-vyoh.* fiancé; new bridegroom; boyfriend.

novus homo [Lat] *NOH-voos-HOH-moh.* (*lit.*, new man) one who suddenly becomes prominent; one released from prison after a pardon.

novus ordo seclorum [Lat] *NOH-voos-OR-doh-seh-KLOH-room.* A new order of the ages (is established): motto on the reverse of the great seal of the United States.

noyade [Fr, from *noyer*, to drown] *nwah-YAHD.* execution by drowning, esp. during the French Reign of Terror, 1793-94.

nu [Yid, from Russ] *noo*. well?; so what?

nuance [Fr, from *nuer*, to shade, from *nue*, cloud] *nü-ÃS*. shade; delicate degree of difference; subtlety.

nudnik [Yid, from Russ] *NOOD-nik*. nuisance; meddler; bothersome person. Also, **noodnik**.

nudum pactum [Lat] *NOO-doom-PAHK-toom*. (*lit.*, nude pact) unwritten or informal contract.

Nuestra Señora [Sp] *NWES-trah-seh-NYOH-rah*. Our Lady; the Virgin Mary.

nuevos cristianos [Sp] *NWEH-vohs-krees-TYAH-nohs*. Neo-Christians, esp. Jewish converts.

nuit [Fr] *nüee*. night.

nulla bona [Lat] *NOOL-lah-BOH-nah*. (*law*) no goods; no possessions or assets.

nullah [Anglo-Ind, from Hindi *nālā*] *NUL-uh*. gully; ravine.

nullius filius [Lat] *nool-LEE-oos-FEE-lee-oos*. (*lit.*, no one's son) bastard.

numen [Lat: *pl.* **numina**] *NOO-men* (*-mee-nah*) command; will; divine writ; local god.

numero [It] *NOO-meh-roh*. number; numeral.

número [Sp] *NOO-meh-roh*. number; numeral.

numéro [Fr] *nü-may-ROH*. number; numeral.

numerus clausus [Lat] *NOO-meh-roos-KLOW-soos*. (*lit.*, closed number) fixed or limited number, as of seats, memberships, admissions, etc.; quota, esp. in reference to limitation on percentage of Jews who could be admitted to universities in pre-World War I eastern European countries.

nunc [Lat] *noonk*. now; —**aut numquam** (*-owt-NOOM-kwahm*) now or never; —**dimittis** (*-dee-MEET-tees*) now let (thy servant) depart; permission to leave; —**est bibendum** (*-est-bee-BEN-doom*) now is the time for drinking; —**pro tunc** (*-proh-TOONK*) (*lit.*, now for then) retroactive decision or action.

nunca [Sp] *NOON-kah*. never.

nuncio [It] *NOON-choh*. papal representative or messenger.

Nusstorte [Ger] *NOOS-tor-teh*. nut cake.

nux vomica [NL: vomiting nut] *NOOKS-VOH-mee-kah.* seed of an E Indian tree containing strychnine, used in medicine.

nyet [Russ] *nyet.* no.

Nynorsk [Norw] *NÜ-norsk.* (*lit.*, New Norse) one of the two official languages of Norway, based on western Norwegian dialects. Also called **Landsmål.** Cf. **Bokmål.**

O

ob [Lat] *ohb.* for; about; over, before; against; because of.

ob [Ger] *ohp.* if; whether.

obbligato [It] *ohb-blee-GAH-toh.* (*lit.*, obligated, bound) (*music*) obligatory; indispensable; a background instrumental or vocal part.

Obers [Ger (Austrian dial.)] *OH-buz.* cream.

Oberst [Ger, from *ober*, above, over] *OH-burst.* colonel.

obi [Jap] *OH-bee.* wide sash worn over a kimono.

obit [Lat] *OH-beet.* he (she) died (followed by a date); obituary.

obiter [Lat] *OH-bee-tehr.* by the way; incidentally; **—dictum** (*pl.* **dicta;** *-DEEK-toom; -tah*) incidental remark; unofficial opinion; (*law*) remark made by a judge on a matter not dealt with in his written opinion.

objet d'art [Fr: *pl.* **objets d'art**] *ohb-ZHAY-DAR.* art object; work of art.

oblast' [Russ: *pl.* **oblasti**] *OH-blust' (-tee)* USSR province or district.

obra [Sp] *OH-brah.* work; project; drama.

obrigado [Port] *oh-bree-GAH-doo.* thank you.

obyed [Russ] *ah-BYET.* dinner.

occhio [It: *pl.* **occhi**] *OHK-kyoh (-kee)* eye.

ochi chorniye [Russ] *OH-chee-CHOR-nee-yeh.* black eyes; dark eyes.

octave [Fr, from Lat *octava*, eighth] *ohk-TAHV.* in fencing, the eighth of eight defensive positions.

octavo [NL *in octavo*, in an eighth (of a sheet)] *ohk-TAH-*

voh. book size of about 6 x 9 inches, made by folding a sheet into 8 leaves.

octroi [Fr, from *octroyer*, to grant, from MedL *auctoricare*] *ohk-TRWAH.* duty; toll; local tax on goods brought in from outside; grant of a charter or constitution by a sovereign.

oculus [Lat] *OH-koo-loos.* eye; round window; —**dexter** (*-DEK-stehr*) (*abbr.* **O.D.**) right eye; —**sinister** (*-see-NEES-tehr*) (*abbr.* **O.S.**) left eye.

odalisque [Fr, from Turk *odalik*, from *oda*, chamber + *-lik*, suffix of appurtenance] *oh-dah-LEESK.* female slave; concubine.

oderint dum metuant [Lat] *OH-deh-reent-doom-MEH-too-ahnt.* let them hate, as long as they (also) fear.

odin [Russ: *fem.* **odna**; *neut.* **odno**] *ah-DEEN* (*-DNAH, -DNOH*) one.

odi profanum vulgus et arceo [Lat] *OH-dee-proh-FAH-noom-VOOL-goos-et-AR-keh-oh.* I hate the vulgar crowd and keep it at a distance.

odium [Lat] *OH-dee-oom.* hatred; —**aestheticum** (*-ys-TEH-tee-koom*) the bitterness of aesthetic rivalry.

oeil [Fr: *pl.* **yeux**] *öy* (*yö*) eye; — **-de-boeuf** (*-duh-BÖF*) bull's-eye; small round window.

Oesterreich [Ger] *ÖS-tuh-ryç.* Austria.

oeuf [Fr: *pl.* **oeufs**] *öf* (*ö*) egg; **oeufs à la coque** (*-ah-lah-KOHK*) (*lit.*, in the shell) boiled eggs; —**brouillés** (*-broo-YAY*) scrambled eggs; —**sur le plat** (*-sür-luh-PLAH*) (*lit.*, eggs on the plate) eggs sunny-side up.

oeuvre [Fr] *Ö-vruh.* work; work of art; literary work: collected works of one person.

offertoire [Fr] *oh-fehr-TWAR.* offertory.

offertorium [MedL, from Lat *offerre*, to offer] *ohf-fehr-TOH-ree-oom.* offering; offering service during Mass; place where collected offerings are kept.

officier [Fr] *oh-fee-SYAY.* officer; —**d'Académie** (*-dah-kah-day-MEE*) officer of the (French) Academy.

officium [Lat] *ohf-FEE-kee-oom.* office; duty; service; vocation.

Oflag [Ger, contr. of *Offizierslager*] *OHF-lahk.* officers' prison camp in World War II.

oggi [It] *OH-jee.* today.

oglavlenie [Russ] *uh-gluhv-LYEH-nee-yeh.* table of contents; contents.

ogon' [Russ] *ah-GAWN'.* fire; **v—** (*v-*) (mil. command) fire!

Ogpu, O.G.P.U. *OHG-poo.* See **G.P.U.**

ohne [Ger] *OH-neh.* without.

Oireachtas [Ir] *EH-rukh-thus.* the Irish Parliament; an annual gathering of Gaelic-speaking people held in Dublin.

oiseau [Fr: *pl.* **oiseaux**] *wah-ZOH.* bird.

ojo [Sp] *OH-hoh.* eye; careful!

Okhrana [Russ] *ah-KHRAH-nuh.* secret police of Czarist Russia.

okimono [Jap] *OH-kee-moh-noh.* decorative things.

Olim meminisse juvabit [Lat] *OH-leem-meh-mee-NEES-seh-yoo-VAH-beet.* It will be pleasant to remember things past.

olio [Sp *olla,* pot, stew] *OH-lee-oh.* mixture; stew; medley.

olla [Sp] *OH-lyah.* pot; stew; **—podrida** (*-poh-DREE-dah*) (*lit.,* rotten pot) a Spanish stew; mixture; medley. Cf. **potpourri.**

ombudsman [Swed: commissioner] *OHM-boodz-mahn.* arbitrator who hears and investigates complaints by private citizens against government agencies or officials.

omega [Gk] *oh-MEH-gah.* the last (24th) letter of the Greek alphabet; hence, the end.

om mani padme hum [Skt] *OHM-MAH-nee-PAHD-meh-HOOM.* In Buddhism, an invocation which loosely means "O Jewel in the Lotus! Amen!"

omne trinum (est) perfectum [Lat] *OHM-neh-TREE-noom (-est)-pehr-FEK-toom.* everything that comes in threefold form is perfect.

omnia vincit amor [Lat] *OHM-nee-ah-VEEN-keet-AH-mor.* love conquers all.

omnibus [Lat, dat. and abl. pl. of *omnis,* all] *OHM-nee-boos.* of or for all.

omnium gatherum [pseudo-Lat, from Lat *omnium*, of all + Eng *gather* + *-um*, Lat suffix] *OHM-nee-oom-GATH-ur-um.* miscellaneous collection; hodgepodge.

on dit [Fr] *ō-DEE.* one says; they say; it is said.

on ne badine pas avec l'amour [Fr] *ō-nuh-bah-DEEN-pah-ah-VEK-lah-MOOR.* you don't banter with love.

on ne passe pas [Fr] *ō-nuh-PAHS-pah.* (*lit.*, one does not pass) they shall not pass; no thoroughfare.

onorate l'altissimo poeta [It] *oh-noh-RAH-teh-lahl-TEES-see-moh-poh-EH-tah.* honor the great poet.

onus [Lat: *pl.* **onera**] *OH-noos* (*-neh-rah*) burden; weight; encumbrance; —**probandi** (*-proh-BAHN-dee*) burden of proof; responsibility for proving.

oolong [Chin] *OO-lohng.* black tea leaves partially fermented.

oom [Du] *ohm.* uncle.

op. cit. Abbr. of **opere citato.**

opera [It, from Lat pl. of **opus**] *OH-peh-rah.* work; work of art; literary work; opera; —**buffa** (*-BOOF-fah*) comic or light opera.

opera [Lat, pl. of **opus**] *OH-peh-rah.* works; —**omnia** (*-OHM-nee-ah*) complete works.

opéra [Fr, from It **opera**] *oh-pay-RAH.* opera; opera house; —**bouffe** (*-BOOF*) comic or light opera; also, **opéra comique** (*-koh-MEEK*).

opere citato [Lat: *abbr.* **op. cit.**] *OH-peh-reh-kee-TAH-toh.* in the work cited.

operetta [It, dim. of **opera**] *oh-peh-RAYT-tah.* light opera; musical comedy.

optimates [Lat, from *optimus*, best] *ohp-tee-MAH-tes.* ancient Roman aristocracy; aristocracy or nobility in general.

optimus [Lat: *fem.* **optima**; *neut.* **optimum**] *OHP-tee-moos* (*-mah*; *-moom*) best.

opus [Lat: *pl.* **opera**] *OH-poos* (*-peh-rah*) work; labor; major work; musical composition; —**reticulatum** (*-reh-tee-koo-LAH-toom*) masonry done in checkerboard pattern, characteristic of earlier Roman period.

ora e sempre [It] *OH-rah-eh-SEM-preh.* now and always.

ora et labora [Lat] *OH-rah-et-lah-BOH-rah.* pray and work.

ora pro nobis [Lat] *OH-rah-proh-NOH-bees.* pray for us.

orate fratres [Lat] *oh-RAH-teh-FRAH-tres.* pray, brothers; in the Mass, a call to prayer.

orbis terrarum [Lat] *OR-bees-tehr-RAH-room.* terrestrial orb; the earth.

öre [Swed]; **øre** [Norw, Dan; all from Lat *aureus*, golden] *Ö-reh.* name of various coins of Scandinavian countries.

oregano [AmerSp *orégano*, from Lat *origanum*, wild marjoram] *oh-REH-gah-noh.* aromatic plant of the mint family, used in cookery.

organon [Gk] *OR-gah-nohn.* instrument; organ; instrument of research or inquiry; title of Aristotle's logical treatises.

organum [Lat, from Gk **organon**] *OR-gah-noom.* organon; (*music*) early form of harmony, consisting of the doubling of parts at one of several musical intervals.

orgullo [Sp, from Germanic] *or-GOO-lyoh.* pride; haughtiness.

oriflamme [Fr, from Lat *aurea*, golden + *flamma*, flame] *oh-ree-FLAHM.* banner; flag; standard; flag of the older French kings.

origami [Jap] *OH-ree-gah-mee.* paper-folding art; decorative object made by folding paper.

origine contrôlée [Fr] *oh-ree-ZHEEN-kŏ-troh-LAY.* bonded and quality-controlled; license for winegrowers.

Ormazd [Pers, from older Pers *Ahura Mazda*] *OR-mahzd.* in Zoroastrianism, the supreme creative deity, opposed to Ahriman, the power of evil.

ormolu [Fr *or moulu*, ground gold] *OR-muh-loo.* a zinc and copper alloy that resembles gold.

Oro y Plata [Sp] *OH-roh-ee-PLAH-tah.* Gold and Silver (motto of Montana).

ortolan [Fr, from Prov; *lit.*, gardener (from its habit of frequenting gardens)] *or-toh-LĂ.* bobolink; an Old World bunting, considered a delicacy.

os [Lat: *pl.* **ossa**] *ohs* (*-sah*) bone; [*pl.* **ora**] (*OH-rah*) mouth.

O.S. Abbr. of **oculus sinister.**

osso buco [It *osso*, bone + *buco*, hole] *OHS-soh-BOO-koh.* marrow bone of veal; Milanese dish consisting of leg of veal with rice cooked in saffron sauce.

osteon [Gk] *ohs-TEH-ohn.* bone.

osteria [It, from *oste*, host, innkeeper] *oh-steh-REE-ah.* inn; tavern.

ostinato [It] *oh-stee-NAH-toh.* (*lit.*, obstinate) constantly recurring musical figure or melody.

Ostmark [Ger] *OHST-mark.* (*lit.*, Eastern region) Austria, during the period of annexation by Germany, 1938-45; (*lit.*, Eastern mark) monetary unit of East Germany.

ostrov [Russ] *AW-struf.* island.

o tempora! o mores! [Lat] *oh-TEM-poh-rah-oh-MOH-res.* Oh, what times! What customs!

o terque quaterque beati [Lat] *oh-TEHR-kweh-kwah-TEHR-kweh-beh-AH-tee.* Oh, three and four times blessed.

ottava [It] *oht-TAH-vah.* (*lit.*, eighth) octave; —**rima** (*-REE-mah*) (*lit.*, eighth rhyme) a rhyme form of eight-line stanzas (abababcc).

où [Fr] *oo.* where.

oublié [Fr] *oo-BLYAY.* forgotten.

oubliette [Fr, from *oublier*, to forget] *oo-BLYET.* secret dungeon open only at the top, into which prisoners were often thrown and left to die.

oui [Fr, from OF *oïl*, from Lat *hoc ille*, that, the same, that he (did)] *wee.* yes.

ousia [Gk] *oo-SEE-ah.* being; essence; substance.

où sont les neiges d'antan? [Fr] *oo-SŎ-lay-NEZH-dã-TÃ.* where are the snows of yesteryear?

outrance. See **à outrance.**

outré [Fr] *oo-TRAY.* outrageous; extravagant; bizarre; extreme; eccentric.

outre-mer [Fr] *oo-truh-MEHR.* overseas; ultramarine; beyond the seas.

outre-tombe [Fr] *oo-truh-TŎB.* beyond the grave.

ouvert [Fr, p.p. of *ouvrir*, to open; *fem.* **ouverte**] *oo-VEHR* (*-VEHRT*) open.

ouverture [Fr] *oo-vehr-TÜR.* overture; introduction; beginning; opening.

ouvreuse [Fr, from *ouvrir*, to open] *oo-VRÖZ.* female attendant who opens doors of theater boxes; usherette.

ouvrier [Fr, from Lat *operarius*, from *operari*, to work] *oo-VRYAY.* worker; artisan.

ovum [Lat: *pl.* **ova**] *OH-voom* (*-vah*) egg; embryo.

oy [Yid] *oy.* oh!, woe!, alas!

oyer and terminer [Anglo-Fr: to hear and determine] *OH-yur-and-TUR-min-ur.* higher criminal court.

oyez [Anglo-Fr] *OH-yay.* listen and hear ye.

ozero [Russ] *AW-zee-ruh.* lake.

P

pabulum [Lat] *PAH-boo-loom.* food.

pace [Lat, abl. of *pax*, peace] *PAH-keh.* by leave of, with permission of; **—tua** (*-TOO-ah*) by your leave.

pacem in terris [Lat] *PAH-kem-een-TEHR-rees.* Peace on Earth: title of an encyclical of Pope John XXIII.

pacífico [Sp] *pah-SEE-fee-koh.* peaceful; pacifist; pacific.

paddy [Malay *pādī*] *PAD-ee.* rice field; rice.

padishah [Pers *pādi*, var. of *pati*, lord + *shāh*, king] *pah-dee-SHAH.* protector; benevolent master; king; emperor.

padre [Sp, It] *PAH-dreh*; [Port] *PAH-druh.* father; priest.

padrone [It] *pah-DROH-neh.* master; employer; patron.

paella [Sp, from Lat *patella*, pan] *pah-EH-lyah.* dish based on rice with chicken or other meat and shellfish.

paesano [It, from *paese*, country] *pah-eh-SAH-noh.* countryman; peasant; compatriot.

pagliaccio [It, from *paglia*, straw; *pl.* **pagliacci**] *pah-LYAH-choh* (*-chee*) character of the Commedia dell'Arte playing the role of clown and deceived husband.

pagus [Lat] *PAH-goos.* district; country.

pain [Fr] *pē.* bread; **—rôti** (*-roh-TEE*) toast.

pais [Gk] *pys.* child; young boy or girl.

país [Sp] *pah-EES.* country; region.

pais [Yid] *PAY-is.* long, curled sideburns worn by some Orthodox Jewish men.

paisano [Sp, from *país*, country] *py-SAH-noh.* countryman; peasant; civilian.

paix [Fr] *peh.* peace.

pájaro [Sp, from Lat *passer*, sparrow] *PAH-hah-roh.* bird.

palabra [Sp, from Lat *parabola*, parable] *pah-LAH-brah.* word; conversation; right to speak.

paladin [Fr, from It *paladino*, from LL *palatinus*, palace official] *pah-lah-DẼ.* knight; defender; champion; paladin.

palaestra [Lat, from Gk *palaistra*, from *palaiein*, to wrestle] *pah-LY-strah.* athletic training grounds and quarters. Also, **palestra** *(-LEH-).*

palais [Fr] *pah-LEH.* palace; building, esp. public building; **—de danse** *(-duh-DẶS)* dance hall; dance palace.

palanquin [Port *palanquim*, from Pali *palanki*] *pah-lahn-KEEN.* portable chair on poles.

palazzo [It] *pah-LAH-tsoh.* palace; building; edifice.

palestra [It, from Lat *palaestra*] *pah-LES-trah.* gymnasium; *(cap.)* a basketball arena in Philadelphia; [Port] *puh-LESH-truh.* lecture; conference.

palette [Fr, from It *paletta*, dim. of *pala*, shovel] *pah-LET.* artist's tablet for mixing paints, usually of wood with a thumbhole.

palio [It, from Lat *pallium*, cloth, pall, orig. given as a prize to the winners] *PAH-lee-oh.* a medieval tourney held annually in Siena.

pallamaglio [It *palla*, ball + *maglio*, mallet] *pahl-lah-MAH-lyoh.* the game of pall-mall.

pallino [It, dim. of *palla*, ball] *pahl-LEE-noh.* in bocce, the small target ball.

pallium [Lat] *PAHL-lee-oom.* large cloak worn by men in ancient Greece and Rome; a cloth band worn over the shoulders by the pope and archbishops.

Palmach [Heb] *pahl-MAHKH.* striking force; advance guard of the Israeli army.

Palmes Académiques [Fr: academic palms] *PAHLM-zah-*

kah-day-MEEK. French order conferred for outstanding service in education or the arts.

paloma [Sp] *pah-LOH-mah.* dove.

palomino [Sp, dim. of *paloma*, dove] *pah-loh-MEE-noh.* white or very light horse.

paltsgraaf [Du *palts*, palace + *graaf*, count] *PAHLTS-khrahf.* a German count palatine; palsgrave.

paludamentum [Lat] *pah-loo-dah-MEN-toom.* cloak worn over the armor by Roman officers.

pampas [AmerSp, from Quechua *bamba*, plain] *PAHM-pahs.* flat, grassy plains of southern South America.

pan [Gk] *pahn.* all.

pan [Sp] *pahn.* bread.

pan [Fr, from Lat *pannus*, cloth] *pã.* flap; lappet; piece, section, side.

panache [Fr, from It *pennacchio*, from *penna*, feather] *pah-NAHSH.* a plume of feathers worn on a helmet or cap.

panaché [Fr] *pah-nah-SHAY.* plumed; striped; a drink made from beer and lemon soda.

panada [Sp, from *pan*, bread] *pah-NAH-dah.* dressing served with roast meat or fowl, made with bread crumbs, milk and seasonings.

Paname [Fr] *pah-NAHM.* (*slang*) Paris.

Panchatantra [Skt] *pun-chuh-TUN-truh.* Five Books: a collection of Indian fables.

panda [Nepalese] *PAHN-dah.* small black-and-white bear-like animal indigenous to China and the Himalayan region.

pane [It] *PAH-neh.* bread.

panem et circenses [Lat] *PAH-nem-et-keer-KEN-ses.* bread and circus games: favorite recipe of Roman politicians and emperors for currying favor with the masses.

Pangloss [Fr, from Gk *pan*, all + *glossa*, tongue] *pã-GLOHS.* optimistic teacher in Voltaire's *Candide*; hence, an optimist.

Panglossa [NL, from Gk *pan*, all + *glossa*, language] *pahn-GLOHS-sah.* (*lit.*, all-tongue, or tongue for all) auxiliary language devised by Lancelot Hogben in 1942.

panne [Fr] *pahn.* breakdown; malfunction, esp. in a motor vehicle.

pannier [Fr, from *pain*, bread] *pah-NYAY.* basket; hamper.

Pantalone [It] *pahn-tah-LOH-neh.* Pantaloon: comic stock character of the Commedia dell'Arte. Also, **Pantalon dei Bisognosi** (*pahn-tah-LOHN-day-bee-soh-NYOH-see*) *lit.*, Pantaloon of the Needy.

pantoufle [Fr] *pã-TOO-fluh.* slipper.

panure [Fr, from *pain*, bread] *pah-NÜR.* finely chopped crumbs used as a covering for baked dishes.

Panzer [Ger, from OF *panciere*, coat of mail, from *pance*, belly, paunch) *PAHN-tsuh.* armored tank, esp. of the German Army in World War II; **Panzerdivision** (*-dee-vee-ZYOHN*) tank corps; tank division.

Pão de Açucar [Port] *PÃ-oo-duh-uh-SOO-kur.* Sugarloaf, highest point on the island in Rio de Janeiro Bay.

papa [Lat, It] *PAH-pah.* pope.

papa [AmerSp, from Quechua] *PAH-pah.* potato; **papas fritas** (*PAH-pahs-FREE-tahs*) fried potatoes. Cf. **patata**.

paparazzo [It] *pah-pah-RAH-tsoh.* (*slang*) free-lance news photographer.

papaya [Sp, from Carib] *pah-PAH-yah.* large yellow melon-like tropical fruit.

Papiamento [Sp, perh. from Port *papear*, to chatter] *pah-pyah-MEN-toh.* a creolized form of Spanish and Portuguese spoken in Curaçao.

papier-mâché [Fr] *pah-PYAY-mah-SHAY.* (*lit.*, chewed-up paper) shredded paper molded to shape with glue; objects made from this material.

papillon [Fr] *pah-pee-YÕ.* butterfly; breed of toy spaniel having widespread ears.

papillote [Fr, from *papillon*, butterfly] *pah-pee-YOHT.* decorative paper wrapper used in cooking to cover the end of the bone of a chop or cutlet.

pappas [Gk] *PAHP-pahs.* a priest of the Greek Orthodox Church.

paprika [Hung, from Croatian, from *papar*, pepper] *PAH-pree-kah.* condiment made from ground sweet red pepper.

Paprikahuhn [Ger, from **paprika** + *Huhn*, chicken] *PAH-pree-kah-hoon.* chicken cooked in a paprika sauce.

paprikas [Hung] *PAH-pree-kahsh.* cooked in paprika sauce.

par [Lat] *par.* equal; alike.

par [Fr, from Lat **per**] *par.* by; through; for, for the sake of; —**accident** (*-ahk-see-DÃ*) accidentally; by chance; —**exemple** (*-eg-ZÃ-pluh*) for instance, for example; —**excellence** (*-ek-seh-LÃS*) best of all; incomparable; —**faveur** (*-fah-VÖR*) please; by your favor; —**hasard** (*-ah-ZAR*) accidentally; by chance; —**ici** (*-ee-SEE*) this way; through here.

para [Sp] *PAH-rah.* for; to; in order to; —**mirar y ser mirado** (*-mee-RAR-ee-sehr-mee-RAH-doh*) in order to see and be seen.

para [Turk, from Pers *pārah*, piece] *PAH-rah.* former Turkish coin, equal to 1/40 piaster.

paradigma [LL, from Gk *paradeigma*, from *para*, beside +' *deiknynai*, to show] *pah-rah-DEEG-mah.* model; pattern; paradigm.

páramo [Sp: barren plain, of pre-Roman origin] *PAH-rah-moh.* high plateau.

parapluie [Fr *para-*, against + *pluie*, rain] *pah-rah-PLÜEE.* umbrella.

parasang [Pers] *PAH-rah-sahng.* Persian measure of length slightly over 3 miles.

parbleu! [Fr *par*, by + *bleu*, euphemism for *Dieu*, God] *par-BLÖ.* egad! by Jove!

Parcae [Lat] *PAR-ky.* the Fates.

pardonnez-moi [Fr] *par-doh-ney-MWAH.* excuse me; I beg your pardon.

parfait [Fr] *par-FEH.* (*lit.*, perfect) dessert made of alternate layers of ice cream and fruit or syrup.

pariah [Tamil *paraiyan*, drummer (with reference to a hereditary function of the caste)] *puh-RY-uh.* outcast; member of the lowest stratum of Indian society.

pari mutuel [Fr] *pah-REE-mü-tü-EL.* mutual betting; type of betting in which winners split the money bet by losers.

pari passu [Lat] *PAH-ree-PAHS-soo.* (*lit.*, at an equal pace) equitably; without favoritism; side by side.

Paris vaut bien une Messe [Fr] *pah-REE-voh-BYẼ-ün-MES*. Paris is well worth a Mass: attributed to Henri of Navarre when he became Henri IV of France by converting from the Protestant to the Roman Catholic faith.

parka [Russ, from Samoyed] *PAR-kuh*. warm, hooded fur (or fur-trimmed) jacket or coat.

parlementaire [Fr] *par-luh-mã-TEHR*. parliamentary; parliamentarian; bearer of a flag of truce.

Parmentier [Fr, after A.A. Parmentier, said to have introduced the potato to France] *par-mã-TYAY*. of food, served or prepared with potatoes.

parmi [Fr] *par-MEE*. among.

parmigiano [It: of Parma] *par-mee-JAH-noh*. Parmesan cheese; a hard Italian cheese usually grated and sprinkled over various foods; **alla parmigiana** (*AHL-lah-par-mee-JAH-nah*) served with melted Parmesan cheese and tomato sauce.

paroimia [Gk] *pah-roy-MEE-ah*. proverb; saying.

parole [Fr, from Lat *parabola*, parable] *pah-ROHL*. password; word of honor; release of a prisoner on his honor before his sentence is fully served.

pars pro toto [Lat] *PARS-proh-TOH-toh*. a part for the whole.

parterre [Fr] *par-TEHR*. (*lit.*, on the ground) in a theater, the part of the orchestra section under the balcony.

parti [Fr] *par-TEE*. party; side, part; choice, decision; basic scheme for the plan of a building, with particulars of style and treatment omitted; **—pris** (*-PREE*) decision or opinion taken in advance; bias.

partie [Fr] *par-TEE*. part, portion; faction; game, match.

partigiano [It] *par-tee-JAH-noh*. partisan; guerrilla fighter in World War II.

partito [It] *par-TEE-toh*. party; side; choice; **—preso** (*-PRAY-soh*) decision or opinion formed in advance; bias.

partout [Fr] *par-TOO*. everywhere.

parure [Fr] *pah-RÜR*. matching set of jewelry or ornaments.

parva componere magnis [Lat] *PAR-vah-kohm-POH-neh-reh-MAHG-nees.* to compare small things with great things.

parvenu [Fr] *par-vuh-NÜ.* upstart; Johnny-come-lately.

pas [Fr, from Lat *passus,* step] *pah.* second element of expression for "not," with *ne* (usually) before the verb; step, pace; **—de chat** (*-duh-SHAH*) (*lit.,* cat step) in ballet, a jump of one foot over the other; **—de deux** (*-duh-DÖ*) dance for two persons; **—glissé** (*-glee-SAY*) glide step; sliding step; **—d'ennemi à gauche** (*-den-MEE-ah-GOHSH*) left-wing slogan: "No enemy on the left" (anything the leftists do is all right; our only enemies are the rightists); **—du tout** (*-dü-TOO*) not at all; **—possible** (*-poh-SEE-bluh*) impossible; incredible.

Pascua Florida [Sp] *PAHS-kwah-floh-REE-dah.* Feast of Flowers; Easter.

Pascuas [Sp] *PAHS-kwahs.* Easter; Christmas holidays.

paseo [Sp] *pah-SEH-oh.* promenade; public walk; ride or stroll for pleasure.

pasha [Turk] *PAH-shah.* high-ranking official in the former Turkish empire.

pashka [Russ] *PAHSH-kuh.* Russian cake usually eaten at Easter.

paso doble [Sp] *PAH-soh-DOH-bleh.* (*lit.,* double step, two-step) a rapid heel-stamping dance; a typical bullfight march which celebrates the kill.

pasquinade [Fr, from It *Pasquino* (name given to an ancient Roman statue which was used for pasting satirical verses)] *pahs-kee-NAHD.* satire; lampoon.

passacaglia [Italianized form of Sp *pasacalle,* orig. street dance, from *paso,* step + *calle,* street] *PAHS-sah-KAH-lyah.* a slow Spanish dance; a musical composition in the rhythm of this dance.

passant [Fr] *pah-SÃ.* passing; pedestrian, passerby; **en—** (*ã-*). See **en passant.**

passé [Fr, p.p. of *passer,* to pass] *pah-SAY.* outdated; outmoded.

passe-montagne [Fr] *pahs-mõ-TAH-nyuh.* hat or helmet

with attached scarf that ties under the chin, usu. worn by mountain climbers.

passe-partout [Fr] *pahs-par-TOO.* (*lit.,* pass everywhere) master key; passkey; ornamental mat for a picture.

passer [Fr] *pah-SAY.* to pass; to put on, slip on.

passetemps [Fr] *pahs-TÃ.* pastime.

passim [Lat] *PAHS-seem.* everywhere; scattered about, as throughout a book.

passionnant [Fr] *pah-syoh-NÃ.* exciting, stimulating.

passionato [It] *pahs-syoh-NAH-toh.* (*music*) impassioned.

passus [Lat] *PAHS-soos.* step, pace; division of a poem or story; chapter; canto.

pasta [It] *PAHS-tah.* paste; dough; soft mass; all forms of macaroni and spaghetti; —**asciutta** (*-ah-SHOOT-tah*) macaroni or spaghetti served with butter and cheese or with a sauce, as distinguished from —**al brodo** (*-ahl-BROH-doh*), in broth.

pastel [Sp] *pahs-TEL.* pie; pastry; tart; a Caribbean dish consisting of minced pork or other meat mixed with a pulp of grated plantains and various tubers, wrapped in a banana leaf and boiled.

pasticcio [It, from *pasta,* dough, mixture] *pahs-TEE-choh.* patchwork; hodgepodge; work assembled from various sources.

pastiche [Fr, from It *pasticcio*] *pahs-TEESH.* work assembled from various sources; hodgepodge.

pastille [Fr, from Sp *pastilla*] *pahs-TEE-yuh.* pill; medicine tablet; tablet-shaped sweet, candy drop.

pastor [Sp] *pahs-TOR.* shepherd; pastor.

pastorale [It] *pahs-toh-RAH-leh.* pastoral music; idyllic music or poem.

pastrami [Yid, from Pol, from Turk] *pah-STRAH-mee.* pickled, smoked beef.

patata [Sp, blend of *papa,* potato and *batata,* sweet potato] *pah-TAH-tah.* potato.

patchouli [Tamil *pacculi*] *pah-CHOO-lee.* Indian perfume.

pâte [Fr] *paht.* paste; a mixture used to make porcelain and pottery.

pâté [Fr] *pah-TAY*. patty; pastry; pie; —**de foie gras** (*-duh-FWAH-GRAH*) goose-liver pie or paste.

pater [Lat: *pl.* **patres**] *PAH-tehr* (*-tres*) father; —**Noster** (*-NOHS-ter*) Our Father; the Lord's Prayer; also, **Paternoster**; —**familias** (*-fah-MEE-lee-ahs*) father of the family; head of the household; patriarch; —**patriae** (*-PAH-tree-y*) father of his country.

patera [Lat] *PAH-teh-rah*. shallow plate; ornament.

pathétique [Fr] *pah-tay-TEEK*. pathetic; (*music*) with pathos or emotion.

pathos [Gk] *PAH-thohs*. suffering; great sadness.

patina [It] *PAH-tee-nah*. coating; a green film that forms on bronze and iron as a result of oxidation.

patio [Sp] *PAH-tyoh*. court; courtyard; paved area in a yard or garden.

pâtisserie [Fr] *pah-tee-s'REE*. pastry; pastry shop.

patois [Fr, orig. clumsy speech, rel. to OF *patoier*, to paw, handle clumsily, from *patte*, paw] *pah-TWAH*. local dialect; rustic speech; jargon.

patres conscripti [Lat: more correctly, **patres et conscripti**, fathers (i.e. patricians) and elect] *PAH-tres-kohns-KREEP-tee*. the members of the Roman Senate; the usual translation, "conscript fathers," is incorrect.

patria [Lat, from *pater*, father] *PAH-tree-ah*. country; homeland.

patrie [Fr, from Lat **patria**] *pah-TREE*. country; homeland.

patron [Fr: *fem.* **patronne**] *pah-TRO* (*-TRUN*) master or mistress; employer; owner; patron; boss.

patroon [Du] *pah-TROHN*. patron; formerly, a Dutch landholder under royal charter in New York and New Jersey.

patte [Fr] *paht*. paw; foot; appendage; flap; leg.

paucis verbis [Lat] *POW-kees-VEHR-bees*. briefly; in a few words.

pavane [Fr, from It *pavana* for *padovana*, of Padua] *pah-VAHN*. stately 16th-century dance; a musical composition in the rhythm of this dance.

pavé [Fr] *pah-VAY*. (*lit.*, paved) pavement; setting in which jewels are closely clustered.

pax [Lat] *pahks.* peace; —**Britannica** (*-bree-TAHN-nee-kah*) British peace; —**Dei** (*-DEH-ee*) peace of God; —**Ecclesiae** (*-ek-KLEH-see-y*) Ecclesiastic peace; same as **Pax Dei**; —**Romana** (*-roh-MAN-nah*) Roman peace; —**vobiscum** (*-voh-BEES-koom*) peace be with you.

pays [Fr] *peh-EE.* country.

paysage [Fr] *peh-ee-ZAHZH.* landscape; countryside.

paysan [Fr: *fem.* **paysanne**] *peh-ee-ZĂ* (*-ZAHN*) peasant.

paz y justicia [Sp] *PAHS-ee-hoos-TEE-syah.* peace and justice.

pazzo [It] *PAH-tsoh.* mad; insane, crazy.

pecadillo [Sp, dim. of *pecado*, sin] *peh-kah-DEE-lyoh.* petty fault; minor transgression. Also, **peccadillo**.

peccato [It] *pek-KAH-toh.* sin; it's a pity!; too bad!

peccavi [Lat, from *peccare*, to sin] *pek-KAH-vee.* I have sinned.

pêche [Fr] *pesh.* peach.

pêcheur [Fr, from *pêcher*, to fish] *peh-SHÖR.* fisherman.

pecorino [It, from *pecora*, sheep] *peh-koh-REE-noh.* cheese made from sheep's milk.

pectiné [Fr, from Lat *pecten*, comb] *pek-tee-NAY.* toothed, like a comb.

pecunia [Lat, from *pecu*, flock of sheep] *peh-KOO-nee-ah.* cattle; livestock; property; money; —**non olet** (*-nohn-OH-let*) money doesn't smell.

pedale [It] *peh-DAH-leh.* pedal; sock.

peignoir [Fr, from *peigner*, to comb] *peh-NYWAR.* dressing gown; robe.

peineta [Sp, from *peine*, comb] *pay-NEH-tah.* large ornamental comb.

peinture [Fr, from *peindre*, to paint] *pẽ-TÜR.* painting; paint.

pekoe [Chin *pek-ho*, white down] *PEE-koh.* fine black tea.

pelagos [Gk] *PEH-lah-gohs.* sea.

pèlerin [Fr] *peh-l'RẼ.* pilgrim.

pèlerinage [Fr] *pehl-ree-NAHZH.* pilgrimage.

pèlerine [Fr] *peh-l'REEN.* fur or cloth cape worn by women.

pelota [Sp] *peh-LOH-tah*. ball; the game of jai alai; —**Vasca** (*-VAHS-kah*) the Basque game of jai alai.

peña [Sp] *PEH-nyah*. cliff; rock ledge; rock.

Penates [Lat] *peh-NAH-tes*. guardians; local or household gods.

penchant [Fr, pr.p. of *pencher*, to lean] *pā-SHÃ*. inclination; liking; tendency.

pendente lite [Lat] *pen-DEN-teh-LEE-teh*. litigation pending; during litigation.

pendule [Fr] *pā-DÜL*. pendulum; clock.

penitente [Sp, It] *peh-nee-TEN-teh*. penitent; one who seeks forgiveness.

pensée [Fr, from *penser*, to think] *pā-SAY*. thought; belief; idea; pansy.

penseur [Fr] *pā-SÖR*. thinker.

pensieroso [It, from *pensiero*, thought] *pen-syeh-ROH-soh*. (*music*) pensively.

pension [Fr] *pā-SYÕ*. boardinghouse; rooming house.

pensionnaire [Fr, from **pension**] *pā-syuh-NEHR*. boarder; boarding student; pensioner.

pentathlon [Gk, from *pente*, five + *athlon*, contest] *pen-TAH-thlohn*. athletic contest consisting of five events: javelin, discus, broad jump, wrestling, and running.

peón [Sp, from Vulgar Lat *pedone*, foot soldier, from *pede*, foot] *peh-OHN*. peasant; laborer; peon; spinning top; (*chess*) pawn; (*checkers*) man; foot soldier; pedestrian.

pépée [Fr, slang var. of **poupée**] *pay-PAY*. doll; puppet; girl.

peplum [Lat, from Gk] *PEH-ploom*. a flounce at the waist of a skirt, falling loosely over the hips; short skirt attached to a bodice.

pepo [Lat: melon, from Gk *pepōn*, ripe gourd] *PEH-poh*. the fruit of a melon, gourd, etc.

pequeño [Sp] *peh-KEH-nyoh*. small; little one.

per [Lat] *pehr*. through; by; for; for each; —**annum** (*-AHN-noom*) annually, each year; —**ardua ad astra** (*-AR-doo-ah-ahd-AHS-trah*) Through difficulties to the stars (Air Force motto); —**capita** (*-KAH-pee-tah*) per person; per head; —**centum** (*-KEN-toom*) percent; for each hundred; —contra (-*KOHN-trah*) on the contrary; on the opposite side; —diem (-*DEE-em*) daily; each day; by the day; —mensem (-*MEN-sem*) per month; —se (-*SEH*) in itself; by nature.

perdrix [Fr] *pehr-DREE.* partridge.

perdu [Fr, p.p. of *perdre*, to lose] *pehr-DÜ.* lost; hidden; hopeless.

père [Fr, from Lat **pater**] *pehr.* father.

perevod [Russ] *pi-ri-VAWT.* translation; translated.

per favore [It] *pehr-fah-VOH-reh.* please.

perfecto [Sp] *pehr-FEK-toh.* perfect; type of cigar with tapered ends.

pergola [It] *PEHR-goh-lah.* area enclosed by plant-covered trellises; colonnade similarly covered.

peri [Gk] *peh-REE.* around; about; near; beyond.

peri [Pers] *PEH-ree.* lovely woman; fairy; sprite.

pericolo [It] *peh-REE-koh-loh.* danger; peril.

peripeteia [Gk, from *peri*, around + *piptein*, to fall] *peh-ree-peh-TEH-yah.* sudden turn of luck or condition which Aristotle considered an essential tragic element; vicissitude.

per me [It] *pehr-MEH.* for me; as for me; so far as I am concerned.

permis de séjour [Fr] *pehr-MEE-duh-say-ZHOOR.* permission to reside in a given place, granted by the police or immigration authorities in some countries.

peronismo [Sp] *peh-roh-NEES-moh.* movement and political doctrine supporting Juan Perón of Argentina; **peronista** (-*tah*) follower of Perón.

per piacere [It] *pehr-pyah-CHAY-reh.* please.

perro [Sp] *PEHR-roh.* dog.

perruque [Fr, from It *parrucca*, wig] *peh-RÜK.* wig; periwig.

persiennes [Fr] *pehr-SYEN.* (*lit.*, Persian blinds) venetian blinds.

persiflage [Fr, from *persifler*, to banter] *pehr-see-FLAHZH.* banter; irony.

persifleur [Fr] *pehr-see-FLÖR.* banterer.

persona [Lat] *pehr-SOH-nah.* actor's mask; person; —grata

(*-GRAH-tah*) acceptable person, esp. as representative
of a country to another country's government; **—non
grata** (*-nohn-GRAH-tah*) unacceptable person.

pes [Lat: *pl.* **pedes**] *pes* (*PEH-des*) foot.

Pesach [Heb] *PEH-sahkh.* Passover.

pésame [Sp] *PEH-sah-meh.* (*lit.*, it weighs upon me) con-
dolences.

pesante [It] *peh-SAHN-teh.* (*music*) heavily; gravely.

pesce [It: *pl.* **pesci**] *PAY-sheh* (*-shee*) fish.

peseta [Sp, dim. of *peso*, weight] *peh-SEH-tah.* monetary
unit of Spain.

peshwa [Marathi] *PESH-wah.* former title of state minister
of the Marathi kingdom in India.

peso [Sp] *PEH-soh.* weight; dollar; monetary unit in many
Spanish-American countries.

pessimus [Lat] *PES-see-moos.* worst; the worst; extremely
bad.

pétard [Fr, from *péter*, to break wind] *pay-TAR.* fire-
cracker; loud or vulgar action.

petit [Fr: *fem.* **petite**] *puh-TEE* (*-TEET*) small, little;
—bourgeois (*-boor-ZHWAH*) petty bourgeois; person
of lower middle class; **—caporal** (*-kah-poh-RAHL*) the
little corporal: Napoleon I; **—chou** (*-SHOO*) little cabbage (term of endearment); **petite marmite** (*-mar-
MEET*) beef consommé, with cubes of chicken and
beef, and finely cut turnips, carrots and celery; **—nègre**
(*-NEH-gruh*) a French pidgin, used in W Africa;
—point (*-PWĔ*) fine needlework; **—verre** (*-VEHR*)
glass of liqueur.

petitio principii [Lat] *peh-TEE-tee-oh-preen-KEE-pee-ee.*
(*law*) begging the question.

petits fours [Fr] *p'TEE-FOOR.* (*lit.*, small ovens) small
cookies and cakes which come in a variety of shapes
and flavors; **petits pains** (*-PĔ*) bread rolls; **petits pois**
(*-PWAH*) peas.

pétroleur [Fr, from *pétrole*, gasoline, petroleum; *fem.*
pétroleuse] *pay-troh-LÖR* (*-LÖZ*) arsonist who starts
fires with gasoline; fire bomber.

petto [It] *PET-toh.* chest; breast; bosom; **in—** (*een-*) in one's breast; in secret.

peu [Fr] *pö.* little; few; **—à peu** (*-ah-PÖ*) little by little; **—de chose** (*-d'SHOHZ*) very little; a trifle.

peut-être [Fr] *pö-TEH-truh.* perhaps; maybe.

pezzo [It] *PEH-tsoh.* piece; part; musical composition; **—concertato** (*-kohn-chehr-TAH-toh*) (*music*) concerted piece; **—duro** (*-DOO-roh*) slice of ice cream; **—grosso** (*-GROHS-soh*) bigwig; big shot.

Pfennig [Ger] *PFEH-niç.* penny; German unit of currency.

Pfund [Ger] *pfoont.* pound.

phantasma [Gk] *FAHN-tahs-mah.* ghostly apparition; phantom.

pharos [Gk] *FAH-rohs.* (*cap.*) island near Alexandria, famous for its lighthouse; lighthouse.

Philosophiae Doctor [Lat: *abbr.* **Ph.D.**] *fee-loh-soh-FEE-y-DOHK-tor.* Doctor of Philosophy.

phos [Gk] *fohs.* light.

phratria [Gk] *frah-TREE-ah.* tribe; brotherhood; fraternity.

phyllon [Gk: *pl.* **phylla**] *FÜL-lohn* (*-lah*) leaf; flower.

physis [Gk] *FÜ-sees.* nature; natural form; creature.́

piacere [It] *pyah-CHAY-reh.* (*lit.*, to please) pleasure; it's a pleasure; favor; **per—** (*pehr-*) please; if you please.

piacevole [It] *pyah-CHAY-voh-leh.* (*music*) in a pleasing manner.

pianissimo [It] *pyah-NEES-see-moh.* (*music*) quietly; very softly.

piano [It] *PYAH-noh.* (*music*) quiet; softly.

pianoforte [It] *pyah-noh-FOR-teh.* (*lit.*, soft [and] loud) piano; pianoforte.

piaster [Fr *piastre,* from It *piastra,* thin sheet of metal, silver coin] *pee-AS-tur.* monetary unit of Vietnam, worth about one U.S. cent; a former coin of Turkey, 1/100 of a lira. Also, **piastre.**

piazza [It, from Lat *platea,* courtyard] *PYAH-tsah.* square; open central area; marketplace; plaza.

pibroch [Gael *piobaireachd,* piper music, from *piob,* pipe] *PEE-brohkh.* bagpipe music, esp. in the Scottish highlands.

picadillo [Sp, from *picado*, p.p. of *picar*, to mince, chop] *pee-kah-DEE-lyoh*. minced meat; hash.

picador [Sp, from *picar*, to prick, goad] *pee-kah-DOR*. a member of the bullfighting team that rides on horseback and goads the bull with a lance.

pícaro [Sp] *PEE-kah-roh*. rascal; rogue; **picaresco** (*-RES-koh*) picaresque.

piccolo [It] *PEEK-koh-loh* (*lit.*, small) little flute; piccolo.

pièce [Fr] *pyes*. piece; portion; room; literary, dramatic or musical work; —**de résistance** (*-duh-ray-zees-TĂS*) main dish at a meal; main event; main feature; —**montée** (*-mō-TAY*) high hairdo.

pied-à-terre [Fr] *PYAY-tah-TEHR*. (*lit.*, foot on the ground) house or apartment maintained for convenience, apart from one's principal residence.

Piedigrotta [It, name of locality near Naples] *pyeh-dee-GROHT-tah*. Neapolitan song festival.

piedra [Sp] *PYEH-drah*. stone; rock.

Pieds-noirs [Fr] *pyay-NWAR*. (*lit.*, black feet) repatriated French Algerians.

Pierrot [Fr] *pyeh-ROH*. (*lit.*, little Peter, Pete) a type of clown.

Pietà [It] *pyeh-TAH*. pity; piety; depiction of the Virgin Mary holding the dead body of Christ.

pietra [It] *PYEH-trah*. stone; rock.

pikinini [Pidgin Eng, from Port *pequenino*, little one] *pee-kee-NEE-nee*. child; children.

pilaf [Turk, from Pers] *pee-LAHF*. rice with meat, fish or poultry, and various seasonings. Also, **pilaff**, **pilau**.

pilikia [Hawaiian] *pee-lee-KEE-ah*. trouble; danger.

pimiento [Sp] *pee-MYEN-toh*. sweet pepper; pimento.

piña [Sp] *PEE-nyah*. pine; pine cone; pineapple; thorn.

pince-nez [Fr] *pẽs-NAY*. (*lit.*, pinch-nose) eyeglasses held on the nose by a clamp.

pinto [Sp] *PEEN-toh*. dappled horse; horse of more than one color.

pioupiou [Fr slang, perh. imitative of chirping of birds] *pyoo-PYOO*. footsoldier.

piquant [Fr: *fem*. **piquante**] *pee-KÃ* (*-KÃT*) sharp; strong; piquant.

pique [Fr] *peek*. annoyance; displeasure.

piqué [Fr] *pee-KAY*. stitched; embossed or ribbed fabric, usually cotton; stung.

pique-nique [Fr] *peek-NEEK*. picnic; outing.

piquet [Fr] *pee-KEH*. a two-hand card game played with a 32-card pack.

pirouette [Fr] *pee-RWET*. turn done on one foot in ballet.

pirozhok [Russ: *pl*. **pirozhki**] *pee-rah-ZHAWK* (*-ZHKEE*) meat- or cabbage-filled puff cake; patty.

pis aller [Fr] *PEE-zah-LAY*. the worst (place) to go; last resort.

piso [Sp] *PEE-soh*. floor; story; pea; —**bajo** (*-BAH-hoh*) ground floor.

pissaladière [Fr] *pee-sah-lah-DYEHR*. a pizzalike crust smothered with onions, anchovies, tomatoes, etc.

pissoir [Fr] *pee-SWAR*. public urinal.

pistole [Fr, from *pistolet*, pistol] *pees-TOHL*. any of various coins formerly used in France, Spain and other European countries.

piton [Fr] *pee-TŎ*. large eyebolt used in mountain climbing for supporting a rope.

pitre [Fr] *PEE-truh*. clown; buffoon.

più [It, from Lat *plus*] *pyoo*. more; plus.

pivo [Russ] *PEE-vuh*. beer.

pizza [It] *PEET-tsah*. large flat crust covered with tomato sauce and mozzarella cheese, and sometimes other ingredients, and baked in an oven.

pizzeria [It] *peet-tseh-REE-ah*. restaurant; pizza shop.

pizzicato [It] *peet-tsee-KAH-toh*. (*music*) played by plucking with the fingers (instead of the bow).

place [Fr] *plahs*. square; place; plaza.

placebo [Lat] *plah-KEH-boh*. (*lit.*, I shall be pleasing) cure-all; pacifier; a medicine containing pleasant though ineffective ingredients.

placet [Lat] *PLAH-ket*. (*lit.*, it is pleasing) an affirmative vote.

placitum [Lat: *pl.* **placita**] *PLAH-kee-toom* (*-tah*) decree; pronouncement; legal decision.

plage [Fr] *plahzh.* beach; shore; seashore.

plaisance [Fr, from *plaisir*, to please] *pleh-ZĂS.* pleasure.

planchette [Fr, dim. of *planche*, plank] *plă-SHET.* small movable board used in demonstrating psychic phenomena.

planh [Prov, from *planher*, to lament] *plahny.* a form of troubadour verse, usually sad and expressing unrequited or unattainable love.

plat [Fr] *plah.* flat; dish; plate; —**du jour** (*-dü-ZHOOR*) dish of the day; daily special.

plata [Sp] *PLAH-tah.* silver; money.

plátano [Sp] *PLAH-tah-noh.* banana; plantain; plane tree.

playa [Sp] *PLAH-yah.* beach; shore.

plaza [Sp] *PLAH-sah.* square; place; marketplace; —**de toros** (*-deh-TOH-rohs*) bull ring.

plebs [Lat] *plebs.* the common people; plebeians.

plein air [Fr] *plĕ-NEHR.* open air; outdoors; a group of French outdoor painters and their works.

pleno jure [Lat] *PLEH-noh-YOO-reh.* with full authority.

plenum [Lat: full] *PLEH-noom.* meeting of the entire membership.

plié [Fr, from *plier*, to bend, fold] *plee-AY.* ballet step in which the feet remain on the floor with the toes facing out at the sides and the knees are bent.

plissé [Fr] *plee-SAY.* pleated; gathered; puckered fabric.

pluie de feu [Fr] *PLÜEE-duh-FÖ.* rain of fire.

plus ça change, plus c'est la même chose [Fr] *plü-sah-SHĂZH-plü-seh-lah-mem-SHOHZ.* the more it changes, the more it remains the same.

plus tôt [Fr] *plü-TOH.* sooner; earlier; **plutôt.** rather.

P.M. Abbr. of **post meridiem** or **post mortem.**

pobeda [Russ] *pah-BYEH-duh.* victory; model name of a Soviet car.

Poblacht na H-Eireann [Irish] *POH-blahkht-nah-HEH-rin.* Republic of Ireland.

pobre [Sp] *POH-breh.* poor.

Pochismo [MexSp, from *pocho*, discolored] *poh-CHEES-moh.* name of a Spanish-English pidgin used along the Mexican-U.S. border. Also, **Pocho** (*POH-choh*).

poco [It, Sp] *POH-koh. little; a little.*

podagra [Gk: trap for the foot, from *pous*, foot + *agra*, a seizing] *poh-DAH-grah.* gout in the foot.

podestà [It, from Lat *potestas*, power] *poh-des-TAH.* magistrate; appointed mayor during Fascist regime.

poêle [Fr, from Lat *patella*] *pwahl.* frying pan; (also, **poile**) stove.

poeta nascitur, non fit [Lat] *poh-EH-tah-NAHS-kee-toor-nohn-FEET.* a poet is born, not made.

pogrom [Russ] *pah-GROHM.* organized massacre, esp. of Jews.

poi [It] *poy.* then; afterward.

poi [Hawaiian] *poy.* staple Hawaiian food prepared from taro root.

poignard [Fr] *pwah-NYAR.* dagger; poniard.

poilu [Fr, from *poil*, hair] *pwah-LÜ.* (*lit.*, hairy one) a French common soldier in World War I.

point d'appui [Fr] *pwē-dah-PÜEE.* fulcrum; point of support or leverage.

pointillage [Fr, from *pointiller*, to point, dot, from *point*, dot] *pwē-tee-YAHZH.* stippling; dotted line.

pointillisme [Fr] *pwē-tee-YEEZ-muh.* a Neo-Impressionist style of painting in which dots of pure primary color are juxtaposed so that the eye blends them into the resultant color.

poire [Fr] *pwar.* pear.

pois [Fr] *pwah.* pea; peas.

poisson [Fr] *pwah-SŌ.* fish.

poivre [Fr] *PWAH-vruh.* pepper.

polenta [It] *poh-LEN-tah.* thick corn-based porridge, sometimes cut into slices and fried lightly.

Polichinelle [Fr, from It *Pulcinella*] *poh-lee-shee-NEL.* Punchinello, or Punch: a character in the Commedia dell'Arte.

polis [Gk] *POH-lees.* city.

Politburo [Russ, contr. of *Politicheskoye Buro*, political bureau] *puh-leet-byoo-ROH.* a former policy committee of the Soviet Union.

politesse [Fr, from *poli*, polite] *poh-lee-TES.* politeness; good manners.

politico [It]; **político** [Sp] *poh-LEE-tee-koh.* political; politician.

politique [Fr] *poh-lee-TEEK.* political; politician; policy; politics.

pollice verso [Lat] *POHL-lee-keh-VEHR-soh.* (with) thumbs down; vote of nay.

pollo [It] *POHL-loh.* chicken; (*slang*) sucker, easy mark.

pollo [Sp] *POH-lyoh.* chicken; (*slang*) handsome, dashing young man.

polonaise [Fr, fem. of *polonais*, Polish] *poh-loh-NEZ.* slow, stately Polish dance; music written for that dance.

polpetta [It, from *polpa*, pulp] *pohl-PAYT-tah.* meatball; fish cake.

polpettone [It] *pohl-pet-TOH-neh.* meat loaf; fish loaf; hash.

Poltergeist [Ger] *POHL-tuh-gyst.* (*lit.*, noise ghost) a ghost that shows its presence by making noises, throwing things around, etc.

pomade [Fr, from It *pomata*, from *pomo*, apple; orig. the term meant "applesauce"] *poh-MAHD.* a scented dressing for the hair.

pomme [Fr] *pohm.* apple; **—de terre** (*-duh-TEHR*) (*lit.*, apple of the earth) potato; **pommes frites** (*-FREET*) fried potatoes; French fries; often shortened to **frites.**

pomodoro [It] *poh-moh-DOH-roh.* tomato. Also, **pomidoro** (*poh-mee-DOH-roh*).

pomposo [It] *pohm-POH-soh.* (*music*) pompously.

poncho [AmerSp, from SAmerInd] *POHN-choh.* square blanket cloth with a center hole for the head, worn as a cape.

pongee [Chin *pun-chī*, own loom, homespun] *POHN-jee.* fabric woven of natural silk with irregular threads visible.

pons [Lat: *pl.* **pontes**] *pohns* (*POHN-tes*) bridge; connecting part; **—asinorum** (*-ah-see-NOH-room*) asses' bridge; something difficult for beginners.

pont [Fr] *põ.* bridge.

ponte [It] *POHN-teh.* bridge.

ponticello [It, dim. of *ponte*, bridge] *pohn-tee-CHEL-loh.* bridge of a stringed instrument.

pood [Russ *pud*, from Low Ger or Scand *pund*, pound] *pood.* measure of weight, approximately 36 pounds. Also, **pud.**

popina [Lat, from Oscan] *poh-PEE-nah.* drinking shop; inn.

popolo [It] *POH-poh-loh.* people; nation.

populus vult decipi, ergo decipiatur [Lat] *POH-poo-loos-voolt-DEH-kee-pee-EHR-goh-deh-kee-pee-AH-toor.* the people want to be deceived, therefore let them be deceived.

poputchik [Russ] *pah-POOT-chik.* travel companion; fellow traveler.

por [Sp] *por.* for; by; because of; each; through; on behalf of; instead of; —**ciento** (*-SYEN-toh*) percent.

porc [Fr, from Lat *porcus*] *por.* hog; pig; pork.

pordiosero [Sp, from *por Dios*, for God] *por-dyoh-SEH-roh.* beggar.

porta [Lat, It] *POR-tah.* door; gate.

portamento [It, from *portare*, to carry] *por-tah-MAYN-toh.* (*music*) glide from one note to another.

porte-cochère [Fr] *port-koh-SHEHR.* covered carriage entrance; covered drive.

portemanteau [Fr, from *porter*, to carry + *manteau*, cloak, mantle] *port-mã-TOH.* suitcase; word formed by contraction of two or more words, e.g. *motel*, from *motor* + *hotel*.

portico [It: *pl.* **portici**] *POR-tee-koh* (*-chee*) colonnade open on one or more sides; porch.

portière [Fr, from *porte*, door] *por-TYEHR.* curtain over a doorway.

porto [It] *POR-toh*; [Port] *POR-too.* port; harbor.

posada [Sp, from *posar*, to stop, rest] *poh-SAH-dah.* inn.

poseur [Fr, from *poser*, to pose; *fem.* **poseuse**] *poh-ZÖR* (*-ZÖZ*) a person who affects a certain pose, attitude or role; affected person.

posse comitatus [Lat] *POHS-seh-koh-mee-TAH-toos.* the local posse; sheriff's posse.

post [Lat] *pohst.* after; behind; —**bellum** (*-BEL-loom*) after the war; postwar; —**diem** (*-DEE-em*) (*law*) after the day; —**factum** (*-FAHK-toom*) (*law*) after the fact or deed; —**hoc ergo propter hoc** (*-hohk-EHR-goh-PROHP-tehr-hohk*) after this, therefore because of this (illogical inductive reasoning); —**meridiem** (*-meh-REE-dee-em*) after noon; in the afternoon; P.M.; —**mortem** (*-MOR-tem*) (*abbr.* P.M.) after death; autopsy; —**obitum** (*-OH-bee-toom*) after death; —**scriptum** (*-SKREEP-toom*) (*abbr.* P.S.) written afterward; note written after closing a letter.

poste de secours [Fr] *POHST-duh-s'KOOR.* aid post; emergency aid station; forward medical station.

poste restante [Fr] *POHST-res-TÃT.* (*lit.*, remaining mail) general delivery.

postiche [Fr] *pohs-TEESH.* superfluously added on; artificial, sham.

postillon [Fr, from It *postiglione*, from *posta*, mail, mail coach] *pohs-tee-YÕ.* coachman who rides on one of a pair or team of post horses; postilion.

potage [Fr, from *pot*, pot] *poh-TAHZH.* soup; vegetable soup.

pot-au-feu [Fr] *poh-toh-FÖ.* (*lit.*, pot on the fire) beef broth; stew.

potlatch [Chinook *potshatl*, gift] *POT-lach.* Northwest Amer. Indian winter ceremonial, often competitive, of giving away property to enhance status.

potpourri [Fr] *poh-poo-REE.* (*lit.*, rotten pot) mixture; medley; hodgepodge. Cf. **olla podrida.**

poulet [Fr] *poo-LAY.* chicken; pullet.

poupée [Fr] *poo-PAY.* doll; puppet.

pourboire [Fr] *poor-BWAR.* (*lit.*, for drinking) tip; gratuity.

Pour le Mérite [Fr] *poor-luh-may-REET.* (*lit.*, for merit) Order of Merit; highest German military decoration under the Hohenzollerns.

pourparler [Fr] *poor-par-LAY.* (*lit.*, for talking) preliminary talk before an official meeting.

pourquoi [Fr] *poor-KWAH.* why.

poussé [Fr, p.p. of *pousser*, to push] *poo-SAY.* (*music*) upstroke of the bow.

pousse-café [Fr] *poos-kah-FAY.* (*lit.*, push coffee) liqueur taken after coffee, usually served in layers of several liqueurs in one glass.

poussin [Fr] *poo-SẼ.* young chicken.

pou stō [Gk] *poo-STOH.* (*lit.*, where I may stay) a place to stand; base of operations.

powwow [AmerInd] *POW-wow.* meeting; conference.

pozhaluysta [Russ] *pah-ZHAH-looy-stuh* or *pah-ZHAHL-stuh.* please; you're welcome.

prado [Sp] *PRAH-doh.* boulevard or promenade; (*cap.*) famous Madrid art museum.

praenomen [Lat] *pry-NOH-men.* first name; given name.

praesul [Lat] *PRY-sool.* prelate; in ancient Rome, the head priest; director, superintendent; patron, protector.

praetor [Lat] *PRY-tor.* Roman magistrate; municipal officer.

pragma [Gk] *PRAHG-mah.* thing; fact; action, deed.

praline [Fr, after Marshal du Plessis-Praslin, whose cook invented it] *prah-LEEN.* sugar-coated almond candy.

prandium [Lat] *PRAHN-dee-oom.* dinner; meal.

pranzo [It, from Lat **prandium**] *PRAHN-zoh.* dinner; meal.

Pravda [Russ] *PRAHV-duh.* (*lit.*, truth) official Soviet Communist newspaper.

pré [Fr] *pray.* meadow; dueling field.

précieux [Fr: *fem.* **précieuse**] *pray-SYÖ* (*-SYÖZ*) precious, valuable; affected in speech or manner.

préciosité [Fr] *pray-syoh-zee-TAY.* preciousness; affectation in speech or manner.

précis [Fr] *pray-SEE.* precise; abstract, summary.

preciso [It] *preh-CHEE-soh.* precise; precisely, of course; (*music*) precisely.

prego [It] *PREH-goh.* (*lit.*, I beg) please; you're welcome; don't mention it.

première [Fr] *pruh-MYEHR.* opening night; first performance; debut; leading role; —**danseuse** (-*dā-SÖZ*) leading female dancer of the ballet.

premio gordo [Sp] *PREH-myoh-GOR-doh.* (*lit.*, fat prize) grand prize.

prenez garde [Fr] *pruh-NAY-GARD.* on guard! beware! be careful!

prensa [Sp] *PREN-sah.* the press; title of many Spanish-language newspapers.

presa [It] *PRAY-sah.* (*lit.*, taking) a mark indicating where various voices join in choral reading or music.

pré-salé [Fr] *pray-sah-LAY.* pre-salted mutton; mutton grazed in salt marshes.

presbyter [Lat, from Gk *presbyteros*, elder] *PRES-bee-tehr.* elder; priest.

presepio [It] *preh-SEH-pyoh.* manger; stable.

presidio [Sp, from Lat *praesidium*] *preh-SEE-dyoh.* garrison; army post; prison.

presto [It] *PRES-toh.* rapidly; immediately; **prestissimo** (-*TEES-see-moh*) (*music*) very fast.

presunto [Sp, It] *preh-SOON-toh.* presumptive; [It] **erede**— (*eh-REH-deh-*); [Sp] —**heredero** (-*eh-reh-DEH-roh*) heir presumptive.

preux chevalier [Fr] *prö-sh'vah-LYAY.* gallant knight.

prévôt [Fr] *pray-VOH.* provost.

prie-dieu [Fr] *pree-DYÖ.* (*lit.*, pray God) prayer stool; in a church pew, support for the knees.

prima [It, fem. of **primo**] *PREE-mah.* first; principal, main; —**ballerina** (-*bahl-leh-REE-nah*) leading dancer; —**colazione** (-*koh-lah-TSYOH-neh*) breakfast; first meal; —**donna** (-*DOHN-nah*) leading lady; principal female opera lead; a woman, or sometimes a man, who overestimates his or her value and demands undue attention.

prima facie [Lat] *PREE-mah-FAH-kee-eh.* (*law*) on first impression; at first sight.

primavera [It, Sp] *pree-mah-VEH-rah.* spring; springtime.

prime [Fr, from It or Lat *prima*, first] *preem.* in fencing, the first of eight defensive positions.

primo [It, from Lat *primus*] *PREE-moh.* first; principal, main; (*music*) principal part; [Lat, abl. of *primus*] first; in the first place.

primogenitus [Lat] *pree-moh-GEH-nee-toos.* first-born (son); the policy or custom of handing down property to the first-born son; primogeniture.

primus inter pares [Lat] *PREE-moos-EEN-tehr-PAH-res.* first among equals.

principe [It] *PREEN-chee-peh*; **príncipe** [Sp] *PREEN-see-peh*; [Port] *PREEN-see-puh.* prince.

printanière [Fr, from **printemps**] *prē-tah-NYEHR.* garnish of spring vegetables.

printemps [Fr] *prē-TĀ.* spring; springtime.

Privatdocent [Ger] *pree-vaht-doh-TSENT.* German university teacher, licensed but not a regular staff member. Also, **Privatdozent.**

prise [Fr, from *prendre*, to take] *preez.* capture; prize.

prix [Fr: *pl. unchanged*] *pree.* prize; price.

pro [Lat] *proh.* for; in behalf of; for the use of; in place of.

proa [Malay] *PROH-ah.* outrigger canoe or boat.

pro bono publico [Lat] *proh-BOH-noh-POO-blee-koh.* for the public good.

proceres [Lat] *PROH-keh-res.* nobility; lords; leaders.

procès [Fr] *proh-SEH.* lawsuit; process; proceedings; — -verbal (-*vehr-BAHL*) minutes; written report of proceedings.

procureur [Fr] *proh-kü-RÖR.* lawyer; prosecutor.

pro Deo et Patria [Lat] *proh-DEH-oh-et-PAH-tree-ah.* for God and Country.

proemium [Lat, from Gk *prooimion*] *PROY-mee-oom.* introduction; prologue.

pro et contra [Lat] *PROH-et-KOHN-trah.* for and against.

profanum vulgus [Lat] *proh-FAH-noom-VOOL-goos.* the common people; fickle crowd.

pro forma [Lat] *proh-FOR-mah.* as a matter of form; as is proper.

projet [Fr] *proh-ZHEH.* project; scheme; draft, design.

pro juventute [Lat] *proh-yoo-ven-TOO-teh.* for youth.

prolegomenon [Gk: *pl.* **prolegomena**] *proh-leh-GOH-meh-*

nohn (*-nah*) introduction; prologue; prefatory or introductory statements.

pro memoria [Lat] *proh-meh-MOH-ree-ah.* by way of memorial; in memory of; as a reminder; memo.

pronto [Sp] *PROHN-toh.* immediately; quickly; [It] ready; hello (on phone).

pro nunc [Lat] *proh-NOONK.* for now; for the time being.

pronunciamento [It] *proh-noon-chah-MAYN-toh*; **pronunciamiento** [Sp] *proh-noon-syah-MYEN-toh.* pronouncement; declaration; affirmation; statement; manifesto.

pro patria [Lat] *proh-PAH-tree-ah.* for country.

proprio motu [Lat] *PROH-pree-oh-MOH-too.* of one's own will; by one's own initiative.

propriété littéraire [Fr] *proh-pree-ay-TAY-lee-tay-REHR.* literary copyright.

pro rata [Lat] *proh-RAH-tah.* according to the rate or ratio; proportionately.

prosciutto [It] *proh-SHOOT-toh.* salt-cured Italian ham.

proshchai [Russ] *prahsh-CHY.* farewell; good-bye. Also, **proshchaite** (*prash-CHY-tyeh*).

prosit [Lat] *PROH-seet.* may it be of advantage; [Ger] *PROH-s't.* to your health!

protégé [Fr] *proh-tay-ZHAY.* (*lit.*, protected) one who is under the patronage or special tutelage of another.

pro tempore [Lat] *proh-TEM-poh-reh.* temporarily; for the time being.

proviso [Lat] *proh-VEE-soh.* condition or provision of an agreement.

provolone [It] *proh-voh-LOH-neh.* light, mellow Italian cheese, often smoked.

proximo [Lat, abl. of *proximus*, next] *PROHK-see-moh.* in or during the next month.

prud'homme [Fr] *prü-DOHM.* prudent or wise man; labor arbitrator.

P.S. Abbr. of **post scriptum.**

pseudes [Gk] *pseh-oo-DES.* false.

psyche [Gk] *psü-KEH.* soul; spirit; mind.

pteron [Gk: *pl.* ptera] *pteh-ROHN* (*-RAH*) wing.

ptoma [Gk] *PTOH-mah.* fall; misfortune; disaster; corpse, cadaver.

ptosis [Gk] *PTOH-sees.* fall, falling; (*grammar*) case.

Pucelle d'Orléans [Fr] *pü-SEL-dor-lay-Ã.* Maid of Orleans: Joan of Arc.

puchero [Sp] *poo-CHEH-roh.* earthen pot; stew.

pud. See **pood.**

pudenda [Lat] *poo-DEN-dah.* (*lit.*, things to be ashamed of) genitals.

pueblo [Sp, from Lat *populus*, people] *PWEH-bloh.* village; town; people.

puée [Fr] *pü-AY.* prostitute.

puente [Sp] *PWEN-teh.* bridge; (*naut.*) deck.

puerto [Sp] *PWEHR-toh.* port; harbor.

puis [Fr] *püee.* then; afterward; next.

puissance [Fr] *püee-SÃS.* power; force; influence.

puissant [Fr: *fem.* **puissante**] *püee-SÃ* (*-SÃT*) strong; powerful; influential.

Pulcinella [It, from *pulcino*, chick] *pool-chee-NEL-lah.* Punchinello or Punch: a character of the Commedia dell'Arte. Cf. **Polichinelle.**

pulque [MexSp] *POOL-keh.* drink made from the fermented juice of the agave plant.

pundit [Hindi *pandit*, from Skt *pandita*, learned (man)] *PUN-dit.* scholar; authority; Brahmin.

punkah [Hindi *pankhā*, fan, from Skt *pakshaka*] *PUN-kuh.* large swinging fan on a rope, usu. worked by a servant boy.

Purana [Skt] *poo-RAH-nah.* (*lit.*, ancient) title of a number of Hindu myths and epics, including the Mahabharata and Ramayana.

purdah [Hindi *pardah*, curtain, from Pers] *PUR-duh.* in Oriental countries, the custom of the seclusion of women; the curtain or screen which serves to hide them.

purée [Fr, from fem. p.p. of *purer*, to strain, make pure] *pü-RAY.* thick strained soup; any thick strained food, esp. a vegetable or fruit.

Purim [Heb, pl. of *pūr*, lot] *poo-REEM.* Feast of Lots: a

Jewish festival in celebration of the defeat of Haman's plot to destroy the Jews.

puta [Sp] *POO-tah.* prostitute.

putain [Fr] *pü-TÉ.* prostitute.

Putsch [Ger] *pootch.* uprising; riot; violent takeover.

puttana [It] *poot-TAH-nah.* prostitute.

puttee [Hindi *paṭṭi,* bandage] *PUT-ee.* leg covering worn esp. by soldiers.

putto [It: boy, child, from Lat *putus*; *pl.* **putti**] *POOT-toh* (*-tee*) cherub, in decorative art or sculpture.

pylon [Gk: gateway] *PY-lun.* tall, slender structure or tower, often used as a marker.

pyr [Gk] *pür.* fire.

Q

qasr [Ar, from Lat *castrum*] *KAH-s'r.* fortress; palace.

q.b.s.m. Abbr. of **que besa sus manos.**

q.b.s.p. Abbr. of **que besa sus pies.**

Q.E.D. Abbr. of **quod erat demonstrandum.**

qua [Lat] *kwah.* as far as; considered as.

quadragesima [Lat] *kwah-drah-GEH-see-mah.* fortieth; the fortieth day before Easter; the first Sunday in Lent.

quadrivium [MedL; in Lat: crossroads, from *quadri-,* four- + *via,* way] *kwah-DREE-vee-oom.* in medieval universities, the upper division of the seven liberal arts, comprising arithmetic, astronomy, geometry, and music. Cf. **trivium.**

quahog [AmerInd] *KWAH-hohg.* a small, hard-shelled clam.

quai [Fr, from Sp *cayo,* key, islet, from Arawak] *keh.* dock; pier; embankment.

Quai d'Orsay [Fr] *keh-dor-SAY.* street in Paris on which the French foreign ministry is located; the French foreign ministry itself.

qualunquismo [It, from *qualunque,* any, anybody] *kwah-loon-KWEEZ-moh.* the ideology of the *L'Uomo qualun-*

que movement, rightist philosophy of Giannini; right-wing ideas or politics.

quand même [Fr] *kā-MEM.* nevertheless; just the same; all the same.

quando [Lat, It] *KWAHN-doh.* when.

quandoque bonus dormitat Homerus [Lat] *kwahn-DOH-kweh-BOH-noos-DOR-mee-taht-hoh-MEH-roos.* sometimes even the good Homer sleeps; even good writers are dull at times.

quante teste, tanti cervelli [It] *KWAHN-teh-TES-teh-TAHN-tee-chehr-VEL-lee.* so many heads, so many minds.

quantum [Lat: as much, how much] *KWAHN-toom.* an indivisible physical quantity.

quantum mutatus ab illo! [Lat] *KWAHN-toom-moo-TAH-toos-ahb-EEL-loh.* how different from his former self!

quantum sufficit [Lat] *KWAHN-toom-SOOF-fee-keet.* as much as is sufficient; a sufficient amount.

quarte [Fr, from It *quarta,* fourth] *kart.* in fencing, the fourth of eight defensive positions.

quartier général [Fr] *kar-TYAY-zhay-nay-RAHL.* headquarters.

quartier generale [It] *kwar-TYEHR-jeh-neh-RAH-leh.* headquarters.

Quartier Latin [Fr] *kar-TYAY-lah-TẼ.* Latin Quarter; the Bohemian quarter of Paris.

quarto [Lat] *KWAR-toh.* (*lit.,* one-fourth) a page size of about 9½ x 12 inches.

quasi [Lat, It] *KWAH-see.* almost; halfway; partly; seemingly; as if; as it were.

quass. *kvahs.* See kvass.

quattrocento [It] *kwaht-troh-CHEN-toh.* 1400's; 15th century.

quattuor tempora [Lat] *KWAHT-too-or-TEM-poh-rah.* the four seasons; Ember Days.

que besa sus manos [Sp: *abbr.* q.b.s.m.] *keh-BEH-sah-soos-MAH-nohs.* (*lit.,* who kisses your hands) respectfully yours: complimentary closing of a letter to a man.

que besa sus pies [Sp: *abbr.* q.b.s.p.] *keh-BEH-sah-soos-*

PYES. (*lit.*, who kisses your feet) respectfully yours: complimentary closing of a letter to a lady.

quebrada [Sp, from p.p. of *quebrar*, to break, split] *keh-BRAH-dah.* ravine, gorge.

que Dieu vous bénisse [Fr] *kuh-DYÖ-voo-bay-NEES.* may God bless you.

que en paz descanse [Sp] *keh-en-PAHS-des-KAHN-seh.* (may he) rest in peace.

que faire? [Fr] *kuh-FEHR.* what to do?

¿qué hora es? [Sp] *keh-OH-rah-es.* what time is it?

queijo [Port] *KAY-zhoo.* cheese; —**da serra** (*-duh-SEHR-ruh*) mountain cheese.

¡que lo aproveche! [Sp] *keh-loh-ah-proh-VEH-cheh.* (*lit.*, may you benefit from it) a hearty appetite!

quelque chose [Fr] *kel-kuh-SHOHZ.* something; some small trifle.

quem quaeritis? [Lat] *kwem-KWY-ree-tees.* whom do you seek?; in medieval drama, the first words to the women gathered at Christ's tomb.

quenelles [Fr, from Ger *Knödel*, dumpling] *kuh-NEL.* worm-shaped soup garnishes made by forcing the ingredients through a pastry bag into the boiling soup.

querido [Sp: *fem.* **querida**] *keh-REE-doh* (*-dah*) dear; beloved.

que sais-je? [Fr] *kuh-SEH-zhuh.* what do I know?

que será, será [Sp] *keh-seh-RAH-seh-RAH.* whatever will be, will be.

queso [Sp] *KEH-soh.* cheese.

questura [It, from *questore*, police chief, from Lat *quaestor*, investigator] *kwes-TOO-rah.* police station; police headquarters.

¿qué tal? [Sp] *keh-TAHL.* what's up?; how goes it?

quetzal [AmerSp, from Nahuatl] *ket-SAHL.* brightly-plumed national bird of Guatemala; unit of currency of Guatemala.

Quetzalcoatl [AmerSp, from Nahuatl] *ket-sahl-koh-AH-t'l.* the feathered serpent god of the Aztecs and Toltecs.

queue [Fr, from Lat *cauda*, tail] *kyoo*; Fr *kö.* line (of persons or things); pigtail.

que voulez-vous? [Fr] *kuh-voo-lay-VOO.* what do you want?; what will you have?

qui a bu, boira [Fr] *kee-ah-BŬ-bwah-RAH.* he who drinks once will drink again.

quiche [Fr, from Ger *Küche*, dial. var. of *Kuchen*, cake] *keesh.* a dish consisting of an unsweetened pastry shell filled with cheese and seasonings; —**lorraine** (*-loh-REN*) a quiche filled with cheese or cream, and bacon.

quidam [Lat] *KWEE-dahm.* somebody; anybody.

quidditas [Lat, from *quid*, what] *KWEED-dee-tahs.* essence; essential quality; subtle distinction.

quid faciendum? [Lat] *KWEED-fah-kee-EN-doom.* what's to be done?

quid novi? [Lat] *KWEED-NOH-vee.* what's new?

quidnunc [Lat] *KWEED-noonk.* (*lit.*, what now?) gossip; busybody.

quid pro quo [Lat] *KWEED-proh-KWOH.* something for something; tit for tat.

Quid rides? Mutato nomine, de te fabula narratur [Lat] *KWEED-REE-des-moo-TAH-toh-NOH-mee-neh-deh-teh-FAH-boo-lah-nahr-RAH-toor.* Why do you laugh? With the name changed, the story is (told) about you.

quien calla otorga [Sp] *kyen-KAH-lyah-oh-TOR-gah.* silence gives consent.

¿quién es? [Sp] *kyen-ES.* who is it?

¿quién sabe? [Sp] *kyen-SAH-beh.* who knows?

quietus [Lat] *kwee-EH-toos.* (*lit.*, quiet, rest) the end; finishing stroke.

qu'importe? [Fr] *kẽ-PORT.* what does it matter?

quinquagesima [Lat] *kween-kwah-GEH-see-mah.* fiftieth; the fiftieth day before Easter; the Sunday before Lent; Shrove Sunday.

quinte [Fr, from It or Lat *quinta*, fifth] *kẽt.* in fencing, the fifth of eight defensive positions.

qui pense? [Fr] *kee-PÃS.* who thinks?

quipu [AmerSp, from Quechua] *KEE-poo.* a cord with knotted, colored strings attached, used by the Incas for keeping records and sending messages.

Quirinal [Lat] *KWEE-ree-nahl.* one of the seven hills of

Rome; a royal palace located there; **Quirinale** [It] (*-NAH-leh*) formerly, a name for the Italian government.

qui s'excuse s'accuse [Fr] *kee-seks-KÜZ-sah-KÜZ.* he who excuses himself, accuses himself.

quisling [Norw, after Vidkun Quisling, pro-Nazi leader in World War II] *KWIZ-ling.* a person who collaborates with his country's enemy.

quisquis [Lat] *KWEES-kwees.* whoever; anyone.

Qui Transtulit Sustinet [Lat] *kwee-TRAHNS-too-leet-SOOS-tee-net.* He who transplanted still sustains (motto of Connecticut).

qui va là? [Fr] *kee-vah-LAH.* who goes there?

qui vive? [Fr] *kee-VEEV.* (*lit.*, long live who?) who goes there?; an attitude of watchfulness (usu. in the phrase **on the qui vive**).

qui vivra verra [Fr] *kee-vee-VRAH-veh-RAH.* he who lives will see.

quod avertat Deus! [Lat] *kwohd-ah-VEHR-taht-DEH-oos.* God forbid!

quod erat demonstrandum [Lat: *abbr.* **Q.E.D.**] *kwohd-EH-raht-deh-mohns-TRAHN-doom.* what was to be demonstrated.

quodlibet [Lat] *KWOHD-lee-bet.* (*lit.*, whatever one pleases) a subtle point or argument; (*music*) a form consisting of quotations of known melodies, arranged in seemingly incongruous order.

quodlibetz [var. of **quodlibet**] *KWOHD-lee-bets.* a style of ceramic decoration in which common objects were painted so as to cast shadows and achieve a realistic three-dimensional effect.

quod vide [Lat: *abbr.* **q.v.**] *kwohd-VEE-deh.* which see: used in cross-references.

quo jure? [Lat] *kwoh-YOO-reh.* by what right?

quomodo? [Lat] *kwoh-MOH-doh.* how?; in what way?

quondam [Lat] *KWOHN-dahm.* formerly; once.

quot homines tot sententiae [Lat] *kwoht-HOH-mee-nes-toht-sen-TEN-tee-y.* so many men, so many minds.

Quousque tandem abutere patientia nostra? [Lat] *kwoh-*

OOS-kweh-TAHN-dem-ah-BOO-teh-reh-pah-tee-EN-tee-ah-NOHS-trah. How long will you abuse our patience?
quo vadis? [Lat] *kwoh-VAH-dees.* whither goest thou?
q.v. Abbr. of **quod vide.**

R

℞ Abbr. of Lat *recipe*, take, used in medical prescriptions.
rabat [Fr] *rah-BAH.* clerical collar; a vest worn beneath the clerical collar.
rabbi [Heb] *RAHB-bee.* master; teacher; Jewish religious leader.
raconteur [Fr, from *raconter*, to tell, recount] *rah-kō-TÖR.* storyteller; man-about-town; nonprofessional entertainer.
radix [Lat] *RAH-deeks.* root.
rafraîchissements [Fr] *rah-freh-shees-MÃ.* refreshments; provisions, supplies.
ragoût [Fr] *rah-GOO.* thick meat stew.
raie [Fr] *reh.* ray, skate (fish); **—au beurre noir.** See **au beurre noir.**
raison [Fr] *reh-ZÕ.* reason; grounds; right; **—d'état** (*-day-TAH*) reason of state; state policy; **—d'être** (*-DEH-truh*) reason for being.
raj [Hindi, from Skt *rājya*] *rahj.* (in India) rule, reign.
rajah [Hindi *rājā*, from Skt *rājan*] *RAH-jah.* king; prince.
rājñī [Skt] *RAHJ-nyee.* queen; princess. Cf. **rani.**
Rajput [Hindi, from Skt *rāj*, rule + *putra*, son] *RAHJ-poot.* a member of a Hindu military caste. Also, **Rajpoot.**
raki [Gk, from Turk] *rah-KEE.* a strong anise liqueur.
rallentando [It] *rahl-len-TAHN-doh.* (*music*) slowing down gradually.
Ramadan [Ar] *rah-mah-DAHN.* the ninth month of the Moslem year; the daily fast observed from dawn to sunset during this month.
Ramayana [Skt] *rah-MAH-yah-nah.* an ancient Hindu epic, relating the adventures of Rama and his wife Sita.
rana [Hindi] *RAH-nah.* rajah; prince.

ranchería [Sp] *rahn-cheh-REE-ah.* rancher's dwelling; group of herdsmen's huts or cabins; Indian settlement.

ranchero [Sp] *rahn-CHEH-roh.* rancher; herdsman.

rancho [Sp, orig., lodging, from *rancharse*, to lodge oneself, from Fr *se ranger*] *RAHN-choh.* ranch; group of herdsmen's huts or cabins; common mess of ranchmen or military personnel.

rani [Hindi *rānī*, from Skt *rājñī*, fem. of *rājan*, king] *RAH-nee.* queen; princess. Also, **ranee.**

ranz des vaches [Swiss Fr] *RÃ-day-VAHSH.* song of the herdsmen; pastoral song played on the alpenhorn.

rapport [Fr] *rah-POR.* affinity; feeling of kinship or relationship.

rapprochement [Fr] *rah-prohsh-MÃ.* a coming together; reconciliation; reestablishment of friendly relations.

rara avis [Lat] *RAH-rah-AH-vees.* rare bird; wonderful or unusual thing.

ras [Amharic] *rahs.* in Ethiopia, a chief; in Italy, after the Ethiopian war, a local Fascist party leader.

Rat [Ger] *raht.* council.

rataplan [Fr] *rah-tah-PLÃ.* sound of a drumbeat; rat-a-tat-tat.

Rathaus [Ger] *RAHT-hows.* town hall.

Rat(h)skeller [Ger] *RAHTS-kel-uh.* restaurant or bar in a basement.

ravigote [Fr, from *ravigoter*, to refresh, invigorate] *rah-vee-GOHT.* a thick sauce based on meat or vegetable stock, herbs and white wine.

ravioli [It] *rah-VYOH-lee.* square pasta patties filled with meat or cheese.

ravissant [Fr, pr.p. of *ravir*, to ravish] *rah-vee-SÃ.* ravishing; alluring; dashing.

razzia [Fr, from Algerian Ar *ghāzya*] *rah-ZYAH.* raid; raid for plunder or for acquisition of slaves.

re [Lat, abl. of *res*, thing, matter] *reh.* concerning; regarding.

real [Sp] *reh-AHL.* (*lit.*, royal) an old Spanish gold coin.

realia [Lat] *reh-AH-lee-ah.* real things; physical characteristics and objects of a culture; real objects used as visual aids.

Realpolitik [Ger] *reh-ahl-poh-li-TEEK.* practical politics; politics based on material factors.

Realschule [Ger] *reh-ahl-SHOO-leh.* secondary school..

Réaumur [Fr, after René A.F. de Réaumur, French physicist] *ray-oh-MÜR.* a scale for measurement of temperature in which the freezing point of water is fixed at zero and the boiling point at 80 degrees.

rebozo [Sp] *reh-BOH-soh.* shawl.

rebus [Lat, abl. pl. of *res,* thing] *REH-boos.* a phrase or word depicted in a series of pictures or symbols.

rebus sic stantibus [Lat] *REH-boos-seek-STAHN-tee-boos.* things staying as they are: a premise for continuing validity of a contract.

réchauffé [Fr] *ray-shoh-FAY.* reheated.

recherché [Fr] *ruh-shehr-SHAY.* carefully researched; recondite, farfetched.

Rechnung [Ger, from *rechnen,* to reckon] *REÇ-noong.* invoice; bill.

Recht [Ger] *reçt.* right; justice; law.

rechts [Ger] *reçts.* right; to or at the right.

recitativo [It] *reh-chee-tah-TEE-voh.* recitative; narrated; spoken part of an opera or music drama.

réclame [Fr, from *réclamer,* to proclaim] *ray-KLAHM.* publicity; notoriety; publicity-seeking; reputation established through advertising.

reconquista [Sp] *reh-kohn-KEES-tah.* reconquest, esp. of the parts of Spain that had been under Moorish domination.

recto [Lat] *REK-toh.* right; to the right; on the right-hand page.

recueil [Fr, from *recueillir,* to collect, gather] *ruh-KÖY.* collection, esp. of literary works; selection.

rédacteur [Fr] *ray-dahk-TÖR.* editor.

redan [Fr, var. of *redent,* from *re-,* back- + *dent,* tooth] *ruh-DÃ.* a tooth-shaped projection in a line of fortifications.

redingote [Fr, from Eng *riding coat*] *reh-deen-GOHT.*

riding coat; frock coat; a woman's dress in the style of a frock coat.

redondilla [Sp, from *redondo*, round] *reh-dohn-DEE-lyah.* quatrain of eight-syllable verses, rhyming *a, b, b, a.*

reductio ad absurdum [Lat] *reh-DOOK-tee-oh-ahd-ahb-SOOR-doom.* reduction to absurdity; disproof of a proposition by proving the conclusion absurd; **reductio ad impossibile** (*-eem-pohs-SEE-bee-leh*) reduction to the impossible; disproof of a proposition by proving the conclusion impossible.

reflet [Fr] *ruh-FLEH.* reflection; shine; highly lustrous glaze.

refrán [Sp] *reh-FRAHN.* proverb; saying; refrain.

refresco [Sp] *reh-FRES-koh.* refreshment; soft drink.

regatta [It *regata* (Venetian dial.)] *reh-GAH-tah.* boat race; gondola race in Venice.

Regenschirm [Ger] *RAY-g'n-sheerm.* umbrella.

régie [Fr] *ray-ZHEE.* direction; government; administration of taxes; state monopoly.

Regierung [Ger] *reh-GEER-oong.* government; executive branch of power.

régime [Fr] *ray-ZHEEM.* government; rule; diet; regimen.

regina [Lat] *reh-GEE-nah.* queen.

regio [Lat: *pl.* **regiones**] *REH-gee-oh* (*-OH-nes*) region; city district.

régisseur [Fr, from *régir*, to direct, rule] *ray-zhee-SÖR.* stage director.

règle [Fr] *REH-gluh.* rule; regulation.

Regnat Populus [Lat] *REG-naht-POH-poo-loos.* The people rule (motto of Arkansas).

Reich [Ger] *ryç.* empire; realm.

Reichsbahn [Ger] *RYÇS-bahn.* the national German railway; **Reichsbank** (*-bahnk*) central bank of Germany; **Reichskanzler** (*-kahnts-luh*) Chancellor of the German Reich; **Reichsmark** (*-mark*) German unit of currency; **Reichstag** (*-tahk*) the lower house of the German legislature; **Reichswehr** (*-vehr*) the German national defense force.

Reine-Marguerite [Fr] *ren-mar-guh-REET*. (*lit.*, Queen Margaret) China aster.

reis [Port, pl. of *rei*, king] *raysh*. a former monetary unit of Portugal and Brazil. Cf. **milreis.**

reja [Sp] *REH-hah*. iron window grating.

relevé [Fr] *ruh-luh-VAY*. raised; exalted; highly seasoned; in ballet, a step in which the dancer rises sharply on the toes.

religieuse [Fr] *ruh-lee-ZHÖZ*. nun.

religieux [Fr] *ruh-lee-ZHÖ*. priest; friar; lay brother.

religioso [It] *reh-lee-JOH-soh*; [Sp] *reh-lee-HYOH-soh*. religious; devout; a monk or friar.

remerciement [Fr, from *remercier*, to thank] *ruh-mehr-see-MÃ*. expression of gratitude; thanks. Also, **remercîment.**

rémoulade [Fr, from It *remolata*, from Lat *armoracea*, horseradish] *ray-moo-LAHD*. a sauce made of mayonnaise and various spices.

remuda [Sp, from *remudar*, to exchange, replace] *reh-MOO-dah*. a relay of saddle horses; saddle horses collectively.

rendezvous [Fr, from *rendez-vous*, betake yourselves] *rã-day-VOO*. prearranged meeting; meeting place.

renegado [Sp, from *renegar*, to deny, renounce] *reh-neh-GAH-doh*. renegade; turncoat.

rente [Fr, from Lat *reddita*, return] *rãt*. annual income; revenue; **—foncière** (*-fõ-SYEHR*) annuity from long-term land rental.

rentier [Fr, from **rente**] *rã-TYAY*. person with a steady income from investments and interest.

renvoi [Fr, from *renvoyer*, to send back] *rã-VWAH*. discharge; adjournment.

répondez, s'il vous plaît [Fr: *abbr.* R.S.V.P.] *ray-põ-DAY-seel-voo-PLEH*. please reply.

repoussé [Fr, from p.p. of *repousser*, to push back or out] *ruh-poo-SAY*. relief work hammered out from behind on a flat metal plate.

Requeté [Sp, independent use of *requete-*, intensifying prefix] *reh-keh-TEH*. a radical organization of the Carlist party in Spain (1833-72); also applied to the Carlist regiments in the Spanish Civil War of 1936-39; a member of either of these groups.

requiem [Lat, acc. of *requies*, rest] *REH-kwee-em*. funeral mass or music.

requiescat in pace [Lat: *abbr.* **R.I.P.**] *reh-kwee-ES-kaht-een-PAH-keh*. may he (she) rest in peace.

res [Lat] *res.* thing; matter; action; **in medias—** (*een-MEH-dee-ahs-*) in the midst of things; in the middle of the story; **—adjudicata** (*-ahd-yoo-dee-KAH-tah*) (see **res judicata**); **—alienae** (*-ah-lee-EH-ny*) things belonging to others; alien property; **—gestae** (*-GES-ty*) things performed; transactions; basic facts; **—judicata** (*-yoo-dee-KAH-tah*) settled matter; closed case; **—nihili** (*-NEE-hee-lee*) a trifling matter; thing of no importance.

respice finem [Lat] *RES-pee-keh-FEE-nem*. look to the end.

respublica [Lat] *res-POO-blee-kah*. (*lit.*, public thing) republic; state.

respuesta [Sp] *res-PWES-tah*. reply.

restaurateur [Fr] *res-toh-rah-TÖR*. restaurant owner or manager.

résumé [Fr] *ray-zü-MAY*. summary, esp. of one's educational and professional experience.

retroussé [Fr] *ruh-troo-SAY*. turned up, esp. of the nose; pug.

revanche [Fr] *ruh-VÃSH*. revenge; return match; the desire on the part of a nation to regain territories or trade advantages lost through war or an unfavorable treaty.

réveillon [Fr, from *réveiller*, to wake up] *ray-veh-YÕ*. midnight dinner on Christmas eve; midnight revelry, esp. on Christmas eve.

revenons à nos moutons [Fr] *ruh-vuh-NÕ-zah-noh-moo-TÕ*. (*lit.*, let us return to our sheep) let's get back to the subject.

revista [Sp] *reh-VEES-tah*. review; magazine; journal.

revue [Fr] *ruh-VÜ*. revue; variety show; survey; magazine; journal.

rex [Lat] *reks*. king; **—Iudaeorum** or **Judaeorum** (*-yoo-dy-OH-room*) King of the Jews.

rey [Sp: *pl.* **reyes**] *ray* (*RAY-yes*) king; **Reyes Católicos**

(-*kah-TOH-lee-kohs*) the Catholic monarchs: Ferdinand and Isabella (1474–1504); **Reyes Magos** (-*MAH-gohs*) the Magi.

rez-de-chaussée [Fr] *ray-d'shoh-SAY.* ground floor.

rial [Pers, from Ar *riyāl,* from Sp **real**] *REE-ahl.* Iranian monetary unit.

ricochet [Fr] *ree-koh-SHEH.* bounce off, as a bullet or echo; rebound.

ricotta [It, from Lat *recocta,* recooked] *ree-KOHT-tah.* a soft white cheese made from whole or skimmed milk.

rideau [Fr] *ree-DOH.* curtain.

ridotto [It: retreat, redoubt] *ree-DOHT-toh.* pleasure resort; music and dance entertainment of 18th-century England.

rien [Fr, from Lat *rem,* acc. of *res,* thing] *ryĕ.* nothing; not at all.

Riesling [Ger] *REES-ling.* a white wine made from a variety of Alsatian grapes.

rifacimento [It, from *rifare,* to redo, remake] *ree-fah-chee-MAYN-toh.* redoing; remaking; copy.

rigatoni [It, from *rigato,* furrowed, from *riga,* furrow, wrinkle] *ree-gah-TOH-nee.* a type of pasta made in short, thick tubes with furrows on the outside.

rigoletto [It, from *riga,* line] *ree-goh-LAYT-toh.* an old Italian round dance.

rigolo [Fr] *ree-goh-LOH.* funny; amusing.

rigor mortis [Lat] *REE-gor-MOR-tees.* stiffness of death; rigidity which sets into a corpse within hours of death.

Rigsdag [Dan] *REEKS-dahkh.* the former Danish parliament, replaced in 1953 by the Folketing.

rigsdaler [Dan] *REEKS-dah-luh.* a former silver coin of Denmark.

rigueur [Fr] *ree-GÖR.* rigor; strictness; precision.

Rig-Veda [Skt, from *ric,* praise + *veda,* knowledge] *REEG-VEH-duh.* an ancient collection of Hindu hymns.

rijksdaler [Du] *RYKS-dah-luh.* a silver coin of Holland. Also, **rijksdaalder** (-*dahl-duh*).

Riksdag. *REEKS-dahkh.* See **Rigsdag.**

Riksmål [Norw] *RIKS-mawl.* (*lit.*, language of the realm) Bokmål.

rilievo [It] *ree-LYEH-voh.* relief, as in sculpture.

Rinascimento [It] *ree-nah-shee-MAYN-toh.* Renaissance; rebirth.

rinçage [Fr, from *rincer*, to rinse] *rĕ-SAHZH.* rinse; rinsing.

Rinderpest [Ger] *RIN-duh-pest.* cattle plague.

Rindfleisch [Ger *Rind*, cattle + *Fleisch*, flesh] *RINT-flysh.* beef.

rinforzando [It] *reen-for-TSAHN-doh.* (*music*) reinforced; accented.

río [Sp, from Lat *rivus*, stream] *REE-oh;* **rio** [It] *REE-oh;* [Port] *REE-oo.* river.

R.I.P. Abbr. of requiescat in pace.

ripaille [Fr] *ree-PY-yuh.* feasting; revelry; debauchery.

ripieno [It] *ree-PYEH-noh.* (*lit.*, a filling in) (*music*) an orchestral accompaniment or background; (*cookery*) stuffing.

riposatamente [It] *ree-poh-sah-tah-MAYN-teh.* (*music*) calmly; with repose.

Rippchen [Ger: *pl. unchanged*] *RIP-ç'n.* sparerib(s).

ris de veau [Fr] *REE-duh-VOH.* sweetbreads.

Risorgimento [It] *ree-sor-jee-MAYN-toh.* (*lit.*, resurgence) Italy's emergence as an independent unified state in the mid-19th century.

risotto [It, from *riso*, rice] *ree-SOHT-toh.* a dish consisting of rice with cheese, chicken or other ingredients added.

risqué [Fr] *rees-KAY.* risky; suggestive; off-color.

rissole [Fr] *ree-SOHL.* a small stuffed pastry, fried in deep fat.

rissolé [Fr, from **rissole**] *ree-soh-LAY.* browned in deep fat.

ritardando [It] *ree-tar-DAHN-doh.* (*music*) gradually slowing.

rite de passage [Fr] *REET-duh-pah-SAHZH.* a ceremony in observance of the passage from one stage of life to another, as at puberty.

ritornello [It, dim. of *ritorno*, return] *ree-tor-NEL-loh.* (*music*) instrumental prelude or refrain in a vocal piece.

ritratto [It] *ree-TRAHT-toh.* portrait, description.

Ritter [Ger: *pl. unchanged*] *RIT-uh.* knight; cavalier.

Rive Gauche [Fr] *reev-GOHSH.* the left bank, esp. of the Seine in Paris, center of student life and artistic and literary activity.

riyal [Ar, from Sp **real**] *ree-YAHL.* Saudi Arabian monetary unit.

riz [Fr] *ree.* rice.

robe [Fr] *rohb.* dress; gown; **—de chambre** (*-duh-SHÃ-bruh*) dressing gown; **—de nuit** (*-duh-NÜEE*) nightgown; **—moulée** (*-moo-LAY*) molded dress; tight-fitting dress or gown.

rocaille [Fr, from *roc*, rock] *roh-KY-yuh.* ornamentation of the Rococo period, usu. consisting of fantastic shapes made of rocks, shells and plants.

Rocinante [Sp, from *rocín*, nag] *roh-see-NAHN-teh.* Don Quijote's horse; any poor horse; nag.

rococo [Fr, from **rocaille**] *roh-koh-KOH.* a decorative style marked by profuse ornamentation, evolved from the Baroque style in 18th-century France.

rodeo [AmerSp, from *rodear*, to go round] *roh-DEH-oh.* a horse show including riding and roping contests; roundup.

rognon [Fr] *roh-NYÕ.* kidney.

roi [Fr] *rwah.* king; **le roi c'est moi** (*luh-RWAH-seh-MWAH*) I am the king; **le roi s'amuse** (*-sah-MÜZ*) the king is amused; **rois fainéants** (*rwah-feh-nay-Ã*) do-nothing kings; **—soleil** (*-soh-LEY*) sun king: Louis XIV.

romaji [Jap] *ROH-mah-jee.* a Roman-alphabet transcription of Japanese.

roman à clef [Fr] *roh-MÃ-ah-KLAY.* (*lit.*, novel with a key) a novel in which a real story is told using fictitious names; **roman fleuve** (*-FLÖV*) (*lit.*, river-novel) a series of novels depicting the life of a single character or group of characters.

romance [Fr] *roh-MÃS.* song, ballad.

romanza [It] *roh-MAHN-dzah.* romance; love ballad.

romanzo [It] *roh-MAHN-dzoh.* novel.

romería [Sp, from *romero*, pilgrim, from LL *romaeus*, from

Gk *romaios*, lit., Roman, from *Roma*, Rome] *roh-meh-REE-ah*. religious pilgrimage.

rond de jambe [Fr] *rõ-duh-ZHĂB*. a ballet step in which a circle is described with one foot.

rondeau [Fr, from *rond*, round] *rõ-DOH*. verse form of three fifteen-line stanzas.

rondo [It *rondò*, from Fr **rondeau**] *RAHN-doh*. a musical pattern in which each part ends with a repetition of the preceding part.

rond-point [Fr] *rõ-PWĔ*. rounded end of a street or building; traffic circle.

ropa [Sp] *ROH-pah*. clothes; clothing.

roquefort [Fr, from the name of a town in S France] *rohk-FOR*. a piquant soft cheese made from sheep's milk.

rosa gallica [NL] *ROH-sah-GAHL-lee-kah*. French rose.

rosbif [Fr, from Eng] *rohs-BEEF*. roast beef.

rosé [Fr] *roh-ZAY*. rose-colored, pink (esp. of wines).

Rosh Hashanah [Heb: Head of the Year] *ROHSH-hah-shah-NAH*. the Jewish New Year.

ros marinus [NL, from *ros*, dew + *marinus*, of the sea, marine] *ROHS-mah-REE-noos*. rosemary.

rossignol [Fr] *roh-see-NYOHL*. nightingale.

rota [Lat: wheel] *ROH-tah*. rotation; turn; ancient Roman court; the court of final appeal of the Roman Catholic Church.

rôti [Fr, p.p. of *rôtir*, to roast] *roh-TEE*. roasted; a roast, esp. of meat.

rôtisserie [Fr] *roh-tee-s'REE*. revolving spit; grill room.

roué [Fr, from *roue*, wheel] *roo-AY*. (*lit.*, one who deserves torture by the wheel) rake; profligate.

rouge [Fr] *roozh*. red; red makeup for the face or lips; —**et noir** (*-ay-NWAR*) red and black: a card game played at a table marked with two red and two black spots on which the players place their bets.

roulade [Fr, from *rouler*, to roll] *roo-LAHD*. (*music*) a lively vocal interlude; (*cookery*) a slice of meat rolled around a filling of chopped meat and other ingredients.

roulette [Fr, dim. of *rouelle*, wheel] *roo-LET*. roller; tracing wheel; gambling wheel; gambling game played with a wheel.

roux [Fr: brownish, reddish, from Lat *russus*, red] *roo.* a butter and flour mixture used as a thickening ingredient.

R.S.V.P. Abbr. of **répondez, s'il vous plaît.**

Rubaiyat [Pers, from Ar pl. of *rubā'īy*, quatrain] *ROO-by-yaht.* a collection of poems by the Persian poet Omar Khayyam, translated (1859) by Edward FitzGerald.

ruble [Russ] *ROO-bl'.* monetary unit of the Soviet Union.

Rückbild [Ger] *RÜK-bilt.* (*ling.*) back-formation.

ruelle [Fr, dim. of *rue*, street] *rü-EL.* lane; alley; narrow passage; narrow space between a bed and a wall.

rumba [Sp, prob. of Afr origin] *ROOM-bah.* a fast Cuban dance.

Rundfunk [Ger] *ROONT-foonk.* radio broadcasting.

Rundschau [Ger] *ROONT-show.* review; show.

rupee [Hindi *rupīyā*, from Skt *rūpya*, wrought silver] *ROO-pee.* monetary unit of India and Pakistan.

rupiah [Hindi *rupīyā*, rupee] *roo-PEE-ah.* monetary unit of Indonesia.

rusé [Fr, from *ruse*, ruse, subterfuge] *rü-ZAY.* sly, devious.

S

S.A. Abbr. of **sociedad anónima; società anonima; société anonyme.**

sábado [Sp] *SAH-bah-doh.* Saturday.

sabaoth [Heb *ç'bhāōth*, pl. of *çābā*, army] *SAH-bah-ohth.* armies; hosts.

sabot [Fr] *sah-BOH.* wooden shoe; clog.

sabotage [Fr, from *saboter*, to kick, from **sabot**] *sah-boh-TAHZH.* damage, interference or disruption, esp. of strategic installations or matériel; undermining of a plan, operation, etc.; to commit sabotage upon; **saboteur** (*-TÖR*) one who commits sabotage.

sabra [Heb, from *sabēr*, prickly pear] *sah-BRAH.* a native Israeli.

Sache [Ger: *pl.* **Sachen**] *ZAH-kheh* (*-kh'n*) thing; cause; topic.

sachem [AmerInd] *SAY-ch'm.* chief; local political boss.

sachet [Fr, dim. of *sac*, sack] *sah-SHAY.* a small sack or envelope filled with perfumed leaves or powder.

Sacrum Romanum Imperium [MedL] *SAH-kroom-roh-MAH-noom-eem-PEH-ree-oom.* Holy Roman Empire.

sadhu [Skt, from *sādhu*, straight] *SAH-doo.* Hindu holy man or monk.

safari [Swahili, from Ar *safara*, to travel] *sah-FAH-ree.* big-game hunting expedition; any long journey made by a group or caravan.

sagamore [AmerInd *sāgimo*, one who overcomes] *SAG-uh-mor.* chief; wise ruler.

Sagittarius [Lat, from *sagitta*, arrow] *sah-geet-TAH-ree-oos.* archer: a sign of the Zodiac.

sahib [Hindi, from Ar] *SAH-heeb.* master: used in India, esp. under colonial rule, in addressing Europeans.

saignant [Fr: *fem.* **saignante**] *seh-NYĂ* (*-NYĂT*) (*lit.*, bleeding) undercooked; rare.

sainete [Sp] *sy-NEH-teh.* farce; playlet.

saint [Fr: *fem.* **sainte**] *sĕ* (*sĕt*) holy; sainted; a saint.

Saint Cyr [Fr] *sĕ-SEER.* famous French military school located in the town of the same name.

sake [Jap] *SAH-keh.* a Japanese alcoholic beverage made from fermented rice.

sal [Lat] *sahl.* salt; —**atticum** (*-AHT-tee-koom*) (*lit.*, salt of Attica) intellectual wit; acerbity; keenness; —**volatile** (*-voh-LAH-tee-leh*) a solution of ammonium carbonate, used as smelling salts.

sala [Sp, It, of Germanic origin] *SAH-lah.* hall; main room; living room; reception room; any large room.

salaam [Ar] *sah-LAHM.* peace: a common salutation; —**aleikum** (*-ah-lay-KOOM*) peace be with you.

salame [It: *pl.* **salami**, from *sale*, salt] *sah-LAH-meh* (*-mee*) a thick, spicy Italian sausage.

salciccia. *sahl-CHEE-chah.* See **salsiccia.**

sale [Fr] *sahl.* soiled; dirty; coarse.

salé [Fr: *fem.* **salée**] *sah-LAY.* salted; coarse; pungent.

salida [Sp, from *salir*, to go out] *sah-LEE-dah*. exit; departure.

salle [Fr, of Germanic origin] *sahl*. room; hall; —**à manger** (*-ah-mã-ZHAY*) dining room; —**d'attente** (*-dah-TÃT*) waiting room; reception room.

salmagundi [Fr *salmigondis*, from It *salami conditi*, pickled salami] *sal-muh-GUN-dee*. a seasoned mixture of eggs, chopped meat, fish, etc.; any mixture or miscellany.

salmis [Fr, contr. of *salmigondis*, salmagundi] *sahl-MEE*. a ragout made with game meat previously cooked, stewed in wine and butter. Also, **salmi**.

salon [Fr, from It *salone*, from *sala*, hall] *sah-LŎ*. reception room; drawing room; art exhibition; distinguished gathering, esp. of literary people.

salpiglossis [Gk, from *salpinx*, trumpet + *glōssa*, tongue] *sal-pee-GLOH-sis*. (*lit.*, trumpet tongue) a garden plant with showy, trumpet-shaped flowers.

salsiccia [It, from *sale*, salt] *sahl-SEE-chah*. sausage. Also, **salciccia**.

saltarello [It, from *saltare*, to leap] *sahl-tah-REL-loh*. a lively Italian dance similar to the tarantella.

saltimbocca [It, from *saltare*, to leap + *in*, in + *bocca*, mouth] *sahl-teem-BOHK-kah*. an hors d'oeuvre made of a small piece of rolled beef browned in deep fat and cooked in anchovy sauce. Also used as a main course.

salud [Sp] *sah-LOOD*. health; to your health!

Salus Populi Suprema Lex Esto [Lat] *SAH-loos-POH-poo-lee-soo-PREH-mah-leks-ES-toh*. Let the welfare of the people be the supreme law (motto of Missouri).

salve! [Lat, from *salve*, imper. of *salvare*, to save] *SAHL-veh*. welcome!; hail!; (God) save. . . !

salvo [It *salva*, from Lat *salve*, hail!] *SAL-voh*. volley of gunfire; broadside; round of applause; salute.

sama [Jap] *SAH-mah*. a suffix appended as a polite form of address to the name of an important personage or deity.

samba [Port, of Afr origin] *SAHM-buh*. a fast Brazilian dance.

samisen [Jap, from Chin *san-hsien*] *SAH-mee-sen*. a three-stringed guitarlike instrument of Japan.

samizdat [Russ, from *sam-*, self + *izdat'*, to publish] a book or other material published and circulated surreptitiously in the U.S.S.R., often in mimeographed typescript.

Sammlung [Ger] *ZAHM-loong.* collection.

samovar [Russ, from *samo-*, self- + *var*, boiler] *suh-mah-VAR.* a special pot used for making tea in Russia and neighboring countries.

sampan [Chin *san pan*, three boards] *SAHM-pahn.* a simple skiff propelled by oars or a single sail.

samurai [Jap] *SAH-moo-ry.* the warrior caste of feudal Japan; a member of this caste.

san [It, Sp, abbr. of santo] *sahn.* saint (used before the name of a male saint).

san [Jap, var. of sama] *sahn.* a title of respect used after a name. Roughly equivalent to Mr., Mrs., Miss.

sanbenito [Sp, after *San Benito*, Saint Benedict] *sahm-beh-NEE-toh.* a prisoner's shirt; during the Inquisition, a yellow robe worn by heretics condemned to die at the stake.

sancocho [Sp] *sahn-KOH-choh.* a kind of stew.

sancta [Lat, fem. of sanctus] *SAHNK-tah.* holy; sacred; sainted; a female saint.

sanctum [Lat, neut. of sanctus] *SAHNK-toom.* private room; retreat; secluded place; —**sanctorum** (*-sahnk-TOH-room*) holy of holies; a place of unassailable privacy.

sanctus [Lat] *SAHNK-toos.* holy; sacred; sainted; a male saint.

sandhi [Skt: a putting together] *SUN-dee.* (*ling.*) phonetic modification of initial or final sounds of words in close syntactical connection, as *I betcha* for *I bet you.*

sang [Fr] *sã.* blood; — -**de-boeuf** (*-duh-BÖF*) oxblood; a dark-red color; — -**froid** (*-FRWAH*) (*lit.*, cold blood) composure; nonchalance; dauntlessness.

sangre [Sp] *SAHN-greh.* blood.

sangría [Sp, from *sangre*, blood] *sahn-GREE-ah.* a cold drink of red wine, sliced fruit, sparkling water and ice.

sanjak [Turk *sancak*] *sahn-JAHK.* district; administrative subdivision of a **vilayet.**

sans [Fr] *sã.* without; — **-culotte** (*-kü-LOHT*) (*lit.*, without breeches) a term applied during the French Revolution to republicans who wore the long trousers frowned upon by the aristocracy; any revolutionary; —**doute** (*-DOOT*) without doubt; certainly; —**façon** (*-fah-SŌ*) without ceremony; informal; —**gêne** (*-ZHEN*) without pretense; unceremonious(ly); casual(ly); —**peur et sans reproche** (*-PÖR-ay-sã-ruh-PROHSH*) without fear and above reproach; chivalrous; knightly; —**souci** (*-soo-SEE*) carefree; nonchalant.

Sansei [Jap *san*, third + *sei*, generation] *SAHN-say.* a third-generation Japanese-American. Cf. **Issei, Nisei.**

santa [It, Sp, fem. of santo] *SAHN-tah.* holy; sainted; a female saint.

santé [Fr] *sã-TAY.* health.

santo [It, Sp: *fem.* **santa**] *SAHN-toh*; [Port] *SÃ-too.* holy; sainted; a male saint.

Santo Oficio [Sp] *SAHN-toh-oh-FEE-syoh.* the Holy Office; the Inquisition.

Sant'Uffizio [It] *sahn-toof-FEE-tsyoh.* the Holy Office; the Inquisition.

são [Port, abbr. of santo] *sã-oo.* Saint (used before a name).

Saorstát [Ir] *SAYR-stoht.* Free State; —**Eireann** (*-AY-run*) Irish Free State.

sapristi [Fr, euphemistic var. of *sacristi*] *sah-prees-TEE.* Good God!: a mild oath.

sarabande [Fr, from Sp *zarabanda*, from Ar & Pers *serbend*] *sah-rah-BÃD.* a slow, graceful, gliding solo dance of Spain; the rhythm and music of this dance, used as one of the movements of the classical suite.

sarape. *sah-RAH-peh.* See **serape.**

sari [Hindi] *SAH-ree.* the common female dress of India, consisting of a long piece of fabric draped around the body.

sarong [Malay] *SAH-rong.* brightly printed cloth worn as a skirt or draped dress by both men and women in the South Pacific.

saros [Gk, from Babylonian *shāru*] *SAH-rohs.* the Chaldean cycle; an eighteen-year cycle of recurring eclipses.

satem [Avestan, hundred] *SAH-tem.* designation of those branches of the Indo-European language family that have in common the sibilant sound of the initial consonant of the word for hundred. See **centum.**

satis [Lat] *SAH-tees.* enough.

Saturnalia [Lat] *sah-toor-NAH-lee-ah.* the festival of Saturn; a time of feasting and revelry observed in December in ancient Rome.

Satyagraha [Skt *satyā,* truth + *graha,* a grasping] *sut-yah-GRUH-huh.* (*lit.,* the true fact or viewpoint) the policy of passive resistance initiated by Gandhi.

saucisse [Fr] *soh-SEES.* sausage; **saucisson** (*-SŎ*) a large sausage.

Sauerbraten [Ger] *ZOW-uh-brah-t'n.* roast meat in sweet-and-sour sauce.

Sauerkraut [Ger] *ZOW-uh-krowt.* pickled shredded cabbage.

sault [OF, from Lat *saltus,* a leap] *soh.* leap; river rapids; waterfall.

saumon [Fr] *soh-MŎ.* salmon.

sauna [Finnish] *SOW-nah.* a Finnish steam bath, in which steam is produced by pouring water on hot rocks.

sauté [Fr, p.p. of *sauter,* to leap] *soh-TAY.* fried slowly in fat or oil; to fry in this manner; something fried in this manner.

sauvage [Fr] *soh-VAHZH.* savage; wild; unrefined.

sauve qui peut [Fr] *SOHV-kee-PÖ.* save (himself) who can; every man for himself.

savant [Fr: *fem.* savante, from *savoir,* to know] *sah-VÃ* (*-VÃT*) scholar; scientist; learned person.

savate [Fr] *sah-VAHT.* (*lit.,* old shoe) a type of boxing in which blows may be struck with the feet as well as the fists.

savoir-faire [Fr] *sah-vwar-FEHR.* (*lit.,* knowing how to do) ability to do, say, and know the right and proper thing effortlessly; **savoir-vivre** (*-VEE-vruh*) (*lit.,* knowing how to live) good breeding; social elegance.

savon [Fr] *sah-VŎ.* soap.

sayonara [Jap] *SAH-yoh-NAH-rah.* good-bye.

sbirro [It, var. of *birro*, prob. from LL *birrus*, red (from the color of some uniforms)] *ZBEER-roh.* policeman; cop.

scaloppine [It, dim. pl. of *scaloppa*, scallop, thin slice, from OF *escalope*, scallop shell] *skah-lohp-PEE-neh.* scallops, esp. of veal, sautéed or broiled, usu. in a wine sauce.

scaramouche [Fr, from It *Scaramuccio*, a stock character in the Commedia dell'Arte, from *scaramuccia*, skirmish] *skah-rah-MOOSH.* cowardly rogue; rascal.

scarola [It] *skah-ROH-lah.* escarole; —**in brodo** (*-een-BROH-doh*) escarole soup.

scena [It] *SHEH-nah.* scene; a dramatic recital passage between singing passages in an opera.

scenario [It, from *scena*, stage, scene] *sheh-NAH-ryoh.* plot or outline of a play or movie.

scène [Fr] *sen.* stage; scene.

Schadenfreude [Ger] *SHAH-d'n-froy-deh.* malicious joy; gloating at another's misfortune.

Schatz [Ger] *shahts.* treasure, wealth; store, stock; sweetheart.

Schauspielhaus [Ger] *SHOW-shpeel-hows.* theater.

schav [Yid, from Russ *shchavel*, sorrel] *shahv.* a cold soup of sorrel and sometimes other vegetables, seasoned with chopped egg, sour cream, lemon juice and chopped scallions.

schema [Gk] *SKEH-mah.* figure; form; plan.

schepen [Du] *SKHEH-p'n.* alderman; magistrate.

scherzando [It, pr.p. of *scherzare*, to play, jest (of Germanic origin)] *skehr-TSAHN-doh.* (*music*) playfully.

scherzo [It, from *scherzare*, to play, jest] *SKEHR-tsoh.* jest, joke; (*music*) a lively, playful composition or passage.

schiksa. See **shiksa.**

Schinken [Ger] *SHEEN-k'n.* ham.

schizzo [It] *SKEET-tsoh.* sketch; drawing.

schlafen Sie wohl! [Ger] *SHLAH-f'n-zee-VOHL.* sleep well!; good night!

Schlagobers [Austrian Ger] *SHLAHK-oh-buz.* whipped cream.

schlemiel [Yid, from Ger, after Peter Schlemihl, title char-

acter of a novel (1814) by Adelbert von Chamisso]
shluh-MEEL. an unlucky person; fool; poor soul. Also,
schlemihl, shlemiel.

schlep(p). See **shlep(p).**

schlimazel. See **shlimazel.**

Schlimmverbesserung [Ger] *S̲HLIM-fehr-bes-uh-roong.* a
bad improvement; an intended gain which only makes
things worse.

schlock [Yid] *shlohk.* (*slang*) cheap; inferior; something
cheap or inferior; junk.

Schloss [Ger] *shlohs.* castle; manor; estate.

Schluss [Ger] *shloos.* end; conclusion; finale.

Schmalz [Yid, from Ger, orig., fat, grease] *shmahlts.* senti-
mentality; exaggerated emotional expression. Also,
schmaltz.

Schmerz [Ger] *shmehrts.* grief; pain.

schmier [Yid, from Ger *Schmiere*, grease] *shmeer.* smear;
paint; (*slang*) bribe.

Schmierkäse [Ger] *SHMEER-kay-zeh.* (*lit.*, smear-cheese)
a kind of soft cheese. Cf. **smearcase.**

schmo [Yid] *shmoh.* (*slang*) a foolish or tiresome person;
jerk. Also, **shmo.**

Schmutz [Ger] *shmoots.* smut; dirt.

Schnapps [Ger] *shnahps.* liquor; brandy.

Schnauzer [Ger, from *Schnauze*, snout] *SHNOW-tsuh.* a
German breed of dogs.

schnell [Ger] *shnel.* rapid; fast; **Schnellzug** (*-tsook*) forced
march; express train.

Schnitzel [Ger, from *schnitzeln*, to cut finely] *SHNIT-s'l.*
cutlet, esp. of veal.

Schnitzelbank [Ger] *SHNIT-s'l-bahnk.* sawbuck; song chart.

schnook [Yid] *shnook.* (*slang*) a mean, insignificant person; dolt. Also, **shnook.**

schnorrer [Yid, from Ger *Schnurrer*] *SHNOR-uh.* (*slang*)
beggar; moocher. Also, **shnorrer.**

schnozzle [Yid *schnoitsl*, snout] *SHNAH-z'l.* (*slang*) nose.

schochet [Heb] *SHOH-khayt.* ritual slaughterer of animals.
Also, **shohet.**

schola [Lat, from Gk *scholē*] *SKOH-lah.* school; —can-

torum (-*kahn-TOH-room*) choir or choral group; part of a church set aside for the use of the choir.

schön [Ger] *shön.* beautiful; good; lovely; fine.

Schottische [Ger, lit., Scottish] *SHOH-tish-eh.* a round dance somewhat like the polka; music for this dance.

schout [Du] *skhowt.* sheriff; local official.

Schrecklichkeit [Ger, from *schrecklich*, frightful, horrible] *SHREK-liç-kyt.* terrorism.

schtick. See **shtick.**

Schuhplatteltanz [Ger] *SHOO-plahtʼl-tahnts.* a Bavarian dance in which the male dancers slap their feet and thighs. Also, **Schuhplattler** (-*luh*).

schuit [Du] *skhoyt.* sloop; canal rig. Also, **schuyt.**

schul. See **shul.**

Schupo [Ger, abbr. of *Schutzpolizist*] *SHOO-poh.* (*slang*) policeman; cop.

Schuss [Ger] *shoos.* (*lit.*, a shot) in skiing, a straight run down a slope at full speed.

Schuster [Ger] *SHOOS-tuh.* cobbler; shoemaker.

Schutz [Ger] *shoots.* defense, protection.

Schutzstaffel [Ger: *abbr.* SS] *SHOOTS-shtah-fʼl.* (*lit.*, protection staff) the Nazi elite guard, which served as Hitler's bodyguard and as a police force.

schuyt. See **schuit.**

schwa [Ger, from Heb *shewā*] *shvah.* name of a Hebrew masoretic point indicating a weak vowel sound; used in linguistics to denote the sound of a reduced unstressed vowel, as in tart*a*n, lin*e*n, rob*i*n, butt*o*n. Also, **shwa.**

Schwanengesang [Ger] *SHVAH-nʼn-guh-zahng.* swan song. Also, **Schwanenlied** (-*leet*).

schwarz [Ger] *shvarts.* black; gloomy.

Schwarzes Korps [Ger] *SHVAR-tsʼs-kor.* Black Corps; members of the **Schutzstaffel.**

schweigen Sie! [Ger] *SHVY-gʼn-zee.* be quiet!

Schwein [Ger] *shvyn.* pig; swine.

Schweinehund [Ger] *SHVY-neh-hoont.* (*lit.*, pig dog) scoundrel; blackguard. Also, **Schweinhund** (*SHVYN-hoont*).

Schweizerkäse [Ger] *SHVY-tsuh-kay-zeh.* Swiss cheese.

Schwyzer-Tütsch [Swiss Ger] *SHVEE-tsuh-tüch.* Swiss German.

scientia [Lat, from *scire*, to know] *skee-EN-tee-ah.* knowledge; science; —est potentia (*-est-poh-TEN-tee-ah*) knowledge is power.

scilicet [Lat, contr. of *scire licet*, it is permitted to know] *SKEE-lee-ket.* namely; to wit.

scintilla [Lat] *skeen-TEEL-lah.* spark; tiny particle; jot.

scire facias [Lat] *SKEE-reh-FAH-kee-ahs.* [*lit.*, make (him) know] a legal writ requiring a person against whom a judgment has been rendered to show cause why it should not be executed.

sciuscià [It, slang, from Eng *shoeshine*] *shoo-SHAH.* shoeshine boy, esp. in Italy after World War II.

Scoppio del Carro [It] *SKOHP-pyoh-del-KAR-roh.* (*lit.*, the explosion of the cart) an annual Florentine festival.

Scorpio [Lat] *SKOR-pee-oh.* scorpion: a sign of the Zodiac.

scriptum [Lat: *pl.* **scripta**] *SKREEP-toom* (*-tah*) script; something written.

scungilli [It] *skoon-JEEL-lee.* scallops of abalone.

scurra [It, from Lat] *SKOOR-rah.* buffoon; jester.

scusi [It] *SKOO-see.* excuse me; I beg your pardon.

scutum [Lat] *SKOO-toom.* shield.

sdegno [It] *ZDEH-nyoh.* disdain; indignation; anger.

se [It] *seh.* if.

séance [Fr] *say-ÃS.* (*lit.*, sitting, session) a spiritualistic session, esp. one in which a medium makes contact with the dead.

se battre contre les moulins [Fr] *suh-BAH-truh-KÕ-truh-lay-moo-LÉ.* to do battle with windmills.

sec [Fr: *fem.* **sèche**] *sek* (*sesh*) dry.

secco [It: *fem.* **secca**] *SEK-koh* (*-kah*) dry.

séchiste [Fr, from *sec*, dry] *say-SHEEST.* drypoint engraver.

seconda volta [It] *seh-KOHN-dah-VOHL-tah.* (*music*) again; a second time.

seconde [Fr, fem. of *second*, second] *suh-GÕD.* in fencing, the second of the eight defensive positions.

secrétaire [Fr] *suh-kray-TEHR.* writing desk; secretary.

secundum [Lat, neut. of **secundus**] *seh-KOON-doom.* second; according to; following.

secundus [Lat, from *sequi,* to follow] *seh-KOON-doos.* second; following.

Seder [Heb] *SAY-dur.* (*lit.,* order, division) in Judaism, a ceremonial feast observed on the first night of Passover.

sedes [Lat] *SEH-des.* seat; chair; see.

Sefer Torah. See **Sepher Torah.**

segno [It] *SEH-nyoh.* sign; signal.

seguidilla [Sp, dim. of *seguida,* sequence, suite] *seh-gee-DEE-lyah.* a lively Spanish dance for two persons.

seguro [Sp] *seh-GOO-roh.* sure; certain; —**servidor** (*-sehr-vee-DOR*) (*abbr.* S.S.) your faithful servant; yours truly: used in closing a letter.

se habla español [Sp] *seh-AH-blah-es-pah-NYOHL.* Spanish is spoken (here).

Sehnsucht [Ger] *ZAYN-zookht.* desire; yearning.

sehr [Ger] *zehr.* very; very much.

seicento [It] *say-CHEN-toh.* the 1600's; the 17th century.

Seidel [Ger] *ZY-d'l.* a large beer mug, often with a hinged lid.

seigneur [Fr] *seh-NYÖR.* lord; feudal master.

sein [Ger] *zyn.* (*verb*) to be; (*noun*) being; existence; (*adj.*) his; her; its.

Seite [Ger: *pl.* **Seiten**] *ZY-teh* (*-t'n*) side; face; page.

sejm [Pol] *saym.* the Polish parliament.

selah [Heb] *SEH-lah.* a word of uncertain meaning occurring in many of the Psalms, presumed to be a musical direction or a signal for a pause.

selene [Gk] *seh-LEH-neh.* moon.

selle [Fr] *sel.* saddle.

seltzer [adaptation of Ger *Selterser,* abbr. of *Selterswasser,* water of a village near Wiesbaden] *SEL-tsur.* mineral water; carbonated water.

semaine [Fr] *suh-MEN.* week.

semana [Sp] *seh-MAH-nah.* week; —**Santa** (*-SAHN-tah*) Holy Week; the week preceding Easter.

Semmel [Ger] *ZEM'l.* breakfast roll.

semolina [var. of **semolino**] *sem-uh-LEE-nuh.* flour milled from durum wheat, used in making macaroni.

semolino [It] *seh-moh-LEE-noh.* coarsely ground flour; semolina.

semper [Lat] *SEM-pehr.* always; —**Fidelis** (*-fee-DEH-lees*) Always faithful (motto of the U.S. Marine Corps); —**Paratus** (*-pah-RAH-toos*) Always prepared (motto of the U.S. Coast Guard).

semplice [It] *SEM-plee-cheh.* simple; unadorned.

sempre [It] *SEM-preh.* always.

sen [Jap, Indonesian, Cambodian] *sen.* monetary units of Japan, Indonesia and Cambodia.

Senatus Populusque Romanus [Lat: *abbr.* **SPQR**] *seh-NAH-toos-poh-poo-LOOS-kweh-roh-MAH-noos.* the Roman Senate and people.

senda [Sp] *SEN-dah.* path; trail.

senhor [Port] *suh-NYOR.* Mr.; sir; gentleman; **senhora** (*-ruh*) Mrs.; madam; lady; **senhorita** (*-REE-tuh*) miss; young lady.

se non è vero è ben trovato [It] *seh-nohn-eh-VEH-roh-eh-ben-troh-VAH-toh.* (even) if it's not true, it's a great discovery.

señor [Sp] *seh-NYOR.* Mr.; sir; gentleman; **señora** (*-rah*) Mrs.; madam; lady; **señorita** (*-REE-tah*) miss; young lady; **señorito** (*-toh*) young gentleman.

sensu bono [Lat] *SEN-soo-BOH-noh.* in a good sense or meaning; **sensu malo** (*-MAH-loh*) in a bad sense or meaning.

senza [It] *SEN-tsah.* without.

separatio a mensa et t(h)oro [Lat] *seh-pah-RAH-tee-oh-ah-MEN-sah-et-TOH-roh.* separation from bed and board; legal marital separation.

Sephardim [Heb, from *Sepharad*, a region mentioned in the Bible, thought to refer to Spain] *suh-FAR-deem.* Spanish and Portuguese Jews: distinguished from **Ashkenazim.**

Sepher Torah [Heb] *seh-FEHR-toh-RAH.* (*lit.*, book of law) a scroll of the Torah, used for public reading in the synagogue. Also, **Sefer Torah.**

sepoy [Anglo-Ind, from Hindi *sipahi*, from Pers *siphāhī*, soldier, from *sipāh*, army] *SEE-poy*. in India, a native soldier; infantryman; policeman. **Cf. spahi.**

septimana [Lat, from *septem*, seven + *mane*, morning] *sep-tee-MAH-nah*. week.

septime [Fr, from Lat *septima*, seventh] *sep-TEEM*. in fencing, the seventh of eight defensive positions.

Septuagesima [Lat] *sep-too-ah-GEH-see-mah*. seventieth; the seventieth day before Easter; the third Sunday before Lent.

Septuaginta [Lat] *sep-too-ah-GEEN-tah*. (*lit.*, seventy) a Greek translation of the Hebrew scriptures done by seventy scholars around 275 B.C.

seq. Abbr. of sequens, sequentes or sequitur.

sequens [Lat: *pl.* **sequentes;** *abbr.* **seq.**] *SEH-kwens* (*-KWEN-tes*) (the) following.

sequitur [Lat: *abbr.* **seq.**] *SEH-kwee-toor*. (*lit.*, it follows) logical conclusion or following remark.

sera [Lat, It] *SEH-rah*. evening.

sérac [Swiss Fr] *say-RAHK*. ice formation caused by crossing of two crevasses in a glacier.

seraglio [It *serraglio*, combining MedL *seracula*, lock + Turk *seray*, palace] *seh-RAH-lyoh*. harem.

serai [Pers: palace] *seh-RY*. inn; resting place; caravansary.

serape [MexSp *sarape*] *seh-RAH-peh*. a heavy blanket worn as a shawl or wrap by peasants in Latin America. Also, **sarape.**

serdab [Ar *sirdāb*, from Pers *sardāb*, ice cellar] *sehr-DAHB*. a secret chamber in an Egyptian tomb, usu. containing a statue of the deceased.

serdtse [Russ] *SYEHR-tsuh*. heart.

serenata [It, from *sereno*, the open air (*lit.*, serene)] *seh-reh-NAH-tah*. serenade.

sereno [Sp] *seh-REH-noh*. serene; clear; a watchman.

sergent de ville [Fr] *sehr-ZHĂ-duh-VEEL*. police constable.

seriatim [Lat] *seh-ree-AH-teem*. in series; one by one.

serment [Fr] *sehr-MĂ*. oath; promise.

serra [Port, from Lat *serra*, saw] *SEHR-ruh*. sierra; mountain range.

serré [Fr, p.p. of *serrer*, to press, crowd] *seh-RAY*, serried; crowded together.

serviette [Fr, from *servir*, to serve] *sehr-VYET*. napkin; briefcase.

servitor [Lat] *SEHR-vee-tor*. servant.

servus [Lat] *SEHR-voos*. slave; (your) servant; at your service.

sestetto [It] *ses-TAYT-toh*. composition for six voices or instruments; sextet.

sestina [It, from *sesto*, sixth] *ses-TEE-nah*. a poem of six stanzas of six lines each, ending in a three-line envoi.

Sexagesima [Lat] *sek-sah-GEH-see-mah*. sixtieth; the sixtieth day before Easter; the second Sunday before Lent.

sforzando [It, from *sforzare*, to force] *sfor-TSAHN-doh*. (*music*) emphatically.

sfumato [It, from *fumare*, to smoke] *sfoo-MAH-toh*. in art, the use of subtle gradation of color to soften the contours of a figure.

sgraffito [It, from *s-*, ex- + **graffito**] *zgrahf-FEE-toh*. a decorative method of incising a design through a surface coating to reveal a different color in the base.

Shabuoth. *shah-boo-OHT*. See **Shavuoth.**

shah [Pers] *shah*. king; ruler of Iran.

shaitan [Ar: enemy] *shy-TAHN*. devil; evil spirit; Satan.

shako [Hung *csákó*, from MHG *zacke*, point, peak] *SHAH-koh*. a stiff military hat of high cylindrical shape, with a visor and a plume or pompon on top.

shalom [Heb] *shah-LOHM*. peace: used as a salutation. *Also,* **sholom;** —**aleichem** (*-ah-LAY-khem*) peace be with you.

shaman [Tungusic, perh. from Pali *samana*, Buddhist monk] *SHAH-mahn*. a medicine man, or a priest or priestess, among primitive tribes, esp. in N Asia.

shammash [Yid, from Heb] *shah-MAHSH*. caretaker or sexton of a Jewish synagogue. Also, **shamus.**

shamus [prob. from *Séamas*, Ir form of *James*; in last sense, by confusion with **shammash**] *SHAH-m's*. detective; policeman; caretaker or sexton of a Jewish synagogue.

shan [Chin] *shahn.* goodness; the practice of goodness or virtue.

shantung [after a province in NE China, where orig. made] *SHAN-tung.* a heavy natural silk fabric; a cotton or rayon fabric imitating this.

sharab [Ar] *shah-RAHB.* wine; alcoholic spirits.

shashlik [Russ, of Turkic origin] *shahsh-LEEK.* small pieces of meat and vegetables broiled or roasted on a skewer. Cf. **shish kebab.**

Shavuoth [Heb] *shah-voo-OHT.* Feast of Weeks: a Jewish festival. Also, **Shabuoth.**

shchi [Russ] *shchee.* cabbage or sauerkraut soup.

sheikh [Ar *shaikh*, old man] *shaykh.* a chief or headman in Arab countries.

sheitel [Heb] *SHAY-t'l.* a wig worn by certain Orthodox Jewish married women.

shekel [Heb *sheqel*] *SHEK'l.* an ancient silver coin of the Hebrews; (*slang, usu. pl.*) money.

shen jen [Chin] *SHEN-jun.* the spiritual side of man.

sherif [Ar *sharif*, exalted] *sheh-REEF.* chief; prince; leader. Also, **shereef.**

shibah. *SHIV-uh.* See **shivah.**

shibboleth [Heb, said to mean "freshet"] *SHEE-boh-leth.* a Biblical word used as a test by the Gileadites to identify the fleeing Ephraimites, who purportedly could not pronounce the sound *sh*; any test word, catch phrase or peculiarity of behavior that distinguishes the members of a group.

shikari [Hindi, from Pers] *shee-KAH-ree.* in India, a big-game hunter.

shiksa [Yid] *SHIK-suh.* a non-Jewish girl or woman. Also, **schiksa.**

shillelagh [Ir] *shuh-LAY-lee.* a heavy walking stick; a club or cudgel.

shinto [Jap, from Chin *shin tao*, way of the gods] *SHIN-toh.* a major Japanese religion based on ancestor worship.

Shir Hashirim [Heb] *SHEER-hah-shee-REEM.* Song of Songs.

shish kebab [Turk] *SHISH-kuh-bahb.* small pieces of meat and vegetables broiled or roasted on a skewer. Also, **shish kabob.** Cf. **shashlik.**

Shiva [Skt, lit., the auspicious] *SHEE-vuh.* the destroyer: a major Hindu deity. Also, **Siva.**

shivah [Heb] *SHIV-uh.* (*lit.*, seven) a mourning period of seven days, observed by Jews upon the death of a parent or close relative. Also, **shibah.**

shlemiel. See **schlemiel.**

shlep(p) [Yid, from Low Ger] *shlep.* to drag; carry; idler, loafer. Also, **schlep(p).**

shlimazel [Yid, from *shlim*, bad + *mazel*, luck (from Heb)] *shli-MAH-z'l.* an unlucky person; a poor wretch. Also, **schlimazel.**

shlomp [Yid, from Ger *Schlumpe*] *shlohmp.* slut; slattern; sloven.

shmateh [Yid] *SHMAH-tuh.* rag; cheap dress.

shmegehgeh [Yid] *shmuh-GEH-guh.* fool, schlemiel.

shmo. See **schmo.**

shnook. See **schnook.**

shnorrer. See **schnorrer.**

shofar [Heb] *shoh-FAHR.* a ram's horn used to announce Rosh Hashanah and Yom Kippur.

shogun [Jap, from Chin *chiang*, lead(er) + *chün*, army] *SHOH-goon.* military leader; any member of the dynasty that ruled Japan, with the Emperor as nominal ruler, from the 12th century to 1868.

shohet. See **schochet.**

shoji [Jap] *SHOH-jee.* a screen of wood and paper or silk, used as an interior partition.

sholom. See **shalom.**

shproty [Russ] *SHPRAW-tee.* sprats.

shtick [Yid] *shtik.* piece, bit; a person's specialty, hobby or eccentricity. Also, **schtick.**

shto [Russ] *shtoh.* what; that; which; anything.

shtoonk [Yid] *shtoonk.* stinker; scoundrel.

shul [Yid] *shool.* (*lit.*, school) synagogue. Also, **schul.**

shvartzeh [Yid] *SHVAR-tsuh.* black; Negro.

shwa. See **schwa.**

si [Fr, from Lat **sic**, so, thus] *see.* if, whether; so, so much; yes (in answering a negative question); [Sp] if, whether.

sí [Sp, from Lat **sic**, so, thus] *see.* yes; indeed.

sì [It, from Lat **sic**, so, thus] *see.* yes; indeed.

sic [Lat] *seek.* so, thus; as quoted.

sic passim [Lat] *seek-PAHS-seem.* thus everywhere; scattered throughout as here.

Sic Semper Tyrannis [Lat] *SEEK-sem-pehr-tee-RAHN-nees.* Thus be it ever to tyrants (motto of Virginia).

sic transit gloria mundi [Lat] *seek-TRAHN-seet-GLOH-ree-ah-MOON-dee.* thus passes the glory of the World.

sic vos non vobis [Lat] *seek-VOHS-nohn-VOH-bees.* (*lit.*, thus you do, but not for yourselves) others take credit for the work you do.

sidi [Ar] *SEE-dee.* chief.

siècle [Fr] *SYEH-kluh.* century; age, era; —**d'or** (*-DOR*) golden age.

Sieg heil! [Ger] *zeek-HYL.* hail, victory!

siempre [Sp] *SYEM-preh.* always; still, yet.

sierra [Sp] *SYEHR-rah.* saw; mountain, mountain range.

siesta [Sp, from Lat *sexta* (*hora*), sixth (hour), midday] *SYES-tah.* nap; afternoon rest.

sieur [Fr, from Lat *senior*, elder] *syör.* lord; sir; your lordship.

sigillum [Lat] *see-GEEL-loom.* seal.

siglo [Sp] *SEE-gloh.* century; age, era; —**de oro** (*-deh-OH-roh*) golden age.

signora [It] *see-NYOH-rah.* Mrs.; madam; lady.

signore [It, from Lat *senior*, elder] *see-NYOH-reh.* Mr.; sir; gentleman; lord. Also, before a name or title, **signor** (*-NYOR*).

signorina [It] *see-nyoh-REE-nah.* miss; young lady.

signorino [It] *see-nyoh-REE-noh.* young gentleman; master.

Sikh [Hindi] *seekh.* (*lit.*, disciple) a member of a Hindu religious sect that renounces the caste system and forbids magic, idolatry and pilgrimages.

silex [Lat] *SEE-leks.* flint.

silla [Sp] *SEE-lyah.* chair; saddle.

s'il vous plaît [Fr] *seel-voo-PLEH.* please; if you please.

sim [Port, from Lat **sic**, so, thus] *see*. yes; indeed.

similia similibus curantur [Lat] *see-MEE-lee-ah-see-MEE-lee-boos-koo-RAHN-toor*. similar (ailments) are cured by similar (remedies); fight fire with fire.

similiter [Lat] *see-MEE-lee-tehr*. likewise.

simoom [Ar *semūm*, rel. to *samm*, poisoning] *see-MOOM*. a hot, dusty wind blowing from N Africa. Also, **simoon** (*-MOON*).

simpatico [It]; **simpático** [Sp] *seem-PAH-tee-koh*. congenial; friendly; pleasant; winsome.

simplex [Lat] *SEEM-pleks*. simple; plain.

simulacrum [Lat] *see-moo-LAH-kroom*. likeness; copy; image.

sine [Lat] *SEE-neh*. without; **—die** (*-DEE-eh*) (*lit.*, without a day) adjourned or tabled until an unspecified future date; **—qua non** (*-kwah-NOHN*) (*lit.*, without which not) a necessary condition or indispensable need.

sinfonia [It] *seen-foh-NEE-ah*. symphony.

Singspiel [Ger] *ZING-shpeel*. operetta with spoken dialogue; drama with little music.

Sinn [Ger] *zin*. sense; thought.

Sinn Fein [Ir] *SHIN-FAYN*. (*lit.*, we ourselves) the Irish nationalist movement that led to the establishment in 1922 of the Irish Free State.

sino [It] *SEE-noh*. as far as; up to; until.

sinus [Lat] *SEE-noos*. cavity, hollow; fold; bay.

si parla italiano [It] *see-PAR-lah-ee-tah-LYAH-noh*. Italian spoken (here).

Si quaeris peninsulam amoenam, circumspice [Lat] *see-KWY-rees-peh-NEEN-soo-lahm-ah-MOY-nahm-keer-KOOM-spee-keh*. If you seek a lovely peninsula, look about you (motto of Michigan).

sirdar [Hindi *sardār*, from Pers] *seer-DAHR*. in India, Pakistan and Afghanistan, a military chief, general; formerly, the British commander of Egyptian armies.

sirocco [It, var. of *scirocco*, from Ar *sharq*, east] *see-ROHK-koh*. a hot, dry wind that blows annually across Italy from Africa; any similar hot, dry wind.

sitar [Hindi] *see-TAR.* a double-stringed instrument of India.

sitz bath [adaptation of Ger *Sitzbad,* lit., seat-bath] *ZITS-bath.* a bathtub in which one may sit so as to immerse only the hips and thighs in warm water; a bath so taken.

Sitzkrieg [Ger] *ZITS-kreek.* (*lit.,* sitting war) the period of relative inactivity during World War II, 1939–1940, after Poland fell.

Siva. *SHEE-vuh.* See **Shiva.**

si vis pacem, para bellum [Lat] *see-vees-PAH-kem-PAH-rah-BEL-loom.* if you want peace, prepare for war.

sixte [Fr, adaptation of Lat *sexta,* sixth] *seekst.* in fencing, the sixth of eight defensive positions.

sjambok [Afrikaans *sambok,* from Malay *cambok,* from Hindi *cābuk*] *shahm-BOHK.* a heavy whip, usu. made of rhinoceros hide.

skald [Icel] *skawld.* a minstrel of Viking times.

skazka [Russ, from *skazat',* to say, tell] *SKAH-skuh.* a folk tale, usu. in verse form.

skoal [Scand, rel. to Dan *skaal,* bowl] *skohl.* to your health; a toast; to toast.

skopeo [Gk] *skoh-PEH-oh.* to look at; behold.

Skupshtina [Serbo-Croatian] *SKOOP-shtee-nah.* the Yugoslav parliament.

slalom [Norw: slope-track] *SLAH-lohm.* a downhill ski race over a zigzag course.

slivovitsa [Serbo-Croatian *sljivovica,* from *sljiva,* plum] *slee-voh-VEET-sah.* an E European plum brandy. Also, **slivovitz** (*SLIV-uh-vits*).

smearcase [Ger *Schmierkäse,* from *schmieren,* to smear, spread + *Käse,* cheese] *SMEER-kays.* any soft cheese, such as cream cheese.

smetana [Russ] *smyeh-TAH-nuh.* sour cream.

smoking [Fr, from Eng *smoking (jacket)*] *smoh-KEENG.* tuxedo.

smorgasbord [Swed *smörgåsbord,* from *smörgås,* sandwich + *bord,* table] *SMÖR-guhs-boord.* elaborate buffet and hors d'oeuvres table; any miscellaneous collection.

snorkel [Ger *Schnorchel*] *SNOR-k'l.* a device for taking in and expelling air underwater used by divers and submarines; to swim or cruise underwater by the use of such a device.

Sobranje [Bulg] *suh-BRAH-nyeh.* the national assembly of Bulgaria.

sobriquet [Fr] *soh-bree-KAY.* nickname. Also, **soubriquet.**

soccus [Lat] *SOHK-koos.* a soft slipperlike ballet shoe worn by actors in Roman comedy.

sociedad anónima [Sp: *abbr.* **S.A.**] *soh-syeh-DAHD-ah-NOH-nee-mah.* (*lit.*, anonymous society) joint-stock company; corporation; **sociedad en comandita** (*-en-koh-mahn-DEE-tah*) limited partnership.

società anonima [It: *abbr.* **S.A.**] *soh-cheh-TAH-ah-NOH-nee-mah.* (*lit.*, anonymous society) joint-stock company; corporation.

société anonyme [Fr: *abbr.* **S.A.**] *soh-syay-TAY-ah-noh-NEEM.* (*lit.*, anonymous society) joint-stock company; corporation.

socle [Fr, from It *zoccolo,* wooden shoe, pedestal, from Lat *socculus*] *SOH-kluh.* a low, flat pedestal for a statue or column; plinth.

soeur [Fr] *sör.* sister.

sofrito [Sp, from p.p. of *sofreír,* to fry lightly] *soh-FREE-toh.* a thick, seasoned sauce used as a base for paella and other dishes.

sogno [It] *SOH-nyoh.* dream.

soi-disant [Fr] *swah-dee-ZÃ.* self-styled; so-called; pretended.

soie [Fr] *swah.* silk.

soigné [Fr, from p.p. of *soigner,* to take care of] *swah-NYAY.* meticulously done or made; elegantly simple; well-groomed.

soirée [Fr] *swah-RAY.* evening; evening party.

Sokol [Czech] *SOH-kohl.* (*lit.*, falcon) a Czech gymnastic society; a member of this society.

sol [Sp] *sohl.* sun; unit of currency in Peru.

solarium [Lat] *soh-LAH-ree-oom.* an open or windowed space within a building for taking the sun.

soldado [Sp] *sohl-DAH-doh.* soldier.

soldat [Fr] *sohl-DAH.* soldier.

soldato [It] *sohl-DAH-toh.* soldier.

solfa [It, from the musical syllables *sol, fa*] *SOHL-fah.* the set of syllables *do, re, mi, fa, sol, la, ti* (or *si*), *do,* used for singing the musical scale; to sing using these syllables; rigmarole.

solfeggio [It, from **solfa**] *sohl-FEJ-joh.* a singing exercise; singing of the musical scale.

soma [Gk] *SOH-mah.* body.

sombra [Sp] *SOHM-brah.* shade; shadow.

sombrero [Sp, from *sombra,* shade] *sohm-BREH-roh.* hat; wide-brimmed hat.

sommelier [Fr] *soh-muh-LYAY.* wine steward.

somnus [Lat] *SOHM-noos.* sleep.

sonata [It, from *s(u)onare,* to play, sound] *soh-NAH-tah.* a musical work in three or four movements, often with piano accompaniment; —**allegro** (*-ahl-LEH-groh*) usually a first movement, consisting of exposition, development and recapitulation.

sonatina [It] *soh-nah-TEE-nah.* a short sonata.

sonde [Fr: plumb line, from *sonder,* to plumb, sound] *sōd.* a rocket or balloon probe.

Sonderdruck [Ger] *ZOHN-duh-drook.* reprint; special printing.

son et lumière [Fr] *SŌ-ay-lü-MYEHR.* (*lit.,* sound and light) a pageant or spectacle featuring music, floodlighting and fireworks.

songe [Fr] *sōzh.* dream; reverie.

son mariachi [Sp *son,* sound, rhythm + **mariachi**] *sohn-mah-RYAH-chee.* a popular round song and dance.

sopa [Sp] *SOH-pah.* soup; —**de fideos** (*-deh-fee-DEH-ohs*) noodle soup; —**de gallina** (*-deh-gah-LYEE-nah*) chicken soup.

sopher [Heb: *pl.* **sopherim**] *SOH-fehr* (*feh-REEM*) scribe.

sophia [Gk] *soh-FEE-ah.* wisdom.

sophos [Gk] *soh-FOHS.* wise.

sophrosyne [Gk] *soh-froh-SÜ-neh.* temperance; moderation.

Sorbonne [Fr] *sor-BOHN.* a famous French university in Paris founded in 1257 by Robert de Sorbon.

sordino [It, from *sordo*, deaf] *sor-DEE-noh*. (*music*) mute. Also, **sordina** (*-nah*).

sordo [It] *SOR-doh*. deaf.

sortie [Fr, from *sortir*, to go out] *sor-TEE*. quick attack, sally; a military flight or mission; exit.

sospiroso [It] *sohs-pee-ROH-soh*. (*music*) sighing; sad.

sot [Fr: *fem.* **sotte**] *soh* (*soht*) foolish; a fool; clown; drunkard.

sotnia [Russ] *SAWT-nyuh*. (*lit.*, hundred) a regiment of Cossack cavalry. Also, **sotnya**.

sottise [Fr, from **sot**] *soh-TEEZ*. silliness; foolishness.

sotto voce [It] *SOHT-toh-VOH-cheh*. in an undertone; whispered.

sou [Fr] *soo*. a former French coin worth about one cent; anything of little value.

soubrette [Fr] *soo-BRET*. maid; silly, coquettish maid of stock comic theater.

soubriquet. *soo-bree-KAY*. See **sobriquet**.

soufflé [Fr] *soo-FLAY*. (*lit.*, puffed up) a casserole dish made with whipped egg whites and baked to a fluffy lightness.

soupçon [Fr] *soop-SŎ*. suspicion; a dash; a mere trace.

soupe [Fr] *soop*. soup; —**à l'oignon** (*-ah-loh-NYŎ*) onion soup; —**du jour** (*-dü-ZHOOR*) soup of the day.

soutane [Fr, from It *sottana*, from *sotto*, under] *soo-TAHN*. cassock.

souteneur [Fr, from *soutenir*, to hold up, maintain] *soo-tuh-NÖR*. panderer; pimp.

soutien-gorge [Fr] *soo-tyĕ-GORZH*. (*lit.*, hold up the throat) brassiere.

soviet [Russ] *sah-VYET*. council; governing body.

soy [Jap *shoy*(*u*), from Chin *shi-yu*: *shi*, salted food + *yu*, oil] *soy*. a spicy sauce prepared from soybeans.

soyez le bienvenu [Fr] *swah-YAY-luh-byĕ-vuh-NŮ*. (be) welcome.

spa [after a resort town in Belgium] *spah*. mineral spring; resort.

spaghetti [It, dim.pl. of *spago*, string] *spah-GAYT-tee*. a food prepared from flour paste, dried in long round strings, and served boiled with any of a variety of sauces.

spahi [Fr, from Turk *sipahi*, from Pers] *spah-EE.* Turkish cavalry irregular; French cavalryman in Algeria. Cf. **sepoy.**

spasibo [Russ] *spuh-SEE-buh.* thanks; thank you.

spät [Ger] *shpayt.* late.

spécialité [Fr] *spay-syah-lee-TAY.* specialty; —de la maison (*-duh-lah-meh-ZŌ*) specialty of the house.

speculum [Lat, from *specere*, to look] *SPEH-koo-loom.* mirror; title of many old books and compositions.

spes [Lat] *spes.* hope.

spiccato [It] *speek-KAH-toh.* separate; distinct; staccato-like playing of the violin.

Spiel [Ger] *shpeel.* play; long-winded oration; pitch; harangue.

spina [Lat] *SPEE-nah.* thorn; spine.

spirito [It] *SPEE-ree-toh.* spirit; animation.

spirituel [Fr] *spee-ree-TÜEL.* spiritual; ethereal; delicate; witty.

spiritus [Lat] *SPEE-ree-toos.* spirit; breath.

Spitz [Ger] *shpits.* (*lit.,* pointed) any of several breeds of dogs having pointed ears and a curved tail, including the chow chow, Pomeranian, and Samoyed.

spokoinoi nochi [Russ] *spah-KOY-noy-NOH-chee.* good night.

sponte sua [Lat] *SPOHN-teh-SOO-ah.* of one's own will.

sporran [Gael] *SPOH-run.* a fur purse worn on the belt by men in the Scottish highlands.

SPQR. Abbr. of **Senatus Populusque Romanus.**

Sprachwissenschaft [Ger] *SHPRAHKH-vis'n-shahft.* linguistics.

Sprechstimme [Ger] *SHPREÇ-shtim-eh.* a combination of speaking and singing which only approximates pitch; dramatic style of declamation.

springbok [Afrikaans] *SPRING-bohk.* a S African gazelle.

spumante [It] *spoo-MAHN-teh.* foaming; effervescent; sparkling wine.

spumone [It, from *spuma*, foam] *spoo-MOH-neh.* a smooth ice cream containing fruit and nuts. Also, **spumoni** (*-nee*).

spurlos versenkt [Ger] *SHPOOR-lohs-fehr-ZENKT.* sunk without trace.

sputnik [Russ, from *s-*, with, together + *put'*, way + *-nik*, suffix of appurtenance] *SPOOT-nyeek.* traveling companion; fellow traveler; space satellite.

sputum [Lat] *SPOO-toom.* saliva.

S.S. Abbr. of **Schutzstaffel; seguro servidor.**

S.S.S. Abbr. of **su seguro servidor.**

Stabat Mater [Lat] *STAH-baht-MAH-tehr.* (*lit.*, the mother was standing) a Latin hymn which is the motif of several music works.

staccato [It] *stahk-KAH-toh.* separate; detached; (*music*) played or sung in such a manner that the notes are abruptly disconnected.

Stad [Du] *staht.* town; city: a suffix of place-names.

Stadt [Ger] *shtaht.* town; city.

Stahlhelm [Ger] *SHTAHL-helm.* (*lit.*, steel helmet) World War I German veterans' organization.

stakhanovism [after A.G. Stakhanov, Russian efficiency expert] *stuh-KHAH-nuh-viz'm.* a system of incentive pay based upon the individual's production, used in the Soviet Union.

Stalag [Ger, contr. of *Stammlager*, group camp] *SHTAH-lahk.* German prisoner-of-war camp in World War II.

Ständchen [Ger] *SHTENT-ç'n.* serenade.

stanza [It] *STAHN-tsah.* room; stanza.

Stati Uniti [It] *STAH-tee-oo-NEE-tee.* United States.

status quo [Lat] *STAH-toos-kwoh.* (*lit.*, state in which) present condition or state; prevalent position.

sta zitto [It] *stah-TSEET-toh.* be quiet!

stella [Lat] *STEL-lah.* star; —**maris** (*-MAH-rees*) star of the sea.

stesso [It] *STAYS-soh.* (the) same.

stet [Lat] *stet.* let it stand: used in proofreading.

stilyaga [Russ: *pl.* **stilyagi**] *stee-LYAH-guh* (*-gee*) in Soviet countries, a young person who imitates the dress and manners of the West.

Stimme [Ger] *SHTIM-eh.* voice; vote.

Stimmtausch [Ger *Stimme*, voice + *Tausch*, exchange] *SHTIM-towsh.* exchange of voice parts in singing.

Stimmung [Ger] *SHTIM-oong.* tuning, key, pitch; mood, disposition; morale; atmosphere; opinion.

stipendium [Lat] *stee-PEN-dee-oom.* stipend; military man's pay.

stoep [Du] *stoop.* stoop; veranda; porch.

stola [Lat, from Gk *stolē*] *STOH-lah.* a long gown worn by Roman women.

stoma [Gk] *STOH-mah.* mouth.

stornello [It] *stor-NEL-loh.* popular song or ballad.

Storting [Norw *stor*, great + *ting*, assembly] *STOR-ting.* the parliament of Norway. Also, **Storthing.**

strada [It] *STRAH-dah.* road; street; way.

strambotto [It] *strahm-BOHT-toh.* a short love poem or lampoon.

strandlooper [Afrikaans] *STRAHND-loh-puh.* S African beachcomber.

Strasse [Ger] *SHTRAH-suh.* street.

stretto [It] *STRAYT-toh.* (*lit.,* tight, narrow) in a fugue, the close overlapping of voices; in an opera or oratorio, an acceleration of the tempo at the end of a movement.

stria [Lat: *pl.* **striae**] *STREE-ah* (*-y*) stripe; groove, furrow, channel; one of the narrow bands between the flutings of a column.

Strudel [Ger] *SHTROO-d'l.* (*lit.,* eddy, whirlpool) a kind of pastry filled with fruit or cheese.

strumento [It] *stroo-MAYN-toh.* instrument. Also, **stromento** (*stroh-*).

Stube [Ger] *SHTOO-beh.* room; sitting room.

stucco [It] *STOOK-koh.* a cementlike mixture of slaked lime and ground stone used as a coating for walls.

Stück [Ger] *shtük.* piece; fragment; selection; musical composition.

Stuka [Ger, contr. of *Sturzkampfflugzeug*] *SHTOO-kah.* a German World War II dive-bomber.

Stunde [Ger: *pl.* **Stunden**] *SHTOON-deh* (*-d'n*) hour; period; lesson.

stupa [Skt] *STOO-puh.* a Buddhist shrine in the form of a dome or pyramid.

Sturmabteilung [Ger] *SHTOORM-ahp-ty-loong.* storm troopers; Brown Shirts; the Nazi strong-arm detachments (1923–1934).

Sturm und Drang [Ger] *SHTOORM-oont-DRAHNG.* storm and stress: a name given to the period of literary revolt and Romanticism of the late 18th century in Germany.

Stuss [Ger] *shtoos.* fuss; ado; nonsense.

sua sponte [Lat] *SOO-ah-SPOHN-teh.* See **sponte sua.**

suaviter in modo, fortiter in re [Lat] *SWAH-vee-tehr-een-MOH-doh-FOR-tee-tehr-een-REH.* gentle of manner, strong in action.

subadar [Urdu, from Pers *suba,* province + *dār,* holder] *SOO-buh-dar.* ruler of a province; military captain. Also, **subahdar.**

subito [It] *SOO-bee-toh.* immediately; quickly.

sub judice [Lat] *soob-YOO-dee-keh.* under judgment; undecided; unresolved.

sub poena [Lat] *soob-POY-nah.* (*lit.,* under penalty) a writ demanding the appearance of a witness in court; subpoena.

sub rosa [Lat] *soob-ROH-sah.* (*lit.,* under the rose) confidential(ly); secret(ly).

subrostrani [Lat] *soob-rohs-TRAH-nee.* See **surrostrani.**

sub sigillo [Lat] *soob-see-GEEL-loh.* under the seal (of confession); in confidence.

sub verbo [Lat: *abbr.* **s.v.**] *soob-VEHR-boh.* (*lit.,* under the word) under oath.

sub voce [Lat: *abbr.* **s.v.**] *soob-VOH-keh.* under the word; under the main entry.

succès de scandale [Fr] *sük-SEH-duh-skahn-DAHL.* success or repute acquired through notoriety or scandal; **succès d'estime** (*-des-TEEM*) honorable success; success as judged by critics and connoisseurs, despite financial failure; **succès fou** (*-FOO*) a raving success, smash hit.

Succoth [Heb] *soo-KOHT.* See **Sukkoth.**

sucre [Fr] *SÜ-kruh.* sugar; [Sp] *SOO-kreh.* monetary unit of Ecuador.

sucrier [Fr] *sü-KRYAY.* sugar bowl.

suède [Fr] *süed.* (*lit.*, Swedish) kid leather, finished with a soft nap surface; a cloth fabric resembling this.

sueldo [Sp] *SWEL-doh.* salary; wages.

sueño [Sp] *SWEH-nyoh.* dream; sleep; **tener—** (*teh-NEHR-*) to be sleepy.

suerte [Sp] *SWEHR-teh.* luck; fortune; lot.

sui generis [Lat] *SOO-ee-GEH-neh-rees.* of its (or one's own) kind; in a class by itself (or oneself).

suisse [Fr] *süees.* Swiss.

suite [Fr] *süeet.* series; set; grouping; sequence; a musical composition consisting of a number of movements in a fixed order.

suivant [Fr] *süee-VÃ.* following.

sujet [Fr] *sü-ZHAY.* subject; individual person; type, sort.

sukiyaki [Jap] *soo-kee-YAH-kee.* a Japanese dish of sautéed meat and vegetables.

Sukkoth [Heb] *soo-KOHT.* (*lit.*, booths) the Jewish Feast of Tabernacles. Also, **Succoth.**

summa [Lat, fem. of *summus*, highest] *SOOM-mah.* highest; compendium; summation; sum; **—cum laude** (*-koom-LOW-deh*) with the highest praise or distinction.

summum bonum [Lat] *SOOM-moom-BOH-noom.* the supreme good.

sumo [Jap] *SOO-moh.* a popular wrestling style practiced by Japanese professionals.

Sunni [Ar] *SOON-nee.* an orthodox Moslem.

sunt lacrimae rerum [Lat] *soont-LAH-kree-my-REH-room.* there are tears for human sufferings.

suo nomine [Lat] *SOO-oh-NOH-mee-neh.* in his own name.

super [Lat] *SOO-pehr.* above; over; beyond.

supercherie [Fr] *sü-pehr-sh'REE.* deception; fraud.

supra [Lat] *SOO-prah.* over; above; before.

suprême [Fr] *sü-PREM.* supreme; (*cookery*) prepared in an especially complex or fancy manner.

sur [Fr] *sür.* on; upon; above; over; about, concerning.

sur [Sp] *soor.* south.

sura [Ar *sūrah*] *SOO-rah.* (*lit.*, step, rung) a chapter in the Koran. Also, **surah.**

surah [var. of *Surat*, a seaport in W India] *SOO-ruh.* a soft silk twill.

sûreté [Fr] *sür-TAY.* security; bond; safety; criminal investigation department, esp. of the Paris police.

sur-le-champ [Fr] *sür-luh-SHĂ.* (*lit.*, on the field) immediately.

sur les pointes [Fr] *sür-lay-PWĚT.* on the toes; toe dancing.

sur le vif [Fr] *sür-luh-VEEF.* lifelike; vivid.

surrostrani [Lat, from *sub*, under + *rostra*, forum] *soor-rohs-TRAH-nee.* in ancient Rome, loafers or idlers who sat about under the speaker's rostrum; also, stenographers who recorded orations. Also, **subrostrani.**

Sursum Corda [Lat] *SOOR-soom-KOR-dah.* lift up your hearts: a phrase occurring in the Roman Catholic Mass and in the Anglican service.

surtout [Fr] *sür-TOO.* above all; especially; overcoat; centerpiece for a table.

su seguro servidor [Sp: *abbr.* S.S.S.] *soo-seh-GOO-roh-sehr-vee-DOR.* your faithful servant; yours truly: used in closing a formal letter.

sussurrando [It] *soos-soor-RAHN-doh.* (*music*) whispering; murmuring.

sustineo alas [Lat] *soos-TEE-neh-oh-AH-lahs.* I sustain the wings (motto of the U.S. Air Force).

sutra [Skt] *SOO-truh.* (*lit.*, thread) rule; verse; treatise; in Hinduism, a collection of moral teachings; in Buddhism, any of the sermons of Buddha.

suttee [Anglo-Ind, from Skt *satī*, good woman] *SUT-ee.* the self-sacrifice of a woman on her husband's funeral pyre; the woman who so sacrifices herself.

suum cuique [Lat] *SOO-oom-KWEE-kweh.* to each his own.

s.v. Abbr. of **sub verbo; sub voce.**

svelte [Fr, from It *svelto*] *svelt.* slender; lithe; fashionably slim.

Swadeshi [Bengali *svadeshī*: *sva-*, self- + *deshī*, native] *swuh-DEH-shee.* in British India, the movement to foster domestic production and keep out foreign goods; (goods) made in India.

swami [Hindi *swāmī*, from Skt *svāmī*, lord, master] *SWAH-mee*. Hindu religious leader or teacher.

Swaraj [Hindi, from Skt *svarājya*] *swuh-RAHJ*. self-rule; self-government.

swastika [Hindi, from Skt *svastika*, good luck sign, from *su-*, good, well + *as-*, be] *SWUH-stee-kuh*. an ancient symbol used in the Orient and by American Indians, consisting of a cross with equal arms, each arm having a continuing crosspiece extending perpendicularly to itself in a clockwise or counterclockwise direction (卍 or 卐); a similar figure (卐) adopted as the emblem of the Nazi party and the Third Reich in Germany.

symposium [Lat, from Gk *symposion*, a drinking together] *seem-POH-see-oom*. banquet; learned gathering; cultural festival.

syn [Gk] *sün*. with; together.

syndicat [Fr] *sē-dee-KAH*. syndicate; union.

T

Taal [Afrikaans, from Du] *tahl*. (*lit.*, speech, language) the Afrikaans language.

tabac [Fr] *tah-BAH*. tobacco.

tabarin [Fr] *tah-bah-RẼ*. a buffoon in 17th-century French comedy.

tabasco [after Tabasco, a state in Mexico] *tah-BAHS-koh*. a hot sauce prepared from ground red peppers.

tabatière [Fr] *tah-bah-TYEHR*. snuffbox; tobacco pouch.

tabi [Jap] *TAH-bee*. a sock with a thick sole and a cleft between the first and second toe for wearing with zoris.

table [Fr] *TAH-bluh*. table; list; **—de matières** (*-duh-mah-TYEHR*) table of contents; **—d'hôte** (*-DOHT*) (*lit.*, host's table) the regular menu, as opposed to à la carte.

tableau [Fr: *pl.* **tableaux**] *tah-BLOH*. painting, picture; tableau, scene; panel; blackboard.

taboo [Polynesian] *tah-BOO*. sacred or prohibited; a sacred or forbidden thing. Also, **tabu**.

tabula rasa [Lat] *TAH-boo-lah-RAH-sah.* (*lit.*, clean slate, erased tablet) a blank mind; a mind without preconceptions.

tacet [Lat] *TAH-ket.* (*lit.*, it is silent) in music, an indication for an instrument or voice to remain silent.

tachisme [Fr, from Gk *tachys*, swift] *tah-SHEEZ-muh.* a style of painting originating in France after World War II, characterized by forceful application of vivid colors; **tachiste** (*-SHEEST*) of or pertaining to this style of painting; an artist who works in this style.

tael [Port, from Malay *tahil*, weight] *tayl.* a unit of weight used in the Far East; a Chinese monetary unit.

Tafel [Ger] *TAH-f'l.* table; board; tablet.

Tag [Ger: *pl.* **Tage**] *tahk* (*TAH-geh*) day.

Tagblatt [Ger] *TAHG-blaht.* daily newspaper. Also **Tageblatt** (*TAH-geh-*).

taiga [Russ, of Turkic origin] *TY-guh.* subarctic forest land covering large parts of northern N America, Europe and Asia.

taikun [Jap, from Chin *tai*, great + *kiun*, prince] *ty-KOON.* tycoon; powerful ruler; wealthy merchant.

taille [Fr] *TY-yuh.* size; waist; formerly, in France, a land tax.

tailleur [Fr, from *tailler*, to cut] *ty-YÖR.* tailor; the dealer at cards; a woman's tailored suit.

tais-toi [Fr] *TEH-twah.* be quiet! Also, **taisez-vous** (*TEH-zay-VOO*).

tajo [Sp] *TAH-hoh.* cut; tear, rip; trench for collecting water during the dry season.

tak tochno [Russ] *TAHK-TOHCH-nuh.* just so; just like that.

talis qualis [Lat] *TAH-lees-KWAH-lees.* such as (it is).

taller [Sp, from Fr **atelier**] *tah-LYEHR.* studio; workshop.

tallis [Yid, from Heb *tallith*] *TAH-lis.* Jewish prayer shawl. Also, **tallith.**

Talmud [Heb] *tahl-MOOD.* (*lit.*, instruction) an encyclopedic work containing the Jewish laws and traditions.

tamales [*pl.* of MexSp *tamal*, from Nahuatl *tamalli*] *tah-MAH-les.* a Mexican dish consisting of chopped meat, red peppers and cornmeal dough, wrapped in cornhusks and steamed.

tamarack [AmerInd] *TAM-uh-rak.* an American larch; the wood of this tree.

tamarind [MedL *tamarindus,* from Ar *tamr-hindī,* date of India] *TAM-uh-rind.* a tropical tree; the fruit of this tree.

tambour [Fr, from Ar *ṭanbūr,* lute] *tā-BOOR.* drum; drummer; a pair of circular hoops fitting one inside the other, used for stretching cloth to be embroidered.

tambura [Pers *tanbūr,* from Ar *tanbūr*] *tahm-BOO-ruh.* an Oriental instrument of the lute family, having a small, round body and a long neck.

tamburitsa [Serbo-Croatian, dim. of *tambur,* drum] *tahm-boo-REE-tsah.* small drum; tambourine; lutelike stringed instrument.

tango [AmerSp] *TAHN-goh.* an Argentine ballroom dance.

tante [Fr] *tät.* aunt.

tant mieux [Fr] *tā-MYÖ.* so much the better.

tanto [It] *TAHN-toh.* (*music*) so much; as much.

tant pis [Fr] *tā-PEE.* so much the worse.

Tantum Ergo [Lat] *TAHN-toom-EHR-goh.* Therefore so great (a Eucharistic hymn of the Roman Catholic Church).

Tao [Chin] *tow.* the way; cosmic order; reason.

tapage [Fr, from *taper,* to strike, slap] *tah-PAHZH.* uproar; noise.

tapis [Fr] *tah-PEE.* rug; carpet.

tarantella [It, from *tarantola,* tarantula, from Taranto, a city in SE Italy] *tah-rahn-TEL-lah.* a lively southern Italian dance.

tarboosh [Ar] *tar-BOOSH.* a tasseled cap worn by Moslem men.

tardando [It] *tar-DAHN-doh.* (*music*) gradually slowing.

tarif maximum [Fr] *tah-REEF-mahk-see-MOHM.* maximum rate.

taro [Polynesian] *TAH-roh.* a starchy root commonly used as food in the South Pacific islands.

tartane [Fr, from Ar *tartaneh*] *tar-TAHN.* a single-masted sailing vessel used in the Mediterranean.

Tartarin [Fr, after a character in a novel by Alphonse Daudet] *tar-tah-RĒ.* a boasting southern Frenchman.

tarte [Fr] *tart.* tart; pastry.

tartine [Fr] *tar-TEEN.* a slice of bread or toast spread with butter or jam.

tartuffe [Fr, after a character in a play by Molière] *tar-TÜF.* hypocrite; a holier-than-thou.

TASS [Russ, abbr. of *Telegrafnoye Agenstvo Sovyetskovo Soyuza*] *tahs.* news agency of the USSR.

tastevin [Fr, from MF *taster*, to touch, taste + *vin*, wine] *tahs-tuh-VĒ.* a shallow silver cup used by a sommelier for tasting wine, often worn hung about the neck.

tatami [Jap] *TAH-tah-mee.* a woven straw mat, used by the Japanese for sitting on the floor.

Taube [Ger: *pl.* **Tauben**] *TOW-beh* (*-b'n*) dove; pigeon.

taupe [Fr] *tohp.* (*lit.*, mole) a brownish-gray color.

Taurus [Lat] *TOW-roos.* the bull: a sign of the Zodiac.

tazza [It] *TAH-tsah.* cup.

tedesco [It: *pl.* **tedeschi**] *teh-DAYS-koh* (*-kee*) German.

Te Deum Laudamus [Lat] *teh-DEH-oom-low-DAH-moos.* We praise Thee, O God: an ancient Christian hymn.

teepee. See **tepee.**

Te hominem esse memento [Lat] *teh-HOH-mee-nem-ES-seh-meh-MEN-toh.* Remember you are a man.

Te Igitur [Lat] *teh-EE-gee-toor.* Thee, therefore: first words of a Eucharistic chant.

telegraphische Adresse [Ger] *teh-luh-GRAH-fi-sheh-ah-DRES-eh.* cable address.

tel père, tel fils [Fr] *tel-PEHR-tel-FEES.* like father, like son.

tempo [It: *pl.* **tempi**] *TAYM-poh* (*-pee*) time; weather; (*music*) speed, tempo.

Tempora mutantur et nos in illis [Lat] *TEM-poh-rah-moo-TAHN-toor-et-NOHS-een-EEL-lees.* Times change, and we change with them.

tempore [Lat, abl. of *tempus*, time] *TEM-poh-reh.* in the time (of).

temps [Fr] *tã.* time; weather.

tempura [Jap] *TEM-poo-rah* or *TEM-prah.* a Japanese dish of deep-fried seafood and vegetables.

tempus [Lat: *pl.* **tempora**] *TEM-poos* (*-poh-rah*) time; **—fugit** (*-FOO-geet*) time flies.

tençon [Fr, from OProv *tensó,* contest] *tã-SŎ.* a poetic debate form. Cf. **tenzone.**

tener es temer [Sp] *teh-NEHR-es-teh-MEHR.* to have is to fear.

tenore di grazia [It] *teh-NOH-reh-dee-GRAH-tsyah.* lyric tenor.

tenson [Fr] *tã-SŎ.* See **tençon.**

tenzone [It, from OProv *tensó,* contest] *ten-TSOH-neh.* a poetic debate form. Also, **tenson.** Cf. **tençon.**

teocalli [AmerSp, from Nahuatl] *teh-oh-KAH-lyee.* (*lit.,* god's house) an Aztec temple, having a truncated pyramid for a base.

tepee [AmerInd (Siouan), from *ti,* to dwell + *pi,* used for] *TEE-pee.* conical tent; wigwam. Also, **teepee, tipi.**

tequila [MexSp, after Tequila, a district in Mexico] *teh-KEE-lah.* a strong Mexican liquor distilled from fermented agave.

terminus [Lat] *TEHR-mee-noos.* end; limit; **—a quo** (*-ah-KWOH*) the end from which; starting point; **—ad quem** (*-ahd-KWEM*) finishing point.

ter quaterque beatus [Lat] *TEHR-kwah-TEHR-kweh-beh-AH-toos.* three and four times blessed.

terra [Lat, It] *TEHR-rah.* earth; soil; land; ground.

terra cotta [It] *TEHR-rah-KOHT-tah.* (*lit.,* baked earth) a type of fired clay; objects made of such clay; earthenware; the rich brownish-orange color typical of this clay.

terra firma [Lat] *TEHR-rah-FEER-mah.* solid ground.

terra incognita [It] *TEHR-rah-een-KOH-nyee-tah.* unknown land; uncharted territory.

terrazzo [It, from *terra,* earth] *tehr-RAH-tsoh.* a kind of flooring made from chips of stone or marble cemented together and polished to a smooth surface; terrace. Also, **terrazza** (*-tsah*).

terre [Fr] *tehr.* earth; soil; land; ground; **—à terre** (*-ah-TEHR*) (*lit.,* earth to earth) commonplace; vulgar.

terrine [Fr, from *terre*, earth] *teh-REEN.* earthenware pot or dish; a pâté of ground pork, veal and liver, seasoned and garnished with strips of pork fat, and baked.

tertium quid [Lat] *TEHR-tee-oom-KWEED.* (*lit.*, a third something) something intermediate between two things; a compromise.

tertius gaudens [Lat] *TEHR-tee-oos-GOW-dens.* third winner; a third person who gains by a difference between two others.

tertulia [Sp] *tehr-TOO-lyah.* party; gathering; social club; circle.

terza rima [It] *TEHR-tsah-REE-mah.* (*lit.*, third rhyme) a verse form used by Dante, consisting of eleven-syllable lines arranged in groups of three, the middle line of each group rhyming with the first and last lines of the following group.

tessitura [It] *tes-see-TOO-rah.* (*lit.*, texture) the major tone pattern in a musical composition.

testa [It, from Lat: jug, earthenware pot] *TES-tah.* head; in botany, the hard outer covering of a seed.

testamento [It, Sp] *tes-tah-MAYN-toh.* will; testament.

testudo [Lat] *tes-TOO-doh.* (*lit.*, tortoise) a shelter formed by Roman soldiers in battle holding their shields so as to overlap above their heads.

tête [Fr, from Lat **testa**] *tet.* head; **tête-à-tête** (*-ah-TET*) (*lit.*, head to head) an intimate or private conversation or meeting.

Teufel [Ger] *TOY-f'l.* devil.

t'fillin [Heb] *t'FIL-in.* a pair of small black boxes containing small parchment scrolls inscribed with verses from Exodus and Deuteronomy, worn by Jewish men at prayer, one on the left arm, the other on the forehead; phylacteries. Also, **tifillin.**

thag [Hindi] *tug.* robber; thug.

thalassa [Gk] *THAH-lahs-sah.* sea.

Thaler [Ger] *TAH-luh.* any of various large coins formerly used in Germany; dollar.

thé dansant [Fr] *tay-dã-SÃ.* tea dance.

theophania [LL, from Gk *theophaneia*, from *theos*, god +

phainein, to appear] *theh-oh-FAH-nee-ah.* an appearance or vision of God or a god.

theos [Gk] *theh-OHS.* god.

thermae [Lat, from Gk *thermai,* pl. of *thermē,* heat] *THEHR-my.* hot springs; hot baths; bathhouse.

Thermidor [Fr, from Gk *thermē,* heat + *dōron,* gift] *tehr-mee-DOR.* the eleventh month of the French Revolutionary calendar; (*cookery*) a style of preparing seafood in brandy.

thermos [Gk] *thehr-MOHS.* hot; a trademark for a vacuum bottle.

thesaurus [Lat, from Gk *thesauros*] *theh-SOW-roos.* treasure; treasure house; collection of ideas; a dictionary of classified synonyms and antonyms.

thespis [after a Gk dramatic poet of the 6th century B.C.] *THES-pis.* an actor; thespian.

thorn [AS] *thorn.* the runic character þ used in Old English and Icelandic to represent the sound *th* as in *thin.*

thug [Anglo-Ind, from Hindi *ṭhag*] thug. See **thag.**

thuggee [Anglo-Ind, from Hindi *ṭhagī,* from *ṭhag,* robber] *THUG-ee.* robbery and murder committed by thugs.

tía [Sp] *TEE-ah.* aunt; old woman.

tiempo [Sp] *TYEM-poh.* time; weather.

tiempo ni hora no se ata con soga [Sp] *TYEM-poh-nee-OH-rah-noh-seh-AH-tah-kohn-SOH-gah.* (*lit.,* neither time nor hour is to be tied with a rope) time and tide wait for no man.

tienda [Sp] *TYEN-dah.* tent; shop, store.

tiens [Fr, from *tenir,* to (be)hold] *tyē.* look here!; hello!; indeed!

tierce [Fr] *tyehrs.* (*lit.,* third) an old measure for wine equal to a third of a pipe, or about 42 gallons; service or prayers at the third hour of the day, or 9 A.M.; in fencing, the third of eight defensive positions.

Tiergarten [Ger] *TEER-gar-t'n.* zoo; game preserve.

tierra [Sp, from Lat **terra**] *TYEHR-rah.* earth; soil; ground; land.

tiers état [Fr] *tyehr-zay-TAH.* the Third Estate; the common people in pre-Revolutionary France.

tifillin. See **t'fillin.**

tilde [Sp, from Lat *titulus*, title, mark] *TEEL-deh.* a diacritical mark over a letter used in some languages, as in Spanish *ñ*, to signify a palatalized *ny* sound (over vowels, a nasal sound, as in Portuguese *irmã*); a similar mark used in dictionaries and other reference works to indicate omission of all or part of a word or phrase.

timbale [Fr] *tē-BAHL.* (*lit.*, kettledrum) food prepared in a drum-shaped mold.

timbre [Fr, orig., bell, drum] *TĒ-bruh.* characteristic quality of a sound, as of an instrument, a bell, or the human voice; tone color.

timbre-poste [Fr] *tē-bruh-POHST.* postage stamp.

Timeo Danaos et dona ferentes [Lat] *TEE-meh-oh-DAH-nah-ohs-et-DOH-nah-feh-REN-tehs.* I fear the Greeks even bearing gifts.

timpani [It, pl. of *timpano*] *TEEM-pah-nee.* kettledrums. Also, **tympani.**

tinctura [Lat, from *tingere*, to dye, tinge] *teenk-TOO-rah.* tincture.

tío [Sp] *TEE-oh.* uncle; old man; guy.

tipi. See **tepee.**

tirailleur [Fr, from *tirer*, to shoot] *tee-ry-YÖR.* sharpshooter; skirmisher.

tirer d'affaire [Fr] *tee-RAY-dah-FEHR.* to help out or pull out of trouble or an embarrassing situation.

tissu [Fr, from p.p. of *tistre*, to weave] *tee-SÜ.* fabric; tissue.

tmesis [Gk: a cutting, from *temnein*, to cut] *TMEH-sees.* a placing of a word between two parts of a compound word; e.g., to do a job any-which-way.

toccata [It, from p.p. of *toccare*, to touch, play] *tohk-KAH-tah.* (*music*) a keyboard composition intended to display the performer's technique.

toddy [Anglo-Ind, from Hindi *tārī*, palmyra palm juice] *TAH-dee.* an alcoholic drink mixed with hot water, sugar and sometimes other flavoring.

toga [Lat] *TOH-gah.* a loose robe worn by Roman men;
   —candida (*-KAHN-dee-dah*) a white toga worn by

Roman candidates for office; —**praetexta** (*-pry-TEKS-tah*) robe of privilege; a white robe with purple trim worn by Roman magistrates and freeborn children; —**virilis** (*-VEE-ree-lees*) manly robe; the adult toga which Roman boys assumed at the age of fourteen.

toile [Fr: linen, canvas, from Lat *tela*, web] *twahl.* sailcloth; canvas; backing material.

toison d'or [Fr] *twah-zō-DOR.* the golden fleece; an order of knighthood in Spain and Austria.

to kalon [Gk] *toh-kah-LOHN.* the beautiful; the good.

tokay [Hung, from the name of the district where it was orig. produced] *TOH-koy.* a heavy sweet white wine.

tokus [Yid, from Heb *tahath*, under] *TOO-k's.* (*slang*) rump; buttocks. Also, **tuches.**

tomo [It, Sp] *TOH-moh.* volume; tome.

tomtom [Hindi *tamtam* (of imitative origin)] *TAHM-tahm.* an Oriental or American Indian drum, usu. beaten with the hands.

ton [Fr] *tō.* tone; style; fashion.

tondo [It] *TOHN-doh.* (*lit.*, round) a painting or sculptural relief of circular form.

tong [Chin *t'ang*, meeting place] *tahng.* secret organization.

topi [Hindi] *TOH-pee.* a pith helmet used in India. Also, **topee.**

toque [Fr] *tohk.* a brimless, close-fitting hat, worn by women; chef's hat.

Tor [Ger] *tor.* gate; fool.

Torah [Heb: instruction, law] *toh-RAH.* the Pentateuch; Mosaic law; Jewish law; books containing the law.

toreador [Sp, from *torear*, to fight bulls, from *toro*, bull] *toh-reh-ah-DOR.* bullfighter.

toreo [Sp] *toh-REH-oh.* bullfighting.

torero [Sp] *toh-REH-roh.* bullfighter, esp. a matador.

torii [Jap] *TOH-ree-ee.* the classic style of entryway to a Japanese place of worship, consisting of two upright posts with two crosspieces at the top, the upper one curving upward.

toro [Sp, from Lat *taurus*] *TOH-roh.* bull; —**bravo**

(-*BRAH-voh*) wild or fierce bull; **toros** (*pl.*) (-*rohs*) the bullfights.

torrone [It, from Sp *turrón*, from *turrar*, to roast] *tor-ROH-neh.* a hard white candy made of toasted almonds, honey and other ingredients; nougat.

Torte [Ger, from LL *torta*] *TOR-teh.* tart; round cake.

tortilla [Sp, dim. of *torta*, cake] *tor-TEE-lyah.* thin, round unleavened bread made from cornmeal, originating in Mexico; in Spain, omelet.

tortoni [It, perh. from the name of an Italian pastry chef in Paris] *tor-TOH-nee.* a light ice cream often containing chopped cherries and other fruits, topped with crushed almonds or macaroons.

tortue [Fr, from MedL *tortuca*] *tor-TÜ.* turtle; tortoise; **—claire** (-*KLEHR*) clear turtle soup.

tortuga [Sp, from MedL *tortuca*] *tor-TOO-gah.* turtle; tortoise.

tosto [It] *TOHS-toh.* soon, quickly; (*music*) rapid, quick.

totem [AmerInd (Ojibwa) *ototeman*, his kin] *TOH-t'm.* an animal, plant or object with which the members of a given tribe associate themselves; a representation of this, serving as the emblem of a tribe.

tot homines quot sententiae [Lat] *TOHT-HOH-mee-nes-KWOHT-sen-TEN-tee-y.* so many men, so many minds.

Totenmarsch [Ger] *TOH-t'n-marsh.* funeral march.

Totentanz [Ger] *TOH-t'n-tahnts.* dance of death.

totidem verbis [Lat] *TOH-tee-dem-VEHR-bees.* in so many words.

touché [Fr, p.p. of *toucher*, to touch, strike] *too-SHAY.* in fencing, an expression used to announce a hit or touch; an expression used to acknowledge defeat in a verbal encounter.

toujours [Fr] *too-ZHOOR.* always; still.

toupet [Fr, dim. of OF *toup*, tuft (of Germanic origin)] *too-PEH.* tuft of hair; forelock; a man's hairpiece; toupee; effrontery, impudence.

tour [Fr, fem. from Lat *turris*; masc. from Lat *tornus*, from Gk *tornos*, lathe] *toor.* (*fem.*) tower; (*masc.*) trip, tour, circuit; turn; lathe; **—de force** (*-duh-FORS*) feat of strength; work of great skill or cleverness.

tourbillon [Fr] *toor-bee-YŎ.* whirlwind; a kind of firework that describes a spiral as it rises.

tourelle [Fr] *too-REL.* turret; small tower.

tournedos [Fr, from *tourner*, to turn + *dos*, back] *toor-nuh-DOH.* round slices of beef fillet.

tournure [Fr, from *tourner*, to turn] *toor-NŬR.* contour; appearance; characteristic shape.

tourte [Fr, from MedL *torta*] *toort.* tart; pie.

tout à fait [Fr] *too-tah-FEH.* completely; wholly; **tout à l'heure** (*-ah-LÖR*) presently, soon; just now, just a moment ago; **tout à vous** (*-ah-VOO*) sincerely yours; **tout comprendre c'est tout pardonner** (*-kŏ-PRÃ-druh-seh-TOO-par-doh-NAY*) to understand all is to forgive all; **tout de suite** (*-d'SŬEET*) immediately, at once; **tout ensemble** (*too-tã-SÃ-bluh*) taken together or as a whole; overall effect; **tout fait** (*-FEH*) ready-made; as is; **tout le monde** (*-luh-MŎD*) all the world; everyone.

tovarish [Russ] *tah-VAH-reeshch.* comrade; friend. Also, **tovarich, tovarisch.**

trabajo [Sp] *trah-BAH-hoh.* work.

traducteur [Fr] *trah-dük-TÖR.* translator; **traduction** (*-SYŎ*) translation.

traduttore, traditore [It] *trah-doot-TOH-reh-trah-dee-TOH-reh.* (the) translator (is a) traitor.

tragédienne [Fr] *trah-zhay-DYEN.* an actress in tragedy.

train de luxe [Fr] *trẽ-duh-LÜKS.* luxury-class train.

trait d'union [Fr] *treh-dü-NYŎ.* hyphen.

tramontana [It, from Lat *transmontanus*, beyond the mountains] *trah-mohn-TAH-nah.* a cold north wind blowing from the Alps across the western Mediterranean; any cold wind blowing from a mountainous region.

tranche [Fr] *trãsh.* slice; cut; **—de vie** (*-duh-VEE*) a slice of life; a realistic work or scene.

tranquillo [It] *trahn-KWEEL-loh.* (*music*) tranquil; soft.

trattoria [It: *pl.* **trattorie**; from *trattore*, host, caterer, from Fr *traiteur*, from *traiter*, to treat, cater] *traht-toh-REE-ah* (*-eh*) eating place, restaurant.

Träumerei [Ger, from *träumen*, to dream] *TROY-muh-ry.* reverie; daydream.

travail [Fr: *pl.* **travaux**] *trah-VY* (*-VOH*) work; labor; a work.

traviata [It, from fem. p.p. of *traviare*, to lead astray] *trah-VYAH-tah.* wayward woman; wanton.

tre [It] *treh.* three.

trecento [It] *treh-CHEN-toh.* the 1300's; the 14th century.

trèfle [Fr, from Lat *trifolium*: *tri-*, three- + *folium*, leaf] *TREH-fluh.* trefoil; clover; the club suit at cards.

treiskaidekaphobia [NL, from Gk *treiskaideka*, thirteen + *phobos*, fear] *trays-ky-deh-kah-FOH-bee-ah.* superstitious fear of the number thirteen.

trek [Afrikaans, from Du *trekken*, to draw, drag, travel] *trek.* long, usually laborious trip; to make such a trip; travel.

tremolo [It] *TREH-moh-loh.* (*music*) tremulous quality; tremble, quaver.

trente et quarante [Fr] *TRÃ-tay-kah-RÃT.* (*lit.*, thirty and forty) a card game, also called **rouge et noir.**

trepak [Russ] *tree-PAHK.* a lively Russian dance.

Trève de Dieu [Fr] *TREV-duh-DYÖ.* Truce of God: a religious law in effect from the 10th to the 13th century, forbidding any form of hostilities on holy days and during certain seasons of the year.

tri [Russ] *tree.* three.

triclinium [Lat, from *tri-*, three- + *clinare*, to incline, recline] *tree-KLEE-nee-oom.* the dining room of a Roman house, providing for nine persons to recline three each on three seats.

tricolore [Fr] *tree-koh-LOR.* tricolor; the flag of the French Republic, consisting of three vertical stripes of red, white and blue.

tricorne [Fr, from Lat *tricornis*, having three horns] *tree-KORN.* a three-cornered hat.

tricot [Fr, from *tricoter*, to knit (of Germanic origin)] *tree-KOH.* a knitted nylon cloth; a kind of worsted cloth.

triduum [Lat] *TREE-doo-oom.* a period of three days of

prayer preceding the feast of the Immaculate Conception.

triennium [Lat, from *tri-*, three- + *annus*, year] *tree-EN-nee-oom.* a period of three years.

triforium [Lat, from *tri-*, three + *forare*, to pierce, make an opening] *tree-FOH-ree-oom.* a gallery above the nave, choir or transept of a Gothic church, consisting of an arch with three openings.

trillo [It, from *trillare*, to trill, ring] *TREEL-loh.* a trill; a ring, as of a bell.

trimestre [Fr] *tree-MES-truh.* trimester; quarter.

Trimurti [Skt *tri-*, three + *mūrti*, shape] *tree-MOOR-tee.* the Hindu trinity of Brahma the Creator, Vishnu the Preserver, and Shiva the Destroyer.

Trinkgeld [Ger] *TRINK-gelt.* (*lit.*, drink money) tip, gratuity.

Trinklied [Ger] *TRINK-leet.* drinking song.

trippa [It: *pl.* **trippe**] *TREEP-pah* (*-peh*) tripe; —**al sugo** (*-ahl-SOO-goh*) tripe in sauce, usu. tomato sauce.

triste [Fr] *treest.* sad, melancholy; **tristesse** (*-TES*) sadness.

tristezza [It] *trees-TAY-tsah.* sadness, melancholy.

triumviri [Lat] *tree-OOM-vee-ree.* in ancient Rome, three officers or magistrates sharing a public function.

trivium [MedL, in Lat, meeting of three roads, from *tri-*, three- + *via*, way] *TREE-vee-oom.* in medieval universities, the lower division of the seven liberal arts, comprising grammar, rhetoric and logic. Cf. **quadrivium.**

troika [Russ] *TROY-kuh.* a Russian carriage or sled drawn by three horses abreast; any group of three persons, nations or the like acting together.

troisième force [Fr] *trwah-zyem-FORS.* third force; any group of nations, political parties or the like constituting an intermediate force between two other groups occupying opposite extremes.

trôleur [Fr, from *trôler*, to stroll, tramp] *troh-LÖR.* vagrant, hobo; **trôleuse** (*-LÖZ*) streetwalker, trollop.

trompe-l'oeil [Fr, from *tromper*, to deceive + *oeil*, eye] *trōp-LÖY.* optical illusion; a décor or art form done in extremely fine detail so as to create an illusion of depth and solidity.

trop [Fr] *troh.* too; too much.

troppo [It] *TROHP-poh.* too; too much.

trottoir [Fr, from *trotter*, to walk, trot] *troh-TWAR.* sidewalk; pavement.

trou-de-loup [Fr] *troo-d'LOO.* (*lit.,* wolf's hole) one of a series of trapholes with pointed stakes in the center, formerly used to foil cavalry attacks.

trou normand [Fr] *troo-nor-MÃ.* (*lit.,* Norman hole) a drink of Calvados after a meal.

trousseau [Fr, from *trousse*, bundle, truss] *troo-SOH.* a collection of linens and lingerie saved by a girl in anticipation of marriage.

trouvère [Fr, from OF *trover*, to find, compose] *troo-VEHR.* a medieval troubadour of northern France.

trovatore [It] *troh-vah-TOH-reh.* troubadour.

trud [Russ] *troot.* work; labor.

truffe [Fr] *trüf.* truffle.

truite [Fr] *trüeet.* trout.

trulli [It] *TROOL-lee.* stone houses of conical shape found in certain regions of S Italy.

tsar. *tsar* (see **czar**); **tsarevna.** *tsuh-RYEV-nuh* (see **czarevna**); **tsarevitch.** *tsuh-RYEH-vich* (see **czarevitch**); **tsarina.** *tsah-REE-nuh* (see **czarina**); **tsaritza.** *tsuh-REE-tsuh* (see **czaritza**).

tsetse [Bantu] *TSEE-tsee.* the fly that causes African sleeping sickness.

T.S.F. [Fr, abbr. of *télégraphie sans fil*] *tay-es-EF.* wireless telegraph; radio.

tsores. See **tzores.**

tsunami [Jap *tsu*, harbor + *nami*, wave] *TSOO-nah-mee.* a large wave produced by an earth tremor or volcanic eruption at the ocean bottom.

tuan [Malay] *TOO-ahn.* in Malaysia, a title equivalent to lord, master, sir.

tuches. *TOO-kh's.* See **tokus.**

Tuileries [Fr] *tüee-l'REE.* a palace surrounded by extensive gardens used by several French kings.

tulipe noire [Fr] *tü-LEEP-NWAR.* black tulip; unique thing, rarity.

tulle [Fr, after Tulle, the city where it was first made] *tül.* a fine net fabric of silk, nylon or acetate, used for hats, dresses, etc.

tumulus [Lat] *TOO-moo-loos.* cairn; conical stone mound.

tundra [Russ] *TOON-druh.* a large treeless plain of the subarctic regions of Europe, Asia and North America.

tu quoque [Lat] *TOO-KWOH-kweh.* thou too: you are guilty of the same offenses of which you accuse me.

turlupin [Fr, after a 16th-century comic actor] *tür-lü-PÉ.* punster, sorry jester; cheat, swindler.

Turnverein [Ger, from *turnen*, to tumble, perform gymnastics + *Verein*, club, society] *TOORN-fur-yn.* gymnastic club.

turrón [Sp, from *turrar*, to roast] *toor-ROHN.* nougat.

tutoyer [Fr, from *tu*, you (*nom.*) + *toi*, you (*acc.*)] *tü-twah-YAY.* to use the familiar forms of address *tu* and *toi*; to address someone in this way; **tutoiement** (*-MÃ*) the use of the familiar forms *tu* and *toi* in addressing someone.

tutti [It] *TOOT-tee.* all; all together; used in music to indicate a passage in which all instruments or voices take part.

tutti-frutti [It] *TOOT-tee-FROOT-tee.* (*lit.*, all fruits) a preserve of chopped mixed fruits; ice cream or other confection flavored with chopped mixed fruits.

tutti i gusti son gusti [It] *TOOT-tee-ee-GOOS-tee-sohn-GOOS-tee.* all tastes are tastes; there is no accounting for tastes.

tutu [Fr, from a child's word for backside] *tü-TÜ.* a short, frilled skirt worn by ballet dancers.

tympani. See **timpani.**

tzar. *tsar.* See **czar**; **tzarevna.** *tsuh-RYEV-nuh* (see **czarevna**); **tzarevitch.** *tsuh-RYEH-vich* (see **czarevitch**); **tzarina.** *tsuh-REE-nuh* (see **czarina**); **tzaritza.** *tsuh-REE-tsuh* (see **czaritza**).

Tzigane [Fr, from Hung *cigány*] *tsee-GAHN.* Gypsy.

tzimmes [Yid] *TSIM-is.* vegetable stew; stewed fruits; fuss, uproar. Also, **tzimmis.**

tzores [Yid] *TSOH-r's.* trouble(s); woe(s). Also, **tsores.**

U

Ua mau ke ea o ka aina i ka pono [Hawaiian] *OO-ah-MAH-oo-keh-EH-ah-oh-kah-AH-ee-nah-ee-kah-POH-noh.* The life of the land is preserved by righteousness (motto of Hawaii).

Übermensch [Ger: *pl.* **Übermenschen**] *Ü-buh-mensh (-sh'n)* superman.

Überschlagen [Ger] *Ü-buh-shlah-g'n.* (*music*) crossing of the hands on the keyboard.

ubique [Lat] *OO-bee-kweh.* everywhere.

ubi sunt [Lat] *OO-bee-SOONT.* where are (they)?

Übung [Ger: *pl.* **Übungen**] *Ü-boong (-g'n)* practice; study; **—macht den Meister** (*-MAHKHT-den-MYS-tuh*) practice makes perfect.

udarnik [Russ] *oo-DAR-neek.* shock worker; a member of a labor force assigned to special emergency projects.

uguale [It] *oo-GWAH-leh.* equal; same (also, **eguale**); **ugualmente** (*-MAYN-teh*) equally; the same; all the same (also, **egualmente**).

uhlan [Ger, from Pol *ulan*, from Turk *oghlan*, boy] *OO-lahn.* a member of the light cavalry in Poland; a member of the German heavy cavalry. Also, **ulan.**

uhuru [Swahili] *oo-HOO-roo.* freedom.

uisgebeatha [Gael] *OOZ-gee-baw.* (*lit.*, water of life) whiskey. Cf. **usquebaugh.**

uitlander [Afrikaans] *OYT-lahn-dur.* foreigner; outlander; in S Africa, a non-Boer white man.

ukase [Fr, from Russ *ukaz. oo-KAHS*]. official proclamation; formerly in Russia, an edict of the Czar.

ukehé [Navaho] *oo-keh-HEH.* thank you.

ukulele [Hawaiian] *oo-koo-LEH-leh.* (*lit.*, flea; perh. in allusion to the rapid running of the fingers over the frets) **a** small stringed instrument resembling the guitar.

ulan. See **uhlan.**

ulema [Ar] *OO-leh-mah.* (*lit.,* learned men) scholars of sacred Moslem law, esp. in Turkey.

ultima ratio regum [Lat] *OOL-tee-mah-RAH-tee-oh-REH-goom.* the final argument of kings: resort to force.

ultima Thule [Lat] *OOL-tee-mah-TOO-leh.* utmost limit; among the ancients, the point farthest north.

ultimo [Lat: *abbr.* **ult.**] *OOL-tee-moh.* in the last or preceding (month): used in business letters.

ultra [Lat] *OOL-trah.* beyond; outside; an extremist; **—vires** (*-VEE-res*) (*law*) beyond the power or authority (of). Cf. **intra vires.**

umbra [Lat: shade, shadow] *OOM-brah.* a region of total shadow in an eclipse; the dark central part of a sunspot.

Umgebung [Ger, from *umgeben,* to surround] *OOM-gay-boong.* surroundings, environment, background; company, society.

umiak [Eskimo] *OO-mee-ahk.* (*lit.,* women's boat) a large boat made of skins stretched over a wooden frame, used for transporting freight and passengers.

Umlaut [Ger *um,* about + *Laut,* sound] *OOM-lowt.* (*phonetics*) assimilation of a vowel to a following vowel; a diacritical mark used in some languages, as in German ä, ö, ü, to indicate a change of sound.

umore [It] *oo-MOH-reh.* (*music*) humor; lightness.

un [Fr: *fem.* **une**] *ü* (*ün*) a; an; one.

un [It, Sp: *fem.* **una**] *oon* (*OO-nah*) a; an; one.

una. See **un, uno,** or **unus.**

una corda [It] *OO-nah-KOR-dah.* (*lit.,* one string) with the soft pedal depressed: a direction used in piano music.

una voce [Lat] *OO-nah-VOH-keh.* with one voice; unanimously.

una volta [It] *OO-nah-VOHL-tah.* (*music*) once; one time.

und [Ger] *oont.* and.

unda [Lat] *OON-dah.* wave.

und so weiter [Ger] *oont-zoh-VY-tuh.* and so forth; etc.

une. See **un.**

Ungeduld [Ger] *OON-guh-doolt.* impatience; **ungeduldig** (*-diç*) impatient.

ungefähr [Ger] *OON-guh-fayr.* casual, accidental; approximate(ly), about.

unguibus et rostro [Lat] *OON-gwee-boos-et-ROHS-troh.* with claws and beak; tooth and nail.

unitas [Lat] *OO-nee-tahs.* unity.

universitas [Lat] *oo-nee-VEHR-see-tahs.* whole; collection; association; university.

uno [Sp, It, Lat (*abl.*); *fem.* **una**] *OO-noh* (*-nah*) one; someone. Cf. **un.**

uno animo [Lat] *OO-noh-AH-nee-moh.* of one mind; unanimously.

Unsinn [Ger *un-*, not, without + *Sinn*, mind, sense] *OON-zin.* nonsense.

Untergang [Ger] *OON-tuh-gahng.* decline; destruction.

Unterseeboot [Ger] *OON-tuh-zay-boht.* U-boat; submarine.

Untersuchung [Ger] *OON-tuh-zoo-khoong.* investigation; examination; search.

unus [Lat: *fem.* **una**; *neut.* **unum**] *OO-noos* (*-nah*; *-noom*) a; an; one.

uomo [It: *pl.* **uomini**] *WOH-moh* (*-mee-nee*) man.

uovo [It: *pl.* **uova**] *WOH-voh* (*-vah*) egg.

Upanishad [Skt *upa*, near to + *ni-shad*, sit down] *oo-PAH-nee-shahd.* one of a collection of post-Vedic philosophical treatises, usu. in dialog form.

upas [Malay] *OO-pahs.* poison; the tree from which an arrow poison is extracted.

upravlenie [Russ] *oo-pruv-LYEH-nee-eh.* direction; administration; government.

uralt [Ger *ur-*, primitive, very + *alt*, old] *OOR-ahlt.* ancient; primeval; **Uralter** (*-tuh*) ancient times, antiquity.

urbi et orbi [Lat] *OOR-bee-et-OR-bee.* (to) the city and the world.

Ursa Major [Lat] *OOR-sah-MAH-yor.* the Great Bear: a constellation; **Ursa Minor** (*-MEE-nor*) the Little Bear: a constellation.

Ursprache [Ger] *OOR-shprah-khuh.* primitive language; parent language, esp. Indo-European.

Ursprung [Ger] *OOR-shproong.* source; origin.

Urteil [Ger] *OOR-tyl.* judgment; sentence, verdict.

urus [Lat, of Germanic origin] *OO-roos.* aurochs.

uscita [It, from *uscire,* to go out] *OO-shee-tah.* a going out; a way out, exit.

usine [Fr] *ü-ZEEN.* factory; mill.

usque [Lat] *OOS-kweh.* up to; until.

usquebaugh [Ir & ScotGael] *OOS-kwee-baw.* whiskey. Cf. **uisgebeatha.**

Ustashi [Serbo-Croatian: rebels] *OOS-tah-shee.* a Croatian terrorist organization that supported the Nazi invasion of Yugoslavia in 1941.

usted [Sp, contr. of *vuestra merced,* your grace; *pl.* **ustedes**] *oos-TED* (*-TEH-des*) you: the polite or formal mode of address.

ut infra [Lat] *oot-EEN-frah.* as (shown or mentioned) below.

ut supra [Lat] *oot-SOO-prah.* as (shown or mentioned) above.

uxor [Lat: *pl.* **uxores**] *OOK-sor* (*-SOH-res*) wife.

V

V. Abbr. of **versus.**

vache [Fr] *vahsh.* cow; (*slang*) cop; (*adj.*) lousy.

vade mecum [Lat] *VAH-deh-MEH-koom.* (*lit.,* walk with me) manual; compendium; book of handy reference.

vae victis [Lat] *VY-VEEK-tees.* woe to the vanquished.

vagón [Sp, from Eng *wagon*] *vah-GOHN.* wagon; carriage; railroad car; —**cama** (*-KAH-mah*) sleeping car.

vale [Lat] *VAH-leh.* farewell.

valet de chambre [Fr] *vah-LAY-duh-SHÃ-bruh.* valet; personal servant.

Valhalla [Icel *valhöll,* hall of the slain] *val-HAL-uh.* in Teutonic mythology, the dwelling place of heroes after death.

Valkyrie [Icel *valkyrja*] *VAL-kee-ree.* one of the mythical young maidens who led heroes into Valhalla; in modern use, a woman who associates with successful or famous men.

vallum [Lat] *VAHL-loom.* wall; rampart.

valse [Fr] *vahls.* waltz.

valuta [It, from *valere*, to be worth] *vah-LOO-tah.* value; currency; exchange rate.

vámonos [Sp] *VAH-moh-nohs.* let's go away; let's get out of here.

vamoose [W U.S., from Sp *vamos*, let's go] *va-MOOS.* scram!; beat it!

vamos [Sp] *VAH-mohs.* let's go.

vanitas vanitatum, omnia vanitas [Lat] *VAH-nee-tahs-vah-nee-TAH-toom-OHM-nee-ah-VAH-nee-tahs.* vanity of vanities, all is vanity.

vaquero [Sp, from *vaca*, cow] *vah-KEH-roh.* cowboy.

vara [Sp] *VAH-rah.* a measure of length equivalent to about a yard.

varia lectio [Lat] *VAH-ree-ah-LEK-tee-oh.* variant reading.

vasco [Sp] *VAHS-koh.* Basque.

vascuence [Sp] *vahs-KWEN-seh.* Basque; Basque language.

Vater [Ger: *pl.* **Väter**] *FAH-tuh (FAY-)* father; **Vaterland** (*-lahnt*) fatherland; Germany.

vates sacer [Lat] *VAH-tes-SAH-kehr.* sacred seer; religious poet.

vaudeville [Fr, from Vau-de-Vire in Normandy, noted for such entertainment] *voh-d'VEEL.* variety show.

vaurien [Fr] *voh-RYĒ.* rogue; ne'er-do-well; rascal.

vavasor [OF, contr. of MedL *vassus vassorum*, vassal of vassals] *vah-vah-SOR.* a feudal lord holding a fief under another lord who was himself a vassal of the king.

veau [Fr: *pl.* **veaux**] *voh.* calf; veal; calfskin.

Veda [Skt] *VEH-dah.* (*lit.*, knowledge) a collection of ancient Hindu sacred writings.

Vedanta [Skt] *veh-DAHN-tuh.* (*lit.*, end of the Veda) the chief Hindu philosophy.

vedi Napoli, e poi mori [It] *VEH-dee-NAH-poh-lee-eh-poy-MOH-ree.* see Naples and die.

vega [Sp] *VEH-gah.* fertile plain.

veh [Yid] *veh*. woe; **—is mir!** (-*is-MEER*) woe is me!

Vehmgericht [Ger] *FAYM-guh-riçt.* (*lit.*, secret court) in medieval Germany, an informal court for trying civil cases openly.

veilleuse [Fr, from *veiller*, to sit up, lie awake] *veh-YÖZ.* night lamp.

veld [Du] *felt.* (*lit.*, field) gently rolling grassland or thinly forested land, as found in S Africa. Also, **veldt.**

velours [Fr] *vuh-LOOR.* velvet; velvety fabric or fur.

velouté [Fr] *vuh-loo-TAY.* (*lit.*, velvety) soft and smooth to the taste; a smooth white sauce.

venaison [Fr, from Lat *venatio*, hunting] *vuh-neh-ZŌ.* venison.

Vendémiaire [Fr, from Lat *vindemia*, vintage] *vã-day-MYEHR.* the first month of the French Revolutionary calendar.

vendetta [It] *ven-DAYT-tah.* revenge; personal or family feud.

Veni, Creator Spiritus [Lat] *VEH-nee-kreh-AH-tor-SPEE-ree-toos.* Come, Creator Spirit: a medieval Latin hymn.

venire facias [Lat] *veh-NEE-reh-FAH-kee-ahs.* (*lit.*, thou shalt cause to come) a legal writ addressed to a sheriff, directing him to summon qualified citizens for jury duty.

Venite [Lat] *veh-NEE-teh.* Come ye: first word of the 95th Psalm in the Latin version (**Venite, exultemus Domino,** Come ye, let us praise the Lord).

veni, vidi, vici [Lat] *VEH-nee-VEE-dee-VEE-kee.* I came, I saw, I conquered: attributed to Julius Caesar after his victory in Pontus in 47 B.C.

ventana [Sp] *ven-TAH-nah.* window.

vente [Fr, from *vendre*, to sell] *vãt.* sale.

Ventôse [Fr] *vã-TOHZ.* (*lit.*, windy) the sixth month of the French Revolutionary calendar.

verbatim [Lat] *vehr-BAH-teem.* word for word; literally; **—et literatim** (-*et-lee-teh-RAH-teem*) word for word and letter for letter.

verbi gratia [Lat: *abbr.* **v.g.**] *VEHR-bee-GRAH-tee-ah.* for example.

verboten [Ger] *fehr-BOH-t'n.* forbidden; prohibited.

verbum sapienti [Lat] *VEHR-boom-sah-pee-EN-tee*. a word to the wise.

verdad [Sp] *vehr-DAHD*. truth; true; ¿no es verdad? (*noh-es-*) isn't it true?; isn't it so? Also, ¿verdad?

verde antico [It] *VEHR-deh-ahn-TEE-koh*. antique green; patina; a green mineral resembling marble, used for decoration.

verdura [It] *vehr-DOO-rah*. greenness; verdure; greens; vegetables.

Verein [Ger] *fehr-YN*. association, club, society.

Vereinigte Staaten [Ger] *fehr-Y-niç-tuh-SHTAH-t'n*. United States.

Verfasser [Ger, from *verfassen*, to compose, write] *fehr-FAH-suh*. writer; author.

Vergissmeinnicht [Ger] *fehr-GIS-myn-niçt*. forget-me-not.

Vergleich [Ger] *fehr-GLYÇ*. comparison; simile.

vergogna [It] *vehr-GOH-nyah*. shame; pity.

verismo [It, from *vero*, true, real] *veh-REEZ-moh*. verism; ultrarealism in art.

veritas [Lat] *VEH-ree-tahs*. truth; —**vos liberabit** (*-vohs-lee-beh-RAH-beet*) the truth shall make you free.

vérité [Fr] *vay-ree-TAY*. truth.

Verlag [Ger] *fehr-LAHK*. publication (of a work); publishing house.

vermicelli [It] *vehr-mee-CHEL-lee*. (*lit.*, little worms) very thin spaghetti.

vermoulu [Fr] *vehr-moo-LÜ*. wormy; worm-eaten.

vermouth [Fr, from Ger *Wermuth*, wormwood] *vehr-MOOT*. an alcoholic beverage of sweet white wine and wormwood or herbs.

vernaccia [It, from the name of a district in Liguria] *vehr-NAH-chah*. a sweet white Italian wine.

verre [Fr] *vehr*. glass; tumbler.

verrückt [Ger, p.p. of *verrücken*, to disturb, derange] *fehr-RÜKT*. deranged; crazy; insane.

vers [Fr] *vehr*. (*noun*) verse; (*prep.*) toward.

Versammlung [Ger] *fehr-ZAHM-loong*. assembly; meeting; convention.

vers de société [Fr] *VEHR-duh-soh-syay-TAY*. society

verse; humorous light verse dealing with contemporary topics.

vers libre [Fr] *vehr-LEE-bruh.* free verse.

verso [Lat] *VEHR-soh.* left; to the left; on the left-hand page.

Versuch [Ger: *pl.* **Versuche**] *fehr-ZOOKH* (*-kheh*) attempt; trial; experiment.

versus [Lat, from p.p. of *vertere*, to turn: *abbr.* **vs.** or **v.**] *VEHR-soos.* opposite; against.

verte [Lat] *VEHR-teh.* turn (the page).

Verwaltung [Ger] *fehr-VAHL-toong.* administration; government.

Verzeichnis [Ger] *fehr-TSYÇ-nis.* list; catalog; inventory; table of contents; index.

vettura [It: *pl.* **vetture**] *vet-TOO-rah* (*-reh*) carriage; hackney coach; taxicab.

vetturino [It: *pl.* **vetturini**] *vet-too-REE-noh* (*-nee*) coachman; hackman.

veuve [Fr] *vöv.* widow; **veuf** (*vöf*) widower.

v.g. Abbr. of **verbi gratia.**

vgl. [Ger, abbr. of *vergleiche*] compare.

via [Lat] *VEE-ah.* road; way; —**Crucis** (*-KROO-kees*) Way of the Cross; —**Dolorosa** (*-doh-loh-ROH-sah*) Way of Sadness: Jesus' road to the Crucifixion; —**media** (*-MEH-dee-ah*) middle way; moderate course.

viaje [Sp] *VYAH-heh.* voyage; trip; **viajero** (*-HEH-roh*) traveler; passenger.

viaticum [Lat, from *viare*, to travel, from *via*, way] *vee-AH-tee-koom.* provisions for a journey; in ancient Rome, travel allowance; the Eucharist, esp. as given to a dying person.

vibrato [It] *vee-BRAH-toh.* (*music*) vibrating; tremulous; a voice or a tone having such a quality.

vice versa [Lat: *abbr.* **v.v.**] *VEE-keh-VEHR-sah.* conversely; in the opposite case.

vichy [Fr, after Vichy, a spa in central France] *vee-SHEE.* mineral water; seltzer.

vichyssoise [Fr, fem. of *vichyssois*, of Vichy] *vee-shee-*

SWAHZ. a cold soup of potatoes and leeks, usu. garnished with chopped chives.

vicomte [Fr] *vee-KŌT.* viscount; **vicomtesse** (*-TES*) viscountess.

victoria [Lat] *veek-TOH-ree-ah.* victory.

vicuña [Sp, from Quechua] *vee-KOO-nyah.* a fur-bearing S American animal; a soft, delicate wool derived from this animal; a coat or other garment made of this wool.

vide [Lat] *VEE-deh.* see: used in textual references; —**ante** (*-AHN-teh*) see before; —**infra** (*-EEN-frah*) see below; —**post** (*-POHST*) see after or further; —**supra** (*-SOO-prah*) see above.

videlicet [Lat, from *videre*, to see + *licet*, it is permitted: abbr. **viz.**] *vee-DEH-lee-ket.* (*lit.*, one may see) namely; that is to say.

video [from Lat *vide(re)*, to see + *-o*, as in *audio*] *VID-ee-oh.* the visible portion of a television broadcast.

vie [Fr] *vee.* life.

vieille [Fr, fem. of **vieux**] *VYEH-yuh.* old; old woman.

viejo [Sp] *VYEH-hoh.* old; old man; **vieja** (*-hah*) old; old woman.

vient de paraître [Fr] *VYẼ-duh-pah-REH-truh.* (*lit.*, has just appeared) recently published.

vierge [Fr] *vyehrzh.* virgin.

Viernes Santo [Sp] *VYEHR-nes-SAHN-toh.* Good Friday.

vieux [Fr] *vyö.* old; old man. Cf. **vieille.**

vigne [Fr] *VEE-nyuh.* vine; vineyard; **vigneron** (*-RŌ*) winegrower.

vignette [Fr] *vee-NYET.* (*lit.*, small vine) a small, decorative design or picture; a short essay or literary sketch.

vilayet [Turk, from Ar] *vee-lah-YET.* in Turkey, a province or district.

villa [Lat, It] *VEEL-lah.* country estate; large residence.

villanella [It, dim. from *villano*, rustic, peasant] *veel-lah-NEL-lah.* a rustic Italian song, usu. sung in parts and unaccompanied.

villanelle [Fr, from It **villanella**] *vee-lah-NEL.* a poetic form consisting usually of five tercets in *a-b-a* rhyme with a final quatrain containing the same rhymes.

ville [Fr, from Lat **villa**] *veel.* city; town.

villeggiatura [It, from *villeggiare*, to vacation in the country, from **villa**] *veel-lej-jah-TOO-rah.* a vacation, esp. one spent in the country.

Ville Lumière [Fr] *VEEL-lü-MYEHR.* the city of light: Paris.

vin [Fr, from Lat *vinum*] *vẽ.* wine; —**blanc** (-*BLÃ*) white wine; —**du pays** (-*dü-peh-EE*) local wine; —**mousseux** (-*moo-SÖ*) sparkling wine; —**ordinaire** (-*or-dee-NEHR*) table wine; —**rosé** (-*roh-ZAY*) pink wine; —**rouge** (-*ROOZH*) red wine.

vinaigre [Fr *vin*, wine + *aigre*, sour] *vee-NEH-gruh.* vinegar.

vinaigrette [Fr] *vee-neh-GRET.* made or served with a vinegar sauce; a small ornamental bottle for holding vinegar or other aromatic liquids.

vincit veritas [Lat] *VEEN-keet-VEH-ree-tahs.* truth conquers.

vinho [Port] *VEE-nyoo.* wine; —**da casa** (-*duh-KAH-zuh*) ordinary wine; table wine; —**seco** (-*SEH-koo*) dry wine; —**tinto** (-*TEEN-too*) red wine; —**verde** (-*VEHR-duh*) green wine.

vino [It, Sp] *VEE-noh.* wine; —**bianco** [It] (-*BYAHN-koh*); —**blanco** [Sp] (-*BLAHN-koh*) white wine; —**da tavola** [It] (-*dah-TAH-voh-lah*) table wine; —**da** (Sp **de**) **pasto** (-*dah-*(-*deh-*)*PAHS-toh*) table wine; a pale dry Spanish sherry; —**nero** [It] (-*NAY-roh*) (*lit.*, black wine) a dark red wine; —**rosato** [It] (-*roh-ZAH-toh*) pink wine; —**secco** [It] (-*SAYK-koh*); —**seco** [Sp] (-*SEH-koh*) dry wine; —**spumante** [It] (-*spoo-MAHN-teh*) sparkling wine; —**tinto** [Sp] (-*TEEN-toh*) red wine.

viola da braccio [It] *VYOH-lah-dah-BRAH-choh.* (*lit.*, viola for the arm) an old instrument of the viol family, held in the arm and supported against the shoulder: forerunner of the modern viola; **viola da gamba** (-*dah-GAHM-bah*) (*lit.*, viola for the leg) an old instrument of the viol family, held between the legs: forerunner of the modern cello; **viola d'amore** (-*dah-MOH-reh*) (*lit.*, viola of love) an early form of bass viol.

violino [It] *vyoh-LEE-noh.* violin.

violoncello [It, dim. of *violone*, bass viol] *vyoh-lohn-CHEL-loh.* cello.

violone [It] *vyoh-LOH-neh.* (*lit.*, large viola) bass viol; double bass.

virginibus puerisque [Lat] *veer-GEE-nee-boos-poo-eh-REES-kweh.* for young girls and boys.

Virgo [Lat] *VEER-goh.* the Virgin: a sign of the Zodiac.

viribus unitis [Lat] *VEE-ree-boos-oo-NEE-tees.* with forces united.

virtù [It] *veer-TOO.* virtue; worthiness; talent; art objects; excellent workmanship.

virtuoso [It, from **virtù**] *veer-TWOH-soh.* masterly; a master of an art or skill.

Virtute et Armis [Lat] *veer-TOO-teh-et-AHR-mees.* By valor and arms (motto of Mississippi).

vis [Lat: *pl.* **vires**] *vees* (*VEE-res*) strength; force.

vis-à-vis [Fr] *vee-zah-VEE.* face to face; facing, opposite; in relation to; a person physically or figuratively opposite; opposite number.

visé [Fr, from p.p. of *viser*, to examine, inspect] *vee-ZAY.* visa; passport.

Vishnu [Skt] *VISH-noo.* the Preserver: a Hindu deity.

vita [Lat, It] *VEE-tah.* life.

vita brevis, ars longa [Lat] *VEE-tah-BREH-vees-ARS-LOHN-gah.* life (is) short, art (is) long.

vite [Fr] *veet.* fast; quick; quickly.

vitello [It: *pl.* **vitelli**] *vee-TEL-loh* (*-lee*) calf; veal; **vitellone** (*-LOH-neh*) an old calf; veal; (*slang*) young, wealthy playboy.

vitrine [Fr] *vee-TREEN.* display case; show window.

viuda [Sp] *VYOO-dah.* widow; **viudo** (*-doh*) widower.

viva [It, Sp] *VEE-vah.* long live . . . !

vivace [It] *vee-VAH-cheh.* (*music*) lively; spirited.

vivandier [Fr: *fem.* **vivandière**] *vee-vā-DYAY* (*-DYEHR*) sutler; purveyor, esp. to the armed forces.

vivat [Lat] *VEE-vaht.* long live . . . !; —**rex** (*-REKS*) long live the king!

viva voce [It] *VEE-vah-VOH-cheh.* (*lit.*, with live voice) out loud; orally.

vive [Fr] *veev.* long live . . . !; hurrah for . . . !; —**l'amour** (*-lah-MOOR*) long live love!; —**la différence** (*-lah-dee-fay-RÃS*) hurrah for the difference! (i.e., between men and women); —**le roi** (*-luh-RWAH*) long live the king!

vixit . . . annos [Lat] *VEEK-seet . . . AHN-nohs.* lived . . . years: usu. inscribed on tombstones.

viz. Abbr. of **videlicet.**

voce [It: *pl.* **voci**] *VOH-cheh* (*-chee*) voice; —**di petto** (*-dee-PET-toh*) (*lit.*, chest voice) natural voice; —**di testa** (*-dee-TES-tah*) (*lit.*, head voice) falsetto; **voci bianche** (*-BYAHN-keh*) (*lit.*, white voices) female voices; contralto and soprano.

vodka [Russ, from *voda*, water] *VAWD-kuh.* a clear liquor distilled from potatoes or grain.

vodun [Haitian Fr, of Afr origin] *voh-DOON.* voodoo.

voici [Fr] *vwah-SEE.* look here; here is (are) . . .

voilà [Fr] *vwah-LAH.* behold!; look there; there is (are) . . .

voile [Fr] *vwahl.* veil; a light silk fabric.

voina i mir [Russ] *vy-NAH-ee-MEER.* war and peace.

voix [Fr: *pl. unchanged*] *vwah.* voice.

volaille [Fr, from *voler*, to fly] *voh-LY-yuh.* fowl; poultry.

volante [Sp, from pr.p. of *volar*, to fly] *voh-LAHN-teh.* a two-wheeled chaise; steering wheel; [It] steering wheel.

Volapük. *voh-lah-PÜK.* world speech: an auxiliary language invented by Schleyer about 1880.

volare [It] *voh-LAH-reh.* to fly.

volata [It, from fem. p.p. of **volare**] *voh-LAH-tah.* flight; rush; sprint; (*music*) a series of rapid notes of embellishment.

vol-au-vent [Fr] *vohl-oh-VÃ.* (*lit.*, flight on the wind) a light pastry shell for filling with meat, fish or vegetables.

volente Deo [Lat] *voh-LEN-teh-DEH-oh.* God willing.

volentieri [It] *voh-len-TYEH-ree.* willingly; gladly. Also, **volontieri.**

volgare [It: *pl.* **volgari**] *vohl-GAH-reh* (*-ree*) the vulgar tongue; vernacular.

Volk [Ger: *pl.* **Völker**] *fohlk* (*FÖL-kuh*) people; nation; tribe; race.

Volksdeutsche [Ger] *FOHLKS-doy-cheh.* members of the German race; Germans living abroad; **Volkskunde** (*-koon-deh*) folklore; **Volkslied** (*-leet*) folk song; **Volkssturm** (*-shtoorm*) people's army: a home defense force in Germany formed toward the end of World War II, consisting of older men and young boys; **Volkswagen** (*-vah-g'n*) (*lit.*, people's car) a German make of automobiles and buses.

volontieri. *voh-lohn-TYEH-ree.* See **volentieri.**

volta [It: *pl.* **volte**] *VOHL-tah* (*-teh*) time; turn.

volte-face [Fr] *vohlt-FAHS.* about-face; reversal of an opinion or attitude.

volteggiando [It] *vohl-tej-JAHN-doh.* (*music*) crossing hands in playing the piano.

volti [It] *VOHL-tee.* (*music*) turn (the page).

voltigeur [Fr] *vohl-tee-ZHÖR.* (*lit.*, vaulter) light infantryman; rifleman.

volventibus annis [Lat] *vohl-VEN-tee-boos-AHN-nees.* (*lit.*, the years turning) as the years go by.

vomitorium [Lat, from *vomere*, to discharge, vomit; *pl.* **vomitoria**] *voh-mee-TOH-ree-oom* (*-ah*) a large opening in a stadium or auditorium through which large numbers of people may enter or leave quickly.

voodoo [Haitian Fr *voudou*, of Afr origin] *VOO-doo.* a system of religious beliefs and rituals based on African tribal religions and containing an admixture of Christian beliefs, practiced chiefly by Negroes of the W Indies. Also, **vodun.**

voortrekker [Afrikaans, from *voor*, before + *trek*, to travel] *FOR-trek-ur.* pioneer.

Vorlesung [Ger, from *vor*, before + *lesen*, to read; *pl.* **Vorlesungen**] *FOR-lay-zoong* (*-g'n*) lecture.

Vorrede [Ger *vor*, before + *Rede*, speech] *FOR-ray-deh.* preface; foreword; prologue.

Vorstellung [Ger, from *vor*, before + *stellen*, to put, set, place] *FOR-shtel-oong.* introduction; opening.

vorwärts! [Ger] *for-VEHRTS.* forward!

vouloir, c'est pouvoir [Fr] *voo-LWAR-seh-poo-VWAR.* where there's a will, there's a way.

vous avez raison [Fr] *voo-zah-vay-reh-ZŎ.* you are right; **vous avez tort** (*-TOR*) you are wrong.

vox [Lat: *pl.* **voces**] *vohks* (*VOH-kes*) voice.

vox clamans in deserto [Lat] *VOHKS-KLAH-mahns-een-deh-SEHR-toh.* A voice crying in the wilderness (motto of Dartmouth College).

vox populi [Lat] *VOHKS-POH-poo-lee.* voice of the people; public opinion; **vox populi, vox Dei** (*-VOHKS-DEH-ee*) the voice of the people is the voice of God.

voyageur [Fr] *vwah-yah-ZHÖR.* traveler; in Canada, an expert woodsman and guide.

voyeur [Fr, from *voir*, to see] *vwah-YÖR.* a peeping Tom.

voyez! [Fr] *vwah-YAY.* look!; see!; **voyons** (*-YŎ*) let's see; come now!

vozhd [Russ] *vawzht.* leader; chief.

vrai [Fr: *fem.* **vraie**] *vray.* true; genuine; real.

vraisemblable [Fr] *vray-sä-BLAH-bluh.* probable; plausible.

vrouw [Du] *frow.* woman; housewife.

vs. Abbr. of **versus.**

vulgaris [Lat] *vool-GAH-rees.* common, vulgar, ordinary.

vulgus [Lat] *VOOL-goos.* the common people; populace; crowd; **vulgo** (*-goh*) commonly; in the manner of the common people.

vulpes [Lat] *VOOL-pes.* fox.

v.v. Abbr. of **vice versa.**

W

Wacht [Ger: *pl.* **Wachten**] *vahkht* (*-'n*) watch; watchman; guard.

wadi [Ar] *WAH-dee.* river; stream, esp. an intermittent stream; oasis.

Wafd [Ar] *wahft.* party; group; the nationalist party of Egypt.

Waffe [Ger: *pl.* **Waffen**] *VAH-feh* (*-f'n*) weapon; arm; firearm.

Wagen [Ger: *pl. unchanged*] *VAH-g'n*. vehicle, conveyance; car, automobile; truck, cart, wagon; carriage; railway car.

wagon [Fr, from Eng] *vah-GŎ*. railroad car.

wagon-lit [Fr: *pl.* **wagons-lits**] *vah-gō-LEE*. sleeping car.

wahr [Ger] *var.* true; real; genuine; **nicht—** (*niçt-*) isn't it so?; right?

Wahrheit [Ger] *VAR-hyt*. truth.

Wald [Ger: *pl.* **Wälder**] *vahlt* (*VEL-duh*) wood, forest.

Walküre [Ger] *vahl-KÜ-reh*. Valkyrie.

walla [Anglo-Ind, from Hindi *-wālā* (suffix of appurtenance)] *WAH-luh*. a person in charge of or occupied with a certain thing. Also, **wallah**.

wallaby [Australian *wolabā*] *WAH-luh-bee*. any of several species of small kangaroos.

wallaroo [Australian *wolarū*] *WAH-luh-roo*. any of several species of large kangaroos.

Wallfahrt [Ger] *VAHL-fart*. pilgrimage.

Walpurgisnacht [Ger] *vahl-POOR-gis-nahkht*. Witches' Sabbath: the eve of St. Walpurgis.

wampum [AmerInd *wampumpeag*, from *wampan*, shiny + *anpi*, string of beads + *-ag*, pl. suffix] *WAHM-p'm*. shell beads, formerly used as money by American Indians; (*slang*) money.

Wanderjahr [Ger: *pl.* **Wanderjahre**] *VAHN-duh-yar* (*-reh*) formerly, year of wandering or traveling; the year spent by a journeyman in travel to gain experience, after serving his apprenticeship.

Wanderlust [Ger] *VAHN-duh-loost*. desire to travel; passion for wandering.

warum [Ger] *vah-ROOM*. why?; wherefore?; **—nicht?** (*-niçt*) why not?

was ist das? [Ger] *vahs-ist-DAHS*. what is that?

Wasser [Ger: *pl. unchanged*] *VAH-suh*. water; waters.

Watusi [Afr] *wah-TOO-see*. a member of a tall, partly Caucasoid people of central Africa; (*l.c.*) a popular dance resembling the frug.

Weh [Ger] *vay.* pain; woe; grief; alas!; —**(ist)mir** [-(*ist*-) *meer*] woe is me!

Wehrmacht [Ger *Wehr*, defense + *Macht*, force] *VEHR-mahkht.* the German armed forces before and during World War II.

Weihnachten [Ger, from *Weih*, consecration + *Nacht*, night] *VY-nahkh-t'n.* Christmas.

Weihnachtsabend [Ger] *VY-nahkhts-ah-b'nt.* Christmas Eve.

Wein [Ger: *pl.* **Weine**] *vyn* (-*neh*) wine; vine.

Weinsäufer [Ger, from *Wein*, wine + *saufen*, to drink, tipple] *VYN-zoy-fuh.* drunkard, tippler, wino.

Weinstube [Ger] *VYN-shtoo-beh.* wine shop; wine cellar; tavern.

Wein, Weib, und Gesang [Ger] *VYN-VYP-oont-guh-ZAHNG.* wine, women and song.

Welt [Ger] *velt.* world, earth; people, society; **Weltanschauung** (-*ahn-show-oong*) world view; philosophy; **Weltansicht** (-*ahn-zict*) world view; philosophical interpretation of reality; **Weltgeist** (-*gyst*) world spirit; spirit of the age; **Weltkrieg** (-*kreek*) world war; **Weltpolitik** (-*poh-lee-teek*) world policy; a foreign policy that advocates worldwide geographic and economic expansion; **Weltschmerz** (-*shmehrts*) world-weariness; pessimism.

wen [Chin] *wun.* culture; letters, literature; —**li** (-*lee*) the classical Chinese language.

wergild [AS *wer*, man + *gild*, payment] *WUR-gild.* formerly, death price; money paid to the family of a slain man. Also, **weregild.**

Wesen [Ger] *VAY-z'n.* being; nature; essence.

Westfälischer Schinken [Ger] *VEST-fay-lish-uh-SHEEN-k'n.* Westphalian ham.

Westmark [Ger: *pl. unchanged*] *VEST-mark.* monetary unit of W Germany.

whare [Maori] *HWAH-reh.* in New Zealand, native hut or house.

wickiup. See **wikiup.**

wie geht's? [Ger, contr. of *wie geht es*] *vee-GAYTS.* how goes it?; how are things?; how are you?

Wiegenlied [Ger: *pl.* **Wiegenlieder**] *VEE-g'n-leet* (*-lee-duh*) cradle song; lullaby.

Wiener Schnitzel [Ger *Wiener*, Viennese + *Schnitzel*, cutlet, chop] *WEE-nuh-shnits'l.* fillet of veal; breaded veal cutlet.

wigwam [AmerInd] *WIG-wahm.* (*lit.*, their house) a hut or lodge made of poles covered with thatching of bark or skins, used by some American Indians.

wikiup [AmerInd *wikiyapi*, lodge, dwelling] *WIK-ee-up.* a rude hut made of brushwood, used by American Indians in the Southwest. Also, **wickiup.**

wildebeest [Afrikaans] *VIL-duh-bayst.* (*lit.*, wild beast) gnu.

Wilhelmstrasse [Ger] *VIL-helm-shtrah-seh.* a street in Berlin, on which formerly were located the offices of the German foreign ministry; the German foreign ministry itself; German foreign policy.

Winterreise [Ger] *VIN-tuh-ry-zeh.* winter journey.

Wissenschaft [Ger, from *wissen*, to know + *-schaft*, suffix of abstract nouns] *VIS'n-shahft.* knowledge; science.

witenagemot [AS *witena*, gen.pl. of *wita*, wise man, councillor + *gemōt*, meeting] *WIT-uh-nuh-guh-moht.* the national council of the Anglo-Saxons.

Wochenschrift [Ger: *pl.* **Wochenschriften**] *VOH-kh'n-shrift* (*-'n*) weekly publication or magazine.

wohl! [Ger] *vohl.* well!; aye!

won [Korean] *wohn.* monetary unit of S Korea.

won ton [Chin *wan t'an*, pastry] *WAHN-tahn.* a dumpling filled with minced meat and vegetables, usu. boiled and served in a soup.

Wort [Ger: *pl.* **Wörter**] *vort* (*VÖR-tuh*) word; **Wortspiel** (*-shpeel*) play on words, pun.

Wörterbuch [Ger: *pl.* **Wörterbücher**] *VÖR-tuh-bookh* (*-bü-çuh*) word book; dictionary.

wunderbar [Ger] *VOON-duh-bar.* wonderful, marvelous.

Wunderkind [Ger: *pl.* **Wunderkinder**] *VOON-duh-kint* (*-kin-duh*) child prodigy.

Wurst [Ger: *pl.* **Würste**] *voorst* (*VÜR-steh*) sausage;
—**wider**— (-*vi-duh-*) tit for tat.

X

xenia [Gk: hospitality, from *xenos*, stranger] *kseh-NEE-ah.*
hotel; motel.
xiphos [Gk] *KSEE-fohs.* sword.

Y

y [Sp, from Lat *et*] *ee.* and; [Fr, from Lat *ibi*] *ee.* there.
yachneh [Yid] *YAHKH-neh.* gossip, busybody.
Yahweh. *YAH-weh.* See **Jahweh.**
Yanqui [Sp] *YAHN-kee.* Yankee; American.
yarmulke [Yid] *YAR-m'l-kuh.* a skullcap worn by Jewish
men, esp. at worship or prayer. Also, **yarmilke.**
yashmak [Turk] *yahsh-MAHK.* veil worn by Moslem
women in public.
yataghan [Turk] *yah-tah-GAHN.* a curved saber with no
guard at the hilt.
yen [Jap, from Chin *yuan*, round thing, dollar] *yen.* monetary unit of Japan.
yenta [Yid] *YEN-tuh.* gossip, busybody.
yentz [Yid] *yents.* to cheat, swindle.
yerba maté. See **hierba maté.**
Yeshiva [Heb] *yuh-SHEE-vuh.* an Orthodox Jewish school.
yeux [Fr, pl. of **oeil**] *yö.* eyes.
yé-yé [Fr, from Eng *yeah-yeah*] *yay-YAY.* of or in the
style of young people or teen-agers.
Yigdal [Heb] *yig-DAHL.* (*lit.*, becomes great) a Jewish
prayer or hymn of faith.
Yildiz Kiosk [Turk] *YIL-diz-KYOHSHK.* palace of the
Sultan.

Yin and Yang [Chin *yin*, female principle; *yang*, male principle] *yin*; *yahng*. in Chinese philosophy, the two opposing and complementary forces of the universe.

Yizkor [Heb] *yeez-KOR*. (*lit.*, be mindful) Jewish memorial service for the dead.

yod [Heb: hand] *yohd*. a letter of the Hebrew alphabet representing the sound *y*; (*ling.*) such a sound produced by consonantization of an unstressed front vowel.

yoga [Skt] *YOH-guh*. (*lit.*, union) a philosophy of self-discipline and withdrawal for the achievement of insight and union with the supreme being of the universe.

yogi [Hindi, from Skt *yogin*, from **yoga**] *YOH-gee*. one who practices or teaches yoga; an ascetic. Also, **yogin** (*-gin*); **yogini** (*-nee*) a woman who practices or teaches yoga.

yogurt [Turk *yōghurt*] *YOH-g'rt*. a food of curdled milk, sometimes with fruits and flavorings added. Also, **yoghurt**.

yoksh [Yid] *yohksh*. buffoon; simpleton.

Yom Kippur [Heb] *yohm-kee-POOR*. Day of Atonement: a Hebrew holiday of fasting and prayers of repentance.

yom tov [Yid, from Heb] *YOHM-TOHV*. (*lit.*, good day) holiday.

yuan [Chin] *yü-AHN*. Chinese government agency; monetary unit of Nationalist China.

yuga [Skt] *YOO-guh*. (*lit.*, yoke) in Hinduism, one of the four ages of the world.

Z

zabaione [It: *pl.* **zabaioni**] *dzah-bah-YOH-neh* (*-nee*) a custard containing egg yolks, sugar and wine. Also, **zabaglione** (*-LYOH-neh*).

zaddik [Heb] *tsah-DEEK*. (*lit.*, righteous) a pious person; leader of a Hasidic group.

zaftig [Yid] *ZAHF-tik*. buxom; having a full figure. Also, **zoftig**.

zager [Yid] *ZAY-guh.* to wheel and deal; act opportunistically.

zaibatsu [Jap] *ZY-baht-SOO.* (*lit.*, wealth-family) a loosely organized power group of Japanese corporations.

zakuska [Russ: *pl.* **zakuski**] *zuh-KOOS-kuh* (*-kee*) hors d'oeuvre.

zamarra [Sp, from Basque *zamar*, sheepskin] *sah-MAR-rah.* a sheepskin coat worn by Spanish shepherds.

zampogna [It, from Lat *symphonia*, harmony, from Gk; *pl.* **zampogne**] *dzahm-POH-nyah* (*-nyeh*) bagpipe.

zapateado [Sp, from *zapato*, shoe] *sah-pah-teh-AH-doh.* heel-and-toe flamenco dancing.

zapato [Sp] *sah-PAH-toh.* shoe; **zapatero** (*-TEH-roh*) shoemaker; cobbler.

zarabanda [Sp] *sah-rah-BAHN-dah.* See **sarabande.**

zarf [Ar] *zarf.* (*lit.*, vessel, sheath) a metal holder, usu. ornate, for a cup or goblet.

zarzuela [Sp, after *La Zarzuela*, a palace near Madrid where it was first performed in the 17th century] *sar-SWEH-lah.* short musical play; musical comedy; —**de mariscos** (*-deh-mah-REES-kohs*) Catalonian shellfish stew.

Zauber [Ger] *TSOW-buh.* magic; spell, charm; **Zauberer** (*-ruh*) magician; **Zauberflöte** (*-flö-teh*) magic flute.

zayim [Ar] *ZY-eem.* chief, leader.

z.B. Abbr. of **zum Beispiel.**

zdravstvuitye [Russ] *ZDRAH-stvooee-tyeh.* hello; how do you do? Often cut down to **zdraste** (*ZDRAH-styeh*).

Zeit [Ger: *pl.* **Zeiten**] *tsyt* (*-'n*) time; age, era; season; **Zeitgeist** (*-gyst*) spirit of the time; social climate of the age; **Zeitschrift** (*-shrift*) magazine; periodical; journal; **Zeitung** (*-toong*); *pl.* **Zeitungen** (*-'n*) newspaper.

zemiroth [Heb] *zuh-mee-ROHT.* (*lit.*, song) traditional Jewish sabbath songs.

zemstvo [Russ, from *zemlya*, earth, land] *ZYEM-stvah.* district council.

Zen [Jap, from Chin *ch'an*, from Skt *dhyāna*, meditation] *zen.* a form of Buddhism practiced in China and Japan which seeks enlightenment through study and meditation.

zenana [Hindi, from Pers *zanāna*, from *zan*, woman] *zeh-NAH-nuh*. in India, the women's quarters.

Zend [Pers] *zend*. (*lit.*, commentary) a Middle-Persian translation and commentary on the Avesta, the sacred scriptures of Zoroastrianism.

Zend-Avesta [Pers] *zend-uh-VES-tuh*. the Avesta together with the Zend: the sacred scriptures of the Parsees.

zendo [Jap *zen*, meditation + *do*, place] *ZEN-doh*. a room used for meditation by Zen monks.

zia [It] *TSEE-ah*. aunt; old woman.

ziemlich [Ger] *TSEEM-liç*. rather; somewhat; —**schnell** (*-shnel*) (*music*) rather fast.

Zigeuner [Ger] *tsee-GOY-nuh*. gypsy.

ziggurat [Assyrian] *ZIG-oo-raht*. an ancient Assyrian temple of pyramidal shape. Also, **ziqqurat** (*ZIK-*).

zingaro [It, from Gk. *Athinganoi*, name of an Eastern people] *DZEEN-gah-roh*. Gypsy. Also, **zigano** (*tsee-GAH-noh*).

zio [It] *TSEE-oh*. uncle; old man.

ziti [It] *DZEE-tee*. a kind of macaroni.

zitto [It: *pl.* **zitti**] *TSEET-toh* (*-tee*) silent, quiet; be quiet!

zizanie [Fr, from LL *zizania*, from Gk *zizanion*] *zee-zah-NEE*. tare, darnel weed; dissension, discord.

zizith [Heb] *tsee-TSEET*. the fringes or tassels worn at the four corners of the tallith.

zloty [Pol] *ZLOH-tee*. monetary unit of Poland.

Zoe mou, sas agapo [Gk] *zoh-EH-moo-sahs-ah-gah-POH*. My life, I love thee.

zoftig. See **zaftig.**

Zollverein [Ger] *TSOHL-fur-yn*. customs union.

zombie [Afr] *ZAHM-bee*. a snake god worshiped by some West Africans and voodooists; a dead person's soul controlled by a magician; one who comes back from the dead by magical powers; a lethargic or eccentric person; a drink made of rum, sugar and lemon. Also, **zombi.**

zori [Jap] *ZOH-ree*. a kind of sandal fastened to the foot by a thong passing between the big toe and the second toe, and around the ankle.

Zouave [Fr, from Berber *Zwāwa*, an Algerian tribe] *zoo-*

AHV. a member of a body of Algerian troops serving in the French army, noted for their colorful Oriental uniform; a member of a similar unit in various other armies; a type of short jacket.

zucchero [It] *TSOOK-keh-roh.* sugar.

zucchetto [It, var. of *zucchetta,* dim. of *zucca,* gourd] *dzook-KAYT-toh.* a small round skullcap of any of several colors, depending on the rank, worn by Roman Catholic churchmen.

zucchini [It, pl. of *zucchino,* dim. of *zucca,* gourd] *dzook-KEE-nee.* a green summer squash.

zueco [Sp] *SWEH-koh.* wooden shoe, clog.

Zug [Ger: *pl.* **Züge**] *tsook* (*TSÜ-geh*) drawing, pulling; traction; train; line, course; troop, platoon, squad; trait, characteristic.

Zukunft [Ger] *TSOO-koonft.* future.

zum Beispiel [Ger: *abbr.* **z.B.**] *tsoom-BY-shpeel.* for example.

zvezda [Russ] *zvyeh-ZDAH.* star.

zwei [Ger] *tsvy.* two.

Zwerg [Ger: *pl.* **Zwerge**] *tsvehrk* (*TSVEHR-geh*) dwarf; midget; pygmy.

Zwieback [Ger] *TSVEE-bahk.* (*lit.,* twice-baked) a crisp biscuit, rusk.